SOCIOLOGY
FOR CHANGING THE WORLD

SOCIOLOGY
FOR CHANGING THE WORLD

Social Movements/Social Research

edited by
Caelie Frampton, Gary Kinsman,
A.K. Thompson and Kate Tilleczek

Fernwood Publishing • Halifax

Smith, George W., "Political Activist as Ethnographer," Social Problems,
Vol. 37, No. 4: 629-648. © 1990, The Society for the Study of Social Problems, Inc.
All rights reserved. Used by permission.

The editors have made every effort to credit and
secure permission to reprint previously circulated materials.
However, as a result of the occasional ambiguities of authorship that
arise in social movement contexts, this has not always proven to be possible.

Editing: Brenda Conroy
Cover Design: A.K. Thompson
Printed and bound in Canada by Hignell Book Printing

Published in Canada by Fernwood Publishing
Site 2A, Box 5, 32 Oceanvista Lane
Black Point, Nova Scotia, B0J 1B0
and 324 Clare Avenue, Winnipeg, Manitoba, R3L 1S3
www.fernwoodbooks.ca

Fernwood Publishing Company Limited gratefully acknowledges
the financial support of the Department of Canadian Heritage,
the Nova Scotia Department of Tourism and Culture and
the Canada Council for the Arts for our publishing program.

 Canadian Patrimoine
Heritage canadien The Canada Council for the Arts
Le Conseil des Arts du Canada NOVA SCOTIA
Tourism and Culture

Library and Archives Canada Cataloguing in Publication

Sociology for changing the world : social movements/social
research / Caelie Frampton ... [et al.].

ISBN 1-55266-183-0

1. Action research. 2. Social movements. I. Frampton, Caelie

HN18.3.S624 2006   303.4'84'072   C2006-900310-6

CONTENTS

for George Smith (1935–1994)

activist, researcher, teacher, friend

*The test for whether or not research has been
successful is the extent to which it enables
people to transform the world.*

Gary Kinsman and George Smith at an
AIDS ACTION NOW! demonstration at
Toronto City Hall in 1988.

CONTRIBUTORS

Some book contributors with other institutional ethnographers. Left to right, back: Adele Mueller, Roxana Ng, Joan Scott, George Smith; front: Dorothy Smith, Gillian Walker, Jennifer Newton, Alison Griffith

Marie L. Campbell

is professor emerita at the University of Victoria. For twelve years she taught research in the graduate program, "Studies in Policy and Practice in Health and Social Services," in UVic's Faculty of Human and Social Development. She has published three books: an edited collection with Ann Manicom, *Knowledge, Experience and Ruling Relations* in 1995; a "primer" on doing institutional ethnography called *Mapping Social Relations*, with Fran Gregor, in 2002; and *Managing to Nurse: Inside Canada's Health Care Reform*, with Janet Rankin, 2005.

William K. Carroll

teaches sociology at the University of Victoria, where he participates in the graduate program in cultural, social and political thought, and teaches critical research strategies in the Sociology Department's undergraduate concentration in social justice. He is a research associate at the Canadian Centre for Policy Alternatives and is active in the Society for Socialist Studies. His books include *Organizing Dissent* (Garamond Press, 1997), *Corporate Power in a Globalizing World* (Oxford University Press, 2004) and *Critical Strategies for Social Research* (Canadian Scholars' Press, 2004).

Kathryn Church

is assistant professor in the School of Disability Studies at Ryerson University. She teaches courses in community organizing and research methods. She also directs the research program for the Ryerson-RBC Institute for Disability Studies Research and Education. It is organized with two foci: the invisible work carried out by disabled people in the course of their everyday/night lives; and disability arts and culture as an evolving activity of the disability rights movement.

John Clarke

has been active in Ontario anti-poverty struggles since he helped to form the London Union of Unemployed Workers (LUUW) in 1983. This organization was brought together by trade unionists who had been laid off during the early 1980s recession. In 1989, the LUUW worked with a range of other organizations in the Province to organize a two week, three pronged March Against Poverty, which converged on the Ontario Legislature from Windsor, Sudbury and Ottawa. The Ontario Coalition Against Poverty (OCAP) came out of this March, and in 1990, Clarke moved to Toronto to become one of its organizers. He has stayed with OCAP since that time.

Caelie Frampton

is a union activist and a graduate student. Currently living in East Vancouver, she worked on the Sociology for Changing the World conference at Laurentian University in her hometown of Sudbury, Ontario. In between organizing with the Teaching Support Staff Union at Simon Fraser University and with Queers United Against Kapitalism, Caelie tries to find time to ride her bike and build community.

Gary Kinsman

has been an activist in gay liberation, AIDS, anti-poverty, anti-war, global justice and socialist organizing over the last thirty-three years. He worked with George Smith in the Right to Privacy Committee, the Canadian Committee Against Customs Censorship, and in AIDS ACTION NOW! He is the author of *The Regulation of Desire, Homo and Hetero Sexualities*, and an editor of *Whose National Security? Canadian State Surveillance and the Creation of Enemies* and of *Mine Mill Fights Back*. He teaches sociology at Laurentian University.

Clarice Kuhling

is a former bargaining team member and executive officer of CUPE Local 3903. She is a PhD candidate in the Department of Sociology at York University and is currently investigating the theory and practice of democracy in relation to social and labour movements.

Alex Levant

is a former executive officer of CUPE Local 3903 and CUPE Toronto Council, and he organized the CUPE 3903 Flying Squad. He is a PhD candidate in social and political thought at York University, working on problems of consciousness and organization in current anti-capitalist struggles in the Canadian state.

Eric Mykhalovskiy

is an assistant professor in the department of sociology at York University. His research focuses on the social organization of knowledge in health and health care. His activist and community-based work focuses on improving health conditions for people living with HIV/AIDS.

Viviane Namaste

teaches at the Simone de Beauvoir Institute, Concordia University, Montréal. She is the author of *Sex Change, Social Change: Reflections on Identity, Institutions and Imperialism* (Women's Press, 2005), *C'était du spectacle! L'histoire des artistes transsexuelles à Montréal, 1955–1985* (McGill-Queen's University Press, 2005) and *Invisible Lives: The Erasure of Transsexual and Transgendered People* (University of Chicago Press, 2000).

Roxana Ng

is an activist, sociologist and professor at the University of Toronto. She has a long history of doing research with and on immigrant women and immigrant communities. She has published three books on the areas related to her chapter in this book. Her current research is on how globalization and restructuring affect immigrant garment workers.

Dorothy E. Smith

is professor emerita at the Ontario Institute for Education/University of Toronto and adjunct professor in sociology at the University of Victoria. She is the author of *Feminism and Marxism: A Place to Begin, a Way to Go* (1977), *The Everyday World as Problematic: A Feminist Sociology* (1987), *The Conceptual Practices of Power: A Feminist Sociology of Knowledge* (1990a), *Texts, Facts, Femininity: Exploring the Relations of Ruling* (1990b), *Writing the Social: Critique, Theory and Investigations* (1999), *Institutional Ethnography: A Sociology for People* (2005), and, with Alison I. Griffith, *Mothering for Schooling* (2005). She did research with and was a good friend of George Smith.

A.K. Thompson

is an activist and PhD student in the department of sociology at York University, where he is earning a degree in troublemaking. He is the author of "Black Bloc, White Riot: Anti-globalization and the Genealogy of Dissent" (forthcoming).

Kate Tilleczek

is an associate professor who teaches sociological methods and the sociology of childhood/youth at Laurentian University. Her research involves understanding the social organization of youth cultures. Schooling, systems of health care, global children's rights issues, and the health of young people are main areas of current research in which forms of ethnographic work with and for children are undertaken. Links between global capitalism and commodification of childhoods is an emerging interest in which Kate's research and activism are targeted.

Cynthia Wright

is an activist and academic. She has served as contract faculty at several Ontario universities and is now at the School of Women's Studies, York University. Her varied research interests include the history and contemporary practice of anti-racist and im/migrant rights campaigns in Canada and internationally, especially those focused on undocumented people. She is currently co-editing an anthology on im/migrant activism and the politics of "no borders." She knew George Smith socially and was a member of his care team.

ACKNOWLEDGMENTS

As is always the case when it comes to books, the editors are deeply indebted
to the contributions of many people — activists, colleagues, students and
friends. We would like to take this moment to formally acknowledge them
and to extend our thanks.

First and foremost, we would like to thank the organizing committee
of the Sociology for Changing the World conference, which was held at
Laurentian University between November 8 and 10, 2002. This conference,
which was conceived as a space for acknowledging and making use of George
Smith's contributions to activist research, provided the necessary impetus
for this volume. In addition to Caelie Frampton and Gary Kinsman, the
conference committee was comprised of Kaili Beck, Stephanie Ouellette,
Sandeep Nagra and Pat Moores. In addition, the editors would like to thank
Evelyne Gervais for her help throughout the early part of this project.

Since even the most well organized conference would be a failure if it were
not for participants, we would like to thank all those who attended Sociology
for Changing the World and helped to engender a climate of lively discussion
and political solidarity. It is our hope that the spirit of those interactions
permeates these pages. Sociology for Changing the World was sponsored by
the Sociology Department at Laurentian University, with the support of the
departments of English, History, Political Science, and Women's Studies,
as well as the Dean of Social Sciences and Humanities, the Vice-President
Academic, the Laurentian University Faculty Association, the Students
General Association and Mine Mill/CAW Local 598. For their support, we
extend our heartfelt thanks. The conference and this collection were made
possible in part through funding from the Laurentian University Research
Fund.

The editors would also like to thank those who helped to organize "Activist
Research and the Sociology of Confrontation," the Department of Sociology
colloquium held at York University in December of 2004. This event, which
provided another opportunity to pursue conference themes, helped us to clarify
our project and made more evident to us the importance of what we were up
to. Particular thanks go to Doreen Fumia and Michael Christenson, as well as
to Lesley Wood, who willingly took on the task of chairing a difficult session.
We would also like to thank the York University Administration and their
security services for making plain what we were all talking about by sending
a spy to monitor our frightful and incendiary proceedings.

There are some people who must be thanked for their assistance and participation in the production of this text. For allowing us to reprint George Smith's article "Political Activist as Ethnographer," we must extend a most grateful thank-you to the University of California Press — producers of the journal *Social Problems*. We are very pleased to have the opportunity to circulate such a crucial text as George's amongst a new generation of readers. For their editorial suggestions and copy-editing skills, which at some points we desperately needed, we wish to thank Melanie Muise and Ellen Vincer. Special thanks must also be extended to Derek Laventure, who helped the editorial collective by setting up a Wiki site on which we could collaboratively craft the Preface and Afterword to this volume despite being separated by great geographical distances. We also thank Sam Bradd, who drew the comic for the Afterword. At Fernwood Publishing, we would like to thank Errol Sharpe, Brenda Conroy, Debbie Mathers and Beverley Rach, each of whom helped to transform an unruly stack of words on paper into the book you are presently holding.

Finally, we would like to thank all the contributors for agreeing to donate their individual royalties from the sale of this book to the Ontario Coalition Against Poverty. Although the sum will not be substantial, we felt that it was important for an anthology inspired by and pertaining to effective activism to be as explicit about its commitments as possible.

In addition to these general thanks, each of the editors would like to express a more personal gratitude.

Caelie Frampton

I would first like to acknowledge Gary Kinsman, who has been an unwavering mentor, profoundly shaping my political thinking and actions. A.K. Thompson has also been crucial in pushing me to get shit done. My student union and TSSU comrades at Simon Fraser University are a radical and dazzling sources of stimulation. Sam Bradd and Marie-Geneviève Lane have offered fierce and unrelenting emotional support. My family in Sudbury also deserves huge thanks for making the coffee and driving around in the snow during weekend-long editing sessions.

Gary Kinsman

I would like to thank the people who have been involved in Sudbury Global Justice, the Sudbury Coalition Against Poverty, the Hunger Clinic Organizing Committee, the Sudbury New Socialist Group, and the Autonomy and Solidarity Network for all the activist support and inspiration they have provided. I would also like to thank the other editors for coming on board and transforming a project that seemed like an almost impossible task into something doable. It has been an important and challenging learning experience working with Andrew, Caelie and Kate. On the home-front, I would like to thank Patrick Barnholden and our wonderful son Mike for indispensable love and support.

A.K. Thompson

In addition to extending my gratitude to the other editors of this volume for their tireless efforts, I would like to thank Himani Bannerji for providing important insight, support and guidance both as a PhD supervisor and as a comrade and friend. It is to Himani — who has always been an equal source of heartfelt encouragement and unsparing critique — that I owe my attentiveness, such as it exists, to the everyday. I would also like to thank my fellow troublemakers in the Autonomy and Solidarity Network for their concurrent pessimism of the intellect and optimism of the will. Finally, I would like to thank K. Mandziuk for reasons that are difficult to specify.

Kate Tilleczek

I would like to thank William and Elliott, my left-handed sons, for their interest in my work — however seemingly oblique. At fourteen and eleven years of age, they are astute teachers and general detectors of ideological crap. I am also grateful to share my days with Ron, who is a loving partner and devoted friend. I especially like it when our philosophical discussions are informed by the everyday. The other editors of this volume — Gary, Andrew and Caelie — all deserve thanks for tugging me earthward and electrifying my work in social science research methods and activism. Finally, and more specifically, I would like to especially acknowledge Gary Kinsman as a true mentor, colleague and friend.

SOCIAL MOVEMENTS/SOCIAL RESEARCH: TOWARDS POLITICAL ACTIVIST ETHNOGRAPHY

C. Frampton, G. Kinsman, A.K. Thompson and K. Tilleczek

A Line of Fault, A Place To Begin

What was a plainclothes university security officer doing taking notes at a forum on research methods? This was the question on the minds of the thirty students, faculty and community activists who came out to "Activist Research and the Sociology of Confrontation," an event hosted by the York Department of Sociology Colloquium Committee in late 2004. The panel presentation, which took place in the university's senate chamber, was meant to provide a space for activist researchers to discuss how to turn their intellectual skills into practical weapons for social change. In addition to this lesson, those in attendance received a concrete example of how relations of ruling are organized at York University. A security officer? At a colloquium event?

How, and by what logic, did the university administration feel compelled to send a security guard to monitor the proceedings? He sat quietly in the back and studiously took notes. What was he going to do with these notes? Why had he been sent to collect them? By what administrative logic were his actions to be justified? Was this act of surveillance a one-off adventure or did it rely upon forms of social organization that determined its course? As those at the colloquium event grappled with these and other questions a disjuncture emerged between the meeting participants and university mandated security surveillance.

For reasons that were not immediately evident, reasons that could — in the first instance — only be speculated upon, the colloquium event managed to antagonize the administration. Why? And how did they decide upon this course of action? Of course, institutions are premised upon sanctioned logics. And nothing comes out of nowhere. The colloquium event took place in the university's senate chambers, a room close to the offices of the York Foundation — a body whose objective is to raise funds for the university. On the board of the York Foundation sits Henry Wu, owner and operator of the Metropolitan Hotel in downtown Toronto. Over the course of the year prior to the colloquium event, Wu had become a target for York activists concerned with the deplorable working conditions at the hotel.[1] On more than one occasion, student activists and outraged faculty paid visits to the offices of the York Foundation to demand that Wu be ousted from the board.

Perhaps it is understandable that the administration believed that a gathering of rabble in a room adjacent to the offices of the York Foundation needed to be put under surveillance. And anyway, the composition of the panel itself posed problems. It's one thing for academics to make boisterous and radical professions from the front of classrooms. It is quite another, however, for the people speaking from the front of the room to be effective organizers, as was the case with this event. In fact, two of the presenters had played active roles in challenging Wu and the York Foundation.

It is worth considering how the colloquium event was situated in relation to an increasingly repressive political climate at York. During the same year, an undergraduate student was effectively expelled for his part in a demonstration against the Israeli occupation of Palestine.[2] Other students, who participated in a demonstration opposing Canadian military and corporate involvement in the wars against Iraq and Afghanistan, found themselves brutally assaulted by police officers who had been called onto campus by the administration.[3] More generally, the administration had turned the screws on student attempts to organize political events on campus.

Through a textual mechanism called "the temporary use of space policy,"[4] the administration effectively made it impossible for student groups to book space or invite speakers to campus. By extending the time required to secure a room on campus and by submitting all incoming speakers to "security assessments," which often led to the requirement that organizers hire security to police their event, the administration managed to put a clamp on student organizing. In the given context, where York had become another zone of conflict in the ongoing battle on Canadian campuses between opponents and supporters of the Israeli occupation of Palestine, the selective application of the regulatory policy helped the administration to avoid potentially damaging public relations scandals.

Given the extensive social relations that could be gleaned from the presence of a single security guard, it seemed fitting that one of the topics scheduled for discussion at the colloquium was the contribution made by the late George Smith to the field of activist research. Smith, who, in his important work "Political Activist as Ethnographer" helped to elaborate a strategy for the production of reliable knowledge for social change, would have been pleased with such a concrete example of the applicability of his method.

⨯ One of the central propositions of political activist ethnography is that, through confrontation with ruling regimes, activists are able to uncover aspects of their social organization. Through forms of engagement that start from the standpoint of the everyday aspirations of their participants, these participants quickly come into contact and conflict with the organizational and administrative logics of the institutions they cross. Through an analysis of the institutional relations movements are up against, more effective forms of activism can be developed. The test for whether or nor not research has been successful is the extent to which it enables people to transform the world. And so it was that, in the relatively minor moment of confrontation in the university senate chamber, the colloquium on research methods itself became a research method. It provided a moment of breach, a point from which to begin investigating both the everyday operations of the institution and the tools and techniques to which it has recourse in those moments when it feels challenged. Although it seemed unlikely, a speaking engagement became a starting point from which people on the outside of the administration's ruling practices could begin looking in on them. Despite what we learned, this moment offers little more than a starting point. Much analysis of the social organization of university security surveillance remains to be done.

Just as the security guard's actions had antecedents, so too did the colloquium event. It was proposed and organized by one of the editors of this volume as a space for the further elaboration of discussions that had begun two years prior. In the fall of 2002, nearly two hundred activists, researchers, students and scholars doing research for progressive social movements gathered at Laurentian University in Sudbury, Ontario, to attend Sociology for Changing the World: Political Activist Ethnography. The conference was exciting and dynamic. In addition to a series of events aimed at breaking the tedium often associated with academic conferences (such as the concurrent activist video festival and dramatic presentations), Sociology for Changing the World also provided room for presenters to explore the content and implications of George Smith's article "Political Activist as Ethnographer" (1990, and in this volume). That gathering, and all the trouble we've managed to cause in its name since then, is the inspiration for this book. Those initial presentations form its sinews; those convictions form its spine.

The Conference and the Book

This book aims to capture the spirit of that conference — the way it brought together researchers, students and activists; the way it paired people very familiar with political activist ethnography with others who had not yet encountered the approach. Like the conference before it, this book invites participants to explore how sociological knowledge can be produced *for* activists, and how activists can make use of and elaborate political activist ethnography as a weapon in our struggles.

The book itself has been produced by an editorial collective working together across geographical distance to edit and write collaboratively. We have different histories and different relations to activism and political activist ethnography, and let's be clear — we don't always agree on everything. Three of us were drawn to political activist ethnography because it resonated with our experiences as activists in various movements. Two of us studied with Dorothy Smith (who produced the context for G. Smith's contributions) in different decades, and one of us worked with George Smith as an activist. One of us had her first major contact with political activist ethnography being part of the organizing committee for the Sociology for Changing the World conference. Finally, one of us came to an interest in institutional and political activist ethnography through feminist theories and qualitative research methods. We have tried to write in as non-monolithic and as dialogical a fashion as possible. Many of the chapters are explicitly practical and outline ways in which political activist ethnography can be used and developed. We have also included a list of critical thinking and discussion questions after most chapters, as well as a glossary of terms that you will find after the Foreword.

This glossary allows readers not yet familiar with political activist ethnography more easy entry into the chapters. In both editing and presentation, our goal has been to make the text as accessible as we can. We realize that, on first read, some of the language used may seem strange and unfamiliar. Nevertheless, our experience has been that many of these terms are very useful to critical social analysis and activism so we hope you will bear with us. It has often been pointed out that ruling relations rely upon a systematic denial of language appropriate to critical social analysis.[5] It is in light of this theft that we offer the glossary. Developing critical social literacy is about discovering and re-discovering forms and ways of thinking and acting that have been denied to us. Many of these words are vital to us when waging the struggles in which we are engaged. They are very useful to us in the practice of changing the world.

To demonstrate this point, let's investigate two words — epistemology and ontology — that are key to grasping political activist ethnography and how it is different from other approaches. Even though we don't use them in our everyday lives, they help us clarify the ways we do research and the commitments we take up as activists. Epistemology refers to the theories of knowledge — how we know what we know — that we use in research and activism. Political activist ethnographers acknowledge that knowledge is produced through a reflexive social process of mutual determination and learning from other people. In other words, we learn from doing, from social practice and from inter-acting with others. Most ruling forms of knowledge subscribe to an objective, value-free approach, pretending that the world can be explored from some disinterested neutral place somehow above or outside the social. This produces a managerial knowledge that then can be used to regulate social problems and movements.

One example clarifies matters here. In response to the widespread rebellions by American Blacks in the 1960s against racism, poverty and police repression, as well as the growth of the Black power movement, which emerged out of the civil rights movement, the U.S. government established a series of commissions and inquiries. Using a structural-functionalist perspective, which dressed itself up as neutral and objective, the influential Moynihan report (1965) argued, that the problem was not actually racism, poverty or police repression but instead that the Black family was "dysfunctional" since it did not look like the white middle-class family.[6] Reports like this mandated state funding to try to "fix" the Black family but did nothing to get at the social roots of racism and poverty.

Most movements challenge these claims to objectivity and value-neutrality by pointing out how they obscure forms of power and the different standpoints making up the social world. The social world is riven with struggles and conflicts, and the social standpoint you take up has an impact on what you can see. How you see a strike, for example, will differ if you start from the standpoint of management, or from that of the union members on the picket lines, or of the police who harass union members when they take action against management. This experience is incredibly different for the various people involved even though the social relations that organize the experience are the same. The trick is to not simply "flip the script" and validate our side but rather to begin mapping these social relations. Throughout this book, we point out how, despite the general aversion outlined above, strands of "objectivity" and "value-neutrality" manage to infiltrate themselves back into social movement research, often causing divisions and problems among activists.

Ontology is a word that points us to investigating the way the social comes into being. Some approaches argue that structures or discourse are what is primary when accounting for the emergence of the social.[7] In these ontologies, agency is transferred from people to thing-like objects that are no longer clearly understood as having been produced by people. In contrast, following from Marx, political activist ethnographers argue that it is "we," as individuals and as groups of people, who, through our own practices, coordinate and produce the social world (D. Smith 2005: 49–73). This implies that we can also collectively change it. The implications derived from these specific conceptions of epistemology and ontology are key to defining the contributions of political activist ethnographers to critical social research and activism.

The chapters in this book come both from conference presenters and contributors who did not attend but who have nevertheless been engaged in the debates that animated the conference itself. The authors include community organizers, professors and graduate students. Like George Smith before them, many of these scholars and researchers are committed activists. We hope this collection captures the excitement and energy of both the conference and the social struggles that have erupted around us. From the protests against the World Trade Organization in Seattle during November of 1999, to the tear-gas filled streets of Québec City in 2001, to the confrontational spirit of the Ontario Coalition Against Poverty and many others besides, this book has been indelibly marked by the convulsions turning our world upsidedown.

Origins of Political Activist Ethnography

As an approach to producing a reliable knowledge of the social in order to facilitate transformative aims, political activist ethnography finds its roots in the work of Dorothy E. Smith. Contrary to the premises of official sociology, which aims to explain people using categorical abstractions like "socialization," "social roles and norms" or "dysfunctionality," D. Smith developed what she called institutional ethnography as a sociology *for* women, *for* the oppressed and — ultimately — *for* people (D. Smith 1987, 1999, 2005). Ethnographic work usually refers to going into another culture or society and learning from people in that culture or society about how their social and cultural worlds are put together. It is based on rich descriptions of how cultural and social practices work. Institutional ethnography proposes a dramatic reversal of the typical paradigm where the sociologist or anthropologist aims to make sense of the curious habits of the Other. Instead, institutional ethnography shows how the practices of ethnography can be turned against ruling institutions in our own society (D. Smith 1987: 151–79, 2002, 2005; Campbell and Gregor 2002). Institutional ethnography is an incitement to return the gaze (Bannerji 1995b) so that oppressed people can look back at their oppressors to see how the oppression they live is socially organized. In institutional ethnography we look upon the lookers to see how they do it.

Institutional ethnography and political activist ethnography have intimate connections to social movements and activism. For D. Smith, the feminist movement of the 1960s and 1970s helped to create the possibility of developing a different way of doing sociology. Since it often relied upon conceptual abstractions that served to occlude the practical dimensions of women's experiences (experiences that often brought them into direct contact with the mundane "how" of the social world), the male tradition of sociology, for D. Smith, began to seem less like a strategy of investigation and description, and more like a practice of ruling. Not only did this sociology neglect to get to the bottom of things, it also on occasion provided a means of either justifying or ignoring social abuses. By drawing on the work of Marx, and of ethnomethodologists (who study the methods people use to produce their everyday worlds) and others,[8] D. Smith helped to turn sociology on its head. Her insistence was simple: rather than contribute to the regulation of people through the application of concepts linked to textual practices (for instance, psychological classifications that can lead to harmful "treatment" regimes, or concepts of "deviance" that construct sex workers and lesbians and gay men as beyond the norm and thus in need of regulation), sociologists should aim to illuminate the textual practices of ruling regimes themselves.

Although her premises are explicitly concrete and despite consistent efforts to clarify and further articulate her approach (most recently, D. Smith 2005), D. Smith has often been read as advocating something akin to feminist standpoint theory, which argues that a feminist standpoint has an almost privileged ability to produce knowledge of the world. Although this characterization amounts to a significant misreading of her work, it is nevertheless one that can be seen repeated in many sociology textbooks and course outlines.[9] At stake in this classification are the grounds upon which we might come to know the world. For feminist standpoint theorists, the unique experiences of women — punctuated by the particularities of given oppressions — provide them with a basis to tell the truth about that experience, its origins and its consequences. This leads to an epistemological approach that can argue that only women can speak the "truth" of their experience, only people of colour can speak the "truth" of their experience and so on. This truth-telling foregrounds narrative and testimony as the raw material of social analysis. Here categories and the differences between them become central. Real lives are transposed into concepts or representations. This begins to dissolve the social relations that link us together, despite our differing social locations. For D. Smith, experiences are crucial. But they cannot be taken to be the "truth" of anything, other than themselves. Rather, social experience is taken to be the starting point for investigation, a place to start investigating the social world from outside the frameworks of ruling discourse. This offers a concrete grounding for a critical interrogation of ruling relations. D. Smith's work makes the social, rather than the "self" seen as separate from the social, the central concern. D. Smith writes that she takes up a women's social standpoint "not as a given and finalized form of knowledge but as a ground in experience from which discoveries are to be made" (2005: 8). As she puts it, "my notion of standpoint doesn't privilege a knower. It does something rather different. It shifts the ground of knowing, the place where inquiry begins" (Smith 1992: 91).

D. Smith is suggesting that people's practical activities in the world, and the practical consciousness that grows from these, influences where they choose to start investigating the world, which in turn shapes what they can discover. In the *Everyday World as Problematic* she draws on Hegel's parable of the master and servant. It is the servant and not the

[handwritten top margin: HEGEL: MASTER & SERVENT ⤷ D SMITH'S ANALYSIS CORRELATES THIS NOTION TO MARXIST VIEWS OF WORKER VS. Bourgeoisie • IT IS THE SERVENT WHO KNOWS practical CONSCIOUSNESS OF HOW TO SERVE THE MASTER • IT IS THE WORKER WHO PRODUCES THE WEALTH of fagasu]

master who has the practical consciousness of how to meet the master's needs since it is the servant who knows how to do the work to meet these needs. Marx extended this to point out that it is workers who have the practical consciousness through their own activities of how the wealth of the capitalists is produced. Building on these approaches D. Smith allows us to see how the practical work and consciousness of women in domestic and reproductive labour, and in the support work they do for men, brings into view aspects of the social world that remain hidden when we take up the social standpoints of men (D. Smith 1987: 78–82). This approach is not intended to privilege the essential experiences of servants, workers or women but rather to allow us to see that starting our investigations from these standpoints produces forms of knowledge that enable us to critically interrogate ruling relations. In relation to women's experiences men can learn from and take up the social standpoints of women by interrogating the ways their own social practices participate in sustaining patriarchal relations. White people can also learn from and take up the standpoints of people of colour to begin to interrogate their own participation in racializing practices (on this, see Bannerji 1995b). This is not an ethical or psychological detour. It is not about asking what it feels like to be the Other. Rather, it is an invitation to explore how the social experiences of the Other are organized.

D. Smith wanted to transform how sociology was done more generally and identified the need for a sociology for women as one vehicle for this transformation. The world of mainstream/malestream sociology, according to D. Smith, is one in which the conceptual world is divorced from everyday experience. This conceptual world is made to operate independently of experience and then aimed at organizing and regulating our worlds. Instead, D. Smith argues for the necessity of beginning with the disjunctures in consciousness that women experience between their own social experiences and the conceptual practices of male domination. People's accounts of their lives are always worked up in relation to social discourse. However, by starting with social experiences of disjuncture, it is possible to call ruling discourses into question. Starting from the everyday world as her problematic, D. Smith demonstrates how one can move from local situations to broader, more extended social relations. Starting from the realm of situated experience, institutional ethnography provides a way of moving from the local to the trans-local.

[handwritten left margin, vertical: 9/5/07 REF: THIS IS B/C SOCIAL INTERACTIONS AT THE INDIVIDUAL LEVEL OF ANALYSIS SERVE AS MICROCOSM TO UPGRADE SCALES OF INTERACTION.]

Political activist ethnography: Extending institutional ethnography
George Smith studied and worked with Dorothy Smith. He was an activist engaged in gay liberation struggles and AIDS activist movements in the 1980s and early 1990s. "Political Activist as Ethnographer" draws upon his experiences as a researcher/organizer in these movements and makes use of the contributions of institutional ethnography in order to outline a form of knowledge production designed explicitly for activism. George

Smith's important contributions to activist sociology were unfortunately cut short through his death from AIDS-related disorders in 1994. More than ten years later, his writing continues to inspire both those who knew him and those encountering his work for the first time. Testament to his continuing impact, the Institutional Ethnography Division of the Society for the Study of Social Problems has recently initiated a George Smith student paper award and had a special section of their November 2005 newsletter devoted to the memory of George Smith.

A number of the contributors to this book directly worked with and learned from George Smith. Others only encountered his work after his death. Throughout the text, we aim to recognize the different impacts George Smith has had and the different readings people make of his work. We have not tried to impose any conventions regarding the interpretation of his writing or life. And, although it is at odds with the current academic fashion of professional address, we allow those contributors who shared a personal relationship with G. Smith to refer to him as "George." Most important to us is that political activist ethnography not become a dogma. Consequently, there are different readings and uses of G. Smith's work reflected in this book.

With political activist ethnography, G. Smith aimed to develop an "insider's" knowledge of ruling regimes based on the daily struggles and confrontations that social movements are already engaged in. His premise was that, even though most social movements are to some extent "outside of" (or in rupture with) ruling relations, political confrontation provides a means for activists to investigate the organizing logic of the ruling regimes they oppose. By providing a concrete practice of mapping out the social relations of struggle — both the dynamics of ruling regimes and of movements themselves — political activist ethnography enables a grounded social knowledge for more effective forms of activism.

In order to begin from where activists develop forms of knowing suitable to the task, G. Smith called for both an epistemological and an ontological shift from conventional sociological research methods. As mentioned earlier, political activist ethnography requires a shift in perspective about how the social comes into being, and an ontological perspective that recognizes how the social world is produced through people's practical activity.

Processes and tools for mapping the social are paramount in moving past positivism — the epistemological approach relying on the methods of the natural sciences to study the social world. But this is not enough. We also need to move past the limitations of philosophical idealism — where ideas and concepts are prioritized over the material practices by which these ideas are produced. The ontological shift proposed by G. Smith is a break from traditional ways of knowing. For example, G. Smith's work encourages us to break with the individualized notions of being elaborated "deeds precede words" If there is no action to the idea, it is nothing.

by liberal philosophy. In its place, he offers us a complex theory of social being rooted not in ideas but in doing and practice. Individuals emerge as social individuals. What is needed is further dialogue about the ways in which the social and individual mutually occur. However, the placement of doing, activity and agency at the centre of this social mapping suggests that these theories of being and knowing are worked out in the practical action (praxis) of everyday struggles. When we speak here of agency, we don't have in mind the individual agency that some liberal philosophers associate with an innate drive for human freedom. Instead, agency, as we envision it, is always related to social action, organization and struggle (see Bannerji 1995b). For instance, the practice of culture-jamming, or of subverting the dress and meanings of capitalist-defined popular culture, can never be simply individual or isolated in character. Invariably, such a practice can be read in reference to the social and cultural contexts created by, for instance, anti-globalization and social justice protests against the capitalist colonization of social space (Bowes 2004).

constructivist Theories would agree. Political activist ethnography takes up this ontological commitment and views people's practices as central to how the social world comes into being, thus recognizing that people have the capacity to change the world. This is in contrast to other ontologies of the social. For instance, one can read Judith Butler's influential poststructuralist *Gender Trouble* (1990) as saying that discourse produces or speaks our gender *through* us. Gender is then a discursive effect. This denies that gender relations are broader social accomplishments (on this see Kessler and McKenna 1978). But if we are simply the puppets of social structures, discourse or "systems," as structuralist and even poststructuralist theories suggest — if "society" and official discourse causes us to act in regulated ways — there is not much hope for social transformation. Our goal is not to deny the social power of the forces of social regulation but to point out that social organization is also based on the activity of oppressed and exploited people ourselves. There is no realm of freedom beyond the social, and this social is produced through the activities of people.

As a result of these contentions, political activist ethnography has a very distinctive methodological and theoretical character. The standard academic distinctions made between "theory" and "method" are here troubled in order to foreground their interrelation as part of an investigative practice. Social movements and their confrontations with ruling regimes become important sites for mapping the social. We wish to trouble the "theory" produced about social movements that takes them as objects of analysis. Rejecting forms of knowledge that posture as being "neutral" and "objective" but hide a standpoint based in ruling social positions, political activist ethnography aims at developing knowledge about social organization from the standpoints of movements for social justice and the oppressed themselves.

Although this book engages in critiques of, and debates with, other approaches to producing knowledge regarding social movements, its focus on how to put <u>political activist ethnography</u> to use in doing research <u>for social movements</u>. This project is pursued at a methodological level and through concrete application to specific movements and struggles.

Troubling Social Movement Theory

As George Smith points out in "Political Activist as Ethnographer," political activist ethnography does not start within the existing academic discourses about "social movements" and "social movement theory." Despite their differences, the various social movement theories all construct social movements as objects of analysis and focus their attention on social movements themselves rather than on explicating the social relations of struggle in which these movements are engaged. In contrast, political activist ethnography is rooted in movement action and experience and does not convert movements or activists into objects of analysis or theory. From here we begin. Nevertheless, some dismantling of social movement theory is necessary given the pervasive problems it can produce for activist based research and knowledge production.

Positioned as the authoritative academic voice on social action, social movement theory (despite moments of insight) has rarely moved far beyond academic discussions. This tradition is based on a hierarchical practice, where the researcher is not required to participate in movements and often writes about them as an outsider. Consequently, the knowledge created by social movement theory is often of little use to activists inside social movements and does not allow them to map out the social relations of struggle. By researching social movements rather than the social world that movements aim to unsettle, social movement theory often reifies activists and movements and establishes regulatory practices within academia by classifying activists and their work. Within new social movement theory, which we investigate more specifically in a moment, some movements are identified as being "new" while others are seen as "old." Some are slotted into the "cultural" while others are seen as having to do with "economics" or "resource allocation." These arbitrary distinctions often result in an inability to describe and account for how social movements actually work and tend to increase the divide between "activist" and "researcher." By critiquing or justifying movements, as if their worth is determined by what an observer thought of them, social movement theory regulates activism by slotting it into categories, rather than explicating the importance of what a movement produces in the social world and what its confrontations with ruling relations bring into view.

Social movement theory can be roughly divided into three recognizable, but overlapping periods. The first period (roughly 1946–1960 with earlier roots), often referred to as "collective behaviour theory," characterized movements as "social problems" in need of explanation. Researchers in this period often relied upon psychological concepts in order to make their evaluations. For example, collective behaviour theory would often understand crowd members as otherwise "normal" people who happened to be reacting in unusual and "irrational" ways while in a crowd. This early theory, which had no contextual understanding of oppression, solidarity or struggle, sought to claim movement participants as "deviant." Consequently, this approach often produced knowledge suitable to the regulation and policing of social movements.[10]

In the post–World War II years, partly as a result of the Black civil rights movement and a series of Third World liberation struggles, social movements began to be conceived in more productive and rational terms. Viewing social movements as extensions of institutional action, "resource mobilization" theorists became the successors to collective behaviour theorists. Resource mobilization theory, which drew upon a certain reading of Marxism (Canel 1992), attempted to integrate political, sociological and economic theories. During this period, social movement theorists examined social action more structurally, while providing some critique of capitalism. The focus rested principally on the capacity of social movements, conceived as rational actors, to mobilize resources in their attempts to advance their struggles. By portraying activism as rational in character, resource mobilization theory began to break from codings of deviance. However, it also tended to narrow our focus on movements to questions of access to "resources" and how these resources were organized and mobilized. In addition to this conceptual delimiting of the scope of investigation, resource mobilization theory continued to construct movements themselves as the object of study.

The 1960s saw an explosion of movement struggles — youth, student, anti-war, feminist, lesbian and gay, ecological, prisoner rights and more — that did not seem to be directly related to questions of class (or at least not the narrow political economy notions of class then prevalent in the left). This moment of insurgency created the basis for new social movement theory influenced by the then emergent post-structural and post-modern approaches to social problems that focus on difference, fragmentation, discourse, language and culture (Canel 1992). These analyses contest Marxism (and sometimes feminism) as no longer relevant, or as "master-narratives" that merely produce the world they seek to "explain." As Otero and Jugenitz argue, "Postmodernism, by denying the existence of real social facts and focusing on the meaning of movements, rather than their causes, challenges the continuing legitimacy of modernist theories, and in particular, of traditional Marxism" (2003: 506). By emphasizing what was "new" and distinctive about these movements, new social movement theory often obscured their connections with earlier forms of organizing (Weir 1993). With a focus on the cultural and identity aspects of these movements, new social movement theory tended to overlook the connections of these movements to class relations and struggles. Often this produced a binary opposition between older movements (which were thought to be based on a narrow notion of class and economics) and these newer movements based on culture and identity. The result was a situation in which it became difficult to grasp the social and historical connections between class and culture (see Bannerji 1995b). This division is in part rooted in the epochal split of the 1960s, constructed as being between the old versus the new left. For instance, within the culture/class binary, lesbian and gay struggles are often classified as belonging to "culture." The result is a theory that disengages these struggles from the material circumstances of queer people's lives. From here it can operate as a regulatory practice that defines cultural issues and identity, but not poverty or class relations, as legitimate queer questions. → new cultural identities: gay community, as a culture.

New social movement theory is often portrayed as a period of deconstruction in which unitary and ruling social categories are taken apart. New social movement theory concentrates on the formation of identities and their trajectories towards collectivity and autonomy, for instance in the feminist or lesbian and gay movements. Unfortunately, this move to deconstruct has, for some, become synonymous with a suppression of class analysis (see Laclau and Mouffe 1985: 159). As a result, new social movement theory has been critiqued for displacing questions of class relations and state formation, and for its rather narrow focus on identity and the cultural (see Adam 1997; Canel 1992; Mooers and Sears 1992). *critique*

Frustrated with the imposition of these theoretical frames, and with the impetus of the global justice movement, some activists and researchers have turned to doing ethnographies of social movements. Despite the promise of this approach, some of these attempts remain trapped within the local (not only as starting point but also as the end point of analysis) and, as such, are unable to make the necessary connections to broader social relations. Some of these ethnographers end up re-imposing aspects of a structuralist or system based analysis, thereby distorting their own attempts to explore these institutional relations in an ethnographic fashion. ↳ NEW SOCIAL MOVTS IMPACT ON ETHNOGRAPHERS (RELATIVELY NEGATIVE)

Others, who have made aspects of the social relations of struggle visible, are still trapped within the confines of social movement theory and especially new social movement theory. In her insightful ethnographic investigation of the Metro Toronto Network for Social Justice, Janet Conway (2004) develops an activist ethnographic approach to coalition building that allows us to see some of the connections between local and more global social relations. She moves far beyond the ethnographic researcher as a neutral and uninterested observer. While she is able to develop an important focus on the importance of the knowledge that social movements produce, her version of activist ethnography is largely inflected by new social movement theory with its emphasis on meaning and the cultural. This approach largely (although not entirely) displaces class relations and is therefore unable to map out the concrete conditions (what we call the social relations of struggle) in which activists find themselves engaged.

In relation to globalization and global justice movements, there has been the emergence of what is referred to as "global ethnography," which uses an extended case method to try to develop ethnographic analyses that can capture the connections between various local settings (Burawoy et al. 2000). This approach acknowledges that ethnographers are participants in the processes they observe, and are in dialogue with others involved in these settings. The global ethnographer also observes settings over extended periods of space and time and views them as part of broader social processes. Despite the insights to be gained from these approaches, global ethnography is not knowledge produced from the standpoints of social movements resisting capitalist globalization. It is a form of knowledge that still takes up the position of observer in relation to these struggles. It is about the movements and their participants and *not* about what these movements learn. As mentioned before there is a shift as inquiry moves from the local to the global, from the "life-world to the system," in which ethnographic investigations are supplanted by the imposition of theoretical constructs of a "system world" (D. Smith 2005: 35–38). The brilliance of the more locally based ethnographic work is subverted by the imposition of system-based theory onto the inquiry.

We find these turns towards activist and global ethnography refreshing and important. At the same time, we feel that political activist ethnography provides a clearer means by which ethnography can be mobilized for activism and for changing the world. This is knowledge that not only interprets the world differently but that can be actively used to transform it (Marx 1975: 423). Political activist ethnography makes very clear that the problem is not the social movement but the ruling social forces within which it is in confrontation.

Currently, there is little writing available that starts from the standpoint of social movements and that develops sociological knowledge for activism. There is no current book for activists, researchers and students that outlines and explores how to *do* social transformation. This is the gap that *Sociology for Changing the World* seeks to fill. It aims to provide a resource and reference point for developing sociologies for progressive social movements. This book is a marked break from those approaches that designate progressive social movements as deviant in character. It is part of the re-orientation of inquiry that instead focuses on troubling and disturbing the social relations of normality (among others on this, see Brock 2003). Breaking free of the conceptualization of deviance this book also does not define social movements as 'objects' to be studied from the outside. Instead, social movements are here engaged as active subjects[11] (as are activists within them) and they are a crucial part of the solution to how we can change the world.

main point of section & book

Mapping the Book's Directions

Following a foreword by Dorothy Smith that outlines George Smith's work and its continuing relevance, *Sociology for Changing the World* is composed of three sections that conform to the movement involved in doing political activist ethnography. The first section, "Beyond Ideology and Speculation," which includes George Smith's "Political Activist as Ethnographer," sets out the distinctive methodological and theoretical features of political activist ethnography and how this approach does not start with speculation or with the ideological, or socially ungrounded, ways of seeing that dominate in society and often in social movements. Instead it begins with people's social practices and experiences. The crucial notions of an epistemological and especially the ontological shift required for this kind of activist research that we have already touched on are set out in this section.

1.

This is followed by "Research as Disruption," which pursues political activist ethnography by explicating how the confrontations of movements with ruling regimes are a crucial resource in mapping out the social relations of struggle in which movements are engaged. Disrupting or breaching ruling relations becomes a crucial form of research as connections are made between ethnomethodological breaching experiments and social movement knowledge creation.

2.

The third section, "Blowing up Social Relations," focuses on how doing political activist ethnography can illuminate social relations and points to paths of action for transforming the world. Covering a diversity of sites of struggle and movement organizing this section allows us to see the insights that can be gained from doing political activist ethnography.

3

This last section is followed by a conclusion by William Carroll and an afterword by the editors, which explores new directions for activist research and catalogues the debates and challenges coming out of this book. We take up the need to move beyond the insider/outsider divide in doing research for social movements and detail some of the regulatory regimes that activist research finds itself up against. We invite you to participate with us in devising ways of subverting these regulatory regimes and developing knowledge for changing the world.

4

We remind readers that the chapters in this book are not unitary or homogenous. Instead, they are diverse and varied expressions of different relations to political activist ethnography. Some contributions are well versed in institutional ethnography. Others are more grounded in the political activist ethnography elaboration of institutional ethnography. Still others make use of modes of investigation in which some institutional and political activist ethnographers are critical. We try to map out some of these dimensions in our section introductions. This expansive approach is crucial to our pedagogical project of making political activist ethnography as broadly relevant as possible to activists and researchers.

Notes

1. On this see the Metropolitan Hotel Workers site at <http://www.metropolitan-hotelsworkers.org/>. (Accessed Dec. 2, 2005.)
2. On this see <www.eye.net/eye/issue/issue_05.13.04/city/york.html>. (Accessed Dec. 2, 2005.)
3. On this see <http://thelink.concordia.ca/article.pl?sid=05/01/25/036244> (accessed Dec. 2, 2005) and the resource page on this at the Autonomy and Solidarity website at <http://auto_sol.tao.ca/>. (Accessed Dec. 2, 2005.)
4. On this see <www.yorku.ca/secretariat/legislation/u_pol/spaceuse.htm>. (Accessed Dec. 2, 2005.)
5. In "A 'Bad Writer' Bites Back," an op-ed written for the *New York Times* on March 20, 1999, Judith Butler makes the following point about difficult language: "Herbert Marcuse once described the way philosophers who champion common sense scold those who propagate a more radical perspective: 'The intellectual is called on the carpet.... Don't you conceal something? You talk a language which is suspect. You don't talk like the rest of us, like the man in the street, but rather like a foreigner who does not belong here. We have to cut you down to size, expose your tricks, purge you.' The accused then responds that 'if what he says could be said in terms of ordinary language he would probably have done so in the first place.' Understanding what the critical intellectual has to say, Marcuse goes on, 'presupposes the collapse and invalidation of precisely that universe of discourse and behaviour into which you want to translate it.'" The point, of course, is not to deliberately obfuscate but rather to recognize that the world of common sense has its own language and the uncritical use of that language will likely serve only to uncritically reproduce the world of commonsense itself. Needless to say, such a reproduction would in nearly every instance be at odds with activist projects.
6. Also see D. Smith, "The Standard North American Family: SNAF as an Ideological Code," in D. Smith 1999: 157–71.
7. For Important examples of structuralist Marxism, see the work of Louis Althusser (1971, 1977). For a poststructuralist focus on social discourse, see Michel Foucault (1979, 1980a).
8. Especially crucial to D. Smith's taking up of Marxism was her re-reading of *The German Ideology* (1976). Crucial to her taking up and moving beyond ethnomethodology was her engagement with Garfinkel's *Studies in Ethnomethodology* (1967) and other work. On the development of D. Smith's approach to sociology, see Campbell (2003).
9. To the best of our knowledge, D. Smith was first lumped together with feminist writers discussing standpoint theory in Sandra Harding's book *The Science Question in Feminism* (1986). It is unfortunately all too common in both sociological and feminist work for D. Smith's contributions to be collapsed into an unlikely amalgam that includes the rather different work of Nancy Hartsock (1985) and Patricia Hill Collins (1990). Also see D. Smith's recent commentary on this problem (2005: 7–26).
10. At the same time Georges Sorel (Horowitz 1961) and others argued from the left for a different understanding of mass psychology and crowd dynamics that

did not classify participants as "deviant." While Sorel's work contains insights it nevertheless has the drawback of collectivizing the psyche in an extrapolative fashion.

11. We use "subject" here in the double-sense of active social agency on the part of oppressed people that Paulo Freire (1970) and Bannerji (1995b) write about but also as "subjects" in the sense that Foucault (1979, 1980a) describes it in much of his work as being the subject of official discourse and discipline. This notion of active agency in our view is always in tension, struggle and transformation.

Foreword

GEORGE SMITH, POLITICAL ACTIVIST AS ETHNOGRAPHER AND SOCIOLOGY FOR PEOPLE

Dorothy E. Smith

This is an emotional topic for me. George Smith and I were very close friends; our collaboration goes way further back than when we both came to Toronto in 1977. In Vancouver we had worked with Marguerite Cassin as political activists for a number of years, mainly in the context of education. In Vancouver we discovered ways of doing things that later, in my own work, became more theoretical, and in George's work, the innovative ways in which he connected activism and ethnography. When I moved to Toronto to take a faculty position in the Department of Sociology of Education at the Ontario Institute for Studies in Education (OISE), George and others from Vancouver, including Marguerite, decided to enter the doctoral program there. They were a powerful group in the department, both intellectually and politically, and George played a leading role. Eventually George and I decided to undertake a research project on the re-organization of skills training (D. Smith and G. Smith 1990). We shared experiences in the field and an intellectual interchange that was deeply valuable for me.[1]

Before preparing my presentation for the conference in Sudbury, I reread George's article, "Political Activist as Ethnographer." I want to reflect on it in a context that has changed somewhat since George wrote it and since he died. The terrain on which social movements go forward and on which struggle takes place has changed. Since I retired, I have been teaching occasionally at the University of Victoria. For a couple of years I taught an undergraduate course there called Research and Social Justice. I start the course by describing a peasant's revolt that took place in England in 1381. I'm not going to give you historical detail on this, but basically you have several hundred men marching on London from the southwest of England. They were protesting against the repression that they experienced from the barons, who were their lords, who owned the land and appropriated their labour. They had at first some success; they attacked and took the Tower of

London, killed some barons and some bishops (who were equally exploitative as overlords) and seemed positioned to make their demands effective.
They were appealing to the king, young, cunning and, unfortunately for
them, two-faced King Richard II. He met with them, assured them that
their grievances would be attended to and persuaded many of them to return
home. Those who didn't, including their leader, Wat Tyler, were then set
upon and murdered. This was a very different organization of a movement
against social injustice from, say, in Seattle in 1999 or in Québec City in
2001. I want to emphasize the difference because the latter movements are
in a world in which the primary modes of organizing are no longer on this
immediate, local, face-to-face basis on which you can march to London and
meet a king and get conned by a king and killed by his forces. Now if you
wanted to march on the World Bank, for example, it is actually hard to find
it and if you did find its head office, you could not be sure in what sense you
had actually found the World Bank in whatever building houses the head
offices of the corporate entity. Wat Tyler and the men he led could break
into the Tower of London and find and kill at least some of their oppressors, but breaking into the head office of the World Bank would not locate
individual oppressors but, for the most part, employees of what George called
a politico-administrative regime, an integral piece of what, following Marie
Campbell and Ann Manicom (1995), institutional ethnographers, call "ruling relations."[2] The ruling relations are those that coordinate our doings and
work in particular local sites with the doings and work of others elsewhere
and at different times; they coordinate trans-locally; they are objectified,
in the sense that they cannot be identified with particular individuals; and
finally, and perhaps most importantly, they are based in and mediated by
texts — printed, written, electronic, film, television, audio and so on.

Contemporary struggles for social justice operate on this ground,
familiar, taken for granted, and yet in its reaches and dimensions of organization only at best partially visible. When George writes about his forms
of activism and ethnography, he is writing about investigations which take
place on the ground of these ordinary yet extraordinary forms of organizing
society; his focus is on what he called "politico-administrative regimes,"
that is, established configurations within the ruling relations organizing and
organized around specific functions. I emphasize this because, for George,
science, the values of science and the importance of scientific research were
central. He did not, however, have to learn the sad lesson that W.E.B Dubois
had to learn in the late nineteenth century.[3] Dubois held at first the belief
of the Enlightenment itself that knowledge as such was transformative. He
believed, when he started his scholarly work and career, that if he drew a
picture of the actual state of living of negroes (that was the term he used)
in Philadelphia by researching their situation and then writing a book that
showed the conditions under which his people lived, that that knowledge
itself would lead to change. He discovered that creating knowledge did not

as such create change; he went on to join his scholarship and teaching more directly in the struggles of his people for justice and equality. George started in a different place; he started with struggle, with activism. But activism on the terrain of the ruling relations needed knowledge of their peculiar properties and organization. The knowledge created by ethnographers of the ruling relations, or institutional ethnographers (as they would now be known), is of the same kind as activists discover in the course of struggle on the terrain of these relations. For the ethnographer who is an activist or the activist who is an ethnographer, there are, George saw, not two kinds of knowledge, the one academic and scientific and the other emerging from the practicalities of struggle. Rather you could pass directly from one to another. Both were grounded in people's actual practices and how they were coordinated as regimes. What the activist learns in the course of his or her engagement with contemporary practices of power is knowledge of the same phenomena that the institutional ethnographer explores.

George was proposing a very different kind of interchange between the academic pursuit of knowledge by the ethnographer and the activist's pursuit of struggle against oppression than that institutionalized in contemporary society. He rejected the production of a knowledge of the social that was indifferent to how it is known in our everyday living practices. The production of academic knowledge has traditionally been for other academics, developing forms of knowledge that are of concern among them but are not intended, even when consciously oriented to the public interest, to be comprehensible or relevant to people in general.

It was not that George believed that knowledge should be created simply for application by activists. He's saying something very different. As activists work increasingly on the terrain of the ruling relations, they are discovering properties and features that the ethnographer can also explore and make observable. The ethnographer can take up the orientation of the activist and focus his or her inquiry on just that organization of power with which the activist engages and knows as practice. He or she can develop ethnographically a knowledge of the workings of politico-administrative regimes that can serve the activist's knowledge by extending and consolidating it. It is not, however, knowledge of a different kind.

Notice that this does not mean being focused on the activist's *issues* as such. It is rather, as an ethnographer, to be systematically investigating and explicating just those dimensions of the ruling relations that constitute the terrain of the activist's struggle. In this way knowledge can be created and developed systematically that makes the kind of working knowledge that the activist acquires explicit and more widely available. The activist's knowledge can be extended beyond the reach of her or his activism; dimensions of the operation of politico-administrative regimes that are implicated in activist experience but not directly accessible can be opened up and displayed by ethnographic investigation.

Established sociology holds generally that a sociology written from the perspective of activist struggle would suffer from lack of objectivity. George adopted a radically different view. He held that a knowledge of the social and, in particular of the ruling relations relevant to activists, could be created by inquiry that was grounded in and investigated people's actual activities or practices. Just as the activist discovers the workings of the ruling relations in the course of struggle, the ethnographer could also explore its practices and relations. What the ethnographer produces as knowledge must be "for real." It must be good enough as knowledge so that activists can rely on it as a guide to aspects of the ruling relations that they must otherwise encounter cold. An academic working as an institutional ethnographer has a responsibility to produce knowledge on which people can rely. If people are going to take the knowledge created by institutional ethnographers seriously, if they're actually going to invest in action on its basis, then the ethnographer just has to get it right. It has to be good though it is always subject to correction originating in the experience of those who are in various ways active in the relations that have been ethnographically explored.

An activist sees the world in terms of what people are doing—what he or she is doing and what others are doing. This is where George starts. So it was central to his project as activist and ethnographer to avoid being snared by concepts that concealed or glossed people's actual practices. It is a critique that connects with Marx and Engels' (1976) much neglected principle that a social science must be grounded in actual people, their actual activities and the relevant material conditions. George rejected a practice identified by Marx and Engels with those they called the German Ideologists, who characteristically substituted concepts for people's actual activities and the relations coordinating them.[4] Concepts rather than people were seen as the agents in history and society. This is a little different from idealism; rather Marx and Engels criticize a way of doing social science that treats the concepts as if they were the reality.

In taking up this critique, George rejected the concept of homophobia as adequate to understand and grapple with the issues of gay harassment in the Toronto of that time. It did not enable gay activists to see how, for example, the raids on bathhouses frequented by gay men had come about. The concept of homophobia forestalled investigation of how the regime worked to enable such actions. His own research (G. Smith 1988b) penetrated the practices and forms of coordinating the work of the police within judicial processes that led to charges laid against the owner of the bathhouse, its manager and the gay men present at the time of the police raid. The kind of language he criticized is common in social movements; indeed it may be important in mobilizing for action. Nonetheless it may actually make it difficult to find out how the relevant dimensions of the ruling relations are actually being put together and hence make it difficult to see what kinds of changes will be effective and how to arrive at them.

The critique of ideology versus science was very central for George. Ideological practices in the use of concepts named and at the same time concealed what was actually going on. They represented actual practices and relations in a kind of abstract space that George wanted to clear away in order that you could get to where you find what people are actually doing in their everyday lives, what they know by virtue of the ways in which they go about in the world. With other institutional ethnographers, George shared the objective of exploring from people's experience of and in our everyday lives into these extended forms of organizing power, which we understand far too little. Even such notions as an "organization of power" must be suspended if we are to investigate the actual practices that bring what we call "power" into being. If the activist's work is to make change; it is the ethnographer's work to make observable and available what is hidden or just out of sight, namely the forms of coordination among people that generate power and shape its character. Those of us who work in universities think we are familiar with how they work but, in fact, we know very little of the actual organization of people's activities that brings into daily being the institutional regime that rules our everyday working lives.

In general, people know very little of the larger scope of the ruling practices that organize our everyday lives. Sure, we can name major organizations such as the World Trade Organization or the World Bank or the International Monetary Fund. We can find out about their policies, political connections and so on. But we have a very limited understanding of the organization of work and textual practices that connect them to what is going on around us or of the very general processes of change in the ruling relations that are currently transforming every aspect of the society we thought we knew. It's this world that George's "Political Activist as Ethnographer" paper hooks us into. His paper tells us to find out about how people's practices are organized in the social relations of ruling much as an activist does, *as they actually are, not as they are theorized.*

The production of social theories that aren't connected to or reflective of people's actual practices is, I think, one of the reasons activists get so fed up with academics. If you're an activist you know a lot about how things work in the area in which you're active even though ideological practices may veil the ways you can talk and tell about them. George's aim as an ethnographer was to get past the barrier of ideology, in the sense that Marx and Engels used in *The German Ideology,* to discover what people actually know about the local practices of a regime they are part of. He pushed the opportunities he had as an activist to find out more about how things work: why, for example, he asked, was government of that time uninterested in possible treatment for AIDS. It was active in preventative education and in providing palliative care for the dying, but treatment was not recognized as programmatic and not therefore funded. Again, he sought an answer not in homophobia, but in discovering the workings of the public health regime that oriented government functions as it did. Treatment for individuals did not come under the jurisdiction of public health authorities, and it was the public health authorities who were responsible for government action on AIDS.

Blame was not, in George's view, useful politically. Rather, inquiry was needed that would uncover how things work to produce the outcomes they did. He began to explore the social organization of treatment knowledge that prevented a knowledge of what was effective in treating AIDS, which was then developing in clinical contexts, being made more generally available in the Canadian health care system. His pursuit of this line of investigation was cut short by his own illness and eventually his death, but his conception of how research should address the problem was typical. He did not deny, of course, that there was homophobia, but held rather that it was a dead end politically, to use the term as an explanation for all the oppressions that gays experienced, including the issue of why treating AIDS was not (at that time) being addressed by government. An ethnography adopting the method that produces knowledge for the activist, could, George believed, discover just how people's practices are socially organized in such a way that things happen as they do, making it then possible to locate where concrete changes might be made.[5]

In his paper he emphasizes that the starting place is not the kind of objectified position that is the starting place of established sociology. He liked to invert Alfred Schutz's (1962) phenomenological notion of bracketing the actual isolating consciousness to enable its experiential exploration as such. George wanted to do the opposite: forget all that stuff about sociology, philosophy, the concepts you get bogged down with in the academic world — forget all that and start looking at what people are actually doing, at what is actually going wrong in their lives as they experience it, at what isn't working for them. You explore the world from there, you begin to look at how it is being put together so that it's happening to people in the way that it does happen to them. In doing that you have a way of looking at the social from the inside but not subjectively. You don't perform the traditional sociological trick of pretending you can see the world from nowhere in particular as if you were outside it. There is no such place. George proposed to bracket those ways of looking at the world that put you outside its reality. For theorizing he substitutes a work of discovery, the writing of an ethnography to display just how people are putting things together so that they work as they do in the actualities of their lives.

When I read George's account (G. Smith 1995), I think "but it's obvious of course, public health, etc." but of course it isn't obvious till the work is done. It's almost a kind of test of an institutional ethnography, once it's done, once you see it, it's obvious. What ethnography discovers is in the same kinds of space in which people live and people are doing their work, and it may be new to you but it's not extraordinary and it doesn't overpower the way you find and discover and experience your world. It adds to and expands our ordinary knowledge. Marie Campbell and Frances Gregor (2002) have used the notion of "mapping social relations" in the title of their book on institutional ethnography. It's a useful metaphor. Making maps is a technical procedure, but for the reader, they bring the world within your reach in a way that enables you to see how where you are is related to where you want to get to and what the way from here to there is like. That's what George's work was aimed at doing. He didn't use the notion of mapping but he would have liked it.

As I mentioned earlier, George did have the notion of a social science. I was studying sociology in England in the 1950s, when sociologists were battling about whether sociology was a science (my bachelor's degree was a B.Sc. (Soc)) and I recoiled at rejoining that issue. George, however, had not been subjected to those wordy battles and was comfortable about doing a science. He was clear that the knowledge produced by what is now called institutional ethnography conformed to the ordinary methodological canons of a scientific enterprise and made the same claims to truth. In producing knowledge relevant to activists, he wanted, as I emphasized earlier, people to be able to count on it. But it was more than that. The ruling relations themselves generalize; politico-administrative regimes aren't just local affairs — they connect and organize trans-locally. Ethnographies of the kind institutional ethnographers develop are exploring the general when they are investigating from particular perspectives.

I emphasize this here because the changes in what George called political-administrative regimes that were already emerging when George and I were working on our research into skills training and he was writing his classic papers oriented to gay politics, go very much beyond how they would have looked then. What seems to be happening is that capital conceived as an organization of the social relations of a mode of production is permeating all aspects of what we have called the ruling relations. This concept of the ruling relations is not a simple reversion to the superstructural theory attributed somewhat doubtfully to Marx. Since Marx's day consciousness and agency have become objectified in social relations mediated by texts — the ruling relations. Until recently there were bases of independence from the interests of capital for an intelligentsia within the professions, universities, health care (in Canada), education, the mass media and in general the public services of government. These should not be exaggerated but they were real. The period of McCarthyism is, oddly enough, indicative of that independence in its attempts to subdue and discipline the intelligentsia in English-speaking North America and — to a large degree successfully — to break an alliance that had been established between the working class and the intelligentsia during the 1930s and 1940s. What we can see goes further and is more fundamental in subordinating public institutions to capital. New technologies of management and administration are reorganizing politico-administrative regimes in ways that integrate them with market processes or simulacra of the market that subordinate their objectives and activities to cost-revenue based financial accountability (McCoy 1999; D. Smith and Dobson 2002). The ambivalences and conflictual character of cultural hegemony that Gramsci identified and analyzed is being resolved into the comprehensive control of capital — a new form of totalitarianism.

If this is indeed the way things are going, we need the kind of scientifically based inquiry that George was putting forward. He proposed a full articulation of the ethnnographer's project with that of the activist engaged in struggle. Institutional ethnography offers ways of exploring and mapping the changing operations of politico-administrative regimes that can extend what activists learn in their practice. If such a possibility is to be realized, teaching and doing research in institutional ethnography needs to be built up and sustained in universities and extended through conferences such as the one represented in this book. This isn't just a matter of developing people's skills and knowledge; it is also essential to building particular studies into more general pictures of the workings of the ruling relations and the changing organization of power based within them. The more general picture is needed to support communities of interest and experience among activists at work in different politico-administrative contexts. We need an ongoing interchange between activists and activist experience and the work of institutional ethnographers both in and outside the academy.

George was both activist and academic. Reflecting on his work from a standpoint in the academy, as I do now, has implications for the development of institutional ethnography in university settings. Teaching the social sciences in universities is a political act. This is not a matter of the expression of specific political values; it is built into the theories and methodologies of every social science. Institutional ethnography is no exception. It is, however, distinctive in proposing a social scientific project that is designed to discover the workings and structures of power *from the point of view of people*'s everyday lives and activities. Developing knowledge from different angles, from different understandings, from different ways of seeing makes possible building towards a more adequate understanding of how these new forms of society are working. The investigations that we can do don't stand by themselves. The different places that we start from feed back into and give us opportunities for discovering not only different aspects but more about how to find about these new technologies of management and administration that are re-forming politico-administrative regimes and the ruling relations in general. It is absolutely in line with George's thinking to imagine a science that could work with and for struggles for social justice because it investigates and makes visible just how power is organized in the multiple sites of struggle that activists engage in the contemporary world.

Notes

1. This introduction draws on papers by George Smith published in 1988b, 1990 and 1995.
2. On ruling relations, also see D. Smith, *Writing the Social: Critique, Theory and Investigations* (1999).
3. W.E.B. Dubois was a sociologist, author and Black activist who lived from 1868 to 1963. One of his most famous books is *The Souls of Black Folks* (1903).
4. See D. Smith (1973) on "the ideological practice of sociology."
5. Among other things, George was exploring, with a group of international scientists, the possibilities of using Bayesian logic to make reliable inferences from clinical observations as an alternative to the standard statistical procedures of contemporary medicine.

GLOSSARY

The editorial collective has compiled this glossary to assist readers in gaining a better understanding of the book. We are not providing definitions of these terms but rather descriptions of their uses by the authors. The ways in which various authors use these terms may be similar, competing or in tension. Many of the terms in this glossary are also interconnected, and we try to make these connections clear. In short, we are interested in what these terms can "do" in the practice of mapping the social relations of struggle. We hope to provide ways through which readers can examine these terms, use them and make them their own. The terms and key words have been derived from the book text, and we have tried to provide some of the multiple ways in which they have been used. In addition, we have tried to synthesize and provide the most cogent explications.

Agency: Agency refers to people's abilities to act in the world. The term is often used in liberal philosophy as a way to represent the essential or autonomous freedom of the individual. In structuralist theory, agency entails being an agent of a social structure, or system, and performing necessary and needed social roles and norms. For some versions of poststructuralism, the agent, or subject, is defined by discourse. Instead, we are using agency to establish people's collective capacities to act in coordinated ways to either reinforce or to dismantle existing social relations. For more on agency, see Bannerji (1995b), where she draws on Marx, Freire and feminism to elaborate a notion of an active sense of agency for the oppressed within a transformative sociology.

Binary: The literary deconstructive theory of Derrida (1978) points to the importance of taking apart and deconstructing the dichotomized oppositions that define many official forms of discourse. For instance, the binary oppositions of man/woman, heterosexual/homosexual, public/private, objective/subjective and inside/outside need to be taken apart in critical social analysis. In relation to gender struggles, the binary opposition of man/woman needs to be organized within the framework of a patriarchal society, and also exploded in a process of social transformation. In this project, we try to link destabilizing and exploding binary oppositions with a more social and materialist grounding while acknowledging that these binaries are used to legitimize certain forms of social relations and social power. We see binaries as not only rooted in discourse and culture, as Derrida views them, but more importantly as rooted in social practices. See the Afterword in this book for our elaboration on exploding the inside/outside binary.

Bracketing: In our usage, this term draws from ethnomethodology, where preconceived notions of the social are set aside for sociological investigations. In ethnomethodology, the natural attitude, common-sense or ideological views are set aside, or bracketed, so that the actual social practices that people use in doing or accomplishing the social can be explicated. For example, the perspective that there are only two genders rooted in biological difference can be bracketed in order to see how people accomplish gender. George Smith extends this to cover the need to bracket pre-existing sociological discourse and theory much more generally. It is only when we bracket ideology, speculation and abstraction that we can recover actual social organization. For more on bracketing, see Garfinkel (1967).

Breaching experiments: Also used in ethnomethodology, these are experiments where social order and normality are disrupted, or breached, in order to learn how social organization is put together. For example, Garfinkel would ask his students to go home to where they lived with their parents and act like boarders to see what social reactions this would produce. From breaching experiments, ethnomethodologists were able to learn about how social order is a continuous social accomplishment and that the social world has an indexical (context-dependent) and reflexive (or mutually determined) character. In this book, Kinsman and Thompson refer to social movement initiatives that breach social relations and challenge institutional relations, in order to learn more about how they are socially organized.

Capital: This is the social relation based on the exploitation of waged and unwaged labour in a capitalist society. Capital is not simply money, investment or a thing but is a social relation between people. To see capital as simply money or a thing is to reify (or thingify) capital, overlooking that capital is based on the active exploitation of surplus value from workers. The "main business" of capital is the accumulation of profit. It is the exploitation of workers (both waged and unwaged) that produces the basis for profit. This use of capital is derived from the work of Marx. For more on capital, see Cleaver (2000); D. Smith and G. Smith (1990), and Kinsman (this book).

Circulation of struggles: In autonomist Marxism (see Kinsman's chapter) circulation of struggles allows us to understand how different struggles have an impact on each other, sometimes circulating the most "advanced" forms of struggle. For instance, certain tactics of direct action and forms of organizing, including affinity groups (small groups that are organized along a basis of affinity, through which people participate in direct actions) and spokescouncils (where representative of affinity groups come together to make decisions), were spread and mobilized around the globe in the years following the Seattle protests against the WTO in 1999. These tactics were then circulated to various points of struggle.

Composition of struggle: In autonomist Marxism, working-class composition (which we can extend to social struggle or movement composition) is used to point to the specific forms of social organization of the working class. These forms of social organization are made clear in relation to capital and ruling relations in specific social and historical periods. For instance, we can look at the composition of struggle by asking the following questions. How integrated is the working class into capitalist relations? How internally divided is the working class and the oppressed? How autonomous is working-class activity from capital? How is working-class struggle in a particular context subversive of social relations? History and shifting forms of social organization therefore become crucial to grasping working-class and social struggles. Capitalists actively struggle to decompose the capacities of working-class struggle by exacerbating and re-organizing internal divisions in the working class and among the oppressed, by ripping apart sources of working-class and oppressed people's power, by fragmenting groups and struggles, by extending social surveillance and by transforming training and skills. These attempts produce new conditions for the possible re-composition of working-class and social struggle. On this, see Kinsman's chapter.

Counter-power: Counter-power, a term used in anarchist and left Marxist activism, refers to forms of organizing that build people's own capacities and forms of power, as opposed to reinforcing state and ruling forms of power. It develops the power of people to do, rather than developing the power over others of state and ruling relations (see Holloway 2002). This form of power develops in distinction from oppressive forms of power and is very often in direct conflict with the logic of capitalism and state relations. See Kinsman and the Afterword in this book.

Dialectics: Focusing on process, conflict and transformation, dialectics is a way of thinking and theorizing. Derived from the work of Hegel and Marx, dialectics insists that the social world never stands still, and neither should our theories of the social. Indeed, the social world is constituted through social struggles and social contradictions; moreover, these lead to social transformation. One crucial aspect of dialectical theorizing is the mediated and inter-connected character of social relations. Each social form of oppression has its own autonomy but is also constructed in and through other social relations. For instance gender, race and class need their own moment of autonomous analysis since sexism is not racism is not class exploitation. At the same time, they can only be fully understood through seeing how racism, sexism and class exploitation in a concrete social and historical sense are organized in and through each other. For more on this use of dialectics, see Bannerji (1995b) and Carroll in this book.

Dialogism/dialogical: There are many voices and dialogues going on around us all the time in society. Dialogism and its variants are central terms used by Russian literary theorist M.M. Bakhtin to get at how "everything means, is understood, as part of a greater whole—there is constant interaction between meanings, all of which have the potential of conditioning others" (Holquist 1981: 426–27). Institutional ethnography and political activist ethnography work to preserve this character of social discourse and interaction. Dialogical works engage with and are engaged by previous works, while anticipating further response. These terms have been taken up in post-modern and post-structuralist theory, where they have often removed language practices from their social and material contexts. Institutional ethnography and political activist ethnography work uses these terms in a more socially and historically grounded fashion and tries to maintain the dialogical character of the social. These terms are found in the chapters by Mykhalovskiy and Church, Kinsman and others. Also see McNally (1997: 26–42) and Smith (1999: 96–130).

Direct Action: Direct actions are forms of social and political action that challenge legal and ruling relations. They do not simply adopt the forms of legitimate, legal action but can sometimes lead to arrest and confrontations with the police. These actions can range from non-violent civil disobedience, to unauthorized strike actions, to squats and occupations of buildings, to forms of targeted property destruction. Direct action support or case work includes the use of these forms of action to get people their social assistance, to prevent evictions or to prevent deportations. In this book, Thompson and Kinsman view direct action as a research practice similar to an ethnomethodological breaching experiment and elaborate on how it can allow for a reflexive materialist understanding of the social. Direct action is also used by Clarke and in the Afterword.

Discourse: This is the social character of language and its connection with relations of social power. Discourse upholds that we can only speak about topics in certain ways. For instance, in the interaction between doctor and patient, it is the doctor who is empowered to diagnose and prescribe a course of treatment. The patient is only allowed to display symptoms and to talk about them, but not to diagnose themselves. This term is commonly identified with the work of Foucault (1974), where it is often focused on the level of statements. D. Smith turns discourse in the direction of the social relations of text-mediated language in our society, whereby texts are used to mediate and coordinate social relations (1999). See the Preface for a description. The term is also used by Namaste, Ng, Wright, Carroll, and Kuhling and Levant in this book.

Epistemology: A term meaning "theory of knowledge," which gets at the *how we know* about the social world that lies behind all theoretical approaches. For example, positivism is one epistemological perspective, a view that assumes that we can know the social world using the same "objective" and "value-free" methods as are used in the natural sciences. Reflexive epistemology views knowledge as being mutually produced through interaction between researchers and the people they learn from. Institutional ethnography and political activist ethnography take up a reflexive epistemological position, arguing the need for a turn away from positivist epistemologies. On epistemology, see our Preface, G. Smith, Thompson and Carroll in this book.

Ethnography: A research strategy common to anthropology and sociology based on entering a culture without preconceived notions and learning from the members of that culture or society about how it is put together. It is used to develop rich descriptions of how culture and the social work. Traditionally applied to "other" cultures, institutional ethnography and political activist ethnography use this way of research as a critical interrogation of ruling relations in our own society.

Ethnomethodology: This is the approach within sociology founded by Garfinkel (1967) that focuses on the study of the methods that people use to make sense of and produce their social worlds. This perspective develops a sustained critique of structural-functionalism and challenges the natural, common-sense view of the world. It views people not as puppets of social structures but as skilled practitioners of their social worlds. In this book, see Kinsman in particular.

Externality: The position of externality is one that is based on being outside of, or on the margins of, the "system." It assumes that it is only from this place that this system can be challenged. However this approach does not fully grasp or recognize that there is no outside to this system. Indeed, the basis for taking up a position of externality is based in the social relations produced within this system. Externality is used in Kinsman's chapter and the Afterword.

The Everyday World as Problematic: Problematic is not the same as a problem. In institutional ethnography, the everyday world becomes the problematic (see D. Smith 1987, 2005) in the sense that questions for investigation arise from the everyday world. As D. Smith points out "defining the everyday world as the locus of a sociological problematic is not the same as making it an object of study" (D. Smith 1987: 90). The everyday world as problematic constitutes instead a lens for research. A crucial aspect of this is that the social relations shaping the everyday world are not simply located in the everyday but are often located in broader, more extended social relations. They are not entirely discoverable within the everyday world and indeed, this is the problematic of the everyday world. A mapping out of how broader social relations enter into the shaping of people's everyday/everynight worlds is required. For example, D. Smith discusses the problematic within small communities affected by capitalist restructuring. She explicates that the logic behind these transformations exists elsewhere (Smith 1987: 94).

Experience: Institutional ethnography inquiry starts within social experience. Experience here is not understood as individual in character or as the "truth." Beginning with people's social experiences can start us in a place that is in rupture with ruling ideologies and social discourses. It grounds us in actual social experience and organization that must be explicated in critical social analysis. This is a crucial part of developing an insiders' knowledge.

Fetishism: In his book *Capital: A Critique of Political Economy* (1962) Marx writes about commodity fetishism. Through this process of fetishization we give supernatural powers to commodities and come to worship things. We can no longer see or remember that it is people who produce the value of commodities. This term has been taken much further in critical sociological investigations to also focus on the fetishization of power and the state. We come to worship power and state relations, forgetting that it is people who produce and make sense of these relations. Holloway (2002) has recently revived an anti-fetishism analysis in his critique of power and state relations.

Ideology: These are social forms of knowledge that are uprooted from, or ungrounded from, the social relations in which they are produced. Given this character, they are useful forms of knowledge for ruling and managing people's lives; the ruling ideas in capitalist society have an ideological character to them. One example is the ideological construction of the "free market" and of "profit," which are separated from the social activities and practices of the people, including waged workers and domestic labourers, who bring them into being. The underlying process of exploitation of surplus value from waged and unwaged workers is thereby made invisible. This ungrounded form of knowledge can also be a problem in social movement theorizing, as we point out in this book. Ideology critique is a key part of Marx's critical analysis of capitalist social relations and is used in this book by many contributors, including G. Smith.

Indexicality: From ethnomethodology, this is the context-dependent character of how people make sense of the social world and how the social world is produced. We interpret and make sense of comments or statements in the social contexts in which we find them. One of the problems of mainstream forms of research and theorizing is that this context-dependent character of the accomplishment of social organization is systematically destroyed. This is carried out with the removal of what people say and do from the contexts in which they say and do them. Institutional ethnography and political activist ethnography try as much as possible to resist this violence of abstraction and to connect doings to their contexts. Indexicality is used by G. Smith and Kinsman.

Insider's knowledge: Institutional ethnography and political activist ethnography as reflexive (mutually determined) epistemological approaches argue for starting within the social and with social experience. These approaches are based on the knowledge of insiders, of the practices of members who produce particular social settings and relations. It is by starting from inside the social world that knowledge of the social world can be produced. This is opposed to the claim that we can start somehow outside of, or above, the social world to develop "objective" and "neutral" knowledge. On this, see G. Smith and Campbell in this book.

Institutional ethnography: Institutional ethnography turns the research strategy of ethnography against ruling institutional relations in our society. D. Smith uses the term 'institution' to demonstrate the complexity and coordination of the intersection of several ruling apparatuses or relations (1987: 160). Starting from the standpoint of a particular group of people (often oppressed and marginalized people) the institutional relations that create problems in people's everyday/everynight worlds are interrogated. Institutional ethnography strives to develop a critical analysis of how these institutional relations are organized so they can be transformed. Central to institutional ethnography is a critique of institutional ideologies, an analysis of the social relations connecting local and more extended relations and a broader notion of work and activity. See D. Smith,

G. Smith, Campbell, Ng and Namaste in this book. For more on institutional ethnography, see Campbell and Gregor (2002) and D. Smith (1987 and 2005).

Internality: This position argues that we always have to be within ruling institutional relations and only argue for reform of these relations. This approach often does not go far enough in its critique of ideology and more traditional research strategies. See Kinsman and Afterword.

Line of fault/disjuncture/rupture in consciousness/bifurcation of consciousness: In institutional ethnography and political activist ethnography this is an important starting point for critical investigation. Oftentimes the social experiences of oppressed people or of social movements exist in rupture with, or in disjuncture with, official discourse and ruling relations. This exists in different although overlapping ways for women, lesbians and gay men, people of colour, working-class people, people living with disabilities and other groups. An example of a rupture in consciousness is when we attend a protest event and the official media coverage of the event has very little to do with how we experienced it. Institutional ethnography and political activist ethnography need to investigate these ruptures in consciousness in terms of how they are socially organized. This notion is used in the writings of D. Smith and G. Smith. Kinsman uses it in relation to social movement struggles. See also Mykhalovskiy and Church, Thompson, Namaste, Wright and Carroll in this book.

Local/extra-local/trans-local: The perspective of the everyday world as problematic starts us in the local world of people's everyday lives. This local interactional world both produces and is shaped by other local interactional worlds that connect together to form more extended social relations. While at one point in the development of institutional ethnography these more extended relations were referred to as extra-local in character, this has now generally been replaced by trans-local, since all these practices and relations, despite occurring across disparate regions, are also locally based. The practice of referring to the extra-local was commonplace in 1990, when G. Smith wrote "Political Activist as Ethnographer" but has now often been superseded by "trans-local."

Mapping social relations: The series of social relations that intrude into and shape local everyday worlds can be mapped out through critical social analysis in institutional ethnography and political activist ethnography work. This mapping is not a neutral or disinterested mapping but is instead an engaged and reflexive map making from the standpoints of the oppressed. This mapping out maintains an indexical (context-dependent) and reflexive (mutually determined) relation to oppressed people's social experiences. This mapping out of social relations is not simply a technical matter, as it is also very much a political and social undertaking. On mapping the social, see D. Smith (1987, 1999, 2005) and Campbell and Gregor (2002). This approach is extended to mapping social relations of struggle by Kinsman in this book.

Materialism: D. Smith and G. Smith are influenced by the historical and social materialist method developed by Marx. This is not a limited or narrow notion of materialism that is reduced to the influence of the material and of objects where the "economic" determines all. Instead, Marx's explication of historical and social materialism as outlined in his "Theses on Feuerbach" (1968) develops a synthesis of the best features of philosophical idealism with that of materialism. This notion of materialism is based on sensuous human social practices. At the same time, while noting the material impact of ideas it does not give power to ideas separated from the material social relations they are produced in, which is what philosophical idealism does.

Monological: This is the attempt to impose one authoritative expert voice over, or on top off, the multiple dialogical interactions going on in society. This authoritative voice over is often the voice of ruling. This term comes from the work of Russian literary theorist Mikhail Bakhtin (1981). Institutional ethnography and political activist ethnography work to oppose this monological character of ruling discourse. Also see D. Smith (1999).

Ontology: These are the assumptions relating to *how the social comes into being* that inform all theories and ways of writing the social. Some theories put forward a structuralist or discursive ontology, whereby it is social structures or discourse that determine the social and brings it into being. Institutional ethnography and political activist ethnography adopt the ontological perspective common to both Marx and ethnomethodology that views the social world as being produced and brought into being through the social practices of people. George Smith refers to this as making the ontological turn. This position is opposed to reification and fetishization within research and theorizing. On ontology see G. Smith, Carroll, and Mykhalovskiy and Church in this book.

Pedagogy: Pedagogy is a term used to describe the study of how we learn and how we are taught. For those engaging in political activist ethnography, this word is often used to talk about exploring how knowledge is produced. In order to investigate how ruling regimes operate, it is essential to be asking how we know. Critical pedagogy, most often inspired by the work of Brazilian literacy educator Paulo Freire (1970), is based on the emancipatory element of education. In opposition to traditional theories of education that reinforce conformity and control and rely on the banking method of the learner as the passive receptacle of authoritative knowledge, critical pedagogy adopts a notion of knowledge that operates to reveal the links between objective knowledge and the regulated norms of society. It argues for an active, producers' notion of knowledge formation in which people as active subjects make connections between knowledge and their worlds. In addition, "[critical pedagogy] begins with the assumption that all people have the capacity and ability to produce knowledge and resist domination" (Darder 2003: 14). Therefore, although pedagogy is most often used to describe the student/teacher relationship, critical pedagogy desires a breakdown of the hierarchies amongst those learning. Under these conditions, teaching becomes a reflexive act. Pedagogy is a useful tool for exploring social investigations between activists and ruling regimes. In this book see Thompson, and Carroll in particular. Critical pedagogy is also used in creative ways in the writings of bell hooks and Himani Bannerji (1995b).

Philosophical idealism: Philosophical idealism is an approach that privileges ideas as central to social explanation but also as separated from the material social relations and practices in which they are produced by people. The classic philosophical idealist claim is from Rene Descartes (2003) — "I think therefore I am," where thought supersedes being and the social relations that create the basis for the thinking "I" are erased.

Political activist ethnography: George Smith extends Dorothy Smith's institutional ethnography approach to more specifically develop sociology for activism and social movements in political activist ethnography. G. Smith suggests that by being located outside of and yet constantly in interaction and struggle with ruling regimes, activists can explore the social organization of power as it is revealed through moments of confrontation. The direction G. Smith's research took was established by the course of confrontation, which in turn was determined by analyzing what he had learned in research that was reflexively organized in relation to movement activism. Political activist ethnography, like institutional ethnography, is based on making an epistemological (from "objective" to reflexive) and an ontological turn (away from ideological and speculative accounts towards the social practices of people). See especially George Smith and Kinsman in this book.

Praxis: Praxis for Marx describes the merging or bringing together of theory and practice. Practice informs theory creation and theory creation informs practice. Further, the combination of theory and practice indicates a move away from simply interpreting the world to acting upon and within it (Marx 1975: 423). This also points to how action and theory are reflexive of each other and not positioned as binary oppositions. See Carroll and Thompson in this book.

Positivism: This is the theoretical or epistemological perspective that argues that the only scientific way to study the human social world is to use the same methods and rules as in the natural sciences, i.e., it is the only way to produce objective and value-free knowledge about the social. Positivism systematically buries the social standpoint taken up in investigating the social world by attempting to obscure the reflexive and experiential dimensions of research. Others, including Marxists, feminists and supporters of sociologist Max Weber, argue that the human social world is different from the realm of the natural sciences and a different epistemology is therefore required. What is needed is a theory of knowledge that takes into account that people have consciousness and can change social practices and relations. In this book, positivism is referred to by Carroll and in the Afterword.

Post-modernism: This is an approach that suggests that we are moving beyond the limitations of modernity and the Enlightenment. While noting important shifts, this approach can suggest that we have moved beyond a capitalist society. Often this approach suggests that we need to oppose all "master-narratives," including those of Marxism and sometimes feminism and that any attempt to grasp the totality of social relations will only lead to totalitarianism. Instead the focus is on questions of fragmentation and social difference, and in general there is a tendency to dissolve social relations. There are different strands of post-modernism, some of which can be more useful for critical social analysis. In general, post-modernism overlaps with post-structuralism. On the limitations of post-modernism, see D. Smith (1999).

Post-structuralism: This is an approach that has moved beyond the limitations of structuralist forms of analysis — especially that of Louis Althusser (1971, 1977). Unitary social structures have been exploded and replaced by fragmentation and difference. There is a focus on discourse, language and the "cultural." The work of Michel Foucault is generally characterized as a form of post-structuralism, as is the deconstructive literary theory of Jacques Derrida. In relation to social movements this approach is especially influential on New Social Movement Theory (see the Preface). There is an influence of post-structuralism on post-modernism and vice versa.

Quantitative methods: These are methods that focus on counting or on quantifying social processes. Often this is based in statistical methods and often (but not always) is informed by a positivist epistemological (theory of knowledge) perspective.

Qualitative methods: These are methods such as interviewing, observational work, visual analysis and critical textual and discourse analysis that are not based on counting. These approaches are often (but not always) based on more reflexive epistemologies (theories of knowledge). Often institutional ethnography and political activist ethnography use these methods but can also use critical quantitative methods.

Radical: This term is used here to mean getting to the root of the problem in social relations and organization (see Rebick 2000). It is not used in the pejorative sense of "extremist" that is often used in official discourse and the mass media.

Recursion: George Smith uses the word recursion to point to the social process through which the same, or similar, forms of social organization are held in place through texts and concepts in ruling forms of social organization. As he writes: "the notion of 'social relations' is involved in discovering the recursive properties of spatial-temporal forms of social organization, especially those that take a textually mediated form." Recursion explicates how the everyday experiences of people can have the same social form as the experiences of others, at other times and places. In his article, George Smith describes the recursive properties of the *Criminal Code of Canada*, which is used by the police to hold the same social form in place through policing practices across the Canadian state.

Reflexivity: This is the mutually determined character of the social world and of knowledge about it. The term comes from the work of ethnomethodology.

Knowledge is produced interactively between someone entering into a social setting and those who are already experts about how this setting is socially produced. It also more generally gets at the interactive and mutually determined character of the social world. This is a form of insider's knowledge. It is also the distinct epistemological perspective taken up in institutional ethnography and political activist ethnography work. On this, see G. Smith in this book.

Reification: This is the social process though which social relations between people get transformed into relations between things. It can be seen as a process of "thingification," in which human agency and activity disappears. This is a pervasive feature of capitalist social relations, in which agency is given to profit, commodities and things and not to the people who socially produce them. Although reification is hinted at in Marx's writings it is more fully developed in the work of Georg Lukács (1968). D. Smith (1999) extends this critique of reification into the realm of sociology and sociological theory to describe how mainstream sociological theory lays out rules and regulations for transforming what people do together in the social world into a series of categories, concepts and things that make the social relations between people disappear and converts them into relations between sociological categories, variables and concepts. For instance, class in much of sociology becomes a classification scheme, a thing and not a social relation between groups of people. In this book reification (and anti-reification) is used in Kinsman and Carroll, among others.

Ruling Relations: D. Smith (1999) and Campbell and Manicom (1995) adopted the term "ruling relations" in order to develop language that moves beyond traditional concepts of power and the state. Ruling relations demonstrate the connections between the different institutional relations organizing and regulating society. Ruling relations combine state, corporate, professional and bureaucratic agencies in a web of relations through which ruling comes to be organized. Key to linking together these different institutional relations are the use of ruling texts in coordinating action in these sites.

Social: In the broadest sense, the social is people's ongoing activities in coordination with the activities of others. Crucial to producing the social are social practices and relations. The distinct realm of the social comes into being in the context of capitalist societies, where a whole range of social problems, contradictions and struggles explode that can no longer be grasped through political economy or psychology. This lays the basis for the emergence of sociology as the study of the social and social problems and also lays the basis for the profession of social work.

Social organization: When distinct forms of coordinating people's activities emerge that are reproduced in many different contexts, we can use the term social organization. Central to social organization are social practices and relations.

Social relations: In institutional ethnography and political activist ethnography social relation is "used not to reference a world, but to orient to it, in the sense in which language conveys the intention (i.e., relevancies) of the user."

First, the notion of social relations is employed in a practical manner to talk about and to investigate the actual practices of individuals, articulated to one another, as forming reflexive courses of action where "different moments are dependent upon one another and are articulated to one another not functionally, but reflexively, as temporal sequences in which the foregoing intends the subsequent and in which the subsequent 'realizes' or accomplishes the social character of the preceding" (D. Smith 1983: 319). These are courses of action that, while coordinated and concerted over time in the activities of people, "are neither initiated nor completed by a single individual" (G. Smith this book).

Standpoint: In institutional ethnography and political activist ethnography, a specific social standpoint is taken up from which to investigate the social. Social inquiry must start from somewhere and institutional ethnography makes this explicit and clear. Starting from the standpoints of the oppressed and exploited can reveal aspects of the social that are not visible from other social locations (see D. Smith 1987, 2005). At the same time, institutional ethnography is not a standpoint epistemology that privileges the social knowledge of a particular social group. Standpoint for institutional ethnography is instead a "transformer," allowing social knowledge to be transformed from particular social locations. The goal is to map the social world from a particular standpoint. On this, see the Preface.

State relations/state formations/the state: The term "the state" is used to describe the government, the military, the police, the law and various levels of bureaucracy. Corrigan and Sayer (1985) point out how the state is not a thing-like object but a series of social relations and a claim to legitimation. To aid in preventing the reification of the state, they suggest we use expressions like state relations and state formation. Many practitioners of institutional ethnography and political activist ethnography use the broader term, ruling relations, which can also include professional and corporate relations.

Text-mediated social organization: This is the ways in which in our contemporary bureaucratic-capitalist society, textual forms of documents and communication (textual here is given a broad interpretation, including TV programs, the mass media and Internet communication) are key means through which social action is mediated, organized and coordinated. Textual forms are crucial to how ruling relations come to be organized. Texts do nothing on their own but are used by people to organize and coordinate social organization. Part of the work of oppositional social movements is to create oppositional texts that can help to organize against ruling relations. On text-mediated social organization see D. Smith (1990b, 1999). On creating oppositional or subversive textual practices see our Afterword.

Part A

BEYOND IDEOLOGY AND SPECULATION

This section sets out the distinctive aspects of political activist ethnography as method and theory and helps to illuminate George Smith as an activist, researcher and teacher. It begins with George Smith's crucial article, "Political Activist as Ethnographer," which initiates political activist ethnography as a specific approach growing out of institutional ethnography. This article requires some contextualization. In his article, Smith engages with how his activism in the gay liberation and AIDS activist movements in

AIDS ACTION NOW! demonstration in downtown Toronto
against proposals to quarantine people living with AIDS/HIV

the early and later 1980s informs his sociological research *for* these move-ments. He moves beyond institutional ethnography as producing knowledge for oppressed people to producing knowledge much more specifically for activism to change the world.

Sites of Struggle: Beyond Ideological Accounts

There are two sites of social struggle specifically investigated by George Smith in "Political Activist as Ethnographer" (G. Smith 1990 and this volume). The first is the mass resistance to the police raids on gay men's bathhouses in Toronto in the early 1980s, when hundreds of men who were in the bathhouses to meet other men with whom to socialize and to have sex were rounded up by the police (McCaskell 1988). The police used the bawdy-house legislation, which can cover not only acts of prostitution but also "acts of indecency" (G. Smith 1988b). Under the *Criminal Code of Canada* to this day sex between men can be considered to be "acts of indecency." Through focusing on the social organization of the police campaign against the baths and against gay sex, George Smith makes visible how they were socially put together through the use of and mediation of the categories and offences outlined in the *Criminal Code* that directed the police against gay sex. George Smith was interested in how these texts were operated and mobilized by people (the police, judges and lawyers), since texts do nothing on their own. This led him to propose that the major goal of the Right to Privacy Committee (RTPC), the defence organization for those arrested by the police that mobilized the community response to the bath raids, needed to be getting rid of the legislation that allowed the police to engage in this criminalization of gay sex (G. Smith 1988b). This type of analysis was vital to developing more effective forms of activism. The RTPC became more effec-tive in its actions the more it investigated questions of social organization and made visible what actually had to be challenged and transformed. On the RTPC and the composition of struggle it mobilized, see also Kinsman's chapter in the next section.

The analysis developed by George Smith is in contrast to the types of speculative or ideological accounts produced at the time of the bath raids. These ranged from the argument that it was the homophobia of the individual cops that led to the smashing down of doors in the bath houses, to theories about how this was all a "Tory plot" because of the upcoming provincial election or speculation that this was just rogue members of the police force doing this without support from their superiors. While some of these approaches had moments of insight they did not actually get at the process of social organization leading to the bath raids and could seriously mislead activism, hindering its effectiveness.

A reflexive-materialist analysis like that developed by George Smith points to the fundamental problem as not the homophobia of individual police officers but rather the social organization of the *Criminal Code* and its relation to police organization and mobilization. Trying to "educate" individual police officers will not get to the root of the problem when changing the law is required. While the conceptualization of homophobia was useful for the gay liberation movement of the early 1970s in contesting definitions of homosexuality as a mental illness, it is limited in reproducing the individualist and psychological aspects of "phobia" from psychological discourse. It therefore obscures social practices and relations (Kinsman 1996: 33–34). Homophobia can come to be seen as the active agent causing troubles for gay men and lesbians, obscuring the actual social organization of the bath raids. In this sense homophobia becomes an ideological or socially ungrounded conceptualization working against analysis of social organization. Instead we have to focus on how what we can come to call homophobia is socially organized and produced by people.

The second site George Smith investigates is the social organization of the denial of AIDS/HIV treatments to people living with AIDS/HIV in the late 1980s in Canada as part of his activism in AIDS ACTION NOW! He explored how this problem in the everyday lives of people living with AIDS/HIV was socially organized, and he came to see that state and social responses to AIDS were then focused on "public health" (isolating the infected from the "general population"), palliative care (compassion while dying) and through viewing AIDS as a "terminal illness" (Kinsman 1997). This did not mandate any infrastructure for getting needed treatments into people's bodies so they could live longer and have a better quality of life. He proposed that AIDS ACTION NOW! take steps to put in place this needed treatment infrastructure and access to treatment information. This meant that the ideological accounts that often informed action around AIDS needed to move beyond explanations of "homophobia," "red-tape" or "AIDS phobia." Effective activism and organizing had to be based on an analysis of how the lack of access to treatments was socially organized. To do this involves important theoretical and methodological shifts.

Epistemological and Ontological Shifts

George Smith, as pointed to in our Preface, outlines two major shifts, from orthodox and "traditional" social theory and methods that are crucial to doing political activist ethnography. Regarding epistemology, he argues for a shift that challenges objective or neutral ways of knowing and learns from feminism to adopt a mutually determined and socially reflexive understanding of the world. The world cannot be known from some objective standpoint outside and above social struggles but only from within the social and by learning from people about how their lives and relations of struggles are put together. Regarding ontology (how the social exists, how it comes into being), he argues for a shift learned from Marx to view the social world as being produced through the social practices of people. This ontological perspective is also compatible with that adopted in ethnomethodology, which focuses on the social practices through which people produce their social worlds (Garfinkel 1967). Eric Mykhalovskiy and Kathryn Church take this exploration of the ontological shift further in their dialogue in their chapter. These epistemological and ontological shifts are crucial to doing institutional ethnography and political activist ethnography and distinguish them from other approaches to theory and method.

This approach allows George Smith to link theory and practice, activism and analysis, thus allowing him to move back and forth between theory and practice, and allowing activism to inform his analysis. George Smith in his own life bridged the divides between activism and theorizing in amazing ways. At times, this major divide in which many of us live our lives seemed to almost effortlessly dissolve for George Smith. At the same time, as Mykhalovskiy points out, this relationship for George Smith was never seamless and was always filled with tension and conflict.

Like many activist-researchers, George Smith also had different ways of writing for his diverse audiences. While "Political Activist as Ethnographer" was directed towards the academic world, including activists located there, he also wrote more specifically to gay and AIDS community and movement activists. We include alongside his major article two "snapshots" of his activist writing. These reproductions are scanned from "In Defence of Privacy: Or Bluntly Put, No More Shit" (circa 1983) and "Talking Politics: The New Militancy" on AIDS organizing in *Rites* magazine (1988). Following his chapter is a selected list of his activist writings.

After writing "Political Activist as Ethnographer" George Smith moved on from his concern with AIDS/HIV treatment access to focus on questions of class and poverty. His institutional ethnography research done with Eric Mykhalovskiy looked at the obstacles people living with AIDS/HIV encounter in hooking up to social service agencies (E. Mykhalovskiy and G. Smith 1994). He also did groundbreaking research on the social organization of the ideology of "fag" in high school contexts (G. Smith 1988b).

Of Pedagogies and Social Organization

But what of George Smith as a particular social individual with multiple impacts on the people around him? In "Of T-Shirts and Ontologies: Celebrating George Smith's Pedagogical Legacies," a delightfully dialogical piece, Eric Mykhalovskiy and Kathryn Church interweave their various encounters with George at the Ontario Institute for Education and as an AIDS activist and researcher. Here, as in Dorothy Smith's Foreword, a more personal connection to George emerges. They describe what they learned from George as a mentor, co-researcher, activist and teacher about doing research and its relation to activism. Each author gives a different sense of George and what they learned from him but both Church and Mykhalovskiy emphasize the ontological shift they learned from George, the importance of starting with social practices and relations and not with ideology and speculation. Mykhalovskiy also raises vital concerns over the new regulatory regimes that are making it more difficult to do activist research in the academy, and Church, drawing on her work with people who have been psychiatrized, raises important concerns about the limitations of conceiving "the textual" simply as written text on the page. Here she emphasizes the need to take up art and cultural production as ways of extending the ability of activist research to engage with people. We return to these questions in our Afterword

Marie Campbell follows this up with "Research for Activism: Understanding Social Organization from Inside It," in which she reflects on the experiences of a street nurse having her work undermined by people in ruling relations, as well as on a participatory action institutional ethnography research investigation regarding the social obstacles facing people living with disabilities. She allows us to see how activists can use institutional ethnography by exploring social organization from our locations within it. This can allow us to develop a social analysis that can provide a solid basis for activism and allow us to see how accounts of the oppressed and of activists are subordinated in ruling accounts. One aspect of effective activism is to be able to analyze how these ruling perspectives are socially organized so they can be challenged and undermined as part of developing effective directions for our struggles.

POLITICAL ACTIVIST
AS ETHNOGRAPHER

George W. Smith

For more than a decade I have been involved as political activist working with individuals who stand outside ruling *régimes* that seek to manage society. From this location, the extra-local organization of an administrative apparatus remains opaque. This is a serious handicap for people who would change how their world is informed, ordered and governed. During this time, I have also studied and worked with a method of doing sociology proposed by Dorothy Smith (1987). I have, in employing her method, used political confrontation as an ethnographic resource. In the early eighties I worked with the Right to Privacy Committee (RTPC), a community-based organization set up to defend people arrested in raids on gay steambaths in Toronto, and more recently, with AIDS ACTION NOW! (AAN!), a community-based, political-action group concerned with improving access to treatment for people who are either living with AIDS (PLWAs) or who are infected with the human immunodeficiency virus (HIV) but asymptomatic (PLWHIVs). This paper sets out a method of using grassroots political organizing as a means of describing how people's lives are determined from beyond the scope of their everyday world. In doing so, it provides a way of exploring, from their standpoint, how the world works and how it is put together, with a view to helping them change it.

Two Studies of Ruling

The discussion of method developed in this paper is focused on two studies: one on the policing of the gay community in Toronto — a study of the 1981 bath raids (G. Smith 1988b); and another on AIDS treatment deficits (G. Smith 1989), a study of the management of the AIDS epidemic in Ontario. Both studies, following D. Smith's method, share the following features: they (1) start from the actual lives of people and undertake an analysis of a world known reflexively; (2) stake out an ontological commitment to a social order constituted in the practices and activities of people; (3) take, as their analytic, the notion of "social relations"; (4) are based on the use of

Here is George looking uncharacteristically corporate in a shirt and tie. He usually wore khaki trousers and T-shirts, and that is probably how most people remember him. But he also possessed a wardrobe of fine suits. I learned about George's sartorial expertise when I worked with him one summer on a research project in which we interviewed government officials and college presidents. George took very seriously the ethnographer's maxim about dressing in a way your informants could relate to and respect. My efforts at dressing up that summer fell far short of George's achievement. The secret, he explained, was not just the quality of the clothes but orchestrating the whole look: if you were going to dress up, you should do it right, with conviction and skill, and if you didn't have the skill, you should try to learn it. In a way, that was pretty much George's approach to everything he did. — LIZA McCOY

meetings with government officials and professional cadres as ethnographic data; (5) analyze texts such as media reports, legislation, internal agency memoranda, annual reports of government departments, in developing a description of how a ruling *régime* works; and (6) illustrate the necessity of bracketing ordinary political explanations — the technique of the materialist *epoché*, as I call it — in order to provide a scientific account of the social organization of a ruling *régime*.

The study of the policing of gay men in Toronto began immediately following the 1981 police raids on gay steambaths in the city and took nearly three years to complete. It examined how the raids were conducted and was written up as the textual analysis of a disclosure document connected with one of the raids. A disclosure document is used to disclose the facts the police intend to use in prosecuting the accused in court. The research examined the social organization of gathering evidence used in the disclosure document, as a mandated course of action (investigation, raid, arrest, trial) shaped by the bawdy-house section of the *Criminal Code*. It explored the ideological practices of inscription in gathering evidence against the steambath patrons, and discovered this work to be embedded in textually mediated social relations. This study had implications for both sociology and gay politics. For sociology, it demonstrated how to undertake research for gay people, rather than treating them as docile objects of study. Secondly, it pointed to the importance of texts in investigating the operations of an extra-locally organized ruling apparatus. Its implications for gay politics stressed the importance of the *Criminal Code* in establishing relations between gay men and the police, and argued for changes in the *Code* rather than using public relations exercises to improve gay-police relations.

The study of the management of the AIDS epidemic in Ontario began in 1988 and is still on-going. Its purpose was to determine how it is that new, experimental AIDS drugs have not been available to people living with AIDS and HIV infection in Ontario. The research discovered and described the social organization of four policy lines in the management of the epidemic: public health policy, AIDS research, palliative care, and treatment. These were investigated as social courses of action occurring over time using the concept of "social relations" as a method of investigation. It became clear early on in the study that the government was basically concerned with public health policy, while the medical profession, organized as small, independent businessmen, was responsible for delivering treatment. Little or no basic AIDS research, as it turns out, is conducted in Canada. What passes for research is product testing of new drugs that, again, is organized within the government's public health mandate. Palliative care is provided by voluntary organizations governed by the concept of compassion for the dying rather than by a mandate directed at delivering life-extending treatments. The medical profession, although responsible for treatment, has generally been unable and/or unwilling to use new, experimental AIDS drugs. This turned out to be, in part, because they are prohibited by public health regulations from using unlicensed treatments and threatened by the possibility of malpractice suits or of losing their hospital privileges should they do so. Consequently, the study's most important finding about the management of the AIDS epidemic, from the standpoint of people living with AIDS or HIV infection, is the lack of an infrastructure to manage the delivery of new, experimental treatments. These findings have directed the work of AIDS ACTION NOW! in designing and in putting in place just such an infrastructure.

A New Paradigm for Sociology

It should be said at the outset that the method of work proposed by Dorothy Smith marks a paradigm shift for sociology because of its unique epistemological/ontological grounding. The sociologist finds herself working with a different method, both ontologically and epistemologically, in relation to the actual world she intends to explore and describe. For Smith, this is a world materially constituted in the practices and activities of people as these are known and organized reflexively and recursively through time. This kind

IN DEFENCE OF PRIVACY
Or bluntly put, No more shit *

free

ACTION!
A Publication of the Right to Privacy Committee
VOL.3 NO.1

Police arrests of ever-larger numbers of gay men in steambaths, parks and restrooms has provoked a discussion of "public sex" in the gay community. This discussion has been cast, however, in terms of the police definition of "public" without the slightest concern for people's right to privacy, especially gay people's. The assumption is that the four walls of a person's bedroom mark the boundary of his/her privacy. Everything else is public. On the one side of this discussion, consequently, are those gays who are essentially anti-sexual and who are prepared to defend the standpoint of the police. On the other side are a number of sexual radicals calling for no-holds-barred sex in public. Neither position takes the right to privacy as an issue. Here, as elsewhere, the police definition of "public" is allowed to set the agenda. What is crucial to this discussion is the way in which terms like "public" are taken out of their ordinary context, given

very easy to see how a very broad definition of "public" cuts down, consequently, on people's privacy. In launching their attack on group sex before the Standing Committee on Justice and Legal Affairs, the police were quite aware that by advocating a broad definition of "public" they were actually infringing on the privacy of Canadians. They believed, however, that this was justified. It helped control organized crime. On the issue of privacy, consequently, Mr. Lafrance, again speaking for the Canadian Association of Chiefs of Police, questioned "whether in the strict and zealous pursuit of privacy protection, the practical ramifications of a change such as this (i.e. to Section 158) have been adequately considered." Underlining the importance of this definition of "privacy" for social control and for the work of the police, he then proceeded to raise the spectre of organized crime: "The adoption of this amendment to the present gross indecen-

the gay community as a criminal minority—in much the same way the Toronto police frame up the Jamaican and Italian communities as criminal. They do this by claiming that gay life in Canada is a creature of organized crime and is rife with drug dealing and illegal weapons. They peddle this story to the media and to government as a means of controlling the sexual lives of gay people.

The police, of course, would argue that they are only enforcing the law, merely doing their job. Their claims to objective law enforcement, however, are shown to be transparently homophobic when considered in the light of recent revelations from Queen's Park on wife beating. So-called domestic disputes involve serious cases of assault, and ultimately account for 40% of homicides in the country. Yet the police lay charges against wife beaters in only 3% of cases. This in spite of the fact that the battered women involved require some form of

Mr. Kilgour: One of the cases that is cited under Section 158 is to the effect that a locked cubicle in a subway washroom into which the public could see is a public place. You would not have any quarrel with that I assume?

RTPC: I guess the problem I am having with it is the question of defining public in terms of public place. It is very—

Mr. Kilgour: Yes, but why can we not be concrete? Do you quarrel with this summary I've just given you?

RTPC: I take the case—

Mr. Kilgour: No, no, but listen, sir. You can only have a discussion if you try to deal with—

RTPC: Yes. Right. Well, I do not know if I would want to agree to that, because it seems to me—

Mr. Kilgour: All right. Okay, the answer is no, then.

RTPC: Yes. Okay.

Mr. Kilgour: Would you agree that a public park to which the public has ... obviously by definition, a public ...

of ontological commitment marks off her work from other empirical and/or radical approaches to sociology because it proposes to investigate social life in terms of how it is actually organized. The social world's pervasive reflexivity requires, in terms of traditional sociology, an epistemological shift because, as ethnomethodology has demonstrated, the sociologist cannot know her world from outside, but only from inside its social organization. The Archemedian point, from which professional sociologists have traditionally launched their investigations, no longer exists in its pristine state. D. Smith, consequently, discovers the problematic of her research from within the everyday world, of which she too is a member (D. Smith 1987). Moreover, her inquiry is best understood as an effort to extend her knowledge as a member of this world (Garfinkel 1967) to its extra-local forms of social organization.

The novel manner in which Smith's work is grounded, the fact that it constitutes a new paradigm for sociology, *ipso facto* presents serious problems for understanding it[1] (Kuhn 1970). This paper, for example, in the way it follows her method has to be read using the interpretative procedures to be found in the paper itself. Employing the standard methods for interpreting sociological discourse is a sure-fire formula for misreading it. Although the social organization of her method starts from and thus takes up the standpoint of women, its ontology and epistemology intends a science of society rather than a form of ideological practice (D. Smith 1990a). Her method, consequently, does not depend on the standard categories of feminist research. For this reason it can be used by all individuals who stand outside political-administrative *régimes* intent on managing society. It is especially useful, moreover, for providing a groundwork for grassroots political action; not only because, as a matter of method, it begins from the standpoint of those outside ruling *régimes*, but because its analysis is directed at empirically determining how such *régimes* work — that is, how they are socially organized.

The Everyday World as Problematic

Rather than starting with sociological or political theory, both studies discussed here began in the everyday world with the actual experiences of actual individuals. The point of starting this way was not to engage in phenomenological analysis but to locate the inception of these investigations with active knowers in the real world. Thus, the "problematic" arose out of the everyday experiences of gay men, in the one instance, and out of those of PLWAs and PLWHIVs, in the other. For these individuals, their knowledge of everyday events situated them on one side of a line of fault separating them from the objective bureaucratic domain of a politico-administrative *régime*.

Ideological practice operates as a set of procedures used to know theoretically, categorically, a social world with a view to administering it. These procedures go forward simultaneously from a number of different spatial-temporal sites. The ways in which they subtend these disparate sites of activity, organizing them into an extra-local conceptual worldview, is an essential constituent of what I have called a politico-administrative *régime*. People more-or-less assimilate these ideological procedures as a form of social consciousness that develops as an everyday feature of their lives. They know, consequently, how to work up accounts of events in the everyday world such that what is seen as relevant both conforms to and intends the practices of a ruling *régime*. Within this kind of matrix the conceptions (i.e., the ideological practice) of a *régime* operate in explanatory fashion to regulate and control events in local settings. Both the bath raids study and the investigation of the management of the AIDS epidemic began with just such ideological explanations used to account for the actions of a politico-administrative *régime*. The first took up the ideology of "gay men as criminals"; the second, the ideology of "AIDS as a fatal disease."

The ideology of a politico-administrative *régime* is ruptured when people know a situation to be otherwise on the basis of their everyday experiences. In the cases of the bath raids and of access to treatments for AIDS, these ruptures occurred along the line of fault separating the local organization of the lives of gay men and of people living with AIDS from the objective, bureaucratic domain of a politico-administrative *régime*. The social organization of the Toronto bath raids, for example, was put together in the ideological practices

Talking Politics: The New Militancy by George Smith

There is a new gay militancy sweeping America that has arisen in the wake of the present AIDS crisis. Activities in the U.S. are being spurred on as well by the recent decision of the U.S. Supreme Court to uphold the criminalization of gay/lesbian sex. In general, this wave of protest is carried forward by concern over wide spread backtracking across the U.S. on the issue of gay/lesbian rights. The target is the homophobia that underlies the organization of the

speech by the chief justice of the Supreme Court.

Increasingly, gay militants in Boston, New York City, L.A., San Francisco, and other parts of the country are opting for direct action strategies to drive home their message to politicians and other members of the ruling apparatus. In New York, ACT-UP (AIDS Coalition To Unleash Power) specializes in attacking the homophobia which underlies the political and bureaucratic

homophobe --rises to deliver his homily, stand in silence. Ordinarily, ushers ask those standing to leave which they have done up to last Nov. That month Dignity's Social Justice Committee uped the ante by deciding not to leave voluntarily. On the first Sunday in Dec., the Cardinal had a detail of 75 NYC cops outside the Cathedral to enforce the seating arrangements. By the time the service was over 11 protestors had been arrested within the precincts of

of the police, which were conceptually coordinated at the local level by the idea of gay men as criminals and the gay community as a criminal minority in the city.

The same sort of rupture occurred with the AIDS epidemic. The medical treatment supplied by the politico-administrative *régime* managing the epidemic in Ontario was ideologically organized by the conception of AIDS as a fatal disease. Palliative rather than aggressive "accelerated care" was the order of the day. The provincial health department, for example, basically allocated funds for hospice care and for psycho-social support for the dying.[2] While most local doctors also followed regimens of palliative rather than accelerated care, PLWAs in Toronto knew through personal contacts and "underground" networking with their counterparts in the United States that people with AIDS could live longer. Contrary to the official prognosis of the politico-administrative *régime* in charge of managing the epidemic, they believed that AIDS was no longer a necessarily fatal illness in the short run.

These kinds of ruptures of consciousness are located in the social relations that produce them. This is where my research began; not in the objective domain of sociological theory, but with everyday events in people's lives. These kinds of problems of knowing — of being told one thing but in fact knowing otherwise on the basis of personal experience — provided a starting point for the research that then went on to explicate how a *régime* works. Essentially, it called for an investigation of ideological practice extending beyond the scope of local settings. In the case of my own work, I formulated the problematic of the police paper as: How is the policing of gay men organized? and with the research on AIDS as: How is the delivery of AIDS treatments in Ontario organized?

The Epistemological Shift: The Rejection of Objective Accounts

D. Smith's use of the notion of "problematic" draws on the epistemological and ontological foundations of her method. The epistemological character of the problematic, the fact that it arises in the everyday world as a problem about knowing, sets the basic framework for the design of the research. The way she uses the term "problematic" is also consistent with her analysis of language as a vehicle for organizing and coordinating the activities of people. This approach is grounded in her studies in the social organization of knowledge that make it conceptually possible to juxtapose the objective knowledge of a politico-administrative *régime* over against the locally organized, reflexive knowledge of individuals in the everyday world. The reflexivity of everyday knowledge was discovered by Garfinkel in his studies in ethnomethodology (Garfinkel 1967). The reflexive knowledge of settings and how they work he identified as "members' knowledge." Even objective knowledge depends upon members' knowledge, although this is never formally recognized in the principles of its construction (Zimmerman 1974).

Her studies in the social organization of knowledge provide for the working out of D. Smith's (1974, 1990a) critique of ideology and, hence, of objectivity. She treats ideology not as a mental phenomenon, but as a form of social organization dependent on texts. Using insights from Marx's (1976) *German Ideology,* she describes the social organization of ideological accounts as being done from a standpoint and, with an objective structure of relevancies located in documents, in a "virtual" reality, outside actual local settings. Ideology operates from here as the imposition of objective, textually mediated, conceptual practices on a local setting in the interest of ruling it. The social organization of this kind of knowledge, moreover, produces the epistemological line of fault between the objective knowledge of a *régime* and, in this instance, the reflexive, everyday knowledge (i.e., knowledge as members) of gay men and of PLWAs.

D. Smith's use of the notion of a "problematic" conceptualizes this line of fault as a topic of research. Her usage depends, first, on the social organization of the standpoint of actual individuals in the real world, which in turn, depends upon the fact that knowing in this everyday world is reflexively, rather than objectively, organized. Objective knowledge is no longer "the truth." Rather, it is a form of knowing used to rule society that contingently, but inextricably, incorporates the standpoint of men. Thus, her feminist critique of objective knowledge, and hence of standard sociology, requires an epistemological shift. This is not a shift from an objective to a subjective epistemology, which some feminists have chosen to make, but rather a move from an objective to a reflexive one where the sociologist, going beyond the seductions of solipsism, inhabits an actual world that she is investigating. It is precisely this epistemological shift that allows D. Smith's method of sociology to embrace the standpoint of those who stand outside a ruling *régime;* whether this be the historical position of women in patriarchal society, the position of gay men and lesbians in heterosexual society, the location of people of colour in a racist society or the standpoint of working people in class society — to name but a few of those individuals who often stand outside a ruling *régime.* D. Smith views the critique of objectivity and the consequent epistemological shift as central to the feminist character of her work.

In terms of my research, the epistemological shift operated in two ways: first, it meant explicating informants' knowledge as socially organized and therefore as constituted reflexively. And second, it meant beginning reflexively from my own, actual location in the world rather than from the objective standpoint of standard sociology.

The Ontological Shift: Rejecting Speculative Explanations

Developing a problematic is part of the work of putting together a research design. This requires not only an epistemological shift but an ontological one as well. The latter involves a change from a generalized world of conceptual and theoretical explanations to the concrete, sensuous world of people's actual practices and activities. For example, in the case of the bath raids, gay men in Toronto speculated that the raids were a direct result of police homophobia. A long-time activist further speculated that this discriminative animus resided not in the upper echelons of the police force, but among the local sergeants, in what he called "the rule of the sergeants." Other activists suggested that the raids were an attempt by the provincial Tory government to win over conservative, rural voters in the up-coming elections. Likewise, with the AIDS crisis, people living with AIDS blamed a lack of access to treatments on the homophobia of the Tory minister of health, or more generally on bureaucratic red tape. In each and every case, the impugning of these kinds of causes was organized conceptually, theoretically, as an interpretation of events that depended on the standard shibboleths of political theorizing, especially among gay men. There was little interest in investigating empirically how the way people were treated came about, either by the police or by the AIDS bureaucracy. Rather than critiquing the ideological practice of these politico-administrative *régimes* as a method of determining how things happen, activists usually opted for speculative accounts. The touchstone of these explanations was the attribution of agency to concepts such as "homophobia" or organizational glosses such as "red tape." These became the "causes" of action or inaction by a *régime*. Instead of events being actively produced by people in concrete situations, they are said to be "caused" by ideas such as "AIDS-phobia."

These kinds of explanations preclude understanding how the world actually works. While they often have a certain force in organizing political reactions to the activities of a ruling *régime*, these kinds of self-activating conceptions obfuscate how things are actually organized. They are not concrete in the sense of being based on a clear understanding of how it was, for example, that the bath raids happened or how it actually was that there was a lack of access to experimental AIDS treatments. At best, these idealist practices treat a politico-administrative *régime* as a black box, the interior workings of which are activated by concepts theorized on the basis of its administrative responses to events in local settings. At worst, as the case of the "rule of the sergeants" or the suggestion that the bath raids were part of a Tory election strategy, they preclude finding out empirically how the internal organization of a politico-administrative *régime* actually works. Because it does not have a concrete grip on how things function, this kind of theorizing is not much help in effectively challenging or changing the workings of a *régime*.

In contrast to these kinds of procedures, research undertaken in a materialist mode produces a different kind of result. The study of policing, for example, documented how the Canadian *Criminal Code* organizes the enforcement of heterosexuality. The "homophobia" of the police, in the first instance, was organized by the law and therefore not necessarily caused by the personalities of police officers. The political implications of this finding are that if gay men are no longer to be regarded as a criminal minority, it is necessary to change the law rather than engaging in public relations efforts to change how the police think. Similarly, the study of the AIDS epidemic revealed that no level of government — federal, provincial, or municipal — had a mandate to manage the delivery of new, experimental treatments to people living with the disease. This lack of a treatment-delivery infrastructure both provided for and hence succumbed to the conception of AIDS as a fatal illness. The situation was viciously circular. The problem of government bureaucracy, in this instance, was not so much a matter of "red tape" and homophobia as it was a lack of a mandate and a managerial infrastructure to deal with the delivery of treatments. What became politically necessary, consequently, was the establishment of a treatment-access infrastructure that supported the efforts of physicians responsible

PROBLEMS IN NON EMPIRICAL SPECULATIONS

EMPIRICAL SOLUTIONS FOR LEGIT /OR THAT LEGITIMIZE (NEED OF?) SOCIAL CHANGE

example

for the delivery of new experimental therapies to people living with AIDS. The political work of AIDS ACTION NOW! in combating the "AIDS as a fatal disease" ideology became the creation of this kind of a treatment-delivery infrastructure, including the relaxation of the regulations governing the federal Emergency Drug Release Program; the publication of *Treatment Update,* a newsletter for doctors documenting recent medical advances in treatments; and campaigning for a government-run AIDS treatment registry.[3]

What these two pieces of research required, as a matter of method, was to move away from the ideological practice of creating speculative accounts, produced in these instances by gay and AIDS activists, to the empirical study of how a politico-administrative *régime* actually works. This move from idealist theorizing and speculation to investigating the everyday world as it is put together in the practices and activities of actual individuals is what is meant by the "ontological shift." This shift is the basis of the critique of speculative accounts and a necessary condition for the formulation of people's experience of an everyday world as problematic. Marx and Engels (1976: 31) set out the basic premises of the materialist aspects of this method in *The German Ideology.* Inasmuch as the epistemological shift formed the core of the contribution of feminism to D. Smith's work, the ontological shift is derived from a study of Marx. It is in this sense that she has developed a Marxist-feminist method for sociology.

The Conceptual Organization of a Reflexive-Materialist Research Method

The fact that D. Smith's method of sociology eschews sociological and political theory as a basis for understanding how politico-administrative *régimes* work is not to suggest that this kind of research is not conceptually coordinated; on the contrary. However, the conceptual basis of the research is reflexively organized within a materialist understanding of a world that is put together in people's practices and activities. It follows, for example, that the ethnographer's language not only coordinates her investigative activities but also the work down the road of writing up her analysis as sociological description. In both instances, the language of method is taken as incorporating the ontological and epistemological shifts described earlier. It is not used, for example, to construct variables as "causes" of social action or to produce objective accounts. Contrary to the claims of objective knowledge as the only "true" reality, D. Smith puts forward the knowledge of members as the basis for understanding how a politico-administrative *régime* actually works. To implement these epistemological and ontological requirements calls for considerable inventiveness, however. The problem is always one of explicating and describing the reflexive, social ontology of the everyday world. Different forms of social organization, different ontological properties, often require different reflexive-materialist methodologies.

"Social Relations" as a Device
for Investigating Social Organization

The everyday world as problematic formulates inquiry as focused on describing the extra-local ideological determinations of local events. Examining these kinds of determinations requires a method of work that can study social organization as this is coordinated and concerted, reflexively and recursively across space and time, in the practices and activities of individuals. D. Smith's device for doing this is the concept of "social relations." This terminology is used not to reference a world, but to orient to it, in the sense in which language conveys the intention (i.e., relevancies) of the user. First, the notion of "social relations" is employed in a practical manner to talk about and to investigate the actual practices of individuals, articulated to one another, as forming reflexive courses of action where "different moments are dependent upon one another and are articulated to one another not functionally, but reflexively, as temporal sequences in which the foregoing intends the subsequent and in which the subsequent 'realizes' or accomplishes the social character of the preceding" (D. Smith 1983: 319). These are courses of action that, while coordinated and concerted over time in the activities of people, are neither initiated nor completed by a single individual.

Second, the notion of "social relations" is involved in discovering the recursive properties of spatial-temporal forms of social organization, especially those that take a textually mediated form (Hofstadter 1979: 127–28). Texts as active constituents of social relations can iterate the particular configuration of their organization in different places and at different times, thereby conceptually coordinating and temporally concerting a general form of social action. Recursion, consequently, is also discoverable in how particular, textually organized, local experiences of people have the same social configuration as the experiences of others, organized extra locally through the same text, at other times and places.[4] The recursive ontology of a generalized course of action, consequently, makes it possible to go from particular events in local settings to a set of general, textually mediated social relations because they have the same social form.

The recursive properties of the social organization of the *Criminal Code*, for example, gave the disclosure document in the bath raid trials the property of coordinating and concerting the same relations the raids themselves did — i.e., they organized a particular set of sexual relations in society. Documents like the *Code* are always designed to organize and coordinate particular forms of organization. In this sense, documents should be read as integral to the social organization of the affairs of people. Thus, both the disclosure documents and the raids, in following the *Code*, had the same recursive relation to it, played out in the enforcement of heterosexuality. Each was an iteration of the social form embedded in the language of the *Code*. Together, all three were doing the same work. Another way of describing this is to point out that the *Code*, the raids and the disclosure document

NOTION OF "SOCIAL REL" IS ACTS A LENS FOR ANALYSIS

had the same social form, the latter being more particular and concrete, and the former more abstract and general.

The notion of "social relations," within this context, operates as a research technique for locating and describing the social form of people's activities over time. It provides a method of looking at how individuals organize themselves *vis-à-vis* one another. The notion of "social relations," in this sense, does not stand for a thing to be looked for in carrying out research; rather, it is what is used to do the looking. It operates as a methodological injunction that requires sociologists to examine empirically how people's activities are reflexively/recursively knitted together into particular forms of social organization. An important discovery of this method of work is the active role documents play in coordinating and organizing people's activities (D. Smith 1984). This discovery provides for the sociologist's ability to investigate and describe networks of co-ordered activities going forward simultaneously across a number of distinct sites of social action. The concept of "social relations" also operates, in this sense, to enter the social world into the sociological text by helping the ethnographer formulate her description of it.

"Régime" as an Investigative
Technique for Studying a Ruling Apparatus

As an adjunct to the conceptual device of "social relations," I have also adopted the notion of *régime* as a mechanism for facilitating an investigation and description of how ruling is organized and managed by political and administrative forms of organization. An everyday feature of our society is how these various institutional sites of regulation and control are merged together to create what I have called, borrowing some terminology from regulation theory (e.g., Agletta 1979), a politico-administrative *régime*.[5] These kinds of *régimes* usually have two interrelated pieces of organization: ① a political apparatus and ② a bureaucracy.

Like "social relations," *régime* is not treated as a reified, theoretical entity that causes social phenomena. It does not tell us anything, consequently, about how governing and ruling practices work, except to provide for investigative procedures that go beyond what is meant by "the state" to include multiple sites of administration following a distinctive mode of regulation. The notion of a politico-administrative *régime* operates as an heuristic device for investigating empirically how ruling works, how the lives of people are regulated and governed by institutions and individuals vested with authority. This is not to suggest that there is a uniformity or a seamless materiality to the work of ruling. On the contrary, the basic ontological properties of ruling relations (i.e., a *régime*) can only be known empirically through investigation. The paper on policing, for example, did not set out to elaborate a theory of policing, such as the "moral panic" theory (Hall et al. 1978), but to study how the policing of gay men works. Likewise, the study of the management of the AIDS epidemic was not intended to produce a theory about the political economy of health care (e.g., McKinlay 1984). Again, describing the managerial or administrative response to the AIDS epidemic was an empirical matter. It was necessary to look and see to find out just how these *régimes* worked.

My research into the management of AIDS treatments in Ontario provides one example of what I mean by a *régime*. Efforts to control the epidemic involved putting into operation an enormous armamentarium, comprising, in addition to the work of family physicians, public health agencies, palliative care institutions, clinical research facilities and so forth, most of which were staffed or in various way supervised by members of the medical profession. The joining together of the sites of these diverse organizations by various systems of communication, but especially through the use of documents, created an AIDS politico-administrative *régime* in Ontario with legal authority to manage the epidemic. By way of comparison the *régime* investigated in the policing paper was restricted more or less to the state apparatus, involving basically the legislature, the police, the judiciary and other members of the legal profession. A standard feature of this *régime* was that it had legal authority to enforce the practice of heterosexuality.

The Concept of the Materialist Epoché

The notion of an *epoché* is taken from Schutz's (1973) procedures for grounding phenomenological sociology by bracketing the everyday world in order to abstract and analyze social phenomena. What is being recommended here is precisely the opposite: a bracketing of sociological theory, political ideology and other abstract and abstracting practices of traditional sociology so as to leave social phenomena, for the purpose of analysis, concretely embedded in the social organization of the everyday world. The materialist character of these procedures follows from Marx's social ontology (Lukács 1978; Gould 1978). Marx of course, was interested in investigating particular social forms of economic organization, such as the social relations of production and capital. This, unfortunately, is read as requiring the production of objective accounts. In the first of the Theses on Feuerbach, however, he makes it very clear that he is proposing a new materialism that ontologically speaking, is very different from previous materialisms. The chief defect of the latter, he claims, "is that things, reality, sensuousness are conceived only in the form of the *object*, or of *contemplation*, but not as *human sensuous activity, practice*, not subjectively" (Marx and Engels 1976: 6). To follow Marx here, consequently, requires setting aside both the standard procedures for producing objective accounts, as well as the practice of starting with political or sociological theory (i.e., the realm of contemplation) in designing and carrying out a piece of social research. What the sociologist who wishes to investigate "human sensuous activity" must avoid is the laying on of an objective or conceptual framework as a method of understanding.

[margin, handwritten, left side:] BRACKETING BASICALLY REMOVES IDEOLOGICAL NOTIONS IN ORDER TO SINGLE OUT SOCIAL PHENOMENA FOR EMPIRICAL ANALYSIS.

Access to the Field

The work of the activist ethnographer, organized by the everyday world as problematic, is to explore and to describe the extra-local organization of the social relations of management and administration. It is the various sites of this extra-local organization that constitute the terrain of the fieldwork. Approaches to research methodology vary according not only to those features of the social world being studied but to the ontological and epistemological premises that are presupposed by the research design. Access to a politico-administrative *régime*, given the conceptual framework of Dorothy Smith's sociology, takes place somewhat differently from other fieldwork methods. She calls her method "institutional ethnography."

Starting from a Standpoint
Outside a Politico-Administrative Régime

Following D. Smith's ethnographic method, the ethnographer finds herself located quite unlike a participant observer, for example, because the participant observer, although a participant in the setting, does not give up his objective (i.e., observer) position as social scientist when he comes to describe it. The same kind of criticism can be launched against ethnomethodology in terms of its objective use of "members' knowledge" compared to people's "knowledge as members of a setting." In beginning from the local historical setting of people's experiences, a Marxist-feminist ethnographer must start in a reflexive fashion from inside the social organization of not only her own world but by extension the social world she intends to investigate. The latter, furthermore, is not truncated at the boundary of a local setting but extends in a contiguous fashion beyond the purview of the everyday. In investigating this extra-local realm it is the local experiences of people that determine the relevancies of the research, that point to the extra-local forms of organization that need investigating.

In the case of my own work, my research was given direction by the on-going confrontation with the authorities. It was this that determined what piece of the puzzle I should study next. The first step in the research, consequently, was not a study of the relevant sociological literature. The focus of my investigations did not arise theoretically in this way. Nor did I start by trying to construct a bird's-eye view of a *régime*. I never collected data using a standard protocol with the intention of making sense of it later. Nor was my access to the field organized from within a politico-administrative *régime*, using university affiliations or organizational structures close to hand. I did not go about arranging interviews from my office, using my professional credentials to gain entree to the field, for example.

Let me elaborate further. In the research on the management of the AIDS epidemic in Ontario, it was the frustration over the lack of experimental treatments for people living with AIDS that led, first, to the investigation of government activities and, second, to the discovery that government intervention in the epidemic was first and foremost grounded in public health legislation. Contrary to what many Toronto PLWAs believed, based on their experience with Canada's socialized system of medicine, the government had no legislative mandate to provide new, experimental treatment for individuals. With this discovery, public health relations came into view for me as the preoccupation of the politico-administrative *régime* managing the epidemic. It was this preoccupation that resulted in the government being concerned almost entirely for the uninfected and about the spread of the disease, on the one side, and on the other, doing precious little for those who were already infected, sick or dying — apart, of course, from some financial support for palliative care.

This discovery did two things. First, it identified a major source of the problem of access to new treatments. Second, it raised the question of what other social relations were involved in the management of the epidemic. These discoveries had the effect of focusing the politics of AIDS ACTION NOW! very concretely on the delivery of treatment. It would have been extraordinarily easy to move from studying the social relations of treatment to examining the social relations of public health policy. The government's public health policy was open to criticism, and for the sociologist looking at the management of the epidemic, this was what was going on — i.e., what was there to be researched. This is what a bird's-eye view approach would have been like with PLWAs, themselves, becoming objects of study (e.g., as "risk groups" or "vectors" of infection). Organizing entry to the field from the standpoint of PLWAs and PLWHIVs outside the politico-administrative *régime* meant that this was not the way my investigation developed. The examination of the social relations of public health, consequently, apart from the realization that the government's preoccupation with this issue was detrimental to PLWAs, did not become a topic of research.

Contemporary Politico-Administrative Régimes Provide Access to Sites of Official Activities

Starting from the standpoint of people living with AIDS or HIV infection, i.e., from outside a politico-administrative *régime*, raises the question of how to get access to the field. This problem is exacerbated by the confrontation taking place with the *régime* itself. Conversely, however, there is the problem for the *régime*, given the extraordinary complexity of our present-day world, of devising administrative policies on paper that will be effective at the local level without creating a political backlash. Royal commissions, for example, have long been established as an administrative device for handling this kind of problem. Politico-administrative *régimes* in Canada have developed an increasing capacity, mainly as a result of changes in administrative practice, to involve the public in policy decisions. Two examples from my research could be the hearings of the police budget subcommittee of metropolitan Toronto and the consensus conference on AIDS organized by the Province of Ontario. Access of this sort is typical of corporate liberal governments, especially for groups that are protected and legitimated by human rights legislation.[6] Recently in Ontario, these rights have been extended to homosexuals. Nonetheless, access to a *régime* is still a very slippery terrain shaped by practices of confrontation and negotiation.

Régimes legitimate cadres of local leaders as "representatives" of various local community organizations. In this process, community groups often end up functioning as the local extension of the management system of government, at least to the extent that government makes them party to its policies and funds their activities.[7] The concept of "community," in this context, should not be understood as a geographical area, the existence of a Chinatown or a gay ghetto notwithstanding. Rather, it operates as a conceptual device used to coordinate political relations among local groups and between these groups and a *régime*. While political strategies for managing local communities constantly require adjustments within a *régime*, it is not surprising that, on the one hand, AIDS activists can and have legitimately demanded more say on the part of PLWAs and people infected with HIV in the development of AIDS policies and programs. Similarly, we might have expected that politicians and senior public health bureaucrats in Ontario would have taken a more inclusive approach to the interests of community-based AIDS organizations. For me as an activist interested in conducting an ethnographic study of the criminal-justice system and of the AIDS bureaucracy, these administrative forms of organization provided a practical entry point to the field from the standpoint of those whose everyday lives are at the mercy of this kind of politico-administrative *régime*.

The data for both the study of policing and the study of the management of the AIDS epidemic in Ontario were gathered in this way. There was a considerable difference, of course, between getting entree to the police and the criminal justice system, and getting access to the Ontario AIDS bureaucracy. In the beginning, access to the criminal justice system and the police came through the defence of those arrested. To begin with, there were the first person accounts by those arrested of the activities of the police during the raids (White and Sheppard 1981: 12–14). Later, there were meetings with defence attorneys resulting in descriptions of how the criminal-justice system works. And then, there was the work of attending court. The closest I came to actually interrogating the police was participating on an open-line talk show with the staff inspector who organized the raids.

The second stage of these investigations involved presenting briefs and making presentations to various components of the criminal-justice system, including the police-budget subcommittee of Metro Toronto, the police commission and the House of Commons standing committee on justice and legal affairs. In the latter instance, questioning by members of parliament led me to do a more intensive study of the public/private distinction, especially as it then related to the *Criminal Code* (G. Smith 1983a). The third stage of my investigations involved consultations with experts on the police, such as city politicians and criminologists, and reading the academic literature on policing (e.g., Hall et al. 1978). Shortly after the raids, the City of Toronto commissioned a study of the relations between the police and the gay community (Bruner 1981), and the police commission, in an unrelated initiative, had a management consulting firm study the administration of the force (Hickling-Johnston 1981–82). Both of the resulting reports provided useful information on the organization of policing in Toronto. While these investigative activities were driven by the RTPC's political strategy, as activist ethnographer with an eye for exploring social relations, I also used them to begin to make visible for myself, and eventually for others, the lineaments of the social organization of policing resulting in the bath raids. These procedures led from the local everyday world of gay men in Toronto to the different sites of *régime* activity as these became relevant. Access was driven by political confrontation and was mobilized from the standpoint of gay men outside the *régime*.

The investigation of the AIDS bureaucracy took much the same form in that it began with the experiences of PLWAs and with efforts to trace the social relations organizing their experiences beyond the boundaries of the local everyday settings of their lives. Again professionals, in this case doctors, helped sketch the social infrastructure of the local organization of the AIDS bureaucracy, for example, the relations between family physicians and medical specialists/researchers in hospitals or how the budgetary organization of hospitals worked. Some of the early political activities centred on the ethics of placebo-controlled trials, and involved communicating, for example, with the institutional review board (IRB) of the University of Toronto and the College of Physicians and Surgeons of Ontario to demand that patients not be forced into clinical trials to get treatment. This was the second focus of the research.

Third, there were meetings with government officials, such as the deputy minister of community health, and later participation in a province-wide consensus conference on the management of AIDS in Ontario. Unlike the bath raids, knowledge of the organization of the AIDS bureaucracy also came from other community-based groups during meetings to establish our bases of unity and thus to set our common political agenda. Fourth, entree to the AIDS bureaucracy was secured through meetings with officials from the health protection branch of the federal government and through presentations to the Toronto Board of Health and to the federal minister of health and welfare. Finally, the organization of the management of the epidemic was accessed through textbooks on topics such as bio-medical ethics (Levine 1986), the design of clinical trials (Spilker 1984), the AIDS bureaucracy (Panem 1988) and the history of the medical profession in the United States (Starr 1982). The Guidelines on Research Involving Human Subjects put out by the Medical Research Council of Canada (1987) helped distinguish between the social relations of treatment and those of the AIDS research involved in testing pharmaceutical products.

In general, access to the field was negotiated outward from the local circumstances of gay men or PLWAs to the various work sites of both the criminal justice system and the AIDS bureaucracy. I never set up separate, formal interviews with bureaucrats, politicians and professionals or with gay men and people living with AIDS in order to collect data. Rather, the route of access was determined by the course of confrontation, which in turn was determined, especially in the research on AIDS, by the analysis of the data.[8] Thus the research had a reflexive relation to the political struggles of people. Data gathering, nevertheless, was a reactive rather than a proactive process. In every instance, the research constituted an exploration of the administrative and political sites of a particular *régime*, starting from my location in the everyday world.

Meetings, Events and Conversations as Access to the Social Organization of a Régime

The data collection did not involve standard ethnographic practices like interviewing subjects, although individuals working in a *régime* were treated as knowledgeable informants. Meetings, events and conversations usually stood in for interviews. Meetings, I should point out, did provide opportunities to ask questions directly about how things worked. There was, nevertheless, a variety of meetings. Some were held with professionals who saw themselves on the side of ordinary people. Others were held with bureaucrats, professionals and politicians who, although often perfectly well intentioned, took up the standpoint of the *régime* as an ordinary feature of their work. An example of the former could be the meetings that the Right to Privacy Committee held, for a year or more, with the half-dozen or so attorneys who worked at developing common defence strategies for those who had been arrested in the bath raids. An example of the latter could be the meetings of the treatment and clinical trials working group responsible for creating a position paper for the Ontario AIDS consensus conference. The latter included federal and provincial government bureaucrats, representatives from the pharmaceutical industry, AIDS researchers, primary-care physicians treating people with HIV infection, PLWAs and myself as a representative from AIDS ACTION NOW! The research was never a study of these people; they were never the object of the research. Rather, it was the social organization of the *régime* that constituted my object of study.

In using these kinds of face-to-face occasions to collect data, what I was trying to recover was the knowledge of informants as members who worked within the *régime*. This meant treating what people said as reflexively related to the social organization of their work within a political or administrative apparatus (e.g., my being interviewed, as activist, by the researcher hired by the City of Toronto to investigate relations between the police and the gay community). It is also important to point out that, in participating in these kinds of meetings with a view to acquiring the knowledge of members of the setting, I listened to what was said using the notion of social relations and the procedures of the materialist *epoché* to explore the social organization of a *régime*.

An event, as opposed to a meeting, could be something like attending court or a lecture on the ethics of clinical trials. AIDS ACTION NOW! for example, had monthly meetings where doctors and other individuals were invited to make presentations at community meetings. A major event in the study of the management of the epidemic was attending the Fifth International Conference on AIDS in Montréal in June 1989. Because they also occur at specific times, TV shows and radio programs on AIDS constituted other events of this sort. An example that comes to mind are the quarterly reports on AIDS produced by the Public Broadcasting System in the United States.

Conversations with individuals working within a politico-administrative *régime* took place sporadically, mostly with professionals giving accounts of what was taking place with a view to proffering their own strategy of what should be done. These conversations could be quite insightful. One victory which AAN!, in part, took credit for was the change in the federal government's Emergency Drug Release Program (EDRP) — designed to provide compassionate release of unlicensed drugs — to include new, experimental AIDS treatments. Among AIDS activists this change represented just a modification in the government's attitude — a little less homophobia, or AIDS-phobia, perhaps, nothing more. A former dean of medicine did not describe it to me this way, however. His account was that the regulations of the department had been "relaxed" to accommodate access to new AIDS treatments. PLWAs were getting a kind of service that other individuals in Canada with serious ailments had heretofore not been able to get. The questions I then set about trying to answer on the basis of this conversation were: What were these organizational changes? How did the EDRP really work? During these kinds of face-to-face encounters, a major technique of accessing the knowledge of my informants as members of a *régime* was to employ the device of the materialist *epoché*. This meant bracketing my own political or sociological theories and speculative accounts as part of a procedure for making sense of what people had to say on its own terms. This allowed for treating informants' knowledge as reflexive.

Documents as Access to the Social Organization of a Régime

An essential ontological property of a politico-administrative *régime* is that it is a textually mediated form of social organization (D. Smith 1987). Investigating how an administrative *régime* works, consequently, involves more than just face-to-face methodologies, such as attending meetings or speaking with officials. It also requires treating texts as actively coordinating

social relations (D. Smith 1982), especially extra-local forms of organization, like those that organize policing or coordinate the operations of an
AIDS bureaucracy. To recover these ontological properties of documents it
is necessary to read them not for their meaning as such, although this is
important, but for how they organize people's lives. This meant examining
how the language of documents operates as a conceptual coordinator of social
action. For example, an important coordinator of the bath raids was the
Bawdy House Law, especially its notion of "indecent act." It was how this
concept coordinated the work of the police during the bath raids that made
the enforcement of the law the enforcement of heterosexuality. Similarly,
the notion of "the general public," embodied in the *Health Protection and
Promotion Act* of Ontario, with its conception of "the health of the people of
Ontario," coordinates the social relations of public health that exclude the
interests of those who are already infected or ill. It was this form of extra-
local social organization that gave credence to the charge of government
homophobia in the treatment of PLWAs.

Official documents, whether these are particular pieces of legislation,
memoranda, manuals, forms, letterhead paper, etc., if they are read to reveal
the organization they coordinate, provide access to the social relations of a
politico-administrative *régime*. The letterhead on a letter from the Ontario
Ministry of Health, for example, indicated that the AIDS Section is part of
the Public Health Branch of the Ministry of Health. This is where the provincial AIDS coordinator has her desk and from where the provincial assault
on the epidemic is coordinated. A reading of the Ontario *Health Protection
and Promotion Act* makes it clear that this section, given its location in the
bureaucracy, has no mandate to deliver new, experimental treatments to
PLWAs.

The organization of the media also provided an entree to politico-administrative *régimes*, particularly as they constituted the terrain of confrontation
between a *régime* and those whose lives it sought to administer. Reporters
covering the AIDS beat often asked questions of individuals in the AIDS
bureaucracy that helped solve puzzles for me posed by its opacity. A serious problem with the media was that news stories were constructed with a
view as to what is news. This meant that they had to be deconstructed twice
over. Once, to substruct the ideology of news and a second time to explicate
the ideology of a *régime*. Part of the political confrontation with a *régime* is
managing the media. It took a long time for AAN!'s media committee to get
the print, radio and TV media to move from a palliative care frame (i.e.,
human interest stories on the dying) to the issue of access to experimental
treatments. It goes without saying that the study of the media's treatment of
the AIDS issue was itself part of the investigation of the *régime* managing the
AIDS epidemic. Early on in the epidemic, the media was the most important
purveyor of *régime* ideology. Nonetheless, the media could also be a useful
source of data. During the early part of my research, for example, I learned

[Handwritten marginal note: Read through a lens that reveals how language organizes ppl's lives.]

a good deal from the CBC's "Ideas" series on AIDS (Allen and Jones 1987–89). Another source of media information was "off the record" conversations with reporters covering AIDS-related stories. Through the use of the telephone and their status as media workers, good reporters were often able to access various sites of an administrative *régime* almost instantaneously, making it possible for them to provide good accounts of how it worked. Finally, the media also provided access to a *régime* when it provoked public pronouncements by officials in reaction to news stories.

The reading of various kinds of official documents, from the media to government reports, often depended on the assistance of bureaucrats and professionals (i.e., knowledgeable informants) who worked on a day-to-day basis within a ruling apparatus. Like face-to-face access in the field, I took up these documents reflexively, using the insights of these individuals as a means of extending my own member's knowledge of the organization of a politico administrative *régime*. This was an important method, as the scope of the research expanded, of tracking social relations beyond the local settings of people's lives. The disclosure document, for example, prepared for the trial of the "keepers" in the bath raids, gave spatial-temporal access to the social relations of policing in the way in which, for example, it spoke of the "accused" in the bath house setting as someone who was later identified as "John Doe."[9]

Data Collection and Analysis

There were two kinds of activities that gave direction to the collection of data. First, there was confrontation with a *régime* and second, the ongoing analysis of the data itself. The constant political confrontation between the Right to Privacy Committee or AIDS ACTION NOW! and its respective politico-administrative *régime* operated, as I have already said, to prioritize the sites of investigative work. These political forays, often designed on the basis of the analysis as it had so far developed, continued to orient the collection and examination of data from the standpoint of the problematic of the research. The collection and the analysis of the data were also treated as informing or contextualizing one another in directing the research. These were just two of a number of reflexive research strategies I pursued. The success of our political strategies — as in the proof of the pudding is in the eating — was a measure of the competency of the analysis in organizing effective political interventions.

The on-going study of the data was intended to extend my working knowledge of a *régime*. In every instance, this involved the acquisition of the knowledge members of the setting had, with the kind of reflexivity that entailed. My ethnographic work, in this respect, was intent on describing, from inside, the social organization of a world that was constantly emerging, and one of which I, too, was a member. As I investigated this world, attending to how politico-administrative *régimes* were socially organized, i.e., to their ontology, it was common to come upon gaps in the reflexive properties of my knowledge. This was a little like coming across a word in a sentence that did not make sense. Situations like this usually occurred when someone said something that failed to fit properly with my understanding of how things worked. Needless to say, it involved an acquired ability to "see" organization in people's talk and in the text of institutional documents. These procedures depended, first, on invoking the materialist *epoché* whereby both political and sociological theory were bracketed so that I had to make sense of settings on their own terms and, second, on treating people who worked in the *régime* as knowledgeable informants. It was always important to remember that simply in order to hold their jobs they had to know their way around the *régime* I was interested in investigating and describing but knew little about. These procedures, however, did not require me to believe the ideological accounts produced by a ruling apparatus; what it did require was to be able to sketch the form of social organization that produced them.

An example of this kind of failure of understanding follows: At one point I served on an institutional review board to determine whether a protocol for a proposed clinical trial of a new AIDS treatment was ethical. Even though I had studied the protocol carefully, had read widely in the ethics of clinical trials and had thought I understood the issues involved, during the review board discussions I was left behind by the medical practitioners. Despite my efforts, my members' knowledge of the medical aspects of clinical trials was simply inadequate. I needed more medical training to know how things worked. Almost invariably, these gaps in understanding provided keys to unlocking puzzles I confronted in putting together an account of the social organization of a *régime*. This example also points to the fact that at some juncture in the research, simply because it was a piece of research and that the political fight had moved on, I had to determine that the state of my knowledge was adequate for the purpose of describing the lineaments of a *régime*. Acquisition of members' knowledge of a setting could go on forever.

The materialist *epoché* (i.e., bracketing procedures), which places the emphasis on acquiring members' knowledge, was also necessary in reading documents. Data collecting procedures that retained the reflexivity of the setting were needed to give a document its intended (or members') reading from inside the professional or governmental agency that produced it (Garfinkel 1967: 186–207). An important assumption here was that a document had an intended reading that was reflexively related to the forms of social organization it helped coordinate. It is a common observation among lawyers, for example, that while lay people might be able to read the *Criminal Code*, they do not understand it. This is because they do not understand how the criminal-justice system works. My research was like trying to understand the *Criminal Code* by talking with informants who could tell me how the law worked so that I could use the *Code* to understand, for example, what

The importance of knowledgeable informants contribution to truly understanding the grey areas that require specialized input

was going on in court. This basically is what the paper on the policing of gay men is about. The same kinds of interpretive problems arose with the management of the AIDS epidemic. The example I have already given is about trying to understand clinical trial protocols. Another would be seeing the operations of the provincial ministry of health as reflexively organized in relation to the Ontario *Health Protection and Promotion Act*. Here, rather than lawyers, it was bureaucrats and doctors, operating as my knowledgeable informants, who continued to enlighten me.

The reflexive technique in handling documents was to treat them as active constituents of social relations (D. Smith 1982). It was possible to see, for example, how the *Criminal Code* coordinated the enforcement of heterosexuality. Conversely, in the AIDS study, it was possible to see how provincial legislation like the Ontario *Health Protection and Promotion Act* failed to coordinate the management of access to experimental treatment for those who were infected. This kind of textual analysis was based more generally on an understanding of language as operating reflexively, conceptually to coordinate and concert forms of social organization (G. Smith 1990). In the study of policing, for example, the enforcement of heterosexuality was conceptually organized by the notion of "indecent act," and in the AIDS study the social relations of palliative care organized by the voluntary sector, from psychosocial support groups to the running of hospices, were coordinated by the concept of "compassion." Indeed, the slogan used by fundraisers for one Toronto hospice was, "Give compassion a home." While there are important physical aspects to the social organization of the management of the AIDS epidemic — e.g., buildings, offices, labs, technical equipment, computers, etc. — the genesis of this social organization was produced and reproduced in language, either as talk or text. In every instance, language was social organization. Thus, the study of a form of social organization became, in part, a study of its language.

IDEOLOGICAL CIRCLE TECHNIQUE

One technique for investigating how language reflexively coordinates the work of a *régime* is to examine its ideological practice. This conceptually organizes the creation of accounts that intend the management of people's lives. D. Smith has labelled the reflexivity of this process the ideological circle. For example, in the undercover investigation of the gay bath houses (see Figure 1), the notebook inscription procedures used by the police were designed to know the operations of a bath house not in order to have sex but to regulate its operation. The *Criminal Code* concept of "indecent act," which the police used to describe bath house activities, intended raids on these premises where people's activities violated the forms of social organization the *Code* aimed to preserve — in this case, a heterosexual society. In Figure 1 the account (Box C) intends the social organization conceptualized in the *Criminal Code* (Box D).

In the later stages of writing up my research, it was possible to embed the data in a wider set of social relations by reading the relevant documents

Figure 1
Smith's Ideological Circle Applied to the Undercover Investigations of the
Steambath

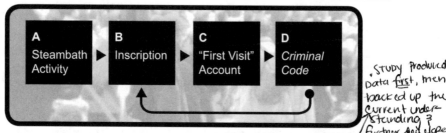

[Handwritten margin notes, right of figure:] · STUDY Produced Data *first*, then backed up the current under standing ? further developed

and/or literature. Instead of starting with a review of the literature, this was ~~most~~ *theoretical analysis.* left to the end of the research so that the analysis of the data could provide a structure of relevance for the reading rather than the other way round. For example, my ability to understand the social relations of treatment in research- *· Flipping theory & research.* ing the management of the AIDS crisis was enhanced by reading an interview with the new head of the Human Subjects Review Committee (i.e., IRB) at the University of Toronto, which described this distinction in some detail.

[Left margin, rotated:] FOCUS OF ANALYSIS. TERMINOLOGY FOCUS

This ability to embed the description of people's activities in a wider set of social relations depended, as I have already pointed out, on an important ontological property of social courses of action — their recursivity. The work of the police in raiding the steam baths, for example, was an iteration of a course of action coordinated by the language of the *Criminal Code*. The history of gay men is replete with these kinds of raids. The same was true of the court appearances by the accused. The social form of particular law enforcement activities at a local level operates as a copy of the social organization constituted in the legislation. The same was true in the AIDS study. The legislation organizing the government's role in the provision of health services provided for forms of public health management in local settings that disregarded the need for experimental treatments of people infected with HIV. Again, this was true in multiple settings across Ontario. Local medical services operated as a copy of the social form of the service envisaged by the legislation. The organization of these social relations, consequently, was recursive. This ontological property of social relations made it possible, in examining a particular instance at a local level, to move to a description of a general form of organization, to social relations as a general course of action coordinated by texts. Methods of traditional "objective" sociology depend on the procedures of inductive statistics to accomplish this level of generality.

[Left margin, rotated:] ONTOLOGICAL NATURE OF SOCIAL RELS DISCOVERED THROUGH SIMILARITIES TO BE USED TO ALLOWS FOR GENERALITY

Discussion

The two pieces of research that I have used to illustrate this method of ethnographic investigation need to be kept in perspective. I think of investigating a politico-administrative *régime* as an ordinary part of the day-to-day work of challenging and transforming a ruling apparatus. It is also important to underline the fact that because of the use of the materialist *epoché* these kinds of studies, although they take up the standpoint of ordinary people, do not in themselves, produce a political analysis or a "political line." Doing this kind of research is not the practice of "vanguard politics." On the contrary, research studies of this sort are designed to be written up, published and made available to all members of a grassroots organization for their political consideration. They are not in some sense special or unique. Rather, they are intended to provide, on a day-to-day basis, the scientific ground for political action. Lastly, because the problematic arises along the line of fault between a politico-administrative *régime* and the local everyday settings of people's lives, it also lies along the disjuncture of class relations in our society.

The results of these two studies placed in perspective some of the things already known about the policing of gay men and the management of the AIDS crisis in Ontario. They provided, however, for a systematic understanding of these insights. Overall they gave the political work of activists a scientific basis. The policing paper, for example, pointed clearly to the homophobic character of the *Criminal Code of Canada* and to its role in the enforcement of heterosexuality. While this might seem to be obvious, changing the *Code* was not something with which the gay community or gay liberation politics had concerned itself in the decade prior to the bath raids. Efforts at changing the law were aimed instead at human rights legislation.

Similarly, the analysis of the management of the AIDS epidemic revealed that there were no mechanisms in place, apart from the work of primary-care physicians and a few hospital clinics, to deliver new, experimental treatments to those infected, sick or dying with the disease. The problem of "AIDS-phobia" or of bureaucratic "red tape" arose, not so much because health professionals and bureaucrats were not doing their job but because they were not prepared to redesign the health-care delivery system to meet the challenge of AIDS and of HIV infection. This analysis provided a basis for an AIDS politics that systematically took up the work of putting this kind of infrastructure in place.

The understanding of a *régime* that is able to provide for concrete, easily operationalized political strategies depends upon the epistemological and ontological shifts required by Dorothy Smith's feminist method. Because both studies ground their descriptions empirically in the actual operations of a ruling *régime*, they provide a scientific rather than an ideological basis for developing political strategy. It is when political strategies are grounded in theory — sociological or political — that there is a strong tendency for them to misfire, or worse yet, backfire. Grassroots organizing is better based on a sociology committed to describing how society actually works.

Some Selected Activist Writings by George Smith

Smith, George. Circa 1983. "In Defence of Privacy or Bluntly Put, No More Shit." *ACTION!* (publication of the Right to Privacy Committee) 3, 1.

Smith, George. 1985. "Policing Sex in St. Catharines." *ACTION!* (publication of the Right to Privacy Committee) February.

Smith, George. 1987. "Talking Politics: Vancouver PWA Coalition Shows the Way." *Rites* (Toronto) 4, 6 (Nov./Dec.).

Smith, George. 1988. "Talking Politics: The New Militancy." *Rites* (Toronto) 4, 8 (Feb. 6).

Smith, George. 1988. "Talking Politics: Socreds Make Strange Bedfellows." *Rites* (Toronto) 5, 1 (May 8).

Smith, George. 1988. "Talking Politics: Double Blind Inertia, Diary of an AIDS Activist." *Rites* (Toronto) 5, 4 (Sept. 9).

Smith, George. 1989. "From Pentamadine to Dextran Sulphate." *AIDS ACTION NEWS!* (publication of AIDS ACTION NOW!, Toronto), January 6.

Smith, George, and Darien Taylor. 1990. "A Treatment Registry, One More Step in Managing the Delivery of AIDS Treatments." *AIDS ACTION NEWS!* (publication of AIDS ACTION NOW!, Toronto), 10, June.

Notes

1. I have chosen to call D. Smith's method a new paradigm not only because it is based on a new epistemological/ontological combination, but because on reading Kuhn (1970: 150) it seemed that his discussion of competing paradigms in science had captured the kinds of difficulties many people appear to have understanding Smith's work:

    > These examples point to the third and most fundamental aspect of the incommensurability of competing paradigms. In a sense that I am unable to explicate further, the proponents of competing paradigms practice their trades in different worlds…. Practicing in different worlds, the two groups of scientists see different things when they look from the same point in the same direction. Again, that is not to say that they can see anything they please. Both are looking at the world, and what they look at has not changed. But in some areas they see different things, and they see them in different relations one to the other. That is why a law that cannot even be demonstrated to one group of scientists may occasionally seem intuitively obvious to another. Equally, it is why, before they can hope to communicate fully, one group or the other must experience the conversion that we have been calling a paradigm shift. Just because it is a transition between incommensurables, the transition between competing paradigms cannot be made a step at a time, forced by logic and neutral experience. Like the gestalt switch, it must occur all at once (though not necessarily in an instance) or not at all.

2. I do not want to suggest here that this kind of treatment was inappropriate or a waste of money. On the contrary, it was desperately needed. The problem however was that the province apart from the establishment of AIDS clinics could do little to intervene in treatment policy.

3. A treatment registry is, in the first instance, a list of new, often experimental treatments for various diseases available to doctors seeking new and improved

treatments for their patients. AAN! proposed the development of a registry where doctors would provide feedback on the success of the suggested treatment with a view to eliminating treatments that did not work well in favour of those that appeared to be effective.

4. Hofstadter in his discussion of recursive processes gives a couple of examples that are useful here. First he described recursion as "nesting and variations on nesting. The concept is very general. (Stories inside stories, movies inside movies. paintings inside paintings, Russian dolls inside Russian dolls (even parenthetical comments inside parenthetical comments!) — these are just a few of the charms of recursion)" (Hofstadter 1979: 127). What is important to emphasize here is how a story inside a story for example is part of the larger story and therefore has something of the same form. Here is another example from Hofstader (1979: 128): "When you listen to a news report on the radio, oftentimes it happens that they switch you to some foreign correspondent. 'We now switch you to Sally Swumphly in Peafog, England.' Now Sally has got a tape of some local reporter interviewing someone so after giving a bit of background she plays it. 'I'm Nigel Cadwanader here on scene just outside of Peafog, where the great robbery took place, and I'm talking with...' Now you are three levels down — it may turn out that the interviewee also plays a tape of some conversation. It is not too uncommon to go down three levels in real news reports, and surprisingly enough, *we* scarcely have any awareness of the suspension" (Hofstadter 1979: 127–28). Again, each level of this *news* report is about the "same" story. This is a requirement for each level to be nested in the next. Otherwise the report would be incoherent. These moves are not unlike, for example seeing how a bath raid is nested in the bawdy-house section of the *Criminal Code*; and how the disclosure document, in turn, is embedded in the raid, etc. A film on the bath raids could have just this structure if it set out to mimic its social organization.

5. The notion of *régime* in *regulation* theory denotes the form of regulation of a mode of production. *My* usage is not tied to a mode of production but of reproduction in the sense that the social world is ongoingly reproduced in the reflexive practices and activities of people. A *régime* is a stable form of organization with a distinctive mode of regulation provided by particular institutional forms, networks and explicit or implicit norms. The notion of a *régime* is not used as an entity with causal or functional properties.

6. There are, of course, groups not politically organized as a community, or community groups not legitimated by government funding. In the first instance, these include environmental groups, anti-abortion groups, consumer protection groups, tenants organizations and so forth. The second category includes anti-racist groups like the Toronto Black Action Defence Committee. While they belong to one of the above communities, the "community" that is systematically left out of these arrangements is working-class people as such.

7. In Ontario, for example, the executive directors of community-based AIDS groups sit on the provincial AIDS advisory board, and at the national level officials from the Canadian AIDS Society, an umbrella organization of community-based AIDS groups, operates as an interface between management structures at the local level and federal government agencies and departments.

8. A major difference between the police paper and the paper on the management of the AIDS epidemic was that the former was written after the fact, whereas the latter was written up as events unfolded and hence was more useful in determining political strategy.

9. Throughout the paper on the policing of the gay community in Toronto, I use John Doe as the pseudonym for the accused.

OF T-SHIRTS AND ONTOLOGIES: CELEBRATING GEORGE SMITH'S PEDAGOGICAL LEGACIES

Eric Mykhalovskiy and Kathryn Church

George Smith led a life of scholarly activism. He did it with grace, vision and much accomplishment. While George was often very busy with his own research and activist work, he took seriously his role as teacher and mentor. This chapter speaks to his legacy as a pedagogue.

We each met George at different moments in the stream of his and our own lives and work. We learned similar as well as different things from him in a variety of ways. Beginning with our early engagements with his influential article, "Political Activist as Ethnographer," in this chapter we reflect on how we have reckoned with George's approach to institutional ethnography and activism. We describe the influence he had on our approaches to doing activist research and explore key moments of learning focused on questions of ontology, managing access to the "field," doing empirical inquiry and studying social organizations rather than individuals. George was committed to building a robust practice of activist scholarship informed by principles of institutional ethnography inquiry. In the spirit of this aim we close the chapter with questions about the relationship between institutional ethnography and activism that we continue to wrestle with in our own work.

First Meetings

Kathryn

My first encounter was not so much with George Smith as with a T-shirt that he wore. It occurred in 1990 when I was a doctoral student in sociology at the Ontario Institute for Studies in Education in Toronto. The setting was Dorothy Smith's course on the social organization of knowledge, a large seminar comprised primarily of women. Dorothy arrived each week accompanied by George, who assisted her throughout. They entered my life as I was making crucial transitions: from western to central Canada, from psychology to sociology, from a liberal to a more radical politics. I was unsettled theoretically, methodologically and in other ways.

Dorothy's lectures suggested that her approach made a significant break with the kind of sociology that I was being taught by other instructors. There was no more obvious sign of this than the T-shirt that George frequently wore to class.[1]

"I have made the ontological shift," it declared, boldly.

"Bully for you!" I thought, already angry.

George's T-shirt reinforced my sense of exclusion from students within the department who seemed to have privileged access to a special way of thinking and talking. Because the rest of us never quite "got it," we were considered deluded and pitiable. I preferred to mill about with the great unwashed, those of us who looked at each other in bewilderment and said, "What ontological shift?"

So, this was a difficult beginning in what turned out to be a much longer process of continually coming into the everyday world as problematic and institutional ethnography. My story positions George problematically. Let me soften that by saying that I have since become deeply grateful to him for that seemingly offensive T-shirt. Of all the things that were said in that classroom more than a decade ago, it is that bold slogan slashed across George's chest that I have never forgotten. Nor have I ever been released from grappling with the ontological shift.

Eric

I first met George in 1989 during a job interview for AIDS ACTION NOW!'s Treatment Information Exchange. By then George's activism had moved from his earlier work on the Right to Privacy Committee to HIV/AIDS. Unlike many others who at the time were concentrating on transmission issues or palliative care, George focused his efforts on making treatments available to people living with HIV/AIDS. His efforts were central to challenging the state and the medical research establishment in Canada to take seriously the health of people infected with HIV. At the time of my interview I was working as a secretary in the Ontario Legislature. A year earlier I had completed a master's degree in sociology at York University. It was a time of transition for me; I was struggling desperately to create a meaningful work life. By some good fortune I was offered the job.

What followed was a period of intense collaboration with George. For two years I was the coordinator of what became the Canadian AIDS Treatment Information Exchange, for which George served as a board member. Afterward we worked as co-principal investigators on the Hooking Up Project, a community-based institutional ethnography study of the interface between the day-to-day lives of people living with HIV/AIDS and the organization of the social service system (Mykhalovskiy and Smith 1994). These four years saw some of the most innovative and exciting AIDS activism in Canada. I remember them as a whirlwind of board and committee meetings, demonstrations and community forums, lively discussion and debate, victories and losses.

As I think back to this time I recognize that George saved me from the sociology that had sent me fleeing from the university after my M.A. As a result, he helped to change my life and work. From George I learned about the possibilities of a sociology that could be active in the world in ways I craved for. I learned about that possibility as part of a political and research apprenticeship with George, slowly over time and without reading a lot of books or going to a lot of classes. In AIDS ACTION NOW! meetings, I listened to how George could think about institutional processes that needed to be put in place to manage AIDS treatment and thought to myself, "I want to know similarly." I also worked with George on research that immersed me in what he would call "thinking organizationally" as we sought to figure out and transform problems of access to social services faced by people living with HIV/AIDS.

I am so very glad to have learned about institutional ethnography as activist research from George and from a place of tension with the university. It helped prepare me for what was to come.

Learnings

Kathryn

While Eric had a sustained working relationship with George, my core learning was distilled into a single encounter. During a coffee break in class, I approached George to ask his advice about situating myself as a researcher with members of the psychiatric survivor movement. He suggested that I stop by his office so that he could give me a copy of the paper that he was working on; he felt it might be of assistance. When I showed up, George handed me pre-publication, *Draft Version 2.0 of "Political Activist as Ethnographer" [ad usum privatum]*. I remember that he was in negotiation with the journal *Social Problems* about revisions to the draft. In class, he talked about the ways in which he felt the editors of the journal were trying to pull his writing into a more conventional sociological framework. I suppose that this was my first glimpse into the politics of publication.

I still have George's original draft. Now fifteen years old, the paper has grown more interesting simply as an object. It is yellowed and musty from being stored in a basement filing cabinet. There is a stain on the front corner where the original staple rusted out and fell off. On the front page I have written what I believe must have been George's home phone number at the time, plus his OISE extension and a note on when he anticipated that the article would be published. In the intervening years, I have reread not just the article but this particular draft, orienting to the words and phrases that I underlined in my very first reading — even though the ink has run and blurred with age. I have been tremendously curious about what I found significant then, what confused me, what upset me. Clearly there was a lot that I did not understand, some that I misinterpreted and some that became the core of my subsequent practice.

It is not difficult for me to remember the passage from *"Political Activist as Ethnographer"* that was most important to me as a doctoral student. Seven lines are clearly highlighted in the draft that George gave to me and quoted strategically early in my dissertation (Church 1993) and the book that grew out of it (Church 1995).

> The first step in the research, consequently, was *not* a study of the relevant sociological literature. The focus of my investigations did not arise theoretically in this way. I *never* collected data using a standard protocol with the intention of making sense of it later. Nor was my access to the field organized from within a politico-admin-istrative regime, using university affiliations or organizational structures close to hand. I did *not* go about arranging interviews from my office using my professional credentials to gain entree to the field, for example. (my italics, G. Smith 1990: 638)

(In the original draft, this passage was not only highlighted but had a line drawn beside it and the word "NOT" written in capitals). It is possible that I have never recovered from reading these words. They changed the shape of my work and that in turn changed my life. The immediate effect was a fundamental shift in my orientation to my doctoral research. Up to that point, I had been paralyzed by the thought that I needed to have my project pretty much figured out before I actually did anything. This meant situating myself theoretically, steeping myself in and coming to terms with the literature. George's words de-centred the literature, and this freed me to activate my project — not as a knower but as someone intent on investigation and discovery. Dorothy Smith's articulation of institutional ethnography in Tim May's new methods text (D. Smith 2002) has a section entitled, "Research as discovery," which begins with the following sentence:

> In institutional ethnography, the researcher is permitted to learn, perhaps must learn from each interview what may inform and change the subsequent interview, even when the same topics or questions are introduced each time. (27)

A wonderful sense of continual process and alertness to the unexpected becomes possible with this orientation. It has become fundamental to how I do research.

Eric

My own copy of "Political Activist as Ethnographer," like Kathryn's, is worn and written upon, filled with underlines, marginal notes and questions about such things as "recursion" and what makes an account "objective." It's not a draft version but a published offprint, something I was very proud to receive from George I'm not quite sure when. I've read the text many times in many places, each reading bringing new insights and shifting my understanding of institutional ethnography and of activist sociology. And so it was with my reading done in preparation for this writing. As I read through the article I was struck by two things. The first is a question pencilled in the right-hand margin of the first page: what is an ontological shift? The second is my recognition of how I have come to read the article as a place to turn for ways to think about the knowledge relations created, implied and disrupted by activist scholarship.

Like Kathryn I too remember the bold announcement of George's T-shirt: "I have made the ontological shift," although my experience of it was somewhat different. George's sartorial gestures never really operated as markers of exclusion for me. Instead, they engendered feelings of invitation. George's T-shirt and his work welcomed me to a sociology that spoke to my reservations with the academy and that buttressed my intellectual predispositions with a coherent body of thought and research practice.

In "Political Activist as Ethnographer," George provides his interpretation of Dorothy Smith's sociology as a reflexive-materialist method. He draws on two of his investigations, one on the policing of gay men, the other on the management of the AIDS epidemic, to describe the epistemological, ontological and practical/technical shifts involved in doing a sociology that "uses political confrontation as an ethnographic resource" (G. Smith 1990: 629).

When I first read the article and encountered the sociology that has come to be called institutional ethnography I didn't know much about ontology. Since that time, what George describes as "the ontological shift" has come to have an important organizing presence in my own work. In his article, George argues for an activist sociology whose ontology shifts from a world of generalized concepts and theories to a concrete world produced through the activities of actual people (G. Smith 1990: 633). His argument is based on Dorothy Smith's interpretation of Marx's materialism, which he extends in relation to his own experiences of developing a program of activist research.

I have a distinct recollection of the sense of possibilities that flowed from my discussions with George about Dorothy's interpretation of Marx. Her work replaces the heritage of cumbersome and determinist base/superstructure divisions with a singular ontology of the social understood as actual people's activities coordinated across time and place. Here was a way of thinking about the social as a world produced by actual people that could be researched as such and transformed. In "Political Activist as Ethnographer," George invokes this materialism to argue for an activist research practice that rejects speculative accounts in favour of an approach committed to careful empirical investigation of ruling relations. The ontological shift, as he elaborates it, enables a research move into the world as empirically investigable.

Kathryn

Even as it gave me permission to discover, reading "Political Activist as Ethnographer" gave me permission to privilege the "field" over the university. Specifically, it released me from organizing my research through OISE as the primary site. In terms of the psychiatric survivor community, my university affiliations and professional credentials were more hindrance than help anyway. I needed something closer to street credentials, which I definitely did not have. I entered into the survivor community on legitimacy that I borrowed from one recognized survivor leader, who introduced me to others, who tested me in various ways and from whom I began to take instructions about how to be in the community.

During the time that I was a doctoral student, I worked for several survivor organizations, one of which hired me to track the participation of psychiatric survivors in a government consultation on the prospect of community mental health services legislation. This consultation became the focus of my doctoral research. As George suggested, my investigative activities were driven by the political strategy of psychiatric survivors and survivor organizations attempting to use the consultation process to confront the government on issues that were pressing for their community.

After my doctorate was complete, I took on a research contract with a community organization. That led to another contract and before too long I began to understand that, although somewhat haunted about it, I actually was choosing to work as an independent researcher from outside a "politico-administrative regime." George never knew how seriously I took him — enough to spend ten years making a living without university resources and actively de-centring my professional credentials. During that time, most of my contracts came through psychiatric survivor organizations doing community economic development. I had no particular interest in the area. I became knowledgeable about it because it was what the organizations were doing, and I was working off their agenda.

Being a contract employee cleaned up the survivor-professional power relations in a useful way. If the organization did not like my work, they would not hire me the next time. If I did not like where they were headed, I could refuse the contract. They generated a lot of the grant money themselves. But I also brought them into grants that were organized by university researchers: a three-year project on evaluating community economic development organized out of McGill in Montréal (LaChance, Church, Shragge and Fontan 1999); and a five-year project on informal learning among people excluded from the labour market that was part of a national research network located at OISE (Church, Shragge, Ng, and Fontan forthcoming).

Eric

I remember how different the kind of empirical investigation George was engaged in felt from my earlier involvement in the peace movement, where our research activities were largely limited to an exercise in activist rhetoric, marshalling statistics and other research in debates and related efforts to convince people of a particular line of argument. George's activist research was of a rather different sort. Some might understand his approach as discouraging movement speculation or wonder. I'm not sure it does quite that. In my experience, George's activist ethnography channels that curiosity and speculative energy into discovering the social world as it is being "put together" in actual activities. His work formulates what I like to call an "ethics of empirical investigation," which it both privileges over abstract speculation and seeks to implant in the politics of social movements.

George's activist sociology was also quite different from other models of scholarship on HIV/AIDS that I encountered during the late 1990s. Behavioural scientists, for example, were relatively uninterested in people already infected with HIV, preferring instead to focus their work on transmission issues, often from a perspective over-committed to faulty models of rational action and decision making (for critical reviews, see Bloor et al. 1992 and Bloor 1995). Others had happened upon HIV/AIDS as an opportunity to elaborate the field of cultural studies, at times at considerable remove from the practical problems faced by people living with HIV/AIDS. When sociological studies did turn to people living with the virus, they often did so in ways that objectified them, describing their experiences of illness or their ways of managing stigma and impending death (see Weitz 1991).

"Political Activist as Ethnographer," by contrast, can be read almost as a guide to developing a practice of sociological investigation that does not study individuals. While the empirical point of entry for the studies it describes is the experiences of actual people — gay men and people living with HIV/AIDS — its analytic objective is ethnographic description of the institutional relations that shape those experiences, not accounts of lives led. In our work together, George was always very clear that our object was the interface of everyday life and ruling practices, or the operation of what he called a politico-administrative regime, not the experiences of people living with HIV/AIDS.

I think it is also important to distinguish this organization of inquiry from other forms of ethnographic study that treat the activities of social movements as a research object. A particularly salient example of the latter is the work of Barrie Thorne (1983), described in her article "Political Activist as Participant Observer," from which I suspect George may have derived the title for his own article. Thorne details her experiences of doing research on the draft resistance movement in the U.S. in the late 1960s and registers her concerns about publishing results that could harm the movement because of their potential interest to political authorities. George's project, by contrast, was emphatically not about studying movements. In emphasizing this point I am not trying to suggest there is only one way to do activist research; clearly a variety of approaches is needed. But the practice of activist sociology George was cultivating did not objectify social movements or the people who formed them; its focus was the organization of ruling relations they faced, the analyses of which were offered to social movements to act on.

Kathryn

Eric worked closely with George in a rare activist-researcher apprenticeship. By contrast, I worked without an intellectual mentor. Perhaps as a result, I faced at least one difficulty and took at least one turn that George would not have taken. He was a gay man working with other gay men in community organizations that were focused on their issues and needs. I was a former mental health service provider attempting to become an ally of people who viewed me as the oppressor. That is a significant difference. He was an insider with respect to his project; I was an outsider.

Needless to say, establishing trust between me and psychiatric survivors was a big issue. Early on, I had repeated encounters, difficult encounters, in which I was questioned about my attitudes, my values, my feelings and my strength for the work. I had to deal with the trauma of these challenges to my legitimacy, to which I often had no response. Being hit by survivor politics was not a one-time occurrence. I would suggest that it is character- istic of outsider alliances with this particular social movement. Far from being linear and predictable, this relation is marked by ruptures — on both sides. These affected not just my intellectual project but my personal life as well.

Like Dorothy, George placed great emphasis on the texts that emerged in the course of his research. I do not dispute their importance. However, in my own work, I was struck by something else. Observing the legislation consultation gave me a front row seat to watch psychiatric survivors from across the province speak in ways that were more like testimonials than they were briefs to government. The stories they told at the legislative hear- ings were a startling departure from monotonous professional discourse. The effect was to break open the rationality (or, following Bahktin, the monological quality) of the proceedings. I watched how disturbing it was to service providers and government bureaucrats as, over and over again, survivors described their lives in relation to the power and authority of the psychiatric system. I discovered that this practice of speaking from "I" was part of how the movement was put together and fundamental to its politics. I have come to call this "first person political."

When it came time to write, I wanted my dissertation to reflect this form. I wanted to create a "survivor frame" for my writing. Mirroring the testimonial form, I wrote what British sociologist David Jackson referred to as critical autobiography (Jackson 1990). It accomplished many things but most dramatically included the story of the physical and emotional breakdown that I experienced in the midst of my doctoral research and the many meanings that "breaking down" began to have for me. This appears to be one of the breaks I made with George and, as Eric so clearly points out, his commitment to sociological investigation that does not study individuals. It may be that George would have seen my incorporation of the personal as solipsism. But writing academia from "I" was a way for me to express my alignment with this particular social movement.

Writing from "I" also enabled me to identify and portray emotion as an unpredictable and disruptive feature of psychiatric survivor participation in the community mental health system. At the time, most agencies and boards were attempting to implement this policy. Thus, the professional "unsettlement" that I observed in this one consultation exercise was occurring much more generally throughout the service system. My research suggested that taking up survivor participation as merely "representation" on boards or committees was inadequate. It needed to be understood as an "unsettling relation" — as those practices that unsettled the comfortable, taken-for-granted ways that mental health professionals viewed and related to their "clients."

Eric

Kathryn's experiences raise some of the vexing issues about relationships between activism, social movements and research. Like other forms of scholarly critique popular at the time and since, George's work locates an important capacity for political and social transformation in the activities of social movements. In some ways, "Political Activist as Ethnographer" reads as a programmatic statement on doing activist ethnography for social movements. Yet written between its lines are moments of tension that complicate that organization of activist research.

I used to think that "Political Activist as Ethnographer" presented activism and research as seamless activities, nearly indistinguishable, one flowing into the other. Certainly in George's practice, activism and academic research were fully intertwined, but it was not an easy coexistence. In his published writings, George took a certain pride in presenting himself as working in ways unlike other university-based researchers might. To repeat a portion of the quote Kathryn used earlier: "I did not go about arranging interviews from my office using my professional credentials to gain entree to the field" (G. Smith 1990: 638).

While this was certainly true, it was also the case that George was a university-based academic whose location within the professional academy facilitated his research. What I learned about from working with George was a measure of conflict between activist research and the university that is not fully expressed in his article. George's academic career suffered because of the nature of his research work and his commitment to gay rights and AIDS activism. The activities required of the political activist as ethnographer and the obligations of a professional academic career do not necessarily fit well with one another.

George was a person living with HIV/AIDS and a prominent AIDS activist. In some ways, the subject relations he embodied in his research activities were less contradictory than those faced by others trying to produce activist research on HIV/AIDS. As Kathryn notes, George was an insider, he worked from within the AIDS movement, using that location to learn about the operation of a politico-administrative regime and feeding what he learned into the politics of AIDS ACTION NOW! While in his life, doing and using research were fully interwoven, in our conversations about activist ethnography, George often presented the doing of research as quite separate from using its results.

As he put it, the work of the activist researcher was do to a careful, detailed and reliable ethnography of how ruling regimes work. Directly using that knowledge was not his or her responsibility but a matter of concern for movement activists. In some ways this split between research production and use resonates with the metaphor of science that George draws upon to discuss the relationship of scholarship to activism. The ethnographer is concerned with putting in place the "scientific basis for the political strategy of grass-roots community organizing" (G. Smith 1990: 629), but using that research to develop that political strategy lies beyond his or her sphere of responsibility and competence.

I doubt whether George would have argued too strongly against political activist ethnographers enthusiastically participating in efforts to use their research for progressive social transformation. Yet his remarks do suggest an alternative stance, one that values cultivating independence with respect to the activities of social movements. There is something to be said for pursuing political activist ethnography relatively unfettered by the ideological commitments of a given social movement, of not having one's inquiry driven by movement theorizing or engaging too closely in its political work of using research.

This vision of activist/research relations and of a distinction between the figure of the researcher and of the activist rest on a notion of science that I feel underpins George's thought. In my experience, George did not rely on conventional approaches to scientific objectivity but on an understanding of science as an organization of activities that permits the making of reliable knowledge. George wanted the space to create a knowledge of ruling that he could feel confident in, that he could offer movement activists, assured that sound decisions about political strategy could be made on its basis.

In our work on the Hooking Up Project, George always described what we were doing as a sociology *for* people living with HIV/AIDS. This naming strategy did not necessarily refer to the direct addressees of our work. Many people living with HIV/AIDS did not care about what we were on about. Still we had a strong sense of our research as having the potential to "go to work for" people with HIV/AIDS, as having an active life in efforts to change the workings of problematic institutions they faced. In this sense, the politics of our research efforts rested primarily on social movements as direct recipients and readers of our research and on people living with HIV/AIDS as active participants in the research process.

Yet there are ambiguities in this formulation. While I can certainly imagine political activist ethnography as a sociology for social movements, our own work was not "for" the AIDS movement in the sense of starting with the problems it posed. Social movement activists draw on a variety of conceptual resources to think about what is problematic and in need of action. Not all of these resources necessarily align well with the approach taken by institutional ethnography investigation. Movement problematizations can have a particular ideological character or rely on forms of speculation that are discouraged by institutional ethnography inquiry, for example. As George suggests in his remarks about AIDSphobia and bureaucratic red tape, starting political activist ethnography in problems as they have been framed by movements can begin inquiry in the "wrong" place. In the context of HIV/AIDS this is all the more acute now that the AIDS movement is in decline and community organizations have been transformed into service agencies that orient to people living with HIV/AIDS as clients and draw on professional, health policy and other discourses and practices to "serve" them. In my more recent efforts to extend the research I did with George, I have had to trouble and unsettle what community organizations consider problems in need of action (Mykhalovskiy and McCoy 2002; Mykhalovskiy, McCoy and Bresalier 2004). Clearly, identity-based social movements and community organizations are not a shortcut into the everyday experiences and problems faced by those they seek to help.

While in his article George presents a relatively unproblematic version of political activist ethnography, there are clearly potential points of tension between institutional ethnography-inspired ethnography, the routine conceptual practices of social movements and the university. How to think about the political character of activist ethnography as he elaborated it, particularly as regards its relationships to the activities of social movements, potential researcher/activist distinctions and the ground of everyday experience is an ongoing project. We need to continue to build spaces within which to continue developing the tradition of political activist ethnography to which George was so committed. We need to do that in dialogue with related efforts and projects in ways that address the possibilities as well as the challenges of connection between social movement politics and institutional ethnography-inspired activist ethnography.

Enduring Questions

Kathryn

When I think back on my doctoral training, I am amazed that writing, such a fundamental activity for academics, is rarely the subject of formal instruction or discussion. During my time at OISE, aside from a lively circle of female graduate students, Dorothy Smith was the only person who ever mentioned it. "I am more and more persuaded," she wrote on my final paper for her course, "that analysis of this kind is done in writing."

I haven't figured out at all what to understand from this. Maybe it is to fall back on the deconstructive theses that language always refers back to language and social organization. So that exploring social organization involves writing and finding out bit by bit in writing how it may be put together, each next movement forward starting from the previous arrival. But that's as far as I can go right now. I have observed as people write theses using ethnographic or qualitative methods or this method, that there's a two-stage process of writing, sometimes quite distinct, sometimes overlapping. One is that stage of writing to discover and the second is the stage of writing as exposition. Writing to discover often does not produce anything that will work as exposition and it may produce a lot of writing. But exposition can't be done properly until the writing-to-discover-how-to-write is done.

George added to this analysis when he argued that political activist ethnographies "are designed to be written up, published and made available to all members of a grassroots organization for their political consideration."

Once again, he never knew how seriously I took him. My practice as a writer for survivor organizations began inside my doctoral project and flowered to become the core of my work as an independent researcher. Over a decade, I wrote a dozen plain language documents that drew their "data" from conversations: formal and informal, planned and spontaneous, serious and hilarious. My method was to listen to psychiatric survivors over an extended period of time and then, through layers of writing and rewriting, to articulate what they thought, experienced and came to know as a result of creating and running community initiatives.

These reports — their knowledge expressed in a kind of "hybrid" researcher/movement voice — were actively taken up by psychiatric survivor groups engaged in education and advocacy (for a prime example, see Church 1997). Some were used in university classrooms; some circulated internationally. It strikes me now that one of the reasons they were successful is that they preserved and kept visible that base layer of work that Dorothy referred to as writing for discovery. I avoided writing as exposition. I discovered early on that, while highly valued in academia, it tended to shut out the psychiatric survivors that I wanted to reach.

In my search for ways of giving research data back to this community,

I turned to images as well as words. After a tentative video experiment in 1995, my survivor colleagues and I sought out two independent filmmakers and raised almost three hundred thousand dollars in order to produce a documentary quality film. By 1999, we had *Working Like Crazy* in our hands. Developed from the survivor standpoint, this film features six psychiatric survivors who work in survivor-run businesses. Their stories reveal not just the contradictions of social movement involvement in economic development but the multi-dimensionality of the movement itself. Embedded in survivor knowledge and identity, the film challenges prevalent notions of the "mentally ill" (Church, in press).

Since its release, *Working Like Crazy* has had an extraordinary trajectory. We carried it immediately into a series of regional screenings and discussions across Ontario, and from there into the hands of mental health activists halfway around the globe: Northern Ireland, Scotland, England and, most recently, Taiwan (Church, in press). The whole process was fascinating but of most interest to me have been the unique and unpredictable interpretations that audiences have made of the film. For example, its humour was taken up quite differently by psychiatric survivor and "non-survivor" audiences. Professional audiences often perceived its point of view as overtly hostile towards psychiatry, rejecting it as "out-dated" and "one-sided." Other audiences enthusiastically received the film as a tribute to the success of entrepreneurship, eliding almost completely its emancipatory, community-building message.

Through projects such as this, my practice has taught me that story/narrative, performance and/or artwork expand the researcher's repertoire for communicating study results. Audiences are eager for alternative representations of our work. At the same time, they often take up these offerings in ways that are personally meaningful rather than entirely compatible with the collectivist intentions of activist work. As someone oriented to both institutional ethnography and arts-informed research, the complexities of audience response have become my new problematic. George's admonishment to write up, publish and make studies available to grassroots organizations (and other publics) still rings true, but how do researchers use new forms or modalities to address enduring questions of social organization and the relations of ruling?

Linked to this is the dilemma that arises when, as George noted, empirically derived research results push against the speculative accounts that people hold onto as explanatory. It is along this line of fault — specifically the sharp (ideological) boundary that psychiatric survivors draw between themselves and movement "outsiders" — that my working relationship with them finally broke down. After years of collaboration, we failed to resolve the issue of whether I could adequately represent our work to the public. I believed that I could. Survivor leaders believed that I should always be accompanied by one of their own, if only for appearances. At their insistence, for example, the Ontario tour of *Working Like Crazy* was organized around mixed insider/outsider teams. The decision was an unhappy capitulation that did not satisfy my longing for a less essentialist position on the question of "whose voice/knowledge is this anyway?"

This was the moment in which I realized that I needed to leave the borderland location in which I worked with/out the survivor community to establish a broader, more diverse base for my work as a producer of anti-oppressive knowledge. And that decision led me back into the university.

Eric

In the short time since George and I worked together, universities have changed dramatically. Sociologists and others have voiced concerns about how market and other relations are transforming the way universities operate and the way knowledge is being produced within and around them (Kurasawa 2002; Turk 2000; Polster 2002). These changes have profound implications for the possibilities of political activist ethnography, both of the sort described by George in his article and those forms that rely more fully on extramural sources of research funding.

For the past five years, I have worked as a sociologist in faculties of medicine trying to create spaces for imaginative, critical social research on health. It has not always been easy. There has been a clash of research cultures; critical work has an uneasy relationship to places where intellectual activity is highly applied, organized by clinical relevancies and often measured in strict output terms. The cultures of evidence-based medicine and the push for forms of research dissemination, or "knowledge translation," that privilege a service relationship between the academy and sites where policymakers and other "decisionmakers" do their work can distort the range of scholarly inquiry.

At the worst of times, when I have felt most deeply the insecure presence of an activist orientation in my current research, I have imagined the problem as an isolated one, something explained by the peculiarities of working in the health sciences. But I'm afraid that's not the case. All around me and around others working at different sites within the academy—in the social sciences and the humanities—a new research apparatus is emerging that puts activist ethnography, arts-based inquiry and other forms of critical investigation at risk.

My own sense of what is involved is quite partial but includes at least the following: a growing shift toward vocational training within the social sciences and certainly within the professional schools where much institutional ethnography is taught. An aggressive move on the part of the state, through the activities of its funding agencies, to transform universities into centres for producing commercial, applied and/or managerial knowledges.

As part of these changes, an emerging reorganization of the Social Sciences and Humanities Research Council is taking place in ways that borrow heavily from an approach to research funding already established by the Canadian Institutes of Health Research. A rapid expansion of ethical policing of university-based research coordinated conceptually by the Tri-Council policy statement on ethical research conduct (MRC, NRC and SSHRC 1998) and organized by university-based ethics review boards in ways that privilege a formal, proceduralist interpretation of ethics and that potentially discourage ethnographic fieldwork (Van Den Hoonaard 2002).

There is a growing distortion of academic inquiry by relations of research entrepreneurship. Increasingly, the expectation is for faculty members to carry multiple and multi-investigator research grants, to bring monies into home departments and to fund students through grant monies. This organization of research promotes a managerial orientation to knowledge making whereby principal investigators become more and more removed from the actual practice of research and more and more involved in administering the work of others.

None of these relations favour the practice of political activist ethnography. The investigative orientation to the everyday world of which the activist ethnographer is a part, the treatment of ruling as an object of critique rather than a client for research and the complex research relationships with social movements rather than with corporate partners are all largely contrary to these developments and the forms of knowledge they would support.

I paint a bleak picture here, perhaps unduly so. The university research apparatus cannot fully foreclose the possibilities of university-associated activist ethnography. There will always be cracks, points of entry and ways of appropriating emerging discourses of university-based research. With their expertise in how texts operate in ruling relations, institutional ethnographers are well positioned to represent their research efforts strategically. Some already have had success with more recent grant competitions. Still the changes underway are occurring at a rapid pace and we do not yet know nearly enough about them. There is research to be done here, responses, critiques, challenges and transformations to be made. I cannot help but think that George would have been on top of it all.

Conclusion

In writing this chapter — separately and then spliced into dialogue — we celebrate the pedagogical legacies of George Smith. Through Kathryn's narrative line we remember George's transmission of two valuable openings: the permission to engage in research as discovery and the permission to privilege the "field" over the university. Through Eric's narrative line we remember his transmission of a sociology that, beyond speculative accounts, takes the institutional relations that organize experience as empirically investigable. These contributions changed not just our work but our lives. They keep us oriented to a sociology that is active in the world, one that values direct engagement with community and social movement organizations, one that reminds us to inhabit the university not as "home" but more cautiously as a place of increasing tension.

This is the work that we intended to accomplish here. But writing this chapter also surfaced aspects of learning from George that were initially buried. We can see, for example, that Eric's robust apprenticeship with George creates an interpretation of his work that foregrounds questions of science and activist/researcher relationships. Kathryn's more fleeting contact produces an engagement that questions the place of individual lives lived in sociological scholarship and the power of stories in the political work done by social movements. Gender is part of this difference, even as, long ago, it influenced our reactions to George's T-shirt. That relentless T-shirt! Writing these intersecting accounts revealed its significance and that of other kept-objects. Our learning is tacked in place through artefacts that flicker with awakening to the ontological shift: clothing stitched with memories, drafts of papers long-published, tracings of ink long-smudged. All leave tell-tale trails.

We conclude, then, where we began. George Smith led a life of scholarly activism. He did it with grace, vision and much accomplishment.

Critical Thinking and Discussion Questions

1. What role do objects (T-shirts, buttons, posters, banners) play in social movement activism? How can ethnographers interact with objects in learning about and participating in social movement activities?

2. What are the tensions between doing university-based research and doing research for social movements and/or community-based organizations? How might they be resolved?

3. As scholar-activists, what impact does the form of our writing have on what we communicate and how (by whom) we are read? How might our rootedness with grassroots movements shift and change the forms of our academic production?

Notes

1. In her latest book Dorothy Smith writes, "I gave him [George Smith] a birthday T-shirt once with 'I have made the ontological shift' printed on the front. He wore it to work" (2005: 4, Note 2).

RESEARCH FOR ACTIVISM: UNDERSTANDING SOCIAL ORGANIZATION FROM INSIDE IT

Marie Campbell

Specifying the Project of "Analysis" for Activism

The conference on political activist ethnography at Laurentian University in the fall of 2002 encouraged researchers like myself to reflect carefully on what we have learned about research for activism. A decade of working in disability research and with a community-based research team has helped me refine the ideas presented in this paper. In part owing to this work, I am, of course, aware of various kinds of barriers that impede cooperation between academics and activists. Much attention has been focused on power and the problems of power-sharing between academics and activists. While that remains a knotty issue, and I have addressed it elsewhere (Campbell, Copeland and Tate 1999), that is not the point of this chapter. Another longstanding problem is the use of scholarly language in research for activism. Even George Smith's (1990) writing about activist ethnography may not inspire much confidence that academics who are themselves activists can speak accessibly to non-academics. While not dismissing the need to write in an appropriate way for an activist audience, here my focus is on something I consider even more fundamental. The kind of research that George conducted changed the focus of activist-orientated research. It drew our attention to analysis, itself, and to how a particular kind of analysis makes a contribution to activism.

Activists most often use research to support a direction they are taking and to provide evidence favouring their side of an argument or struggle against the other side. But if we catch hold of what George Smith was doing, we see that the research that he conducted offered activists something else. It provided analytic help for activists in thinking about and *determining an effective direction for activism.* My own contribution here is to show what George (and institutional ethnographers in general) mean by "analysis." In what follows, I illustrate how research as George was doing it and as I have learned to do it relates to analysis that works for activism. I use several kinds of data in this project. Excerpts from a study on health care experiences of people with disabilities (Campbell, Copeland and Tate 1999) allow me to demonstrate how I see institutional ethnography contributing insights that can help activists focus their struggles. While my work with a group of disabled people is important to the chapter's message, I remain <u>primarily a researcher and teacher, not an activist</u>. For that reason I turned for help in thinking through my ideas and preparing the conference presentation and the chapter based on it, to my friend and former student, Pat Larson, who at the time was a street nurse working with a consumer-based agency in Toronto. Larson's accounts of one of her own struggles, initiated by an outbreak of tuberculosis (TB) in Toronto's homeless shelters, have been woven into this chapter.[1]

Because of her activist profile, Pat Larson had been involved in the committee of the City's Health Department that is responsible for developing a policy to prevent a TB epidemic. Pat spent months on her contribution to this work, much of it educating her Health Department colleagues. First, she and her street-level colleagues <u>collected evidence</u> about the new and unhealthy situations in Toronto that encourage the spread of TB. They arranged for speakers from various aspects of the field, and discussed and explained the dangers to Health Department staff, who themselves lacked street-level expertise. She contributed hours of work to writing reports and recommendations. When she presented the recommendations to the relevant group at the Health Department, her presentation was (as she says) "sabotaged" by the City Health Department personnel from her own committee. While this was unexpected in the circumstances of collaborative committee work, Pat was familiar with the way that authorities she meets in her position as street-nurse frequently downplay her accounts of troubles faced by the homeless and dismiss her recommendations for action. She finds it uncomfortably commonplace for people in official positions to make hostile and disparaging remarks about her and other activists.

This story can be easily generalized to many different situations that activists face — whether organizing around homelessness as Pat does, or more militantly against war or in anti-globalization struggles. We all know what happens when activists find themselves arrayed on the opposite side of issues from those with the power to take needed action. Official agents of the powerful seem to be acting from a different set of understandings, priorities and positions, which while they may not be spoken, or if spoken be necessarily rational, will nevertheless supersede the activists' views. <u>Activists faced with the task of communicating a controversial view must find ways of impressing on the opposition the importance of this view and the different course of action it requires.</u> In a leadership position, the <u>activist's</u> task is to <u>consider how to approach a problem</u>, <u>what pieces of the problem to concentrate on</u> and <u>what course of action will have maximum impact</u>. *This is where a good analysis is needed.* In Pat's case, after consultation with others involved in related struggles, she took her next steps vigorously and in a variety of ways. Pat knows what that will mean for her own interactions at city hall. People like herself, advocating an alternative perspective, will be treated as wrong, even embarrassingly misguided, and if they persist, they may be seen as dangerous. These are the everyday experiences of activists.

Some Premises of Institutional Ethnography

To move toward my project of explaining analysis, I need to introduce readers to how institutional ethnographers understand the world as a basis for proposing how to explore its specific and troublesome features. It is most important to see that we think of everything that happens as being the product of human activity — of people whose lives and actions are being coordinated somehow. An inquiry in institutional ethnography focuses on the poorly understood "somehow" that organizes people's lives. The theory and language of institutional ethnography identifies *ruling relations* and *ruling practices* as what needs to be explained in specific instances. These terms identify general beliefs in institutional ethnography about how social life is coordinated through the everyday work of people. Let's think about this in the situation described of Pat Larson's struggle to get better services for homeless people. As an institutional ethnographer, I would treat those on the power-holding side of a contested position as holding a ruling perspective, which the other side challenges. The ruling position was held in this case by officials whose minds Pat wanted to change and whose policies she wanted to influence. If successful, activism disrupts the ruling perspective. But the ruling side holds material (E×) resources, including, in some cases, the legitimate capacity to use violence, which it will use in the amount needed to win. We have grown accustomed to seeing a certain level of animosity expressed to people demonstrating on the streets. The violence used against them includes everything from hostility and demeaning verbal abuse to more physically damaging acts.

I suggest that the hostility that Pat Larson speaks about meeting routinely in public committee rooms is merely a different form of the more physical repression of street confrontation. It is important to recognize that both expressions of hostility are a feature of how a ruling perspective is maintained. On the street, physical repression is usually obvious and may be captured for the world to see by television cameras. In offices and committee rooms of Canadian public officials, the lines are more blurred. People of good will are drawn into the ruling perspective and enact it against their own colleagues, even against their own interests. Engaging in confrontation in such meetings or work settings constitutes a different sort of risk than the physical risk to activists' bodies on the street. Both are serious. The ruling practices that are the object of Pat's activism represent a serious risk to democracy, all the more so because they operate quietly; when they "take prisoners" they do so secretly, and when this kind of ruling wins, it wins invisibly. That is the moment that my presentation at the conference and this chapter focus on. My project to illuminate analysis begins by putting a face to the activities of this kind of everyday ruling and shows how these ruling practices operate in our lives.

Terms such as "ruling relations" used by institutional ethnographers are more than the language of theory. Rather, these words reflect what actually happens. They express how everyday life is organized and *that* is what we are interested in. Institutional ethnographers accept that the people taking the opposite sides of a struggle hold conflicting positions not just as a whim. Rather, such conflicting positions are socially organized. *They are grounded and enacted in people's lives and express their different interests.* Pat, for instance, would have no hesitation in declaring that her position on public health policy was embedded in the needs of her constituency of homeless people. The views of those who resisted her recommendations should be understood as similarly grounded in another constituency and its own interests. Institutional ethnographers recognize that they need to approach a problem informed by the everyday/night experiences of the people on whose behalf they are working. We call that a "standpoint in the everyday world" (D.E. Smith 1987), and understanding the world from that perspective is crucial for figuring out the action to be taken. The question that an institutional ethnographer wants to answer is: "what organization of the world organizes and maintains the position that these people live and suffer from, and that my research is helping in the struggle against?" Institutional ethnographers find, account for and use such differences of perspectives analytically. Competing versions of what is happening open the door to research on how those views arise, how they are organized and maintained, what is being accomplished through operating as if one perspective were the right or only legitimate way to see things, etc. The activist ethnographer, using the methods of institutional ethnography developed and taught by Dorothy Smith (1987, 1999), can discover how certain perspectives are embedded in officialdom and how they buttress official actions and discount other knowledge and other actions.

Different Perspectives at Work

While activists might have the urge to classify different perspectives as simply right or wrong, I suggest that we can expect to learn something from seeing how they are embedded within and arise from particular social locations. For instance, that members of the Toronto Board of Health work and live in places where they can avoid seeing street people in any but superficial ways underpins the different perspective they may hold on managing the TB outbreak. Their knowledge comes in sterile packages, reports, statistics and library research. Pat found that they lacked current local knowledge about the increasing level of overcrowding in jails and homeless shelters and the effects of hepatitis C and other infections contributing to a generalized decline in health status of the dispossessed — and how this was implicated in the spread of tuberculosis. Her committee work tried to broaden this narrow perspective on responding to the outbreak of TB. She spoke from a standpoint in the experience of the street people and, as a street nurse, she interpreted their interests in planning for action. When she questioned her committee colleagues about the resistance that they had mounted against her recommendations, one member of the committee, a manager of the TB program, explained that she was obligated to "not make recommendations to City Hall that cost the city more money."

Pat was attempting to influence a course of action undertaken within a public institution, using public funds, implementing public policy. Her concerns about the TB program were intended to address the actualities of the lives of people living on or near the street. Pat's representation of the health problem and how it should be handled would be easily identified with a minority group's interests. It may not be so easy to identify interests within officialdom. Official views are usually presented as being neutral and official actions as being in the public interest, or for the common good. It may therefore be ineffective to challenge them on the level of claims about which view is "right." For activist researchers, that means learning a set of research strategies beyond critiquing differing perspectives and their appearance in public policies. Activists must also learn how to understand and engage with the actions of public administration whereby policies are planned, implemented and evaluated. Ruling interests are enacted routinely through specific administrative practices. When attempting to intercede on behalf of marginalized people, activists must discover how their constituency's interests are being marginalized in routine organizational action.

The resistance to Pat's ideas came at the point where they were moving toward being embedded in organizational policy, through which they would acquire the force of organizational funding. With the recognition that perspectives always have a social location, analytic attention shifts away from what people say to how their views are embedded in practical action. This highlights what people *do*, as well as what they say or believe. The social organization that structures public action was the focus of George Smith's research, and it is also my focus here. When George explored the social organization of AIDS treatments and discovered that they were embedded in public health policy and practices, he saw how they addressed interests that were not those of people with AIDS or HIV. This was a moment of analysis and discovery that turned out to be crucial for George's and his activist group's strategizing.

I now turn to a discussion of data from my own research to demonstrate the kind of analysis I have been describing. I begin by identifying conflicting perspectives on how services are delivered to people with disabilities and how successful they are understood to be. Then I show the official perspective embedded in the mechanisms underlying delivery of these services. My analysis is offered here to suggest how a ruling perspective becomes and stays dominant. In this case, it becomes apparent that the concerns of people with disabilities routinely get subordinated to an official version of their needs and the agency's work, without any intention by agency personnel to discriminate or dismiss what their clients say. We can see how good intentions to serve the public are not enough.

I need to set the stage with a bit of background about the study (Campbell, Copeland and Tate 1999) on the operation of a home support program providing services to people with disabilities. The community-based research team looked at how this program worked and how successful it was, from the perspectives of both service recipients and those who planned, organized and managed, supervised and delivered the services. We discovered, among other things, how beliefs about good practice expressed in policy and program descriptions, or personally, by professional leaders and managers, were often contradicted in actual practice. The situation I have chosen to discuss here concerns the hourly assignment of home support workers to clients with disabilities. The support work to be done was personal service such as bathing, dressing and food preparation. In our research, disabled clients complained that agencies frequently assigned to them workers whom they did not know and who didn't know how to take care of their particular needs. They were of the opinion that the agencies did not appreciate the importance to them (the disabled clients) of having consistency in assigned workers. Yet, from agency officials, we heard assurances that everyone hired to do home support work was trained and adequately skilled. We discovered that both the health care authority and the agencies we studied took "continuity of workers" to be one of the principles underlying their mission for giving good client-centred care. The importance of this principle was documented in policy statements and in union contracts. The staff understood and talked about continuity of workers. More than that, agency supervisors and scheduling clerks insisted that it was a routine feature of their practice to assign workers to the same clients over time. Of course, everybody was attuned to overriding issues of scarce resources and how that, unfortunately, compromised good intentions to some extent.

When we tried to match up our observations of what actually was happening with expressions of organizational beliefs we saw that we couldn't. They continually came apart. Organizational accounts did not usually express what we were seeing. This was especially the case regarding the different perspectives on assigning the same workers consistently to clients. In our field research, we observed the kind of difficulties a "new" worker (meaning, previously unknown to the particular person with a disability) could create for the people who needed specialized attention. We actually saw a client being put at risk by a casual worker who was trying to conduct personal care. It was apparent that the worker was inadequately prepared to handle this client's particular needs, in spite of the documentary evidence of appropriate hiring criteria and supervision.

This example of different perspectives about continuity of workers assigned to clients is the kind of thing that institutional ethnography can investigate. As already discussed above, our theory tells us that a difference in perspectives is actually *organized* somehow. An institutional ethnographer would look for the ruling practices that organize the dominant perspective, and that is the analysis I now turn to: I draw on observations of an agency's home support clerk "scheduling" workers into work assignments, using a computerized system. This fragment of data analysis illustrates how conflicting knowledge about consistent workers arises from knowers differently located in the system, as well as from processes of knowing that are radically different. Some people know from living the experience; others know the situation as it is constituted in texts, for ruling purposes.

The Analysis: How the Standpoint
of Ruling Pervades the Local Setting

In the excerpt of data below, a clerk who assigns workers to clients is talking about what she is doing, for the benefit of a researcher who sits beside her at her workstation. A call has come into the agency and to her desk ordering an increase in home support hours for a regular client of the agency. From the clerk's comments, you can hear that in her assignment work she recognizes the necessity of reducing to a minimum the number of workers whom this client must interact with. She says:

> This lady gets service every evening at eight o'clock. What I need to do now is I need to set up [for extra service] every morning at eight o'clock. I want to use as many of the evening workers as I can to keep the number of workers down. (Campbell, Copeland and Tate 1999: 56)

This comment tells us that the clerk's intention is to assign workers so that "continuity" can be maximized. The observer watches and listens while the clerk scrolls through the computer program looking at lists of workers, their current work assignments and their availability at the newly required time. However, her comments suggest that continuity of workers may not be her only concern. She says, "We have to schedule the most senior worker that is available." For an institutional ethnographer, the notion of "most senior worker" alludes to some social organization external to the relationship between a client and a home support worker. These words are clues to the social relations organized outside this setting and penetrating it, through the knowledge, skills and work organization of the clerk and the technical capacity of the computer. Since this aspect of the social organization is external and not available in the observational setting, it had to be followed up later. It turns out that "seniority" is a reference to a contractual agreement between the agency and the workers' union. What the observer sees in the setting is that "seniority" is the clerk's first priority; it supersedes the clerk's commitment to "continuity," even though at the moment of taking this action, she treats it as a *routine condition of doing scheduling*.

Later, we learn that provisions in the contract allow the seniority clause to be overridden at the discretion of the agency. However, this would add another complication to the busy clerk's already complex and time-sensitive job. There was no mention of this possibility as she searched for the most senior available worker, one whom she hoped this client already knew. As it happened, although she found several workers known to the client, she judged all to be inappropriate for a number of organizational reasons. While I won't extend this data analysis further, it turns out that besides seniority, efficient use of workers' time and an underlying concern about adhering to the agency budget were never far from the clerk's mind. As an ordinary feature of agency life, her commitment to producing continuity for clients is continually superseded by organizational issues that enter into the scheduling process in routine but apparently unnoticed ways.

This analytic fragment about scheduling home support workers illustrates the institutional processes through which ruling practices subordinate and write over experiential knowing. For example, these data show how labour agreements take priority over concerns for clients' comfort (and in the instance we saw, their safety too.) The domination of union rules is a ruling practice vested in legal processes. Managing such agreements is a complex textual process that, because of the power of unions to hold home support agencies to account, automatically supersedes the mission statements about client-centred care. But the instance of seniority being considered first is only one kind of ruling that dominates scheduling. The clerk's scheduling activities, her know-how and familiarity with workers and clients and their wishes and needs, were routinely appropriated to the agency's ruling interests in productivity and efficiency in the use of paid labour. One potential worker was rejected as a possible caregiver to the post-hospitalized woman because it would take her into "overtime" and extra costs; another would have to drive too far, meaning that she would be engaged for longer and cost the agency more than absolutely necessary.

I want to be clear here that *my analysis is not itself a critique.* I am not criticizing this assignment clerk and how she did her work. Nor is my analysis an anti-union critique — the rights of home support workers certainly need to be protected. Nor am I criticizing the agency or the health authority, although of course, they might actually benefit from a critical review of their policies and practices. I am offering this fragmentary analysis as an illustration of the social organization of assignment of workers to clients and how it departs from what is known about it, officially. We get only a glimpse here of ruling practices: in them, the agency's intentions to address clients' interests are being actively subordinated. The tools of ruling are discursive, programmed into texts of all kinds. The discursively organized work process allows the organization's actual priorities to be addressed *first,* by providing, among other things, a computerized list of workers in order of their seniority. It supports the cost-efficient management by listing cumulative hours assigned, assuring that none exceed regularly paid amounts (avoiding overtime pay; avoiding over-booking a casual worker). The clerk's knowledge of the clients, the workers and the city assures that assignments are made in such a way as to avoid wasting workers' paid time in travel. This is how ruling happens and how in local settings ruling practices are employed in ways that reorganize, displace and discount clients' experiential knowledge — of meeting workers they don't know, consistently, of continually having to orientate new workers, of being anxious as workers inexperienced with them and their needs attempt to provide care for them. I am making the point that this social organization of local settings happens in routine organizational practices that, until they are explicated through a conscious application of research methodology, will go unnoticed.

As long as that happens, confrontation on this issue is likely to stay at the level of different perspectives, with clients' voices being subordinated routinely. For instance, doing this scheduling to accomplish organizational goals did not undermine the clerk's belief in her attentiveness to the goal of continuity of workers. Nor did it interfere with the health authority's or agency's claims to give excellent home care to people with disabilities — care that was confidently claimed to be client-centred and to offer continuity of workers. Nothing about the routine practice of assigning "hours of work" to clients would shake the authoritative claim the organization made about its commitment to continuity of care, regardless of what clients said. What we can see in this analysis of discursive organization is that the official knowledge of the nature of care in this setting is (what institutional ethnographers call) "ideological," that is, it arose from sources that were internal to the management of the organization and that were almost entirely split off from the people who were having a parade of different, often "casual" and inexperienced, workers appearing in their homes to provide personal care.

Conclusion

We have made a quick trip from thinking about activists dissenting from an established ruling position, putting themselves on the line on behalf of a constituency whose interests are at stake. I have attempted to show how different kinds of activism are similar in their attempts to disrupt and replace the hegemony of ruling ideas. My particular message here is about how institutional ethnography can help specify the practices of ruling that are operative in any particular struggle. Of course, the specifics of analyzing Canada's part in the World Trade Organization would be different from analyzing consistency of assignment of workers to a home support client. But the framework of the analysis is the same. I have argued that activism can be strengthened by specific knowledge of how ruling interests are substituted for the interests of the activists' constituency. I am recommending a materialist over an ideological (or as George Smith called it, a speculative) analysis. Of course, so much remains to be said about all this. Left unstated as yet is my contention that struggle has room for and needs all kinds of actions, from street protest to new policy development, and the best kind of research to support them. I am not making the claim that institutional ethnography is the only research needed.

I raise this point because I want activism to be a collective effort. In the area of disability activism, I am learning about the debates within the movement about different perspectives and who has or can have the correct line on struggle. In situations like this, institutional ethnography's project of analysis is particularly helpful because it forces analytic attention back to the social organization of what is happening. A claim to knowing based on the knower being in the right category (e.g., disabled) or using the right theoretical conception (e.g., social model of disability or emancipatory research) can fail if the research itself lacks a secure grounding in the everyday world. To be fair, I think that that is the goal of disability theorists — to insist that researchers actually have a knowledge basis in the experience they analyze. But nothing about being "in the know experientially" insulates us from being drawn into a ruling perspective. I suspect that we have all had the experience of seeing someone we know to be "one of us" taking a position that does not represent the interests of our constituency (as we understand them). There are many opportunities for people from our side to take up the ruling perspective as their own. The kind of analysis that I am recommending here clarifies how ruling practices accomplish just that. With that illumination, perhaps we are better prepared to sort out how to authentically take the standpoint of those on whose behalf we want to work.

Critical Thinking and Discussion Questions

1. What are the main problems that activists face in working with academics and how does this article address them?

2. Campbell suggests that the focus for activism should be informed by research; how practical is this suggestion and can you see it being put into practice in the areas of activism with which you are familiar?

3. Identify a setting where you know that some changes need to be instituted. Discuss the problem(s) you recognize there in terms of the ruling relations of the setting. Does identifying what you know and what you don't really understand about the setting's organization suggest what might usefully be researched prior to any action being taken?

Note

1. I want to express my gratitude to Pat Larson, RN, MN, who generously shared her experiences of activism with me and allowed me to use them for my purposes in this chapter. Also, for funding support for the research reported in Campbell, Copeland and Tate (1999), I thank the BC Health Research Foundation, the Social Sciences and Humanities Research Council of Canada/ Human Resources Development Canada, and The Vancouver Foundation.

Part B

RESEARCH AS DISRUPTION

One of our interests in the project of doing activist sociology is a methodological one. As the project emerged, we came to reflect on the ability of this volume to address the emerging practice of sociology more generally. While the entire book provides food for this address, the following three chapters focus on the practice of doing research in a fresh manner. All authors demonstrate how research can be seen *as* disruption and disruption seen *as* research.

In teaching, studying and using research methods, we have witnessed the ways in which methodologies are cut up for the purposes of simplification. This reduction tends to stabilize false faults. However, Thompson, Clarke and Kinsman build channels through these cuts that allow a full flow of the critical notions of transformation, reflexivity, ideology, critique, practice, resistance and pedagogy. They do this by demonstrating how direct action and resistance are already dripping with research insight. Thompson, for example, states that direct action and confrontation allow people to learn something "very concrete about the belly of the beast" and, later, that "it is as simple as knowing your enemy," a line also echoed by Clarke. Thompson then examines the nature of this "knowing" in detail, walking us through the front lines of direct action and the ways in which it can help us to demystify the world. Like Kinsman and Clarke, he argues for the epistemological recognition of the social dimensions of the act of knowing, carried out by people who then extend this act to the mapping of their social locations. Direct action, therefore, becomes a coherent and useful research practice, not an ideological exercise. Thompson's use of the critical pedagogy of Paulo Freire, and the work of G. Smith, D. Smith and K. Marx are apt and cogent. For instance, G. Smith's point that when doing activist research one should "Start where you're at. Map your way outward. Watch the interconnections proliferate" is followed through with examples of how interrogation by the state is itself a potent research moment. From this moment forward, Thompson suggests, "in swallowing us, they expose their squishy insides, their ineptitudes and the causes of their indigestion."

These "squishy insides" are further explored by Clarke through his work with the Ontario Coalition Against Poverty (OCAP). Here, the practicality of research *as* activism and activism *as* detailed research is fleshed out further. The praxis of social justice work is made plain through the activity of OCAP around housing takeovers and the Pope Squat and in resistance to urban redevelopment schemes in Toronto. These are discussed in the context of the neoliberal agenda of systematic removal of social provisions. Uncovered are moments of resistance, ways in which resistance is mapped and future research directions. For instance, Clarke illustrates the moments of praxis in which the homeless secure and hold living space as transformation "from the realm of proposals and demands to carv(ing) out solutions" all the way to the level of legislation. He states that "our grasp of the situation can never be complete as long as we merely focus on our enemies, their plans, alignments and methods of operation. We also must fully evaluate our own capacity for resistance." Clarke clearly shows how direct action is a beginning point for mapping the social organization of struggle. He ends with an elaboration of activist needs for research and provides directions for future research while remaining critical of ideological primacy. Three such directions are a) a detailed understanding of the process of gentrification, b) the coordination and operations needed to undertake the removal of the poor in the process and c) the social history of the workings of the police in the defence of capitalism.

Kinsman's chapter refers and responds to Clarke's latter point in providing and gathering the ways in which activism, ethnography and explorations of social organization work to help us produce new forms of research practice. Kinsman provides "new ways forward" for activists that are based in the praxis of mapping not only ruling regimes in their multinational form but also the social relations of struggle. Political activist ethnography is detailed as a practice and methodology for extending the already present research capacities of activists. The further democratization of research is suggested, and its boundaries pushed through examination of dialogical ways to move beyond speculation. Kinsman, like Thompson, notes that activism is already ripe with research, and here we see concrete strategies for harvesting these fruits. By starting with a political commitment to begin on the side of the oppressed, Kinsman reflects the arguments of both Thompson and Clarke.

DIRECT ACTION,
PEDAGOGY OF THE OPPRESSED[1]

A.K. Thompson

*The more radical the person is, the more fully he or she enters into
reality so that, knowing it better, he or she can better transform
it.* —Paulo Freire

On September 27, 2002, thousands of activists from across the United States
descended on Washington, DC, to challenge the increasing barbarity of the
neoliberal world. In what was to be the first major convergence of anti-globalization and anti-war sensibilities post September 11th, the People's Strike
— as the day was called — targeted both U.S. imperialist military policy and
the IMF/World Bank leviathan.[2] As with previous mass demonstrations in
DC, activists were confronted with sweeping arrests. Among those picked
up and detained were three women who, in the spirit of non-cooperation
that had become a cornerstone of movement activity since Seattle, chose to
delay and frustrate the state's attempt to process them by refusing to provide
identification. Since the police could not process them at the station and
since they could not be released on bail, the Jane Does, as the activists came
to be known, were transferred to a Washington-area women's prison.

As might be expected, this change of venue led the organizers of the
People's Strike — DC's Anti-Capitalist Convergence (ACC) — to begin
coordinating jail visits. Within a few days, their efforts led them to circulate instructions on how to visit the Jane Does over the Internet. Jails,
after all, have rules and, if activists were to be able to visit their comrades,
they would have to know how to approximate good behaviour. Presumably
because of the prison policies they had encountered, the ACC posted the
following "rules for visits" on their website: "30 minutes for each visit,
only 2 adults at a time, No sandals or open-toed shoes. No sweat suits, No
camouflage, No cross-dressing. Women must (appear to be) wearing a bra."
To the end of these regulations, ACC added the following parenthetic note:
"(Unfortunately, this is not a joke)." Indeed.

While the bemusement is noteworthy, I think the encounter with prison
regulations described above has significance beyond providing another

anecdotal basis for despising institutional (hetero)sexism. Apart from the offensive, decidedly unfunny, encounter with yet another expression of the antiquated devotion to outmoded gender categories, what took place in this interaction? Through what process did ACC activists come to know prison visit rules? It is worth considering how direct action and confrontation allowed people to learn something very concrete about the belly of the beast.

Many anti-globalization activists embrace direct action as an effective means of struggle. What is less evident, however, is how direct action might also be the basis for a new kind of thinking. By extending the insights of radical educator Paulo Freire and activist-scholar George Smith, it becomes clear that direct action is not only an effective and courageous means of resistance but a potentially effective research practice and pedagogy as well. Residual commitments to forms of idealist thought,[3] however, currently make it difficult for activists to make the most of this potential.

For readers familiar with Freire and G. Smith, it is important to note that I am not arguing that their positions or approaches are identical or without contradiction. Indeed, Smith (whose writing takes up and extends the themes of institutional ethnography) would probably scoff at some of the existential formulations in Freire's writing. In particular, Freire's idea of an "ontological vocation" and the struggle to "become more fully human" (1996: 25) would likely strike him as an unproductive detour into the snared terrain of ideological thought.

Nevertheless, there are significant points of convergence in G. Smith and Freire's approaches. This is particularly the case with respect to each writer's desire to break down distinctions between various forms of human activity. For Freire and G. Smith, education, research, learning and struggle must each be emancipated from constraint and become aspects of the others. Likewise, both G. Smith and Freire place significant emphasis on the role of confrontation in the process of knowledge production. Both insist, too, that learning must be based on forms of concrete investigation that begin where people are located. How can activists use these insights to help realize the potential of direct action, thus helping us to increase the effectiveness of our disruptions? How might G. Smith and Freire help activists to improve our effectiveness?

"Women must (appear to be) wearing a bra," read the ACC's account. Was the parenthetic qualifier part of the jail's policy? It seems unlikely. Instead, this sentence is probably an expression of a struggle between the rigid jailhouse code and the stern will and defiance of activism. More to the point, it represents a conflict between the letter of the law and the experience of existing within it, of trying to navigate its stipulations. It is not difficult to imagine a member of the Anti-Capitalist Convergence going to the prison and being told that they could not visit their comrades on account of a transgression of one of these rules.

Perhaps the activist went further and challenged the prison official to provide an account of why these rules even existed. It might even have been discovered that the intersection between the projects of incarceration and gender regulation was enshrined in a written policy. And, we might imagine, as the concrete practice of the jail became clearer, the mystifications through which its contours are ordinarily perceived began to fade away. Although this interaction can only be inferred from ACC's disclosure of the policy for prison visits, the parenthetic note reveals something about a confrontation and an active moment of social research.

From the meticulous planning of logistics and scenario committees preparing large actions, to the time individuals spend brushing up on issues raised by structural adjustment programs, activists already engage in extensive amounts of investigation aimed at making the movement more effective. However, as of yet, there has been no systematic attempt to use the experiences of movement participants as the starting point for research, to turn ourselves into conscious, organized and effective researchers. Such an attempt, I feel, would allow for a considerable escalation in the level and effectiveness of struggle. It's as simple as knowing your enemy.

Is activist research of this sort possible? A cursory glance suggests that the general orientation towards direct action within the anti-globalization movement already spontaneously satisfies many of the criteria for effective social research outlined by George Smith. In "Political Activist as Ethnographer," Smith suggests how, since we are located outside of but in constant interaction with "ruling regimes" (like the prison in which the Jane Does were held), activists can explore the social organization of power as it is revealed through moments of confrontation (1990: 641). The confluence between Smith's proposed research method and the practices adopted by activists is intriguing.

How, then, might this capacity for research be clarified and extended in order to provide us with reliable knowledge upon which to base strategic and tactical decisions? For, even as the carnivalesque abundance of the current movement is important as a life-affirming impulse, it remains insufficient as a systematic basis on which to extend disruptive capacities. However, by challenging the formal distinctions between research, education and disruption, by engaging in activism as producers (and not merely critics) of social relations, activists could considerably extend the possibilities of transformative intervention.

It is in light of this possibility that the confluence between the direct action ethos and Paulo Freire's ideas about education as an act of freedom gains special significance. As a practice of resistance, but also as a method of engaging with the world that throws many of its mediations into relief, direct action provides activists with a strategy of moving beyond what Freire, following Alvaro Vieira Pinto, called "limit situations" (1996: 83). By impelling conditions that require actively uncovering how social relations are put together and by forcing ourselves to enter more fully into the social, direct action, in a manner not unlike that advocated in Freire's pedagogy, facilitates the demystification of the world. Even a brief appraisal of activist attempts to visit the Jane Does in jail reveals how this is the case.

The entire Jane Doe situation and the knowledge people gained from it was made possible through a systematic commitment to confrontation. This commitment, which lies at the very heart of the direct action ethos, enabled activists to push against limit situations. In this instance, conflict and learning each began with the ACC's call to action for the day of the People's Strike. In the context of police fears about losing control of American cities since the Battle of Seattle, this call-out led police to organize a massive operation that culminated in the mobilization of hundreds of riot cops. Even before activists had hit the streets, confrontation played a key role in producing the situations that led them to discover the policies that organize visits to DC-area women's prisons, and much more besides.

As many activists have come to realize, police and lawmakers have expanded "confrontation" to encapsulate such a range of activities in the context of anti-globalization protest that one need hardly to do anything at all to wind up in custody. Picked up simply for failing to disperse when they were ordered to, the Jane Does, once arrested, continued their confrontation with police by refusing to comply with the institutional logic and mechanisms through which they would be processed. Finally, by taking an active interest in what was happening to the Jane Does, ACC activists came into confrontation with the bureaucratic mechanisms that regulate interactions between inmates and those who would visit them.

While this small piece of information might not initially seem to be especially important in the fight for global justice, it is useful to consider George Smith's point that when doing activist research, what is learned is determined by the course of struggle itself. Start where you're at. Map your way outward. Watch the interconnections proliferate. Recounting his experience doing research to further gay liberation struggles and AIDS activism, Smith confides that he did not base his work on separate or formal interviews. "Rather, the route of access was determined by the course of confrontation, which in turn was determined ... by analyzing the data. Thus the research had a reflexive relation to the political struggle of people" (1990: 641).

It is clear that confrontation helped to reveal a small but significant piece of the social regulation puzzle by uncovering, in this instance, a connection between gender and the carceral project. What happens, then, if we try to make sense of this small discovery in the context of the anti-globalization movement as a whole? The implications are dizzying. During the People's Strike alone more than 650 activists were arrested.

If one begins counting from Seattle, where approximately 500 activists were picked up, arrests have reached staggering proportions. Nearly 500 activists were picked up in Québec City during demonstrations against the Summit of the Americas. More than 200 were nabbed in New York during protests against the World Economic Forum in February of 2002. Hundreds were booked in each of Genoa, Gothenburg, Prague and other protest venues between 1999 and 2001. On top of this partial list of enormous roundups, we must remember the A16 actions in Washington, DC, where it is estimated that nearly 1200 people were arrested in a week of protests against the IMF and World Bank.

Since the Battle of Seattle, several thousand demonstrators have been granted the opportunity to learn something about the state while spending time in its custody. While the state has seemingly relied on arrest as a means to distract activist energies and break organizing momentum, this regulatory strategy has led in many instances to a new fearlessness amongst activists. The repressive structures of the state, now laid bare through excessive use, do not generate the same trepidation that they did when their machinations were unknown. "Being interrogated by insiders to a ruling regime, such as a crown attorney," George Smith points out, "allows a researcher to come into direct contact with the conceptual relevancies and organizing principles of those bodies" (1990: 640). And so, in swallowing us, they expose their squishy insides, their ineptitudes and the causes of their indigestion. Through the concrete experience of arrest, many activists have come to a better understanding of how the system actually works and have, in a manner of speaking, inoculated themselves against its mystifications.

Although direct action provides the basis for a rigorous materialist epistemology, this is not how most anti-globalization activists currently talk about our project. A result of the contradictions built into our social locations, often white and middle class, many activists continue to start from the perspective and standpoint of ideas. George Smith observes a similar tendency amongst activists fighting against the policing of gay men and those fighting for treatment options for people living with AIDS.

> Rather than critiquing the ideological practice of... politico-administrative regimes as a method of determining how things happen, activists usually opt for speculative accounts. The touchstone of these explanations was the attribution of agency to concepts.... Instead of events being actively produced by people in concrete situations, they are said to be "caused" by ideas. (1990: 634)

As Marx points out, the cause of events is not ideas but rather forms of organized and coordinated social action. To miss this point, he thought, was to undermine the possibilities of effective social transformation. In order to find ways to make the anti-globalization movement more effective, then, it seems urgent to look for strategies to overcome the abstractions of conceptual thought. For, even as activists are often more attentive to the dynamics of the world than most, we are still subject to our own forms of idealist abstraction. Freire has pointed out that abstract thought, whether marshalled by the left or the right, presents itself as a barrier to transformative engagement. "Closing themselves into 'circles of certainty' from which they cannot escape," Freire argues, "these individuals 'make' their own truth." However,

It is not a truth of men and women who struggle to build the future, running the risks invoked in this very construction. Nor is it the truth of men and women who fight side by side and learn together how to build the future — which is not something given to be received by people, but is rather something to be created by them. Both types of sectarian, treating history in an equally proprietary fashion, end up without the people — which is another way of being against them. (1996: 20–21)

Blowing Up a Social Relation

It was during an occupation of the president's offices at the University of Guelph that I first noticed how direct action could be a form of research. Provoked by government plans to increase tuition, the occupation represented an attempt by students to address the growing inaccessibility of Ontario universities. Importantly, although the provincial Tory government had been systematically raising tuition since its election in 1995, by 1997, perhaps in an effort to avoid criticism for its anti-education policies, it left the tuition increase to the "discretion" of individual universities.

Ontario students had been opposing attacks on education for years. However, the "discretionary" tuition increase fundamentally changed the dynamics of student activism. Before 1997, Ontario students would regularly gather on the lawn of the provincial legislature to raise their voices in moral outrage. Since the actual processes involved in implementing educational policy were opaque to most of us, all that was left to protest was a governing "anti-student" ethos. Assembled in front of the legislature, students would learn about "the issues" but could not intervene in the events shaping the future of education. In 1997, with the purported shift in decision-making power from the province to the university itself, many students were provoked into looking closely at our own institutions, perhaps for the first time. A whole world of specificity began to unfold.

Occupation impelled the need for a new kind of knowledge of the university and its social relations. In order to get into the president's offices in the first place, activists had to become familiar with mundane aspects of the building and its operation. A discernable shift in student politics took place. Once a measure of commitment and engagement, being "informed about the issues" was quickly surpassed by the need to develop an intricate knowledge of actual social relations. At organizing meetings leading up to the occupation, activists began compiling lists of things we would need to know in order to proceed: "When do the janitors unlock the door from the stairwell to the administrative floor?" "How many doors lead in and out of the space?" "Will we be able to lock them?" "Once inside, what will we do if administrators or office staff are already there? Is it better, legally speaking, to force them to leave the office before locking the doors or risk the possibility of locking them in and being charged with forcible confinement?"

A process of research and concrete investigation ensued. When investigating the "extra-local realm," George Smith points out that "it is the local experiences of people that determine the relevancies of the research; that point to the extra-local forms of organization in need of investigation" (1990: 638). It was in this manner that we proceeded. Starting from the initial point of local confrontation, activists began looking outward and asking specific questions about the organizational processes that impacted upon the immediate situation.

These organizational processes were often enshrined in and made possible through texts: the *Criminal Code of Canada* and the University's Code of Student Rights and Responsibilities came into view as potentially significant for the occupiers. Since these texts weighed heavily on the local situation and gave it its social character, activists were wise to look at how our planned activities related to them. Continuing well after the action itself, this new approach to confrontation changed the way we understood the university. Resulting from an epistemic shift, research, pedagogy and knowledge production each became important, if under-articulated, aspects of our activist practice.

But students were not the only actors in the confrontation dynamic. Arriving to find locks and chains on their doors and barring the entrance to their offices, administrators began making urgent pleas, backed by threats, that the occupiers not read or tamper with files in the offices. Files, after all, are a critical part of the infrastructure that makes a ruling relation possible. Initially, the administration knew this more than the occupiers did. It was their domain, after all. However, through confrontation, the importance of the files was revealed to the activists as well. In retrospect, we should have been much more curious. The occupation really only began to scratch the surface of what we didn't know about how the university worked.

After assuring the occupiers that hell hath no fury like a bureaucrat whose files have been tampered with, the administration's next course of action was to call the city fire department. With the doors locked, the administration reasoned, the occupation was a fire hazard and posed a threat to the "safety of students." Although, in the end, the firefighters did not intervene, the incident revealed something important about how physical spaces are often regulated. Since then, I have noticed how common it is for authorities to cite fire code violations when evicting activists from squatted buildings or organizing centres. Zoning laws, fire codes, property titles: these are the texts that make it possible for ruling relations to be conducted in, and occupy, actual spaces in the actual world. And because these texts prompt standardized and universal courses of action to address ideologically construed local "situations," they can be mobilized to regulate a multitude of experientially different moments. Given the regulatory capacities they enable for those in power, these texts are thus of supreme importance to activists as well.

The occupation provided us with a way to begin piecing together a concrete understanding of how the university worked. However, despite the intensity of our engagement, learning was not limited to the activists directly involved in the occupation. By forcing the administration to act in ways to which it was unaccustomed, we were able to throw into relief some previously invisible dynamics, which henceforth became evident to everyone on campus. There was a palpable shift in the character of discussions between students. A carefully planned provocation, the occupation produced a pedagogical moment.

It was, however, only with the rise of the anti-globalization movement that I became fully aware of the connections between direct action, pedagogy and the possibility of effective activist research. I began conducting workshops on direct action and street tactics. With an academic background in critical pedagogy and a desire to make struggles against globalization as effective as possible, I became very interested in the problem of designing a workshop that would prepare people to engage in sometimes frightening confrontations. Since many workshops I had attended took place either immediately before, or in the lead-up to, major actions, they tended to focus on lists of things that activists "needed to know": Don't wear contact lenses; don't lose your buddy; remember not to say more than required while under arrest; remove pepper spray with mineral oil followed immediately by rubbing alcohol: our lists were certainly notable for their esoteric contents.[4] Novelty aside, the direct action workshop never strayed too far pedagogically from the banking model of "education" critiqued by Freire. Activists were being equipped with lists of what to know but the more difficult problem of how to know, how to think, still needed to be addressed.

When I began conducting my own workshops, I noticed how participants would not want to begin any activities until I produced a definition of direct action. Although my workshop began with an exercise in which participants were asked to situate themselves in relation to whatever conception of direct action they currently held, for many, this was insufficient.[5] Until I described what I meant by direct action, some participants intoned, there would be insufficient grounds for discussion. To me, this brought to light two related problems. First, despite the fact that everybody talked about it, there continued to be ambiguity about the meaning of direct action within the movement.

Second and more significant, despite being a way of knowing enlisted by the very powers we were fighting, activists expressed a strong desire to start from the standpoint of conceptual knowledge and explain their experiences from there. The workshop setting allowed participants to forget that knowing is an act carried out by people. Instead, what the workshop allowed for was knowledge: the objectified residue of knowing. As workshop facilitator, I was expected to convey this knowledge, now perceived as static, universally applicable and transferable from situation to situation. The social specificities that prompted the initial knowing and the knowing of workshop participants themselves were forgotten in the leap towards abstract thought. Dorothy Smith describes this way of thinking as an important component of contemporary ruling relations. *In Conceptual Practices of Power*, D. Smith explains that, in a ruling relation,

> subjective experience is opposed to the objectively known. The two are separated from each other by the social act that creates the externalized object of knowledge — the fact.... Facts mediate relations not only between knower and known but among knowers and the object known in common.... A fact is construed to be external to the particular subjectivity of the knowers. It is the same for everyone, external to anyone and... is fixed, devoid of perspective, in the same relation to anyone. It coordinates the activities of anyone who is positioned to read and has mastered the interpretive procedures it intends and relies on. (1990a: 69)

Since I was the workshop facilitator, I was cast in the role of dispensing the knowledge particular to "the workshop" — itself a form of social organization with its own conventions and interpretive procedures. Hence, I was called upon to provide a definition of direct action. Such a definition, according to the standards of objectified knowledge, was a universal object that I could dispense; an object that anyone, provided they had come to my workshop, could receive. Needless to say, this approach bears strong and disconcerting resemblance to the "banking" model of pedagogy critiqued by Freire. In this model, knowledge is construed as an object that can be "deposited" into the student, the passive recipient. According to Freire, in the banking model,

> The teacher talks about reality as though it were motionless, static, compartmentalized and predictable or else he expounds on a topic completely alien to the existential experience of the students. His task is to "fill" the students with the contents of his narration — contents which are detached from reality, disconnected from the totality that engendered them and could give them significance. Words are emptied of their concreteness and become a hollow, alienated and alienating verbosity. (1996: 52)

I shuddered at the thought that this "teacher" could be me. Having spent the last several years of my life in the academy, I knew that I was sometimes guilty of "alienating verbosity." But hadn't I been the one pushing workshop participants to generate an account of direct action derived from their own existential experiences? Had I not, further, argued the importance of thinking about the reality of confrontation as a relational dynamism? Was it the workshop itself, with the interpretive structure that it demanded, that led participants to want to set a universal definition of direct action, emptying it of its concreteness? I was perplexed by the disappearance of workshop participants as knowing subjects; subjects who could use their experiences as the basis for developing an understanding of the social. Did the workshop swallow them?

When participants did refer to their experiences, it often took the form of testimony: less about developing an understanding of the world by investigating concrete situations and more about telling a personal truth. While it was good to hear accounts of people's experiences, these did not bring us much closer to an understanding of social relations and how to blow them up. Instead of starting from the standpoint of reified objective "knowledge," these accounts would often go to the opposite extreme and take personal experience as truth. They would start from the standpoint of situated subjectivity and, adopting the narrative voice, which as Freire points out is the defining tool of banking pedagogy (1996: 52), they would then enter "experience" into the realm of objectified knowledge. Often, this would produce a situation where knowledge-objects would stand in sharp contradiction with one another.

What could be done? Following the conventions of post-modern politeness, should we have concluded that the situation leant itself to multiple readings? This seemed depressing: we weren't talking about twentieth-century working-class Irish novels, after all. We were talking about social relations. Surely, there was something concrete here that we could actually know. What seemed to be required, and as George Smith has succinctly outlined, was not a "shift from an objective to a subjective epistemology, which some feminists have chosen to make, but rather a move from an objective to a reflexive one where the sociologist [and, we might add, the activist], going beyond the seductions of solipsism, inhabits the world that she is investigating" (1990: 633).

In *Pedagogy of the Oppressed*, Freire cautions about the shortcomings of both "objectivism" and "subjectivism." What is needed, he maintains, is a form of praxis that breaks down the dichotomy between subject and object; a way of approaching the world that starts from people's experiences but does not end there. This approach plays itself out on the world of objects through a process of broadening and socializing subjectivity. "The more people unveil this challenging reality which is to be the object of their transforming action," Freire argues, "the more critically they enter that reality" (1996: 35). In "entering that reality," which is the object of their activity, the subject ontologically becomes the social. Freire posits the struggle to change the objective in the following way:

> To present this radical demand for the objective transformation of reality, to combat the subjectivist immobility which would divert the recognition of oppression into patient waiting for oppression to disappear by itself, is not to dismiss the role of subjectivity in the struggle to change structures. On the contrary, one cannot conceive

of objectivity without subjectivity. Neither can exist without the other, nor can they be dichotomized. The separation of objectivity from subjectivity, the denial of the latter when analyzing reality or acting upon it, is objectivism. On the other hand, the denial of objectivity in analysis or action, resulting in a subjectivism which leads to solipsistic positions, denies action itself by denying objective reality. Neither objectivism nor subjectivism, nor yet psychologism is propounded here, but rather subjectivity and objectivity in constant dialectical relationship. (1996: 32)

Since I was beginning to suspect that direct action contained a strong revelatory impulse and the possibility of becoming a coherent research practice for the anti-globalization movement, I was frustrated that personal activist experiences were consistently recast in a narrative, story-telling frame. It seemed odd to me that direct action, which had been so pedagogically generative during the occupation at the University of Guelph, could be reduced in workshops to either testimonial utterances or lists of things to remember. Despite the potential of becoming an effective research practice; despite real similarities with Freire's pedagogy and Smith's activist ethnography, in the workshop setting, discussions about direct action erred toward banking and not problem-posing pedagogy, toward abstract and not reflexive-materialist understandings of the social. Why was this so?

Idealism and the Limits of Conceptual Action

Although direct action puts activists in a good position to adopt a problem-posing investigative approach that challenges limit situations, activists nevertheless demonstrate a continued reliance upon conceptual abstraction. This is especially true when activists try to explain what direct action is. So, while activists have managed to confront limit situations and break abstract and solipsistic "circles of certainty" (Freire 1996: 20) through direct action activities, we have not always broken with the idealistic thought structures of liberal philosophy, nor the social organization of facticity of ruling regimes. Rather than existing in dialectical interaction, practice is here ahead of theory. This disjuncture between reflection and action can be traced through the written accounts that activists have produced in the course of their activity.

The following passage, found in the pages of the *Anarcho-Syndicalist Review*, is an excellent case in point. Although as a piece of writing it is exceptionally bad, the frustration experienced in reading it cannot be the result of poor writing alone. Indeed, the solipsistic sentence structures appear to have less to do with literary deficiencies than with an abstract conceptual world spinning out of control. "From an anarchist perspective," Harald Bayer-Arnesan begins:

> Direct action is connected not only to solidarity, but also to what tends to be the precondition for solidarity and the underlying principle of the concept of direct democracy: non-hierarchical human communication. Such communication lies at the root of what direct action always is, individual and collective self-empowerment. As direct action contains its own end, within that self-defined end its meaning is also found. The more the ends are manifested in the means, the more it is direct action. (2000: 11)

Conceptually, this is quite elaborate and complicated. While it's true that not all movement accounts of direct action are this indecipherable, it is important to acknowledge that many activists have had difficulty providing a clear articulation of the term. This passage, then, can be read as a hyperbolic reflection of a more general problem. Given that Bayer-Arnesan's definition of direct action was published in a movement magazine's feature on the topic suggests that the frustration at pinning down a workable definition is not merely the matter of this one writer's anguish or incomprehensibility; not merely the result of lax editorial protocols.

What is at work in this passage? By situating his account within an anarchist perspective, the writer provides the interpretive procedure through which to read the rest of the account. Already, direct action becomes a knowledge-object, the attributes of which vary depending on the standpoint of the viewer. From here, Bayer-Arnesan enters the world of predetermined logical concepts, drawn out in an interlocking constellation of abstract relations. Direct action is connected to solidarity. Solidarity and direct democracy are connected to and have their precondition in non-hierarchical human communication. Non-hierarchical human communication is, in turn, the definition of what direct action always is (individual and collective self-empowerment, remember?). Snap! The circle of certainty closes.

Fortunately, not every attempt to define direct action comes to such unhappy ends. Nevertheless, as a procedural approach to making sense of the social relations in which we engage, many activists begin from the perspective of the concept (self-empowerment, direct democracy, non-hierarchical human communication) and never entirely work our way out. Materials produced by DC's Justice and Solidarity Collective to distribute during the People's Strike show strong signs of this conceptual imbrication. The collective, which functioned as a legal support team for activists during the protest, put together a leaflet instructing demonstrators on how to deal with the possibility of cops showing up at their doors, whether in the lead up to or during the action. Written in convenient point form, the leaflet provided the following instructions:

> Write down the names and badge numbers of all police officers
>
> Write down the names, job titles and departments of any fire mar-

shals, building inspectors, or other government officials that enter with the police or independently

Write down an inventory identifying everything being searched and/or confiscated, where in the center it comes from

The leaflet is standardized knowledge, a textual list of procedures that can be initiated by activists in multiple local settings throughout the action. In order to accomplish this effect, the leaflet follows the conventions of writing adopted by ruling institutions. The effect of this form of writing is to turn specific experiences of encounters with police into a series of universal knowledge claims that then come to organize the practices of activists when the police show up at their door. Dorothy Smith has described how this kind of writing is achieved by transposing the experiences that produce knowledge of an event into universal, "textual time."

In this transposition, the active processes that led to the production of the textual account are rendered invisible. However, while the leaflet by the Justice and Solidarity Collective presents itself in a way that obscures the concrete experiences underlying its knowledge claims, it is important to note how the Collective's attempt to enter activist knowledge into textual time does not entirely work. Indeed, even as they provide universal procedures for activists, the everyday world of experience makes a symptomatic appearance. The leaflet presents general guidelines for coming through police visits as unscathed as possible. The general guidelines are written in such a way as to be useful to activists in a variety of local circumstances. However, the suggestions, in what they anticipate as possible during a police visit, almost certainly emerge directly out of the experience of anti-globalization actions where police have raided convergence centres using the pretence of fire code violations.

In order to trace this process of translation from experiential to textual time and account for the resulting contradictions, it is useful to consider some of the events that surrounded the production of the leaflet. "Ruptures of consciousness," George Smith reminds us, "are located in the social relations that produce them" (1990: 632). Activists in DC, after all, were witness to the kind of raid on a convergence centre anticipated by the JSC leaflet during the A16 actions against the IMF and World Bank.

Although the Justice and Solidarity Collective leaflet begins by talking generally about the "police" coming to "your home or workplace" — a framing which aims to cast its relevance as broadly as possible — by the end, the text has become much more specific. With the introduction of particulars that are neither "police" nor "your home," but rather "fire marshals," and "where in the [convergence] center" confiscated materials came from, the leaflet makes a return to specificity that betrays its attempt to speak in universal textual time.

Evident in the text, then, is a conflict between what people have learned through experience and the social training that has instructed them to convey these experiences in particular ways. Since these sense-making procedures divorce people from their own experiences, this training serves only to blunt the research potential inherent in direct action. Perhaps the leaflet writers were unable to approximate the procedures through which experience enters textual time. Alternately, maybe activist experience itself, especially when it involves encounters with the state, does not easily lend itself to this kind of transposition. In either case, what remains is a trace of the events that were then worked up into abstract knowledge. The leaflet, then, can be read as a symptom of the split consciousness of anti-globalization activists caught between concrete knowledge and ideological thought.

For D. Smith, the bifurcation of consciousness that occurs as a result of the disjunction between everyday experience and abstract commonsense provides a point of entry into an understanding of the social. Especially for those who do not determine the content of ideological thought but must live within it, the inevitable rupture signals the starting point for research. For Freire, the situation is nearly identical. Describing the contradiction of "progressive" educators using inherited pedagogical practices, Freire recounts how the ensuing discord can sometimes provide the oppressed with an opportunity to engage with the world:

> Those who use the banking approach, knowingly or unknowingly (for there are innumerable well-intentioned bank-clerk teachers who do not realize that they are serving only to dehumanize), fail to perceive that the deposits themselves contain contradictions about reality. But, sooner or later, these contradictions may lead formerly passive students to turn against their domestication and the attempt to domesticate reality. They may discover through existential experience that their present way of life is irreconcilable with their vocation to become more fully human. They may perceive through their relationship with reality that reality is really a process, undergoing constant transformation. If men and women are searchers and their ontological vocation is humanization, sooner or later they may perceive the contradiction in which banking education seeks to maintain them, and then engage themselves in the struggle for their liberation. (1996: 56)

Although the contradiction between experience and deposited knowledge functions as a kind of engine that can impel people into action and encourage a more complete engagement with the social, this outcome is not guaranteed. For activists concerned with direct action, then, the task is twofold: begin developing a reliable knowledge of the social and find an effective means of communicating it that does not abide by the conventions of idealist thought.

People's Army an Oxymoron?

Has the anti-globalization movement's commitment to activity helped to develop a reliable and expanded conception of concrete social relations? Has it, further, allowed for this knowledge to be communicated in such a way as to challenge the constraints of abstract and idealist thought? The Black Bloc communiqué, penned by members of the Green Mountain Anarchist Collective (GMAC), helps us to answer these questions. Written in December of 2000, *A Communiqué on Tactics and Organization* reads like a position paper outlining ways in which the Black Bloc can be restructured in order to continue meeting demonstration objectives. "The following document is presented," GMAC begins, "with the intention of furthering the basic effectiveness of our movement, by advocating various tactical practices that we hope will be adopted by the Black Bloc as a whole" (2000: 1).

GMAC is very good at outlining how the concrete situation at demonstrations necessitates specific forms of organizing. They draw out, in considerable detail, how the Black Bloc can become more effective by developing a more formal and tactically reflexive command structure. In order to make these recommendations, they produce detailed accounts of police strategies deployed at actions since Seattle. Recognizing the importance of maintaining control of the streets when trying to disrupt business as usual, GMAC exhorts discipline and organization. "At the present time," they venture, "the mobilization of our forces is done in such a haphazard manner that our ability to combat well trained and disciplined State forces is limited" (2000: 7). In order to overcome organizational and tactical fragmentation, GMAC proposes various command structures and disciplinary techniques aimed at extending activist control over the streets.

In order to make sense of the considerable emphasis placed on control of the streets in this communiqué, it is useful to consider the amount of energy that police and other security forces have put into addressing this precise question. Anti-summit demonstrations since Seattle have taken on the characteristics of medieval sieges. Large perimeter walls were constructed in Windsor during demonstrations against the Organization of American States in June of 2000, in Québec City and in Genoa. During the 2002 meeting of the Summit of the Americas, delegates assembled in a remote mountain resort in Kananaskis, Alberta. In addition to recourse to geographic isolation and the erection of physical barriers, security agencies and private corporations have invested considerable time and money developing "less than lethal" technologies aimed at controlling crowds.

Faced with the challenge of organizing to effectively confront police on the streets, GMAC proposes several measures, including the formation of an elected tactical facilitation force; increased discipline and preparedness within individual affinity groups (including a division of labour between defensive and offensive forces, each outfitted with the appropriate equipment); extending reconnaissance and communications capacities;

implementing a system of reserve forces that can be mobilized at moment's notice; devising extra security precautions (including marking maps in code and using preplanned fluctuating radio frequencies for communication); circulating comprehensive communiqués after every action; engaging in physical fitness training between actions and taking pre-emptive measures to diminish state capacities.

On this last point, *A Communiqué on Tactics and Organization* makes a very deliberate connection between the concrete situation and the forms of activity appropriate to addressing it. Drawing on movement experiences, the Collective writes: "The forces of the State are known to take pre-emptive measures against demonstrators prior to their actions." Given the previously mentioned raids on convergence centres, this can hardly be disputed. Furthermore, says GMAC, the police "regularly infiltrate us and make arrests before any general demonstration or acts of civil disobedience begin." Finally, the police also "start their tactical mobilization long before the sun comes up prior to the demonstrations on any particular day."

> In order to neutralize this advantage, limited elements presently engaged in Black Bloc actions should independently take counter-measures. Here sabotage of police (and when necessary, National Guard) equipment is our best bet.... If one of the primary advantages of the State is their mechanized mobility, then we should strike out against these repressive tools by effective, clandestine means. (2000: 20)

One is struck by the undeniably militaristic inflection of these proposals. While it is unquestionable that — if the goal is to beat the cops on the streets through tactical usurpation — the practice of sabotage would undoubtedly put activists at a greater advantage, the communiqué's analysis of the concrete situation nevertheless misses an important point. Who are the people who will do this sabotage? Where will they come from? The document is somewhat vague: "Such activities should be voluntarily coordinated by separate affinity groups under their own direction" (2000: 20). Roughly translated, this means, "someone else should do it".

So while the document challenges its reader to confront the idealism that, for instance, would eschew a "militaristic tone" (2000: 1), it nevertheless engages in its own form of wishful thinking. Specifically, it anticipates the possibility of turning the Black Bloc into a large, disciplined force capable of engaging in highly specialized and illegal operations against ruling regimes without looking at the broader dynamics of movement building. These too are concrete social relations that must be explored and mapped. While GMAC correctly identifies many of the concrete measures that the state might take to make activists less effective (and does so in a way that obviously makes use of their own concrete experience), their analysis nevertheless casts people as mere numbers who can be slotted abstractly into an action plan. By what force will the masses turn up to the next action in balaclavas? Although GMAC pays meticulous attention to the minutiae of the social organization of their opponents, they are silent on the specific conditions of an equally important and contradictory social force: the people.

The purpose of advancing this critique is not to dismiss GMAC's contribution. However, because GMAC's analysis aims only in one direction, because it engages with questions of social organization without considering corresponding questions of pedagogy, it discloses troubling limitations. In order for direct action to become a research practice and pedagogy for the anti-globalization movement, we must aim in two directions at once.

Specifically, then, the task of direct action activists is to call into question not only the movement's continued reliance on forms of ideological thought but also the tendency to equate the specificities of ruling regimes with the terrain of struggle itself. As both Paulo Freire and George Smith make explicit, there is no doubt that these specificities are important. But social relations of struggle, the dynamics that lead people to mobilize in particular moments and along particular lines, cannot be reduced to a desire to simply negate an understood evil. The connection between knowledge of ruling relations and the forms of action appropriate to unsettling them cannot be taken for granted. It too must be mapped. Direct action, provided that it is focused on and helps to illuminate concrete details, can be one means by which this is done.

Critical Thinking and Discussion Questions:

1. Why have activists insisted upon a definition of direct action and why has that definition continued to elude them?

2. If confrontation is an important principle of activist pedagogy and research, what can we take it to include? What are some examples of "everyday" confrontations that could lead to reliable knowledge of social relations?

3. Why does an exclusive focus on the concrete specificities of ruling regimes make it difficult to envision the social relations of struggle?

Notes

1. I would like to acknowledge and thank several people for their assistance — both direct and indirect — in helping me to develop the ideas in this chapter. I would like to thank Donna Harrison for organizing a session on "emancipatory research methods" as a contribution to the Society for Socialist Studies gathering at Congress 2004. There, I was able to workshop an earlier version of what appears here. I would also like to thank the organizers of the CSA Speakers Series at the University of Guelph and, in particular, Andrew Langille, who furnished me with an opportunity to try these ideas out in front of a wider audience. A personal thank-you goes to my comrade Meredith Slopen, who put up with me and gave me a place to stay during the low moments of the fall of 2002. Meredith also introduced me to the dramatic reading room in the 42nd Street library in New

York. It was in that room that I was first able — thanks to a borrowed laptop — to write the notes that have since become "Direct Action, Pedagogy of the Oppressed."

2. While the People's Strike may have been the first convergence of anti-globaliza-tion and anti-war sensibilities, it was definitely not the last. As the bombs began falling on Iraq, marking George W. Bush's reprise of the Gulf War (this time in the name of anti-terrorism and, ironically, dispossessing Sadam Hussein of his fictive "weapons of mass destruction"), activists in San Francisco adopted anti-globalization strategies to disrupt "business as usual." Their campaign, which resulted in more than 2000 arrests, targeted major roads, bridges and army recruitment centres. Similarly, activists in Italy and elsewhere began a campaign of anti-war disruptions that targeted military freight shipments by blockading rail lines.

3. Idealist thought, brought to its most developed form with the emergence of liberal philosophy, places the human subject at the centre of the world. From here, the Cartesian claim that "I think therefore I am" produces the conditions whereby it is possible to argue that events are caused by ideas. In opposition to this way of thinking, Karl Marx advocated a materialist understanding of human history. Rather than argue that consciousness determined reality, Marx reversed the formulation and traced how material circumstances shaped consciousness. Writing against the dominant ideas of his time, Marx launched the following at-tack against the Young Hegelians in *The German Ideology*: "Since the Young Hegelians consider conceptions, thoughts, ideas, in fact all the products of con-sciousness, to which they attribute independent existence, as the real chains of men (just as the Old Hegelians declared them the true bonds of human society) it is evident that the Young Hegelians have to fight only against these illusions of consciousness. Since, according to their fantasy, the relationships of men, all their doings, their chains and their limitations are products of consciousness, the Young Hegelians logically put to men the moral postulate of exchanging their present consciousness for human, critical or egoistic consciousness, and thus of removing their limitations. This demand to change consciousness amounts to a demand to interpret reality in another way, i.e., to recognize it by means of another interpretation" (1970: 41). Both Paulo Freire and George Smith begin from a materialist conception of human history.

4. This list of things to remember would frequently be repeated in the lead up to any action where there was the possibility of confrontation with police. It was important not to wear contact lenses since chemical agents like tear gas or pep-per spray could become trapped between the lens and the eye, thus causing further damage. Since demonstrations were often chaotic affairs, people were reminded to go with a buddy who could keep track of them. Should they get arrested, people were reminded that, for their own safety and for the safety of others, all they were required to tell the police — should they decide to speak at all — was their name, address and telephone number. In order to remove pepper spray from a demonstrator's skin, activists were told to remember the MOFIBA protocol: mineral oil followed immediately by rubbing alcohol. Fortunately, this treatment also satisfied many activists' love of acronyms.

5. From my initial workshop notes:

    Section 1: What is Direct Action? (a straw poll to get people to self-identify in relation to direct action, to begin building a definition of what direct action is)

    • Who has been at a demonstration where they thought direct action was taking place?

- Who feels they have themselves been involved in direct action? (get people to provide examples)
- Who has been arrested because of these actions? (if there have been arrests, ask who has been convicted)
- Who was at (some event people were likely at not ordinarily understood as direct action but that fits the themes expressed so far, i.e., an effective picket line from a strike) (In this exercise, the number of hands usually decreases with each question until the end, when usually people realize they have more connection than they had previously thought. It is also useful to point out the low number of convictions emerging from direct action scenarios.)

RESEARCHING FOR RESISTANCE: OCAP, HOUSING STRUGGLES AND ACTIVIST RESEARCH

John Clarke

When I spoke at the Sociology for Changing the World Conference at Laurentian University in 2002, I advanced a notion of how research might serve the needs of a resistance that is based in poor communities. I did this from the perspective of someone directly involved in such a struggle. At that time, the Ontario Coalition Against Poverty (OCAP) was up to its neck in an ongoing occupation of an abandoned property in Toronto's West End that became known as the Pope Squat. I put forward some ideas around the kinds of academic study that might equip a movement that utilized the tactic of a housing takeover. It seemed at the time, and remains obvious to me, that the political act of taking vacant property could only be evaluated as a part of a battle against upscale urban redevelopment and the "social cleansing" of low income communities and homeless populations that flows from it. I would like to map out a little more fully and precisely the importance of housing takeovers as a method of resistance. What is said here about takeovers can also be applied, to a considerable degree, to other direct forms of action that might occur in an ongoing struggle to turn back the push to clear out poor communities.

There are at least three sides to the question of taking back vacant housing that speak to the balance of social forces. First of all and very simply, when people affected by homelessness secure and hold living space, they have moved from the realm of proposals and demands and have begun to carve out solutions. Moreover, if this form of social action takes place on a large enough scale, the possibility begins to emerge of some level of legislated concession in the form of recognized "squatters' rights." In Canada, squatting has not made any such breakthroughs but in many European jurisdictions, a partial acceptance of the taking of empty buildings has been attained. In conditions of large scale destitution, such a gain, which would enable significant numbers of people to survive by squatting vacant property, would be a highly favourable development. A housing takeover movement that had sufficient tenacity and that assumed a large enough scale might attain such a victory.

② A second reason to pursue housing takeovers lies in the degree of defiance that they embody. A central element of the neoliberal agenda is the systematic removal of social provision. As social housing is wiped out, tenants' protections obliterated and minimum-wage and social assistance levels pushed down, a resistance movement that includes the practice of taking back housing for those who are put onto the streets points us in a very healthy direction. Sooner or later, the destruction of the social safety net must provoke ubiquitous anger and mass movements of opposition. A readiness to defy property laws and place social rights ahead of them is a very hopeful sign that such resistance is neither impossible nor particularly distant.

③ Finally, the taking of housing is a form of direct action that stands in the very path of the processes of gentrification and the social cleansing of the poor. While present day governments have a general interest in gutting the social wage, including a vast reduction in spending on housing, this is not the primary reason why people are being made homeless and low income housing stock is being eradicated. Urban development is proceeding along lines whereby lavish and upscale commercial, recreational and residential development is supposed to dominate over large areas and, certainly, in the central sections of the cities. Homeless populations are unwelcome as an eyesore that discourages condo buyers and affluent tourists. Housed low income people and the communities they inhabit, often very long standing communities, similarly are at odds with the way in which urban space is to be utilized. Duplicitous nonsense about "mixed neighbourhoods" notwithstanding, an upwardly mobile business and professional population is now colonizing the urban areas that the poor were once allocated, and the "quality of life" expectations and property values of these "pioneers" can only fuel the process of social cleansing.

Housing takeovers, particularly if their scale can expand and they can be linked to other methods of resistance, actually serve to disrupt this whole process of redevelopment. The homeless and poor who resist in this fashion are no longer simply on the receiving end of the social cleansing agenda. They have stopped waiting for the eviction notice to be put on their doors or the cops to come into the park where they are sleeping to terrorize and disperse them. They have taken the path of an effective resistance as an organized entity.

Having set out some of the notions that underlie the housing takeover tactic and having established its importance as a resistance strategy, we approach the question of the research needs of a movement that utilizes this and similar methods. I would first like to mention, however, some issues posed by the present limitations of OCAP's housing actions in Toronto.

The Pope Squat of 2002 was taken during a papal visit to Toronto. A large empty property in the West End was taken with a support crowd of over a thousand people while the Pope addressed his followers at the nearby Canadian National Exhibition grounds. It became home to dozens of homeless people and a symbol of resistance to the housing crisis in Toronto and beyond. The obvious political protection provided by the Pope's visit, coupled with a murky ownership of the property, enabled us to hold the building for three and a half months. Since then, the takeovers we have carried out have not been held for any length of time. They have been important acts in terms of building momentum in the fight for housing, but the balance of forces has, in each case, enabled the police to act as they have seen fit. A takeover in 2004 was of a city owned, six-story property on Jarvis Street in the process of being sold to a condo developer. Yet, even with a mayor who is NDP affiliated and who cultivates an ill-deserved reputation as an ally of the poor, calling the shots, we could not create the conditions whereby the hands of the cops could be stayed. The property was cleared within an hour of a large, inspiring and highly public takeover that was still simply insufficient as an act of political challenge.

Clearly, the housing takeovers we undertake have to become links in a widely supported struggle to arrest the process of upscale urban redevelopment and the resulting social cleansing of the poor. Only when takeovers are carried out in the context of a political campaign for housing and in defence of poor communities can they be elevated from events the politicians leave to the cops and become something that forces political concessions from governments. Such a campaign requires a highly developed understanding of the processes of gentrification and redevelopment. We need to understand in detail the emerging patterns, as well as the corporate entities that drive the process. We have to fully appreciate the links between the developers and other business interests, and the City Hall regime that serves them. We must know in detail how they are removing low income populations and replacing them with affluent colonizers and, then, be able to draw vital general conclusions as to the nature of the process.

In this regard, there is an enormous role for research that is not just sympathetic to the resistance of poor communities but that actually forms a component of these struggles. Army officers and corporate ideologues alike are very fond of reading the ancient Chinese military strategist, Sun Zi. They especially love his comment in *The Art of War*, written in 2,500 BC, that, "If you know your enemy and know yourself, you need not fear the result of a hundred battles."

Keeping this advice in mind, OCAP has a very clear appreciation of the fact that billionaire property owners are driving out poor communities, with the help of an unholy alliance of politicians, bureaucrats, cops and yuppie homebuyers. We also know that this process is driven by the profit needs of capitalism. But Sun Zi would not have congratulated us on our knowledge

(margin handwriting) What is necessary for successfully carrying out a social movement of (tired) Resistance

of the enemy if all we could say was, "there are a lot of them and I think they want to hurt us." We need to deepen our understanding of the process of redevelopment in Toronto. Moreover, not to forget the other side of the ancient advice, we also need to know more about the history and composition of the communities under attack, which form our base, and evaluate clearly their capacity for resistance.

Let me elaborate on the ways in which the fight against the social cleansing of the poor in Toronto could draw strength from research that was motivated and shaped by the need to resist. As we see inner Toronto being gentrified before our eyes, it is easy to grasp the fact that the profit motive is at work. Rich tourists, a well-heeled party crowd and yuppies who like to savour their domestic affluence close to the office are all clear and obvious consumers in this process. However, the process is more complex. If an international trend has emerged to redevelop inner cities, it must be driven in this society by returns on investment. The urban yuppies' choices as consumers are not by any means irrelevant to the process of gentrification, just as the political clout they exercise are clear and important factors in the drive to remove low-income populations. Fundamentally, however, the developers, builders and financiers and their quest for profit are at the heart of the matter.

In *The New Urban Frontier: Gentrification and the Revanchist City*, Neil Smith (1996) outlines the emergence of a "rent gap" in inner cities over much of the globe. It required a lengthy process of capital being drawn away from the urban core and the lowering of property values in this area in order to set the stage for profitable upscale inner city redevelopment. In terms of a resistance movement to counter the assault on poor communities, this distinction is a vital one. As long as we see the upscale colonists and their evil little "residents associations" as the driving force in the process, we understand nothing fundamental about what is going on. If we think right-wing councillors who spew hateful rhetoric directed at the homeless are the main foe, we are sadly disorientated. If thuggish cops with their racist "war on drugs" and violence against the destitute are seen as being at the heart of the issue, we are fumbling. Big capital and its profit needs are driving urban redevelopment and those who serve it are merely its mouthpieces or attack dogs.

N. Smith's international overview is of great help in orientating us, but what we need on the ground in Toronto is an understanding of how that general process has emerged in the neighbourhoods in which the gentrification battle is being fought. It is important to have a clear understanding of the history that has led to the present stage in the war in areas like Cabbagetown, Kensington Market, Lakeshore, the Junction and Parkdale. Depreciation of property values over a long period, the loss of industrial employment that fuelled the exodus of better paid working-class residents and the beginnings of the process of gentrification should all be studied

[Margin notes:]
gentrification : a global trend
→ to deconstruct the cause, must first identify the fundamental actors

"THE RENT GAP"

identify beyond the frontal actors & speculative language

KNOW HISTORY

KNOW YOUR TERRAIN

and understood. If we do not know the terrain on which we have to fight, we are at a severe disadvantage.

The profit needs of capital are always pursued by its flesh-and-blood representatives, who organized into tangible economic, political and bureaucratic entities. We need to have a detailed understanding of these players and the battle plans they are putting into effect. Who precisely are the corporate beneficiaries of gentrification? Who are the developers, the financiers and the builders who profit from upscale redevelopment? What role do the "hospitality" and tourism sectors play in developing the vision and securing these corporate urban goals? What are the links in terms of investment and family connections that hold together the corporate compacts active in this assault?

[handwritten margin note: Questions to ask the fundamental actors? Facts.]

Once we come down from the corporate heights, we start to run into (and need to identify and study) a whole procession of those who grease the wheels of the process of redevelopment — the politicians being among the greasiest. Municipal government is the level that most directly services the needs of profit generated through the property industry. Toronto City Council has its showy battles between right and left, but, at root, both sides serve the same god. A right-wing councillor who denounces the homeless as an ugly blight on the city is debated by more compassionate servants of the developers with NDP cards in their pockets, but not one of them seriously fights for (or even discusses) defending the poor from social cleansing. In the summer of 2004, OCAP took a stand against the removal of street vendors from the streets of Chinatown by city officials. The attempt to drive them out was, in fact, prevented because of the determined resistance of the mainly elderly street sellers themselves. Local "left" city politician Olivia Chow met with a delegation of the vendors and brought to the meeting a veritable "who's who" of the local business interests. While she played the role of wise and caring "neutral party" during the meeting, she was entirely clear in her subsequent public statements that she fully supported the driving out of poor vendors because business and the developers wanted it so.

The fundamental loyalties of those who sit on City Council are easy to establish once you get beyond their political flavours. We need, however, to know more about how they are actually incorporated into the redevelopment process. Some interesting informant has been sending us e-mails outlining the dinner companions from the development industry of one progressive light on Council. While we can't stop social cleansing with tidbits like this, the career, social and family connections that bond the corporate and political players will bring us closer to an understanding of how these people operate and what they have in mind.

Nor should we fail to see and study the massive role of the municipal bureaucracy in all this. At its senior levels, it organizes the work of shaping and regulating Toronto according to the needs of property. It drafts the bylaws and policies that encourage some uses of Toronto's land base while

precluding others. It ensures that office blocks and "multi faceted recreational complexes" can be built while rooming houses and other forms of
low-income housing stock are wiped from the face of the earth. It sends out
the "bylaw officers," who drive homeless people from parks, from empty
buildings and from under bridges, and arms these officials with the legal
pretexts for this social cleansing. Who are these people and how are they
linked to the property owners? This is a group of people we need to put
under a very powerful microscope and who need to be understood in serious
detail.

Then there are the ultimate "servers and protectors" of profit-making,
the police. They are the muscle that carries out the ugliest aspects of social
cleansing. In the late 1990s, OCAP was involved in a successful fight to prevent
the closing of a homeless shelter in the downtown. Part of our campaign
involved picketing businesses that had pressured the city into closing the
shelter. Police were often in attendance at these events and, on one occasion,
a staff sergeant with the 52 Division told me that the "removal of vagrants
from the downtown" was his most important duty. He was most clear that
this was necessary to meet the needs of business investment. David Boothby,
a former Toronto Police Chief who was a liberal reformer compared to Julian
Fantino, also considered crackdowns on panhandlers a major priority for
his force and pointed to the concerns of major downtown merchants as the
reason for this.

The working links between the police and key corporate interests need
to be explored and the cops' role as the shock troops of gentrification fully
examined. Police officers attend meetings of yuppie residents' associations
in the central part of the city on an ongoing basis and have detailed discussions with these people over campaigns of action when it comes to harassing
the poor and homeless. It is not enough to know the cops defend capitalism
and attack workers and poor people. The actual history and workings of the
process have to be studied and understood.

The redevelopment of Toronto and the driving out of established poor
communities is unfolding on a scale that precludes it being an entirely
improvised process. Uncovering the plans that shape this and subjecting
those plans to serious analysis is a vital task. We see corporate and city
plans floated in the media all the time. For a period it was the "revitaliza-
tion of Yonge Street" in the very heart of the city that was the issue. Now
the "rejuvenation of the waterfront" is a veritable obsession that we are all
supposed to care about. Only detailed research and analysis can strip away
the duplicitous covering that cloaks the reality of this agenda. We need to
precisely translate their talk of balanced, healthy and thriving communities
and lay bare their plans to transform poor areas of the city in ways that serve
only the interests of profit-making.

Just as much study must go into analyzing the sweeping out of the poor
so as to replace them with higher income functionaries, consumers and

residents. We know low-income housing stock is being depleted through a combination of social cutbacks and zoning restrictions. We know that one of the largest social housing complexes in the country, Regent Park, is about to be obliterated and transformed into a "healthy mix" of market-value and rent-geared-to-income (RGI) units. Somehow, the RGI component seems to be slipping away as the day for the bulldozers to show up gets closer. Low income housing stock is not being removed and prevented merely because it is not something governments want to spend money on. It is also the case that a lot of very big moneyed interests have other ideas about how the land base that might be used to house the poor should be utilized. In every area of this city where the process of income based population transfer is taking place, there is more at work than greedy yuppies and mean spirited cops. The work of upscale colonization is being planned, implemented and monitored with the blessing and active assistance of municipal planners. We have had the need and opportunity to see enough City Hall documents to know that the patterns that underlie this process could be discerned and interpreted if they were skilfully and thoroughly scrutinized.

The coordination of operations to clear out the homeless and destitute are even more stark and worthy of study. The plans of action are based on clear tactical appraisals made in official quarters, where there is a theory that the homeless come to inner Toronto because some level of provision exists for them. The network of shelters, drop-ins, street patrol services and health and welfare agencies that exist are allegedly a magnet that draws in those who might otherwise head off in other directions. Some even characterize this position with the slogan "Don't feed the animals!" This scorched earth approach to "solving" the homeless crisis is largely wrong headed, even from the standpoint of its own hateful frame of reference. The truth is that destitute people gather in the inner core of cities because distances that have to be covered on foot are minimized and because the concentration of population in those areas makes the acts of survival they must engage in somewhat more viable. Moreover, Toronto is climatically a better option than all other major Canadian cities with the exception of Vancouver. Closing down the services in Toronto will not, in and of itself, convince the homeless to pack up their misery and leave.

If the assumptions that underlie the removal of services to the homeless are shaky, they are nonetheless implemented with dreadful and often life-threatening effect. Through its powers to fund social agencies, the City of Toronto is now working to hamper the ability of the street patrol services to provide hot soup and blankets to people on the streets through a bylaw that limits the allocation of homeless shelters on a ward by ward basis. Drop-in facilities are being squeezed both because the city wants to remove the homeless from the core over time and because, in the meantime, a strategy is being pursued of minimizing their visibility. Drop-ins, or day shelters, as they are sometimes called, are not in favour with the social engineers in

City Hall because they encourage some mobility during the day among the homeless population. Round-the-clock shelters are more favoured by city officials.

I am writing these lines when the issue of removing the homeless from sight (if they can't actually be removed from the city) has emerged as a hot issue. Rather like the spectacle of homeless people sleeping outside the White House has enraged the reactionaries of America, the presence of homeless "rough sleepers" in Toronto City Hall's Nathan Phillips Square has inflamed the passions of our local social reactionaries. Overt right-wingers and a shamefaced and dubious left-wing on Council this week worked together to put forward a bylaw that would ban the homeless from sleeping in the Square. The ongoing presence of the homeless at City Hall has been identified by the politicians, very rightly, as a livid monument to their neglect of and culpability in the crisis of homelessness. Since they have no intention of confessing their guilt or atoning for their sins, they have handed the homeless over to the cops and will leave the messy details to them.

The attempts by the authorities to clear Nathan Phillips Square (that OCAP and others will fight tooth and nail) has serious symbolic significance in another sense as well. (The clearing of the square has been maintained and the homeless encampment has not been able to re-form there.) It is a green light to every cop, bylaw officer, vigilante merchant and residents' association in Toronto to target the homeless they wish to remove from their sight. If the local government leads the assault, who will feel any need for restraint in such matters? For a long time, the city's own enforcers have moved to clear homeless people from anywhere they will be an "eyesore." Municipal "park ambassadors" ensure that precious green space is not taken over by the homeless while the dogs of yuppies defecate in the parks with impunity. Homeless youth who hate and fear the crowded, unhealthy and sometimes violent shelter system have bandied together to minimize their suffering and danger by forming "families" and building encampments under bridges. They are swept away under city bylaws and out of concern for their "safety and well being." ← Ref: Discursive justifications

From the Mayor and his closest advisors to the paid thugs who roll up their sleeves and provide the service of physical intimidation, they are all working according to a detailed plan to drive out the homeless. It is a battle plan, in fact, that has been developed and that is being put into effect with some care and precision. It is another aspect of urban redevelopment that needs to be assessed and compared to operations of its kind in other times and places. It needs to be understood from the standpoint of developing methods to challenge and defeat it.

If we are talking about the role of serious analysis in comprehending and resisting urban redevelopment, let's not forget the question of how class politics on this front intersects with the broader neoliberal agenda of capital. The destruction of the social wage has massively curtailed income maintenance protections. Social housing provision is a shadow of its former self. The general removal of barriers to profit-making has meant that the upwardly mobile stake their claim to space presently occupied by the poor under circumstances where both the scale and depth of poverty continues to increase. The poor are being driven out at a time when their alternatives following such removals are substantially reduced. The political creation of destitution occurs and expands just as the developers decide the homeless must be swept under the rug. Ramifications and connections in this situation have to be made much clearer in setting our goals and framing our demands.

We live in a time when the virulence of the neoliberal onslaught has created a veritable crisis of opposition in the very organizations that workers and poor people looked to as representing their interests. Trade unions, under their existing leaderships, have not been able to organize consistent or effective resistance to the weakening of workers' rights and the gutting of the social wage. Social democratic parties and their parliamentary representatives have gone from the notion of reforming capitalism to a "third way," which imposes the neoliberal project on populations with a touch more tact and more incrementally than the overt conservatives. The role of this misleadership is also of great importance in exploring the redevelopment equation in Toronto. The last mayor, Mel Lastman, became too crude and obvious to be a suitable front man for the developers, but his NDP successor, David Miller, is doing a much better job for them. The patterns of accommodation that come to the surface around the mayor's office are worthy of the most serious study and consideration.

The passage of the bylaw that bans the homeless from Nathan Phillips Square was an object lesson in this role of the social democratic parliamentarians in implementing the public policies that make possible the process of social cleansing. As is the norm in municipal politics, the measure was taken to a standing committee of the Council to be put forward as a recommendation. The mayor took the chair and his NDP allies on Council vied with each other to parade their support for the crackdown on the destitute people sleeping in the Square. Deliberations at the committee stage require the tedious ordeal of public deputations, and it might have been expected that the line up of liberal academic and social agency speakers would have created some unease in the ranks of the NDP. After all, this is the very social layer that constitutes their electoral and campaign support base. It was not, however, the overt right-wingers on Council who led the way in defending the crackdown. It was the "left-wing" of the Council that championed the driving out of the homeless.

This factor of the "soft" left sitting in the political driver's seat is one of some importance. It should be stressed that, while the NDP-led mayor's office provides the main impetus in all this, many key figures who have long been held up as progressive voices on Council work within their own wards and areas of responsibility to make their contributions to redevelopment. I have already mentioned Olivia Chow's total support for an ugly war on poor, mainly elderly street vendors. All across the city, the mayor's political allies are working with yuppie resident and business associations to find "solutions" to the presence of homeless people that are to the liking of the upwardly mobile and that serve the corporate interests that frame their expectations.

FACADES OF NEUT- RALITY

The great value of entrusting fake reformers with the implementation of social regression is that they are better able to neutralize potential opposition. Last summer, during OCAP's above-mentioned challenge to the removal of homeless people from their encampments under two city bridges, we held a picket at a luxurious home in the ultra wealthy Rosedale neighbourhood. This was the venue for a decadent giving of thanks to those who had worked to put David Miller in the mayor's office. A veritable who's who of the labour movement and a corresponding selection of the movers and shakers in the left agency world made their way through our picket line. None of these people had any concern that homeless people were being attacked in this fashion. Miller was simply a better electoral choice that his predecessor, and any attempt to embarrass or publicly pressure him was an act of gross political irresponsibility. The unspoken implication of their position was that if Miller had to send in a legalized goon squad to drive out some homeless youth, this was a price worth paying in order to preserve their political alliance with him. Of course, the labour leadership hardly set the city alight with militant resistance during the life of the previous mayoral regime. Now, however, a degeneration into the realm of overt collaboration means that those driving the agenda of redevelopment have little to worry about. For the present, even the theoretical possibility of resistance to their plans coming from the labour movement has been removed.

o shift in social agency to sellout to corporate allegiance

Upscale redevelopment is unfolding as those who are placed to initiate and lead movements of resistance are playing the role of blocking such oppositional directions. The union leaders keep a lid on their members and stifle broader community upsurge. The bureaucracies of the social agency world accept the reshaping of their operations so as to remove and redirect services that might provide the poor and homeless with any cohesion and capacity to resist. The gatekeepers of official multiculturalism, funded by governments to contain indignation in "their" immigrant communities, ensure that those they are appointed to speak for remain atomized and ineffective. This increased role of those in positions of leadership and influence over communities under attack is a very important element of the present situation. The overcoming of this massive impediment will require not just an oppositional practice but a detailed analysis that includes a study of the particular situation as well as of historic and contemporary comparisons.

In light of the kind of politically motivated and partisan research that I am advocating, I want at this point to deal with a potential misinterpreta-

no kidding

tion of my argument. I am not at all trying to create the impression that we are somehow trying to study and arrive at an understanding of a process of redevelopment that should be regarded as all powerful and unstoppable. On the contrary, we work for an understanding of the attack and its architects in order to hunt out weaknesses and to find the openings that will point us towards winning strategies and methods. However, our grasp of the situation can never be complete as long as we merely focus on our enemies, their plans, alignments and methods of operation. We also must fully evaluate our own capacity for resistance, including and especially, by finding such resources within the communities under attack.

(ex. summary)

RACISM

In Toronto, poor communities are being pounded by a removal of social provision and the upscale colonization process. However, these areas of the city have a long-standing history of opposition to such forces. In highly multicultural Toronto, moreover, there is a diversity to such opposition potential that needs to be examined very seriously. OCAP has done a very significant amount of organizing, for example, in the Dixon and Kipling area in the north-western part of the city, a part of town containing a large Somali community. These people have fled the most dreadful conditions of oppression and dislocation in their own country only to encounter exclusion and racism here. Well over 90 percent of Toronto's Somali community lives in poverty. Those who bring to Canada professional qualifications find that these are discounted, and they are forced to accept employment of the lowest paying and most exploitative kind.

Discussing

Thrown into this situation of needless poverty, the community has been overtly targeted on a racist basis by the security staff of property management companies in the buildings where they raise their families. Their children are subjected to gross intimidation and harassment by the police. This reaches the point where young Somalis are unable to enjoy the basic freedom of movement and peace of mind that would be considered normal within a community not so singled out and abused. They become targets as soon as they step outside their front doors; indeed, it is not always necessary for them to leave their homes in order to face such intrusion.

Several years ago, OCAP was approached by people at Dixon and Kipling with allegations that police officers were going into homes and Somali-owned restaurants in order to bully people. In some cases, it was alleged, cops were actually stealing the belongings of local Somalis in the process. Four OCAP members attended a community meeting that had been organized to deal with this issue. During the course of it, a couple of young Somali men burst into the room and breathlessly explained that such an incident was underway right at that moment. The meeting hastily adjourned, and its participants moved to the front of a nearby apartment complex where two cops were being confronted by an angry crowd of Somalis. Taxi drivers from the community were ferrying in more and more people to bolster this spontaneous mobilization, and the crowd size was growing rapidly. Angry accusations of racism and theft from the community were being thrown at the cops. Only a panic-stricken operation to send in reinforcements enabled the two officers to make their getaway from the scene, and even then, pepper spray had to be used.

This incident did not solve the problems in the area of police brutality and harassment by any means. However, by all accounts, it had a positive effect for some time in terms of promoting caution on the part of the police when they dealt with the local community. It was not an event that was directly connected to urban redevelopment, but it did give a glimpse of a very powerful and concrete means by which an impoverished and targeted community can resist. It was a telling and sadly fleeting example of how people can break through the sense of atomization that renders them powerless in the face of attack and take action in their own defence.

Of course, the follow up to such an incident would be hasty meetings between the police and some government-funded agency that purports to speak for the community that would produce the modicum of empty gestures necessary to defuse the potential for struggle that had shown itself. This is all the more reason why such examples of real community action must be evaluated and understood so as to find within them the means to create a more generalized and widespread mood of resistance that can't be contained or neutralized.

OCAP's work with street vendors in the Chinatown area at Dundas and Spadina relates more directly to the issue of urban redevelopment and holds a wealth of lessons for those who might be ready to study its ramifications. As we found ourselves trying to mobilize legal support and street actions to defend the vendors, we soon began to understand that something larger and more fundamental to the life of the Chinese community in the area was underway. This was not the first time that Chinatown had faced serious attack from the forces of urban development. In the post-war years, shortly after the repeal of the *Chinese Exclusion Act*, a major drive was initiated in several Canadian cities to remove their Chinatowns. The areas close to downtown Toronto occupied by Chinese homes and businesses where slated for "improvement." The newspapers of the day were full of racist diatribes against the alleged dirt, disease and immorality of the Chinese area. Toronto's present City Hall actually stands on a part of Chinatown that did, in fact, succumb to this attack. The intended total sweep of the area, however, was turned back by the resistance of the community.

Today, the same allegations of unsanitary and unsightly conditions are being hurled at a few dozen elderly street vendors who bother no one as they eke out an existence. It is clear, however, that the vendors are only the first point of contact for the developers' attack. Small storeowners are also being targeted for harassment by city bylaw officials. The Chinese-language media is taking up story after story about making Chinatown more attractive to tourists and new residents or businesses. The present thriving street market that caters to local people in the area is simply "outdated" in the estimation of the corporate boosters. A focus on condos, trendy boutiques and high-class restaurants is emerging. In the words of one local resident who spoke to us, "they are turning this place into a Chinese Yorkville."

I hope that the example of the attack on Chinatown shows the need for research that can, in much more detail than OCAP has been able to do, explore the nature of the present redevelopment drive. Such research would examine historical settings, evaluate the nature of the community under attack and, thereby, assist a movement of resistance to develop the strategies needed to fight back successfully. Chinatown's struggle is, of course, only one illustration. We need to shed light on the capacities for resistance that exist in all communities under attack by the agenda of redevelopment.

Finally, supportive research must explore points of comparison that exist as lessons of the past or as present-day examples. The 1930s were a period of mass, militant opposition to social abandonment. Direct action methods were adopted on a massive scale to win relief for hungry families, to block evictions and to oppose coercive slave-labour schemes for the jobless. The history and methods of this movement still have enormous relevance today. We should also pay considerable attention to present-day struggles, particularly those raging in the oppressed countries of the globe. The road blockades conducted by the unemployed in Argentina and the mass land takeovers by the Landless Peasant Movement (MST) in Brazil are but two examples from which those of us challenging social cleansing here in Toronto could learn a vast amount. However, it's not enough just to read the inspiring, agitational accounts of these bold actions. We need a detailed understanding of how these powerful movements took shape and how they function if we are to consider properly how some elements of their approaches can be incorporated into our work.

In what I have written above, I have moved beyond the immediate question of the housing takeovers that first got me involved in the project that has culminated in this book. I have tried to show how such direct methods of resistance to redevelopment are factors in a class-based social conflict fought out over the utilization of urban land space. I have pointed to some ways in which academic research could arm social movements with knowledge and perspectives that would enormously enhance the capacity to resist effectively.

Capital's agenda for the inner city is a brutal and inhuman one wherein a thin layer of the highly privileged are to enjoy their "quality of life" at the expense of many others. Homeless people will be banished to human warehouses at the periphery and long standing poor communities will be broken and dispersed to make way for those with the money to buy into a very restricted paradise on earth. From within the communities under attack, resistance has already emerged. Those fighting back do not have the high connections and the legions of researchers that those leading the attack have at their disposal. They do, however, need a generalized understanding and detailed knowledge of what they are up against. A form of research that is based on open support for communities that refuse to be socially cleansed has an important role to play, and its emergence as a clearly defined trend is long overdue.

Critical Thinking and Discussion Questions

1. What elements of social control exist in the academic world and how might research that is pursued in the service of struggle be conducted in light of constraints entailed by these elements?

2. What barriers and tensions might academic researchers and social movement activists encounter when attempting to build working relationships?

3. What issues might arise with regard to standards, legitimacy and the academic value of research if academic research takes sides and actively assists poor communities?

MAPPING SOCIAL RELATIONS OF STRUGGLE: ACTIVISM, ETHNOGRAPHY, SOCIAL ORGANIZATION[1]

Gary Kinsman

I dedicate this chapter to Dr. Jennifer Keck, 1954–2002, a friend, colleague and social justice activist who taught in the Social Work Department at Laurentian University, and my dear friend left gay liberation activist Greg Pavelich, 1951–2003.

I think of investigating a politico-administrative regime as an ordinary part of the day-to-day work of challenging and transforming a ruling apparatus. (G. Smith 1990: 646)

Political Activism and Institutional Ethnography

Institutional ethnography and political activist ethnography have been vital to me in my sociological work on struggles against oppressive sexual and gender regulation, national security and ruling relations (Kinsman 1995, 1996, 1997, 2000, 2003a, 2003b, 2004). Central to this work is developing an analysis that helps to produce the conditions for more effective activism for changing the world. Making visible and critically analyzing social organization is crucial to this project.

A political commitment to taking up the side of the oppressed and exploited is key to institutional ethnography and political activist ethnography. The world is investigated to disclose its social organization so that it can be transformed from these standpoints. This connection between investigating social organization, activism and social transformation is what attracted me to institutional ethnography as a left queer activist and graduate student involved in resistance to the bath raids in the early 1980s. This is also where I came to work with and to learn from George Smith.

George Smith's work generally (G. Smith 1988b, 1998), and especially "Political Activist as Ethnographer" (G. Smith 1990 and this volume),

Police confront global justice protestors at the Organization of American States meeting in Windsor, June 2000. Photo by Casey Desilets

extended institutional ethnography systematically to developing sociology *for* social movements and *for* activists. He builds on the insider's knowledge of social movement activists and uses political organizing and confrontation with ruling regimes as valuable resources in developing sociology. Political activist ethnography draws upon the research and theorizing about the social world and how it is organized that is already "going on" in social movements (see Clarke and Thompson this volume). While there are often limitations to this research, it is an everyday/everynight part of the life of social movements whether explicitly recognized or not. Activists are thinking, talking about, researching and theorizing about what is going on, what they are going to do next and how to analyze the situations they face, whether in relation to attending a demonstration, a meeting, a confrontation with institutional forces or planning the next action or campaign.

Social movement life is not separate from research, although this is often the way it is posed in academic circles and mirrored in movement circles. This position replicates theory/research, theory/practice and research/activism divides without acknowledging that there is already grassroots research taking place. Political activist ethnography requires working against the standard binary oppositions of theory versus practice and researcher versus activist constructed through academic disciplines, professionalization and institutionalization (D. Smith 1987, 1999). In a Gramscian democratic sense (Gramsci 1971), movement activists are also intellectuals (with an organic relation to social movements and struggles), researchers and theorists. There is much to be learned from movement organizers and activists and from their confrontations with ruling regimes. Political activist ethnography makes these practices more explicit, critical and focused on social organization and its transformation. This extends the capacities of movement activists to do more effective forms of research — which are at the very same time more effective forms of activism.

Political activist ethnography also requires challenging the "common-sense" theorizing that can often be ideological in character — uprooted from actual social practices and organization[2] — put forward in movement circles, as George Smith points out in "Political Activist as Ethnographer." For instance, we need to challenge approaches that lead us away from addressing the forms of ruling social organization we are struggling against, such as the disappearance of class relations from mainstream gay movement analysis or the obscuring of gender or race relations in union and other movements.

In some movement theories, as addressed by George Smith, concepts such as "homophobia," "AIDSphobia" or "red-tape" are given agency as the social world is reified and fetishized (Lukács 1968; D. Smith 1999: 45–69; Holloway 2002), and social relations between people are transformed into relations between thing-like concepts or categories that seemingly act independently in the world. Reification and fetishization are major problems in ruling discourse, and they can also limit and contain the theory and practice of social movements. George Smith was profoundly committed to an anti-reification approach that made visible social organization and how people can resist and transform social relations. We have to constantly resist in our research and activism giving agency and power to things.

In this chapter I apply the insights of "Political Activist as Ethnographer" in developing one way of elaborating this work through mapping the social relations of struggle in which movements are involved. Following a sketch of aspects of political activist ethnography, I outline what mapping the social relations of struggle entails. I point out how insights drawn from autonomist Marxism can aid in explicating the social capacities of struggle, and I use the resistance to the bath raids and the global justice movement as examples of how this can be done. As an integral part of this, I point to connections between social movement activism and the ethnomethodological practice of breaching experiments in the production of knowledge; also, I point to activist language in relation to the effectiveness of activism. Finally, I raise questions and draw conclusions regarding overcoming binary oppositions between research and activism and the need to develop an activist pedagogy for social transformation. This is intended as a beginning point for dialogue and not the final word.

"Political Activist as Ethnographer," despite its many insights, marks only a beginning point for developing political activist ethnography. Many questions remain: how to build this type of research into the everyday organizing of social movements; how to make doing this research more participatory; and how to build dialogical,[3] multi-voiced and non-monological discussions into movements that can link diverse research, analysis and discussions. There are also major questions about acquiring funding for political activist ethnography research, since it develops knowledge for movements and for activism, which many official bodies will not be interested in funding. I return to some of these questions in the conclusion.

Mapping Social Relations of Struggle

Mapping out the social relations of struggle in which a movement situates itself is crucial to developing knowledge *for* social movements. I take "mapping out" from Dorothy Smith's use of "mapping" and Marie Campbell and Fran Gregor's use of "mapping out" in their primer on institutional ethnography (D. Smith 1987, 1999, 2005; Campbell and Gregor 2002). From the standpoints of oppressed groups or social movements we map out the social relations that participate in the oppression or marginalization of the oppressed group or movement. This is a crucial aspect of the method of doing an institutional ethnography.

It is a mistake, however, to see this mapping out of social relations as simply a technical matter, since it is also very much a political and social undertaking. As Roxana Ng has suggested there are also dangers with the possible colonialist, imperialist or orientalist (see E. Said 1979; S. Amin 1988) connotations of "mapping" as developed by the white European-derived powers, who mapped the world from their standpoints. The mapping I am arguing for is not a "neutral" or disinterested mapping. It is instead an engaged and reflexive (mutually determined) mapping from the standpoints of the oppressed and social movements. This mapping out maintains an indexical (context-dependent) and reflexive relation to social movement organizing and confrontations with ruling regimes. Activists must be able to locate themselves within these mappings of social relations of struggle; these maps are used to further their analysis of the situations they face as they chart paths and move forward in their/our struggles. Later on in this chapter, I provide ideas for doing this mapping in diagrams of the social relations of struggle that are involved in the resistance to the bath raids and the global justice movement in its confrontations with capitalist globalization (Figures 1 and 2). You may wish to briefly explore them now and come back to them in more detail later.

Mapping out the relations of struggle is crucially about mapping out the ruling relations that oppressed people and movements confront. But it is not only an analysis of ruling relations. Fixating on the operation of ruling relations, or official discourse (Foucault 1979), as in much Foucauldian oriented work, can obscure possibilities for resistance and transformation. As Clarke suggests in this volume, we also need to examine our own capacities and resources. Central to the mapping out of the relations of struggle there also needs to be an analysis of the social organization of opposition, resistance and transformation — of the sources of agency that can bring about social transformation. This aspect of political activist ethnography, however, remains underdeveloped.

The Social Organization of Struggle:
Composition, Cycle and Circulation

In elaborating on the area of resistance and transformative agency in political activist ethnography, insights from autonomist Marxism can be very useful. Autonomist Marxism is a current within Marxism that learns from workers' struggles and focuses on developing working-class (in a broad sense, including the work of domestic, reproductive and student labour) autonomy and power in a capitalist society (Cleaver 2000; Dyer-Witheford 1999: 62–90; G. Kinsman 2005a). Autonomy is seen as autonomy from capital, autonomy from the official leadership of the trade unions and political parties, and the capacity and necessity of groups of workers who experience different oppressions acting autonomously from others (Blacks from whites, women from men and queers from straights). → diff definition

Autonomist Marxism shares with institutional and political activist ethnography a deeply rooted revolt against political-economy readings of Marxism (D. Smith 1999: 29–44; Cleaver 2000), which reify the social world, give all power to capital and ruling relations, and reproduce in our analysis the focus of capitalism on the "main business" of making profit. They do not make visible the agency of workers and the oppressed. Autonomist Marxists share with institutional and political activist ethnographers a wider notion of "work," one not reducible to labour power as a commodity in a capitalist society. For both approaches this is influenced by the theoretical discoveries leading up to the wages for/against housework struggle. The analytical basis for this approach was created through the work of autonomist Marxist feminists like Mariarosa Dalla Costa and Selma James (1972) and Silvia Federici (1975), who make visible the significance of the work of housewives in reproducing the commodity labour power for capital (also see D. Smith 1987: 165–66; Lilley and Shantz 2004). There is also ontological compatibility between autonomist Marxism and institutional and political activist ethnography approaches since both view the social world as being produced through the social practices of people. These areas of overlap and similarity, despite tensions, make autonomist Marxism a productive approach from which to learn in extending how political activist research can map out the social relations of struggle relating to the agency, capacities and power of the oppressed. *[margin note: ontological similarity of social construction]*

Autonomist Marxism develops a number of useful tools for thinking through class and social struggles. As long as these terms are not understood as monolithic in character and are used in the concrete social and historical sense of pointing to social relations that need to be investigated, they can be very helpful in our struggles and theorizing. These terms also need to be extended and complicated to deal more fully with race, gender, sexuality, ability and other lines of oppression.

Autonomist Marxist theorists and activists use the expression "working-class composition" (Cleaver 2000; Dyer-Witheford 1999: 62–90; G. Kinsman

[margin: following constructionist scholarship]

[margin: marxist questions]

2005a), which we can extend to social struggle or movement composition, to highlight the specific forms of social organization of the working class in relation to capital and ruling relations in specific social and historical periods. For instance, autonomist Marxists ask: how integrated is the working class into capitalist relations; how internally divided is the working class; how autonomous is working-class activity from capital; and to what extent does working-class struggle subvert social relations in particular contexts. Unlike in many Marxist applications, the "working class" is not a thing, an object or classification; it is always in process and exists in struggle (Cleaver 2000; Dyer-Witheford 1999; D. Smith 1987, 1999). It is continually chang-

[margin: this is following]

ing, is in the process of remaking itself and is being remade. History and shifting forms of social organization therefore become crucial to grasping working-class and social struggles.

For example, capitalists actively struggle to decompose the capacities of working-class composition through exacerbating and re-organizing internal divisions in the working class, including along lines of race, gender, sexual-

[margin: ignoring working class struggles through focus on intersectionality]

ity, nation and language; through ripping apart sources of working-class and oppressed people's power; through fragmenting groups and struggles; through extending social surveillance; and through the transformation of "training" and "skills" (D. Smith and G. Smith 1990). These attempts to decompose working-class struggles produce new conditions for the possible re-composition of working-class struggle and power. The process of class composition, decomposition and re-composition constitutes a cycle of struggle within autonomist Marxism (Cleaver 2000; Dyer-Witheford 1999: 62–90; G. Kinsman 2005a). It is crucial to grasp where we are situated in these cycles of struggle in order to evaluate our own sources of power and weakness and identify how to move forward. If we are in a period of a downturn in the composition of working-class struggle it may be more difficult for us to wage the struggles that are needed to meet people's needs.

[margin: cycles of struggle demonstrate how to make across boundaries]

For autonomist Marxists, circulations of struggles illuminate the ways through which different struggles have an impact on each other, sometimes circulating the most "advanced" forms of struggle. For instance, we can look at how early radical and socialist feminist struggles had impacts in multiple movements and settings, including within union movements, leading to the formation of women's caucuses and women's autonomous organizing within the unions. We can also see this in terms of how certain tactics of direct action and forms of organizing, including affinity groups (small groups that are

[margin: ex: Seattle WTO protest]

organized along a basis of affinity through which people participate in direct actions) and spokescouncils (where representative of affinity groups come together to make decisions), were spread and mobilized around the globe in the years following the Seattle protests against the WTO in 1999 (Notes from Nowhere 2003; Yuen, Katsiaficas and Burton-Rose 2004; Hurl 2005).

In summary, autonomist Marxism has been explicated here as it provides useful additions and extensions as to how part of mapping out the social relations of struggle needs to be addressing our own powers and capacities in relation to the social composition of struggles, the cycles of struggles we are located in and the circulation of struggles between different movements. In the next sections, I clarify how these notions can assist us in concrete social investigations.

Within and against Ruling Relations

[handwritten: Political activist maps → sketch conflict of ruling relations ? social mvts]

Political activist mappings of the social relations of struggle are not the same as critically investigating the set of ruling relationships that oppressed people confront, which institutional ethnography more typically focuses on. It is instead a mapping of the social struggles themselves, a relational sketch of the conflicts between ruling relations and social movements. *[handwritten: Institutional ethno. → analyzes the relation of opp ? ruling.]*

[handwritten in left margin, bottom to top: Marx's Capital is ex. of how to change system]

Social movements and class and social struggles are not simply outside of capital or ruling relations, but are also internal to reshaping the ground upon which ruling strategies are deployed. Social movement activism and organizing can shape the options of governance for ruling agencies, forcing the adoption of different strategies. This can be seen in the classic example from Marx's *Capital*, of working-class revolt and organization closing off the option of raising the rate of the exploitation of surplus value from workers through the lengthening of the working day (the absolute strategy). This forced the capitalist class to develop a new, relative strategy (based on the application of technology to production, speeding-up production and "scientific"-management technologies) (Marx 1977: 307–672).

The bath raids that George Smith writes about were themselves a response within ruling relations to the growth and public visibility of gay men's communities and of queer sex, which had moved beyond the "private" realm to which the 1969 *Criminal Code* reform attempted to confine them (Kinsman 1996: 288–345). The massive resistance to the bath raids and the composition of struggle built around this pushed back the forces regulating queer sexualities and opened up social space for the emergence of broader gay and lesbian community formation. This resistance and cycle of struggle made widespread use of the bawdy-house legislation and mass police arrests very difficult for a period of time, forcing the police to re-focus on more individual and dispersed arrests on "indecent act" and other charges (Kinsman 1996: 344–45). Social movement activism undermines previous strategies of regulation forcing the elaboration of new strategies of management, which create new terrains of social struggle.

Political activist ethnography allows activists to map out the social relations that they are engaged with in their struggles. This mapping of the institutional relations and obstacles that movements are facing identifies the contradictions that exist in ruling relations and illustrates the weak points that can be actively challenged. It also entails mapping out possible allies and alliances with other social forces that can be effective in transforming the ruling relationships. This process begins from where movement activists are with their practices, insights and questions, with what they are confronting, with what they are learning and with what their knowledge is. It does not, however, begin from the speculative or ideological perspectives that sometimes hegemonize movements, as George Smith points out.

Mapping the Relations of Struggle of the Bath Raids — A Sketch

In elaborating on mapping the social relations of struggle, I first look back at one of the sites of struggle that George Smith writes about: the resistance to the bath raids in Toronto in the early 1980s. I was involved in this struggle, it took place in the historical past and we can look at it in a somewhat different way than some of the current struggles we are engaged in (see Figure 1).

The starting place for this mapping is the rupture in experience between gay men who were arrested in the early 1980s and the police who were directly engaging with them. This is tied into the line of fault created between gay men and our supporters and the police at the demonstrations against the raids. As the doors to the bath house cubicles were smashed down by the cops (Nicol 2002), what the gay men who were sitting in the cubicles or having sex in the bath houses experienced directly were these individual cops and their unwanted incursion into the social and erotic spaces these men had created for themselves (G. Smith 1988b; McCaskell 1988). Some activists produced an analysis of the homophobia of individual cops as the problem, which often had something to do with people's immediate experience of, and reading of, what happened to them. As George Smith points out, this experience however, was socially organized through and connected to a broader set of social relations, mobilized through the *Criminal Code* and police organization. Taking up the experiences, the standpoint, of gay men in the bath houses and those resisting the raids in the streets, we can begin to see, using political activist ethnography, the process of social organization of the raids.

First, I paint in the ruling relations that are implicated in this struggle. There is the police force itself, and as George Smith points out (1988b, 1990), there is a whole process of social organization behind this, not just the individual officers who would be most visible to the men being arrested. There is the *Criminal Code*, and its bawdy-house section, which ties together the police, the courts, the criminal justice system, the work of lawyers and the social organization of the law, which in turn is tied into a broader series of state relations (see Figure 1).

Regarding the legal system it should be clarified that lawyers are on different sides, at different points of time and in different positions, of/in this divide. There were not only the crown attorneys and their agents, who were working trying to convict these men, but also many defence lawyers, who worked with the Right To Privacy Committee (RTPC), trying to win victory for these men in their court cases. Much was learned from these lawyers about the social organization of the law and the criminal justice

Figure 1
Sketch of the Social Relations of Struggle Surrounding the Bath Raids

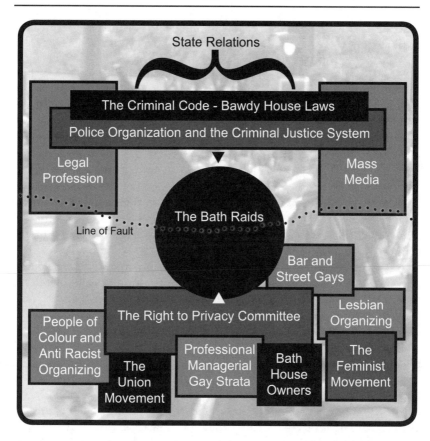

system. The whole defence campaign, with major public and fundraising activities outside the courtroom, was remarkably successful. At the same time there also were tensions between the defence lawyers and the RTPC, for example, when lawyers came up with legal strategies such as making deals that were politically unacceptable to the RTPC. The relation with defence lawyers could itself become a terrain of struggle since the work of lawyers is articulated within a legal system and legal ideology that is part of the organization of sexual oppression and class exploitation. Confrontations with ruling relations can even take place within working relations with lawyers.

Another site of struggle was the mainstream media and how they portrayed/framed (Fishman 1988) the bath raids and the resistance to them. This spans the line of disjuncture between the gay movement and ruling relations. As George Smith points out, the mass media becomes an important terrain of confrontation. Managing (or attempting to manage) media coverage can be crucial to activism in communicating with broader layers of people (G. Smith 1990: 643). The massive resistance and composition of gay movement struggle was able to win types of framing in the mainstream media that facilitated the extension of the struggle. Much of the mainstream media took up a relatively positive framing of the gay struggle against the raids, allowing more people to learn about and to participate in this struggle.[4]

These are some of the institutional relations that the RTPC was up against and sometimes implicated within. The initiatives of the RTPC challenged these relations, but this was also simultaneously part of researching and learning more about these relationships. What George Smith examines is this field of struggle and these political confrontations as a major site of research and knowledge production.

Even though George Smith in "Political Activist as Ethnographer" tends to write about this research as almost individual in character, it had a more collective character. It was not simply that George Smith was coming to these conclusions, many other people in the RTPC were as well, and this was connected into the political development of the RTPC. At first, following the bath raids, many people in the RTPC wanted to simply argue that bath houses are not bawdy houses, had nothing to do with prostitution, and therefore, these police raids were just totally invalid. What members of the RTPC, and George Smith in particular, began to realize was that it was the organization of the *Criminal Code* that allowed the police to engage in these types of raids and activities. If we did not grasp how the bawdy-house law in the *Criminal Code* enabled the police to make these arrests, we would not be able to combat this police repression. Popular education conducted in the RTPC developed an analysis that it was the bawdy-house laws themselves, and especially the construction of gay male sex as acts of "indecency," that had to be directly challenged. The ability of the cops to be able to engage in these activities had to be removed if the struggle was going to succeed. Skirting the issue of the *Criminal Code* and the bawdy-house legislation would be to fail to address the way in which the attacks were socially organized and would severely limit the composition of struggle that the RTPC could mobilize and coordinate.

The actual organizing of the RTPC and its strengths and capacities is also key to mapping out the social relations of struggle (also see McCaskell 1988). The tactics the RTPC engaged in included marches to go onto Toronto's Yonge Street, when it was then illegal to have marches on this street, other rallies and demonstrations, media conferences, deputations and fundraising for legal defence. By organizing hundreds of people in compact groups, including through the linking of arms, we learned that we could prevent the police from confining us to the sidewalk when we turned onto Yonge Street. In the orbit of the RTPC, a gay and lesbian self-defence street patrol emerged to work against violence against gay men and lesbians, and it also assisted in the marshalling of demonstrations. The RTPC had several committees, including public action, fundraising, legal support and communication, which for instance, monitored the media, organized media releases and conferences and produced *Action!*, which included some of the more activist writings of George Smith. Major decisions were made in large assemblies that, after the major raids in early 1981, had more than a thousand people at them. The first meetings of the public action committee after the raids had hundreds of people in attendance.

Beyond "Outside" and "Inside"

In exploring the social relations of struggle, activists encounter a series of social relations that are not always entirely distinct. This comes back to the discussions at the Sociology for Changing the World conference about "us versus them" and "inside and outside" distinctions and how these oftentimes change in relation to people's implication and complicity in institutional relations. While we may be in rupture with ruling relations on one front, we may be fully inside ruling relations on another. The RTPC itself was an alliance of different social forces coming out of the gay and, to some extent, lesbian communities. This group included the bath and bar owners and middle-class professionals and managers. When there was a mass movement and the RTPC was a mass organization, with hundreds of people involved in its discussions and activities, the interests of the bar owners, professionals and managers, which were sometimes quite distinct from those of the larger number of working-class, bar and street gays in the RTPC, were held in check and subordinated to this mass struggle and organizing. When it became much less of a dynamic organization, when the cycle and circulations of struggle had died down, with only dozens of people involved, the interests of these strata became more distinct and defining. A process of class stratification (or what I refer to as the emergence of a queer professional managerial strata) grew out of the resistance to the bath raids and shifted the political character of the RTPC (Kinsman 1996: 5–6, 381–82).

There were also links with other movements and allies — the feminist movement, the anti-racist movement, the union movement — that strengthened the RTPC's composition of struggle. But it is important for us to analyze concretely how these alliances and circulations of struggles were made. For instance, it was not spontaneously, nor without organizing, that Wally Majesky,[5] then head of the Metro Toronto Labour Council, came to speak out against the bath raids. Because I knew activists in the Canadian Union of Postal Workers (CUPW), I learned that it was gay postal worker activists who raised the issue of opposing the raids at the Metro Toronto Labour Council and persuaded the Labour Council to adopt this position. The self-organizing of gay activists in the union movement, which may not be visible from the locations of gay activists more rooted in the gay movement or in gay community formation, is also quite important to flesh out in strategizing around activism.

Another vital aspect to the circulation of struggles at the time of the bath raids was that many people from the Black and South Asian communities were also facing police repression and came out against this repression of the gay community. A limited common front against police repression was formed between a number of groups experiencing police arrests and violence at the time. We also experienced the largest ever contingent of gay men, organized by the RTPC and by Gay Liberation Against the Right Everywhere (GLARE), in the Toronto International Women's Day march in March 1981, following the bath raids. Important connections were made by many gay men in the context of the need to support the feminist movement since the feminist movement was supporting them. Since these gay men were also in motion challenging social forces of oppression this was a social context far more conducive to the circulation of struggles than when large numbers of gay men and other groups are not in motion.

Beginning to Map Struggles against Global Capitalism

The mass resistance to the bath raids that George Smith writes about took place in the early 1980s. As Dorothy Smith points out in the Foreword, ruling relations have been transformed since then and have become more extensively trans-locally organized. I suggest that political activist and institutional ethnographies are now even more important than in the past since, with the development of new forms of capitalist globalization, social power is organized on a more international level and no longer in local communities, regions or nation-states. The nation-state has been superseded in important respects as a framework in which capital is organized and as a framework in which working-class and social struggles can be contained (Hardt and Negri 2000, 2004). We have seen the generation of a whole series of new "global" and "regional" organizations through which capital and ruling relations come to be organized. At the same time, capitalist globalization also works through an intensification of aspects of nation-state formation. This includes the tightening up of border restrictions against migrants, immigrants, refugees and people of colour, and assaults upon the poor and the rights of workers (Sharma 2000, 2001; McNally 2002; Hardt and Negri 2000, 2004; and Wright in this volume). Crucial to the current waves of capitalist globalization are the attempts to convert more aspects of our social and "natural" worlds into commodities (including water, seeds, education and services) and a further colonization of the global commons. We are witnessing a new enclosure movement, which is extending the commodification of our lives while pushing more and more people off the land and separating people from access to various means of production (McNally 2002: 69–92). New forms of poverty *and* proletarianization are being produced through this process.

We desperately need political activist and institutional ethnographic work on the social organization of capitalist globalization and struggles against it. Developing this analysis on a global level, however, presents difficulties. We need to always link the local and the global in processes of social organization accomplished by people and to see the importance of these mediating linkages. At the same time it is vital not to reduce the global to the local, or vice versa. Rather, we should aim to develop an analysis that sees the links between social relations moving from the multiple local interactional worlds in which we live and struggle, to the extended social and institutional relations that are produced through these multiple local interactional relations. Protests organized against a meeting of the WTO in a particular city, for instance, are not simply global events but also occur in particular local settings, just as global relations are always accomplished in local settings and have impacts in people's local worlds. Global ruling relations are directly linked into more regional and local forms of "rationalization" and "restructuring," which have direct impacts in people's everyday/everynight lives (Sears 2003: 1–29; Kinsman 2005b; and Ng this volume). We must move beyond abstraction both in relation to the global and the local (see Conway 2004; A.K. Thompson forthcoming), which are both accomplished by people, even though it is often harder for us to grasp trans-local social relations.[6] Below is one way in which making these local/global connections can be seen in a preliminary sketch of social organization:

> A study by Dawn Currie and Anoja Wickramasinghe (1998) begins with the everyday experiences of women garment workers in factories in a Free Trade Zone in Sri Lanka. [They]… describe the long hours, the stress, the effects on their health, job insecurity and "the growing casualization of work" as women experience them. They go on from this account to locate such experiences in economic policies of Sri Lanka in the changed global economy and the complex of communication and management created by transnational corporations specializing in textiles. The latter locates Sri Lankan textile factories in a worldwide hierarchical division of the labour of fashion production articulated to different markets (Cheng and Gereffi 1994). From there connections can be made with the organization of design and advertising in the fashion industry that establish the perennially changing and market-differentiating norms of style, colour and so on. (D. Smith 2002: 39)

This analysis needs to be developed beyond the language of economics and markets, but it connects the local and global through social organization and relations. Another illustration of how this is done is in Ng's contribution in this book.

Since I have been involved as an activist in the global justice movement, I outline a very preliminary sketch of some of the social relations of struggle that this movement faces (see Figure 2). I only address aspects of these relations of struggle here and hope others will take this analysis much further

Figure 2
Sketch of the Social Relations of Struggle Engaged in by the Global Justice
Movement

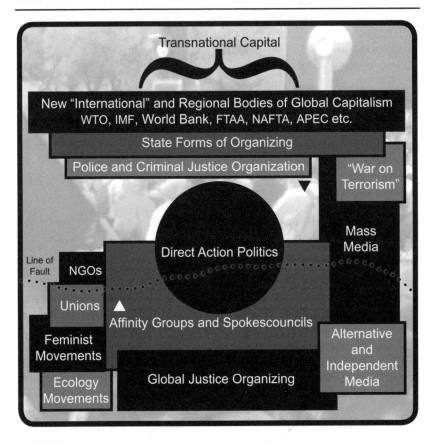

(on this, see Thompson this volume and Choudry 2004). Most crucially
for me, the more radical — radical as in getting to the root of the problem
— currents in the global justice movement have once again made possible
the naming of capitalism as the problem and have made resistance to the
social relations of capitalism actual again, starting with the Zapatista revolt
(Midnight Notes 2001; Notes from Nowhere 2003). The protests inside and
outside the WTO meetings in Seattle in 1999 and in Cancun in 2003 were
also highly effective in obstructing the progress of capitalist globalization
(Independent Media Centre/Big Noise 2000; Independent Media Centre
2003; Yuen, Burton-Rose and Katsiaficas 2004: 48–71, 109–25).

The line of fault from which this investigation begins is the disjuncture between the commitment of global justice activists to work against
poverty and exploitation and to expand democracy into new areas, and the
actuality of capitalist globalization, which intensifies exploitation, poverty

and major areas of oppression, restricting the limited forms of current democratic participation (Choudry 2004). The social relations of struggle that the global justice movement finds itself within include the emerging international bodies of global capitalism: the World Trade Organization (WTO), the International Monetary Fund (IMF), the World Bank, the Group of 8 (G8), regional agreements such as the proposed Free Trade Area of the Americas (FTAA), the North-American Free Trade Agreement (NAFTA) and the Asia Pacific Economic Cooperation (APEC). We need more institutional ethnography work for activists done on the operations of these institutions and the linkages between them.

These international and regional forms of capitalist organizing rest on the organization of state, corporate, professional and other ruling relations and the identification of "national security" with defence of these institutions of global capitalism, especially in the context of the new "war on terrorism." In the years prior to 9/11, it became common for police forces in Canada to use pepper spray and to engage in new forms of criminalization of global justice protests, beginning with the Vancouver protests against APEC in 1997 (Pearlston 2000; Pue 2000). Of course, throughout these years, in the experiences of indigenous protesters, far more overt state violence was mobilized.

Given the increasing criminalization of political dissent integral to capitalist globalization, activist currents within global justice movements find themselves up against the police and the criminal justice system in critical ways. The use of direct action by thousands of activists in Seattle in 1999, combined with mass demonstrations, surprised the police, who responded violently when they were ordered to clear the streets. The composition of struggle mobilized in Seattle was based on the development of a series of skills and capacities mobilized through Internet communication networks, affinity groups, spokescouncils, street medics, legal support teams and a series of alliances and solidarities built between networks of activists coming out of different movements (ecological, feminist, anti-racist, international solidarity, anti-poverty and radical labour) (Hurl 2005). Direct action protests have led to the creation of a great deal of useful and insightful analysis of police, jail and criminal justice system organization. This could be further extended using political activist ethnography (see Thompson this volume).

The police and authorities, however, also perform their own research. They learn new responses aimed at neutralizing the impact of direct action protests, how to decompose this social organization of struggle by arresting people prior to the actions even starting, attacking or shutting down centres where activists gather (see Thompson this volume) and encircling people who gather in the "green zones" for non-direct action festivities.

Simultaneously, protesters use tactics to try to outmaneuver police responses. For instance, snake marches can move in any direction to try to disrupt events or parts of cities. While activists have learned a fair bit about police and criminal justice organizations and how to resist these, more focused political activist research linked to these struggles is required.

In summary, the global justice movement has been at its most effective when a series of different social forces and modes of struggle have intersected. For instance, in Seattle and Cancun we saw the coming together of direct action protests (including in Cancun within the security zone) and large mass protests by trade unions and peasant organizations (in Cancun). This created a space for protests by representatives of some "Third World" countries inside the meetings. This composition of struggle led to the breakdown and cancellation of these meetings. Global justice mobilizations have been at their weakest when direct action protests have been isolated and separated off from the actions (or more likely inaction) of larger mass organizations, which has often led to the mass arrests of activists.

Activism, Which Activism?

Some of the reasons for the difficulties of global justice organizing, especially after 9/11 in the U.S. and Canada, have been the growing divergencies between the differing social interests and forces that compose the "movement," along with the success achieved by ruling strategies in trying to decompose the composition of social struggles mobilized for global justice. The global justice movement has a range of strands and possible allies, including unions, feminist groups, community organizations, ecological groups, "Third World" organizations and NGOs. There is a range of forces engaged in global justice organizing: mass organizations of struggle include the Landless Rural Workers Movement of Brazil, the Piqueteros in Argentina, the Zapatista communities in Mexico, radical union movements in South Korea and other countries; direct action activists in the North; the union movement in the North with its more moderate and limited agenda than many of the previously mentioned movements; and various nongovernmental organizations (NGOs). At times these diverse and somewhat contradictory currents maintain certain types of alliances and push struggles forward. At other times the differences between groups come to the fore and usually isolate the more radical of these groups, leaving them more vulnerable to state repression. State, corporate and professional regulation can penetrate and transform the character of NGOs, converting them into professionalized, bureaucratic and pro-capitalist forms of organizing (Ng 1996; Walker 1990; Kinsman 1997). Choudry describes how:

> Another disjuncture exists between the language and priorities of a professionalized NGO stratum which privileges particular forms of activity such as lobbying and policy analysis, and the dynamics and aspirations of many grassroots movements. In turn a disjuncture exists between experience and claims to speak for the interests

of communities and people for whom NGOs have no mandate to represent. (Choudry 2004: 6)

This produces the basis for some of the major differences within global justice organizations, i.e., divisions over how far to go in resisting the policies of capitalist globalization and over the forms of struggle that should be used. Often the leadership of northern mainstream unions and the major northern NGOs has attempted to reform the relations of capitalist globalization rather than to radically transform them. Our mapping out of the social relations of struggle facing global justice organizing must include the differential tying in of "oppositional" social forces to state and capitalist relations. The global justice movement needs more focused institutional and political activist ethnography on the social organization of unions, NGOs and other organizations, starting from multiple and varied social locations. It must link this research with a more overall transnational analysis. As Choudry also suggests, we:

> need to uncover and understand the antagonisms and conflicts which exist between and within NGOs and social movements, and to identify the ways in which these are organized, and in whose interests. But, in order to do so... we need to extend institutional ethnography, to transnationalize and democratize it, in order to explicate an increasingly complex and transnational web of actors involved in "anti-globalization" activism. (Choudry 2004: 5)

As Choudry points out, many NGOs are regulated through state legislation or subcontractual relations with state agencies, or through developing consultative relations with bodies like the World Bank or the WTO (Choudry 2004: 12), which leads to the mobilization of very different interests than those mobilized by more grassroots activist movements. Choudry suggests that there is no common "we" of the global justice movement and that the divergent class and social interests need to be recognized as different social projects. The same tensions and conflicts exist within other sites of social and class struggle, as John Clarke illustrates in his contribution to this book, where the moderate and social democratic left has at times been complicit in attacks on the homeless and the poor, and have undermined and isolated the radical anti-poverty activism of groups like the Ontario Coalition Against Poverty (OCAP).

These tensions tie back to questions that emerged at the Sociology for Changing the World conference and that Marie Campbell raises in her chapter in this volume. In some of the sessions, there was ambiguity and controversy over what "activism" is. Activism can refer to a range of different activities and different relationships to social struggles. When talking about activism some people are talking about NGOs and service organizations, whereas others are referring to OCAP or global justice organizations that organize in an explicitly anti-capitalist fashion. How can we develop knowledge that understands that certain parts of movements are much more implicated in ruling relations than other parts? And what does this entail regarding the types of research that we are doing and for whom?

One way in which sections of the global justice movement have tried to address the need to build alliances and to link the global and local is to move beyond a politics defined by "summit hopping." Instead they have become involved in local organizing against the everyday impacts of capitalist globalization, including poverty, homelessness, deportations of immigrants and refugees, social service cuts and defence of health-care and education. This locally grounded organizing is vital but needs to be combined with the continuing circulation of struggles based on more central confrontations with the emerging institutions of global capitalism (Hurl 2005), such as those in Seattle, Prague, Québec City, Genoa, Cancun and Santiago (against APEC in Nov. 2004).

Attempting to Rip Apart the Movement — "Bad" Versus "Good" Protesters

The declared "war on terrorism" has been rather effectively used to disrupt the composition of global justice struggles, making it a much more difficult terrain upon which to organize, especially in the U.S. and Canada. One strategy for undercutting the composition of this struggle has been the generation of a division between "good" and "bad" protestors and between "legitimate" and "illegitimate" forms of protest. Activists need more critical work on the social organization of this "war on terrorism," which is simultaneously a war on dissent.

A major ruling response to the composition of the global justice movement struggles that came together in Seattle (that started during the first day of the actions themselves) was the division of the movement between good and bad protestors, often coded as non-violent and violent protestors. The "violence" in this case was the breaking of some Starbucks and Nike windows. For many people who did not attend the Seattle protests or had no access to alternative sources of information, the only available media framing of these protests was the "violence" of the protestors smashing a few windows. The mass police violence and the use of tear gas and pepper spray that day conveniently disappeared.

The global justice movement confronts multiple problems with an increasingly concentrated corporate ownership of the mass media, which have often framed the global justice movement with special attention to its "violent" character, focusing on the small amounts of property destruction that have occurred at some demonstrations. This ignores the systematic forms of social violence that are organized through capitalist globalization, including poverty, homelessness and cuts in social programs, and the police and state violence mobilized against protestors (McNally 2002: 244–49). To suggest that the small-scale and targeted property destruction that some activists engage in is the introduction of violence into this setting is to forget that capitalist social relations are already saturated with social violence. Along with some state and other political forces, the mass media divide the movement into good and bad protestors, an attempt to associate global justice organizing with political and social deviance (Fishman 1988). The media and official framing of the global justice movement as violent and as being composed of bad protestors is in part an attempt to prevent alliances from being built between different activists and movements, an attempt to separate young direct action activists from more mainstream currents in union leadership and in NGOs. Global justice activists must work to overcome these divisions.

In response to this framing of global justice activism in the mainstream media the movement has facilitated the creation of worldwide independent media sites, which are important sources of information and connection that people cannot otherwise get. This important resource needs to be extended to become a basis for continuing recompositions of struggle in relation to the mass media and the Internet (Dyer-Witheford 1999: 116–29: Cleaver 1998; Kidd 2004). While the generation of independent media has been crucial, they unfortunately, in current circumstances, cannot communicate their messages to a mass audience.

At the same time, activists, influenced by the structuralist analysis of the news media associated with the "propaganda model" of Chomsky and Herman (2002), sometimes understand the mainstream media as too monolithic and corporate controlled to bother confronting. This leads to an inadequate analysis of how journalism is socially organized as a work process (Fishman 1988). Despite the ever-growing concentration of media ownership, there are still spaces for disruptive, albeit momentary, intervention and media activism in these relations. Action grounded in an analysis of the social organization of journalism and media will lead to more effective forms of media activism that intervene into the social organization of the mainstream media, while building more effective alternatives.

Activist Breaching Experiments:
Disrupting Research and Disruption as Research

Part of the activism that the RTPC engaged in, part of what the radical currents in the global justice movements engage in and a day-to-day part of many activist movements have similarities to an ethnomethodological breaching experiment. Such experiments were developed by Harold Garfinkel to learn more about how social organization is put together through disrupting it, or breaching it, and learning from the social reactions that resulted (Garfinkel 1967). For instance, he asked his students to go home and to act as boarders with their parents. In some cases, this so disrupted "normal" relations at home that it caused tensions and fights. Lessons were learned about the fragility of "social order" and how this depends on a process of continuous social accomplishment of relations producing a home or household situation. In extending Garfinkel's work in relation to the social construction of gender, Kessler and McKenna (1978) learned from pre-operative transsexuals, who in major ways breach the "natural attitude" towards gender in this society that there are only two "opposite" genders based in biological difference. Kessler and McKenna showed that gender is based not on biology but on the ongoing social practices of gender attribution we engage in, i.e., how we talk, how we manage our public appearances, how we manage our private bodies, how we talk about our personal pasts and other practices (112–41).

It was also through these breaching experiments that ethnomethodologists were able to learn about the indexical and reflexive character of the social world, mentioned earlier. For these breaching experiments and for its opposition to the portrayal of people as "cultural dopes" in mainstream sociological theory, ethnomethodology came to be labelled as a "subversive" current within sociology.

In activism, these breaching experiments are situated in the life and cycles of struggle of movements that are confronting social and institutional relations. Through disruption the objective is to learn more about how these relations are socially organized so they can be more effectively challenged and transformed (see Thompson in this volume). Initially, when the feminist movement against violence against women initiated take-back-the-night marches (especially when these were not sanctioned by law or state), thereby disrupting the patriarchal relations prescribed for women, feminists learned a great deal from the responses they provoked. Another example of a movement breaching experiment could be a militant demonstration outside a police commission meeting, combined with an official deputation inside, to see what can be learned from troubling these institutional relations. Similarly, direct action protests aimed at disrupting organizations like the WTO have learned a fair bit about the social organization of the police, the criminal justice system and the WTO itself. This is a concrete way of learning more about how ruling relations are organized and can make visible the possible weak links in these relations. If we can begin to see social movement activism as a more political and collective practice of breaching experiments, it becomes another way of thinking through how knowledge is produced within social movements. Action and research can be directly linked together. These breaching experiments are not simply possible on local interactional levels, which was the situation in Garfinkel's proposals to his students, but can also occur on a more trans-local basis, e.g., in the extended social relations that the global justice movement confronts.

Politically situated breaching experiments become a central way of mapping out the social relations of struggle from the standpoints of organizing and activism. The very capacity to undertake these forms of research are tied to the composition and cycles of struggle involved in social movement mobilization and organization. There is a radically different relationship here between theory and practice than in traditional academic constructions. Sometimes when we talk about research and activism in the academic world we replicate distinctions around notions of consciousness and activity that are detrimental to our objectives. We can fall back on research as being an analysis, or a particular form of consciousness, and activism as about doing things "out there," which leads to a divorce between consciousness and practice. If we begin to recognize that consciousness always has a direct living relationship to what people are doing, we grasp ways in which theory and practice, consciousness and knowledge production are connected. We are talking about actual relations, research, knowledge, people and bodies involved in cycles and compositions of social struggles. Social movement breaching experiments are attempts to do research and to simultaneously alter the relation of social forces in favour of movement struggles. We produce knowledge as we change the world.

The Social Organization of Language and Activism: "Whose Streets, Our Streets" Versus "Whose Cops, Our Cops"

Movement based breaching experiments can also lead us to think through the politics of language and its relation to activism. As George Smith suggests in another context, "in every instance, language was social organization. Thus, the study of a form of social organization became, in part, a study of its language" (G. Smith 1990: 645). While George Smith was writing about the social organization of ruling relations, I am exploring the ways in which language can coordinate and push forward (or not) the social organization of activism. George Smith in his critique of the limitations of the language of homophobia and AIDSphobia already focused our attention on questions of language and activism.

The slogan of "Whose streets, our streets" is chanted on global justice and other demonstrations as people actually take over the streets. This is on one level a breaching experiment, as it is usually violating the law and bending ruling definitions of social space. Movements of people exert more collective social power by taking over the streets, instead of being confined to sidewalks. Taking over the street is direct practice and captures an incredible amount of power and energy with people taking more social space and engaging in more effective forms of political activism. This slogan is performative, since it accomplishes the social act of taking the streets.[7] People learn in practice that they have the power to disobey laws and social normality, and people learn that they can exert their own power much more effectively when they establish some control over the streets. On the other hand, disrupting social conventions and the law can provoke a police response of arresting those people taking over the streets or moving them back onto the sidewalks.

In Seattle and at other demonstrations since then, people have tried to use the same formula to approach other questions. Another slogan I have heard is "Whose cops, our cops,"[8] which is usually chanted when activists are confronted by a massive wall of riot cops. This chant does not work as a slogan, it is not linked to practice, and it also does not work as any form of analysis because it is not reflexively tied into the same type of social practice as "Whose streets, our streets." It is a slogan that entirely misunderstands the social organization of the police, who are not organized in any democratic fashion (Scraton 1985) and certainly are not accountable in any way, shape or form to global justice protestors, who are one of the cops' central targets.

We can see here very different illustrations of the dialogical and reflexive use of language in relation to activism. "Whose streets, our streets" is an affirmation of counter-power as people engage in doing it. "Whose cops, our cops," while it is based on the same linguistic formula, is divorced from practice and does not develop a useful analysis of social organization. This slogan and activism around it are not going to get the police to defect and come over to the protestors' side, at least not in current circumstances. This slogan can also lead to some disorientation in global justice organizing on those occasions when the police are not violent. This can lead to an ideological distinction between "good" cops and "bad" cops, an analysis that is not grounded in how the police are socially organized. The reflexive and dialogical relation of language to our organizing and what it can or does not coordinate in our compositions of struggle become an important terrain of the social relations of struggle we need to investigate. Most of the time activists pay little attention to the precise character of the slogans and chants that we use. My argument is that paying attention to the rhythm and language of struggle is an important part of mapping the social relations of struggle with which we are engaged. In this context while "Whose streets, our streets" has a radical dynamic leading towards the emergence of experiences of counter-power, "Whose cops, our cops" serves only to disorient us and weaken our struggles.

Challenges, Questions, Pedagogy

Activists in movements are searching to move forward in new ways. Lately, what the academic world offers is often grounded in postmodernism and poststructuralism. With their focus on interpretation and re-interpretation, these approaches are unable to map out the social relations of movement struggle. Despite the insights we can see in some new social movement theory influenced by these approaches (see the Preface), postmodernism and poststructuralism provide little grounding for social movement activism as they tend to produce theory disconnected from practice. In contrast, as activists and researchers, we need to move beyond the binary oppositions between theory and practice. We need theory connected to and constantly transformed and enriched by practice that can assist us in mapping out social relations of struggle, identifying sites where progress is possible and developing strategies for fighting to win our struggles. Political activist ethnography can be very useful in extending the capacities of activist researchers and in clarifying that these activists in movements are already doing research. They are already intellectuals when they are active in social movements. There is an important need for political activist and institutional ethnography work *for* activism. We need to identify the questions and areas of social organization that need to be further researched for the progress of movements and struggles. Political activist and institutional ethnography are alternative ways of doing sociology that are not fixed or dogmatic and thus are able to be continually open-ended and remade as new voices and new movements come forward to join in struggles for social transformation.

Political activist research builds on and extends the research capacities of movement activists and aids in subverting the binary oppositions of research versus activism and of inside/outside distinctions that often ensnare activists and researchers who attempt to produce knowledge for social transformation. We need to move beyond the inside/outside dichotomy, beyond arguing for either absolute "externality," outside ruling relations, or absolute "internality," inside ruling relations. By starting instead inside social relations and social organization we begin with our double and simultaneous engagement with social relations of ruling and resistance to them. This allows us to grasp the social relations of struggle in which we are involved (also on this, see the Afterword).

A further challenge is to discuss how we can democratize research and knowledge creation and distribution practices within social movements. This is something that George Smith raised but was never resolved in the RTPC or in AIDS ACTION NOW! How can we make doing research much more democratic, much more linked into collective forms of analysis, much more linked into effective forms of activism? How can we transform doing research from a monological enterprise organized around the university-trained and "connected" researchers to becoming a much more dialogical project with many centres and many voices weaving together an analysis of the social relations of struggle movements face?

This perspective also raises issues about the pedagogy of activism and teaching. We have to think about education and teaching as much broader than what is taught in the classroom. What happens in social movements is very much about pedagogy, teaching, learning and knowledge production. We can actually begin to democratize our notions of education and knowledge creation in a more profound way. If we are committed to developing a sociology for changing the world, it is vital that it is not just about developing a brilliant analysis in the university world, it also has to be about developing a relationship to social movements. These movements are the social forces that can provide the composition of struggles — the resources, the energy, the dynamic, the rhythm and the initiative to change the world (see Thompson in this book and the Afterword).

Moving beyond interpretation, ideology and speculation to actual social organization and social relations, a sociology for changing the world can produce more effective knowledge for activism organically linked to movements capable of changing the world. As Marx once put it, "The philosophers have only interpreted the world, the point, however, is to change it" (Marx 197: 423).

Critical Thinking and Discussion Questions

1. How can mapping out the social relations of struggle be useful for social movement activists?

2. How can autonomist Marxism be useful for doing political activist ethnography?

3. Many social movements confront the mainstream mass media. How can social movements engage with the media as a terrain of struggle?

Notes

1. This chapter is based on bringing together, updating and transforming two talks. The first was delivered at the Putting Institutional Ethnography Into Practice conference in Victoria in June 2002. I thank Stephanie Ouelette for word processing and making sense of my notes for this talk. The second was given at the Sociology for Changing the World conference in Nov. 2002. This was transcribed by Caelie Frampton. Revisions are also influenced by the talk I gave at the Activist Research and the Sociology of Confrontation session at York University, Nov. 26, 2004, referred to in the Preface.

2. "Ideology refers to all forms of knowledge that are divorced from their conditions of production (their grounds)" (Bologh 1979: 19). On ideology, also see the work of Dorothy E. Smith (1990a, 1990b) and the work of Himani Bannerji (1995b) and her articles on the ideological construction of India (1994) and (1995a).

3. Dialogism and its variants are central terms used by Russian literary theorist M.M. Bakhtin to get at how "Everything means, is understood, as part of a greater whole — there is constant interaction between meanings, all of which have the potential of conditioning others" (Michael Holquist 1981: 426–27). Also see David McNally (1997: 26–42); Dorothy E. Smith (1999: 96–130).

4. This is now more difficult to achieve given the growing corporate concentration of media ownership.

5. Wally Majesky is shown speaking at the rally against the bath raids at the St. Lawrence Market in Nancy Nicol *Stand Together* (2002).

6. See Dorothy Smith's "The Ruling Relations" (1999: 73–95) for analysis of the textual construction of capital that maintains this as an active social accomplishment by people mediated through texts.

7. Performative is used here to get at language that accomplishes a social act. I do not use this in the same sense as Judith Butler, who largely uses it to refer to a discursive effect. Instead I view performative as a social accomplishment (see D. Smith 1999: 107–109).

8. Both "Whose Streets, Our Streets" and "Whose Cops, Our Cops" are used in the first section of *This is What Democracy Looks Like* (Independent Media Centre/Big Noise 2000).

Part C

BLOWING UP SOCIAL RELATIONS

We have called this section "Blowing Up Social Relations," a phrase referenced in numerous anarchist discussions on terrorism. It is thought to have been originally proclaimed by a Russian socialist, who — writing a polemic against the nineteenth-century anarchist factions who were engaged in explosive terrorist acts against the Czar — declared: "You can't blow up a social relation." The author's point was simple: attacking infrastructure, even if it is of more than symbolic importance, cannot do away with a system. Without far-reaching reorganization of social relations, cutting off the head of the king never prevented another from sprouting in its place.

On this point, we largely concur. However, there is something to be said for the possibility of blowing up social relations. This potential clamour takes place in two ways. First, since a social relation is a coordinated practice that requires a kind of orchestration between two or more people or institutional points, it is possible to imagine how an intervention at the intersection might lead — at least metaphorically — to an explosion, a kind of rupture in continuity and efficacy of the social relation. Second, since social relations tend to be largely invisible from within local settings and since the trans-local coordination of relations of ruling are not immediately visible from the standpoint of the everyday, the process of "blowing up a social relation" can be conceived of as a strategy of illumination. In this second sense, "blowing up" entails a process of mapping in order to figure out how to intervene most effectively. Each of the chapters in this section is written with the aim of doing just that.

The following section provides some concrete applications of the research methods and practices built on throughout this book. While each of these research experiments cover what might be considered familiar ground within the sociological literature, they nevertheless stand as distinct contributions by virtue of starting, not with abstract categories of analysis, but rather with the concrete experiences of people embroiled in specific moments of conflict.

To start, Viviane Namaste's discussion of the relationship of transsexual Québécois people to several ruling regimes breaks down the ways in which constant negotiation is required in the everyday. This chapter provides a description of how ruling relations can be conveniently flexible in order to suit their own needs, clearly demonstrating a lack of institutional consistency. In a similar fashion to George Smith's analysis of the lack of institutional coordination of getting AIDS/HIV treatments into the bodies needing them, Namaste pinpoints how the lack of institutional coordination regarding sex, gender and identification creates problems in the everyday/everynight worlds of transsexuals. Interestingly, Namaste also shows the importance of documents and how these are used to regulate proof of gendered identity and in turn can create barriers to social integration.

Roxana Ng makes the connection between activist projects and research strategies explicit in her account of globalization and female garment workers. Having worked on a campaign to address deplorable labour standards within the garment industry over ten years, Ng is able to start from the problems of workers in the trade as they become actualized in managerial processes and the social organization of production. From the experiences of garment workers themselves, she is able to quickly move to the sphere of coordinated trans-local social relations often referred to as "globalization." By tracing seemingly abstract problems back to their points of origin in concrete practices, Ng is able to propose practical modes of resistance.

In Cynthia Wright's chapter, the question of the politics of border policing in the post-9/11 era is taken up from the standpoint of non-status people and their supporters. Wright investigates the manner in which the clampdown on borders and the criminalization of migrant populations has been achieved through concrete textual practices, both legal and administrative. She also elaborates on the strategies devised by activists to combat this repression and concludes with proposals about areas in need of further research.

While Ng's article provides a means of mapping social relations spatially, Clarice Kuhling and Alex Levant's chapter aims instead at mapping these relations temporally. Taking as their focus the plight of Canadian trade unions under neoliberalism, Levant and Kuhling outline how activity within trade unions has been systematically curtailed through institutional and textual practices originating in the post-war period. Kuhling and Levant propose that flying squads — autonomous political formations of union members — provide a way to both enable trade union militancy and to call into question the legalistic and bureaucratic sphere of expert knowledge that has turned many contemporary unions into service organizations.

Each of the authors in this section has a different relation to political activist ethnography and institutional ethnography. Viviane Namaste and Roxana Ng are both very invested and experienced with the work of institutional ethnography, even though they each approach institutional ethnography somewhat differently. For Cynthia Wright, Clarice Kuhling and Alex Levant, the commitment to political activist ethnography has been a more recent development. While Wright knew and worked with

George Smith, her chapter in this volume is a rare instance in which she directly articulates her work in relation to the concerns of political activist ethnography. For Kuhling and Levant, political activist ethnography has provided a useful complement to their ongoing and prior concerns with union activism and class analysis.

While each of their chapters takes on the task of applying the insights of political activist ethnography in a slightly different manner, they all share the commitment to starting their investigations from the standpoint of those directly affected. From there, they each make recommendations about how the knowledge gained in and from struggle can be practically applied in order to come up with effective strategies of resistance aimed at confronting specific problems and transforming social relations. As this section illustrates, the enemy is never abstract.

CHANGES OF NAME AND SEX
FOR TRANSSEXUALS IN QUÉBEC:
UNDERSTANDING THE ARBITRARY
NATURE OF INSTITUTIONS

Viviane Namaste

The specific case study of political activist ethnography to be discussed here concerns the change of name and sex for transsexuals in Québec. Transsexuals are individuals who are born in one biological sex but who identify as members of the "opposite sex." They take hormones and undergo surgical interventions to modify their primary and secondary sex characteristics. Transsexuals are both male-to-female (MTF), individuals who are born male but who live and identify as women, and female-to-male (FTM), individuals who are born female but who see themselves and who live as men.

Obviously, the process of changing one's sex is complicated. It involves fundamental adjustments to all aspects of one's life: the physical body (modified through hormones and surgery) as well as social life more generally (employment, housing, education). Access to health care remains difficult for transsexuals: people are regularly refused services outright, are unable to find the information and resources they need to begin a process of sex change or cannot find support throughout the process (Namaste 1995, 1998, 2000).

These difficulties are compounded by the situation transsexuals face with respect to their legal documents. All transsexuals go through a period of time in which their legal identity does not correspond to the physical image that they present to the outside world. For example, male-to-female transsexuals function and live in the world as women, but many have papers which indicate that they are biologically male. Research on access to health services indicates that such a dilemma creates an inordinate amount of stress for transsexuals (Namaste 1998). Indeed, many transsexuals interviewed about their access to services stated that they preferred to pay cash when seeing a doctor, as opposed to presenting a health card that was in the name and legal identity of their biological sex (Namaste 1998). A provincial needs assessment of transsexuals in Québec revealed that people will go to extraordinary lengths to avoid presenting legal papers that will identify them as transsexuals. Of twenty-seven individuals interviewed, five had obtained false documents in order to access health care and education without divulging their transsexuality (Namaste 1998).

That transsexuals will forge their identities in order to avoid being labelled transsexuals within different institutional sites demonstrates the importance they accord to moving through the world in their chosen sex and gender. It also provides a useful opportunity to reflect on the institutional management of sex. As ethnomethodologists in the discipline of sociology have shown (Zimmerman 1975), the institutional world relies on documents extensively. Documents are used to establish proof of identity for citizenship, for travel and for access to health care, to name only a few examples. Yet what happens when one's identity documents do not correspond to one's social gender? How do institutions manage such a discrepancy? Furthermore, what kinds of knowledge do we have about how institutions rely on documents of sex? What kinds of knowledge is lacking? As ethnomethodologists have shown, the project of critical sociology includes an analysis of the "seen but unnoticed" phenomena of everyday life (Garfinkel 1967). What elements and functions of sex and gender are seen but unnoticed in our everyday institutions?

Asking these questions about the relations between sex, documents and institutions is a useful starting point in the development of a critical activist research agenda. And it is here that political activist ethnography has much to offer. Specifically with regards to transsexuals, political activist ethnography can offer an analysis of how institutions manage sex through documents. Such knowledge is important for transsexuals in a variety of ways. In the first instance, it confirms that their experience of the institutional world, a dissonance between their sense of themselves and how they are positioned based on their documents, is valid.[1] Moreover, such political activist ethnography can help transsexuals understand how institutions function in concrete terms. This knowledge is useful for the kinds of demands they can make upon the state and its institutions in the work of social change.

Transsexuals and Identity Papers in Late 1990s Québec

In the course of conducting a provincial needs assessment of transsexuals and transvestites with respect to HIV/AIDS in Québec in 1997–1998, I quickly learned that a gap between the social and psychological identity of transsexuals and their legal papers represented a significant barrier to their social integration (Namaste 1998). Participants informed me, for example, that they avoided going to a medical clinic, since their health care card was in their biological name and they would be subject to embarrassment and possible ridicule and violence when their name was called. Alternatively, interviewees stated that they did not go to school because they were unable to change the names on their school records and were thus forced to disclose their transsexual status. This information raised the important question, then, of the legal and administrative procedure for name and sex change in Québec.

The law states that, in order to change their name and sex, a transsexual individual must have undergone a surgical intervention of the genital organs involving their structural modification and destined to change their sexual characteristics (*Code civil du Québec* 1991: 28). It should be underlined here, perhaps especially to the anglophone reader, that the process of name change and sex change are to occur simultaneously in Québec, which is to say after surgery on the genitals. This legal framework reflects a civil code jurisdiction. In English Canada, which functions under a common law jurisprudence, a change of name for transsexuals is permitted even before genital surgery. These different practices for name and sex change in Canada reflect the differences between common and civil law (Kouri 1973, 1975; Greffier 1975; Salas 1994).

If the law declares that there is to be a structural modification of the genitals before transsexuals can change their name and sex, what does that mean in concrete terms? Which surgery, or surgeries, are required to fulfill this requirement of a structural modification? Importantly, at the time of conducting my research (1997–1998), there was a gendered aspect to the interpretation of this law. The *Direction de l'état civil* (Office of Civil Status), the centralized government agency responsible for civil status, name change and sex change, stated clearly at the time that for MTFs, the construction of a vagina was required (Namaste 1998). Yet what was required for female-to male transsexuals? At the time of my research, the *Direction de l'état civil* gave conflicting and inconclusive answers in this regard. Some FTM transsexuals were not told what surgeries were required in order to proceed with a change of name and sex; others were given contradictory information.

FTM participants I interviewed informed me that prior to 1996, the surgeries required included a hysterectomy, an ovariectomy (removal of the ovaries), a mastectomy and hormone treatment. However these men maintained that since 1996, the Office of Civil Status had interpreted the text of the law differently. In January 1998, they required a vaginectomy (the closure of the vagina), the justification for which, however, was not evident. Regardless, this change in the interpretation of the law was a result of an administrative practice at the *Direction de l'état civil* and not the result of a consultation with FTM transsexuals or with surgeons or professionals working with these men. One FTM recounts his experience upon discovery of the new interpretation of the law:

Okay, vaginectomy. When I received that letter, I said, my God, what is a vaginectomy? I mean, since this entire transition, I know what are the operations required. And the next operation is a phalloplasty (construction of a penis), but what is a vaginectomy? So I made an appointment with the surgeon who operated on me. And the doctor said, well that is impossible, we don't do vaginectomies on transsexuals. It's impossible, it's an operation which is only practised on cases of extreme cancer. And anyway, they can't take all that tissue away because the doctor needs some to make the, to be able to do the phalloplasty. So he wrote a letter which said that, exactly, that it's been twenty five years he's practised these operations, and it's the first time a request like this is asked for a case like this.

Upon receiving the letter from the *Direction de l'état civil*, this FTM spoke with the office. They explained that he could be exempted from a vaginectomy for medical reasons, with an authorization. They might refuse his request, but he could win in tribunal. So he wrote a letter to this effect, which said that he would not undergo a vaginectomy because of his health. They called him to tell him that his request had been refused. According to him, the vaginectomy had been replaced by the criterion of a phalloplasty: "The Office of Civil Status had changed their mind. It was no longer a vaginectomy, it was a phalloplasty."

These administrative matters became more complicated. In April 1998, Civil Status changed its interpretation and application of the law once again, this time demanding the reconstruction of male sexual organs. Yet they refused to specify what surgeries were required to attest to this reconstruction. During one consultation with the office, they explained that FTMs needed to have male sexual organs in order to be considered men before the law and that they also needed to be able to urinate standing up (Namaste 1998). When I asked for the justification of this criterion, they could not explain the link between an individual's legal sex and their behaviour in a restroom.

My research reveals not only a lack of explicit information in this regard but an application of the Québec law that is neither obvious nor uniform. During a telephone consultation in October 1997, the Office of Civil Status could not tell me what surgeries were required to attest a structural modification of the genital organs: "I cannot list the operations for you. Each case is different." During a meeting in January 1998, on the other hand, I was informed that FTMs needed to have a hysterectomy, an ovariectomy, a double mastectomy and a vaginectomy. In April 1998, I was once again informed that each FTM case is unique and it is impossible to enumerate the surgeries required. The experiences of FTM transsexuals and my research clearly indicate that within the course of a year, diverse and contradictory criteria were necessary for a name and sex change. This clearly speaks to a lack of protocol in this domain.

In the late 1990s, FTM transsexuals in Québec could not change their papers because protocols and policies in this regard did not exist, changed regularly or were interpreted differently. The complexity of this situation is a function of its administration. As sociologists have demonstrated, government administration often lacks cohesion. Grant Jordan (1994: 2) summarizes the situation in Britain, but his remarks are equally pertinent for the practices of the *Direction de l'état civil* in Québec:

> Where one might expect bureaucratic rigidity there is *ad hoc* improvisation. British public administration is made up by Governments as they go along. It is characterized precisely by features that might be least expected: uncertainty, inconsistency, disorder.
>
> It is surprisingly difficult to prove this. An account of confusion reads very much like a confused account. Since there is no ordered pattern to British administration, the more detailed knowledge that is gathered serves to emphasize the weakness of our understanding.

Jordan's remarks illustrate the complexity of administrative practices with regards to name and sex change for female-to-male transsexuals in Québec in the late 1990s.

Uses and Applications of Political Activist Ethnography

In terms of its method, this research applies the important tenet of institutional ethnography that a problematic is to be investigated according to the standpoint and experience of those within the everyday world. Beginning with a simple reading of the law with respect to name and sex change for transsexuals, for example, would have eclipsed the complexity of the situation. A researcher who reads the text of the law could easily conclude that administrative protocols do exist in which transsexuals can change their identity papers. However, by beginning with the experiences of transsexuals themselves, the critical sociologist learns that while such a possibility exists on paper, the change of name only after genital surgery has important repercussions for the ability of transsexuals to integrate into Québec society. Furthermore, research that begins with the experience of everyday transsexuals also reveals that, despite a clear law in this area, the practical reality for FTM transsexuals is quite a different story. In this regard, the issue at hand is not one of the law *per se*, but rather its interpretation and application. Such a research focus thus requires a method that turns its attention to the concrete elements of everyday government administration.

An examination of the daily workings of government administration, taken from the standpoint of the transsexuals located outside of it, provides further evidence as to the specific reasons for these practices. Such an orientation is important. In the case of FTM transsexuals in late 1990s Québec, the research clearly shows that the interpretations of the law with respect to name and sex change for FTM transsexuals by the *Direction de l'état civil* are completely arbitrary. This knowledge is important and offers a useful nuance to the explanations offered by some FTM transsexuals themselves, who understood such practices as a form of hatred or contempt for transsexuals. The research shows that government administration of name and sex change is clearly based on misinformation with respect to FTM transsexuals but is not necessarily grounded in attitudes of vilification. Here, my research parallels that of George Smith (1995: 22), who maintained that AIDS activists in the late 1980s often viewed a lack of infrastructure with respect to experimental AIDS drugs through "speculative accounts" of homophobia or bureaucratic red tape. Smith's investigation illustrated how the workings of the government were a result not so much of homophobia *per se*, but rather reflected a public health bias that understood AIDS according to a model of palliative care. In a similar manner, my research shows that the workings of the *Direction de l'état civil* regarding name and sex change for FTM transsexuals emerge from practices which are, in the final instance, arbitrary.

This emphasis on the arbitrary nature of interpretations of the law allows for a broader analysis of how a social institution operates. Furthermore, this perspective is useful in helping to identify sites of future political activism for transsexuals in Québec. The research process itself involved a certain amount of interface between transsexuals and the government. Interviews with bureaucrats sent a clear message that their policies, as well as the changing interpretations of their policies, were under close scrutiny both by individual transsexuals as well as health researchers. The transsexuals with whom I spoke indicated frustration at the situation and pressed me to meet with representatives of the *Direction de l'état civil* in order to get clear answers to their questions. The research report served a useful function in this regard by providing clear documentation of the arbitrary interpretation of the current law in the case of FTM transsexuals. As George Smith argues, political activist ethnography is not to be understood as political activism in and of itself. However, the method is "intended to provide, on a day to day basis, the scientific ground for political action" (G. Smith 1995: 32). In this regard, the research was an integral part of helping to identify the current problems in the workings of one particular institution and how these prevented transsexuals from integrating into Québec society.[2]

Lack of Coordination among Different Institutions: Implications for the Social Ordering of Experience

The institutional marginalization of transsexuals in Québec is further noteworthy when we consider more than one institution. Indeed, different institutions in Québec, for example, civil status and/or health, administer their affairs with respect to transsexuals independently, without consideration of the policies or practices of other institutions. The transsexual person can get completely lost in an administrative abyss, the requirements of one institution excluding the individual from another. Several examples illustrate this problematic. Federal prisons, for instance, require that an individual be followed and evaluated by a team from a gender identity clinic (Correctional Services Canada 1991). Yet because these clinics refuse to evaluate transsexuals who work as prostitutes (Namaste 1998; 2000), many prostitutes do not have access to hormones in federal penitentiaries. To take another example, representatives of gender identity clinics will not authorize access to hormones to drug users, telling them that they need to deal with their drug use before they can obtain services related to transsexualism. Yet drug detoxification or rehabilitation programs do not respect the identities of transsexuals, do not have sufficient training in this area or never address this question (Namaste 1995, 2000). The result is that transsexual addicts are refused services from detoxification programs and from gender identity clinics.

A similar situation exists with the *Direction de l'état civil*, which requires that the surgery be achieved before the name can be changed. Yet in order to obtain the surgery, one must demonstrate that one is well integrated into society, a fact evidenced by work or full-time studies. Access to employment, however, requires identity documents. Transsexuals who cannot find jobs cannot have access to surgery. One participant summarizes this situation:

> It's simple, really, the government isn't doing anything. You begin the process, to get your operation and all that, you begin, and even if you're okay, the government doesn't pay for it, you have to see a private surgeon, but a private surgeon, you have to pay for that. What's left for you to do? You know, no work, nothing, problems with your identity, all that, at a certain point, it's a vicious circle. You have to go, and you need money really quickly and you say "Aie calvas!" What's left for you to do? You want to dance, but dancing with a penis is rough. So what's left? Prostitution. You can't do prostitution long without ending up taking drugs. The result is that you have to take drugs and then you're hooked. You can't get your operation, and when you come back into the system to ask for help they say to you, "Oh no. You're a prostitute." Do you see how it works?

This quotation explains how transsexuals are marginalized because they are caught between institutions. Somewhere in the gaps between health care, civil status and employment, transsexuals must manage to survive.

This quotation is also important, however, because it illustrates how there is currently a two-tiered system of health care for transsexuals in Québec. Gender identity clinics require that an individual work or study full time in order to demonstrate social integration. Yet such work demands identity papers that correspond with one's appearance. As long as the person does not work, they do not have access to surgery. These administrative practices have distinct consequences for different transsexuals. Individuals who begin a transition with a significant work experience, a unionized job or a job in the government can often change sex and keep their position. In this way, they can enroll in the program of the gender identity clinic, are eligible for surgery and can change the name and sex on their papers. A young transsexual who works as a male clerk in a grocery store, however, does not have the same kind of job security when the person wants to begin to work as a female clerk. If fired, getting another job is not easy, especially given her papers. If she does not work or if she begins to work as a prostitute, she will not have access to a gender identity clinic and thus will not be able to change her papers. In this way, the administration of health services for transsexuals actually favours individuals who have stable employment. Youth find themselves the most marginal within transsexual communities. A political activist ethnography, based in the everyday experience of different transsexuals, illustrates the manner in which institutions reproduce class relations. Specific identity documents of name and sex, and the administrative procedures which govern their modification, favour the lives of individuals with stable employment and middle-class cultural capital. This case study exemplifies George Smith's (1995: 25–26) discussion of a "materialist epoché," in which an examination of how the everyday world functions, beginning with the standpoint of people located within it, explains how dominant social and economic relations are realized.

Further Development of Institutional Ethnography and Its Methodology

The data I have presented clearly indicate that it is necessary to understand the complex workings of a network of institutions: civil status, health, education, employment. Indeed, transsexuals in Québec find themselves marginalized as a result of the policies of individual institutions, but also as a result of the connection, or perhaps more accurately, the lack of connection and the absence of coordination between different institutional elements of social life. Studies in the field of institutional ethnography frequently limit themselves to one particular institution. Roxana Ng's (1988) study of immigrant women workers focuses on one particular employment agency; Dorothy Smith's (1987) research examines how the experiences of women and mothers, and the work they do in the home, are shaped by the institution of education; and Gary Kinsman (1995) considers the institutional management of homosexuality through a focus on law and state security. In all of these cases, the focus of analysis is on one specific institution. Such an approach has a great deal of insight to offer, particularly with respect to the kind of detail it can provide in understanding how institutions operate. Yet analysis that restricts itself to one institution can be limited to the extent that it does not understand the links or the lack of connection among different institutions, as well as the attending consequences for the institutional ordering of experience. To return to the case of transsexuals in Québec, we can observe that the difficulties they confront in integrating into Québec society result not simply from problems with one specific institution. Their difficulties need to be understood with respect to the ways in which different institutions relate to each other, especially the lack of coordination among them.

These examples of institutional dissonance parallel George Smith's (1995: 21) political activist ethnography work with people living with HIV/AIDS in Ontario who were confronted with "ruptures of consciousness" in their daily lives. They knew from personal experience and friends that AIDS was not necessarily a fatal illness in the short term, but the information they received from government, as well as its policies emphasizing palliative care, did not acknowledge such a possibility.

A visual image may assist our understanding here (see Figure 1). The lack of coordination among certain institutions creates a situation in which transsexuals are completely shut out from the institutional world. Gender identity clinics, for example, are mandated to evaluate transsexuals and to provide recommendations for surgery. Indeed, any individual who wishes to have genital surgery must provide two letters from recognized psychiatrists or psychologists authorizing such an intervention. The gender clinics, then, offer services of evaluation and recommendation that are intimately linked to a person's legal identity. Recall that transsexuals can only change their papers after genital surgery. In this regard, the approval or refusal of a gender identity clinic has tremendous implications for the lives of transsexuals, effectively determining who can change their papers. Transsexuals who are prostitutes, unemployed or drug users, for instance, cannot receive an authorization for surgery from gender identity clinics (Namaste 1998; 2000). In concrete terms, such individuals can access neither the services of a gender clinic, nor those of the Office of Civil Status. Within the visual provided in Figure 1, a wall between gender identity clinics and Civil Status represents such a lack of coordination among these institutions.

While some institutions are quite distinct, others are more closely related. In Figure 1, the institutions of the prison, the law and immigration are similar in their management of transsexuality in a variety of ways: a criminalization of prostitution in the law means that many transsexuals who work as prostitutes end up in prison (Namaste 1998, 2000). In a parallel manner, access to immigration and citizenship is complicated when it is discovered that an individual is working as a prostitute in Canada (Namaste 1998, 2000). In these institutional sites, a common professional discourse exists that frames transsexual prostitutes and drug users in terms of morality, deviance and the criminal. Figure 1 offers an arrow pointing to each institution to symbolize such collaboration. This type of institutional operation is qualitatively different than that discussed above, in which

Figure 1
Lack of Coordination by Different Institutions for Transsexuals in Québec

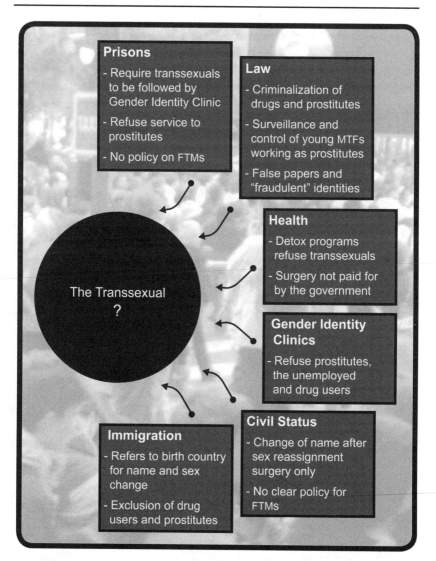

different institutional sites remain disparate and disconnected.

Figure 2 is taken from Dorothy Smith's (1987: 171) work on the reproduction of mothering and class relations within education. For Dorothy Smith, the experience of individual mothers is shaped by specific forms of work organization of mothering and teaching, in turn related to professional discourse and the bureaucratic organization of education itself. She illustrates the ways in which different forms of teaching reproduce class

Figure 2
Smith's Model of the Social and Material Relations of Mothering and Education

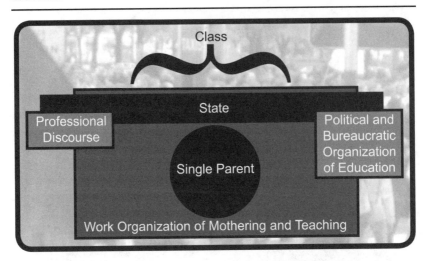

relations. Figure 3 builds on this model but offers an important nuance. Dorothy Smith's schema focuses on the single institution of education. My own research on transsexuals in Québec, beginning with the standpoint of transsexuals themselves, invokes a variety of institutional sites: law, prisons, immigration, health care, civil status and gender identity clinics. Figure 3 offers a visual representation of the ways in which these varied institutions shape different elements of experience for transsexuals in Québec. In some instances, such as those of law, immigration and prisons, there is a similar professional discourse at work. However, in different locations of the everyday world, such as gender identity clinics, civil status and health care, there is a noticeable lack of connection among these institutions and the professional discourses that they generate and with which they operate. Conceptions of civil status and identity papers, for example, are not fundamentally connected to matters of health care in government discourse and practice (Namaste 1998, 2000). Yet for transsexuals, these aspects of everyday life cannot be separated. The inability to change their identity papers pushes transsexuals to the margins of society: it prevents them from obtaining employment, it impedes their continued studies, it marginalizes them in health care, it forces them to live in poverty. The reproduction of class relations thus occurs not only as a result of one specific institution but also as a result of how different institutions are not coordinated.

These visual images seek to raise important questions with respect to the methodology of institutional ethnography. As the case of transsexuals demonstrates, the everyday world is lived in and through a variety of different institutional sites. In some instances, the lack of coordination among

Figure 3
Institutional Ordering of the World for Transsexuals in Québec

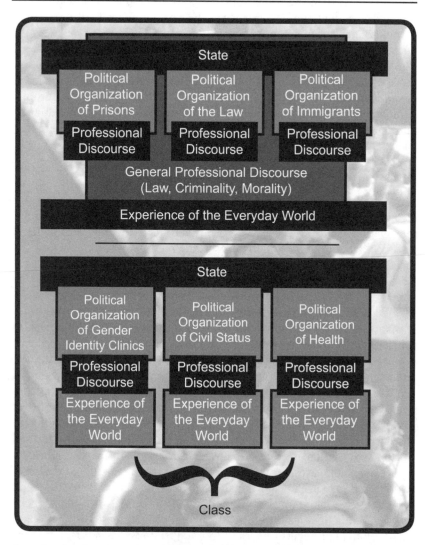

these institutions creates problems for people outside of ruling relations. To be even more precise, the lack of coordination among institutions is, in fact, what locates some individuals outside of ruling relations. Given this information, practitioners of institutional ethnography ought to devote some attention to the development of methodologies that allow us to understand the relations between different institutions, as well as their impact on the ordering of social experience. Everyday life is marked, of course, in and through different institutional contexts: education, employment, health care, civil status, the law. If political activist ethnography as outlined by George Smith seeks to understand the everyday world from the perspective of people, then the framework needs to develop a methodology that acknowledges that one's experience of the world is shaped not just by one particular institution, but by a variety of institutional sites. These sites may function in concert, or there may be a significant disjuncture among them. The empirical data presented in this paper, based on the standpoint of FTM transsexuals in Québec in the late 1990s, offers some concrete evidence of the political importance of such methodological reflection. As institutional ethnography and political activist ethnography develop and expand in the future, I suggest that it is important they consider these kinds of methodological questions in their research.

Concluding Reflections

This article has offered a case study of political activist ethnography. My research with transsexuals in Québec during the late 1990s offers important information as to how specific government departments administered matters related to transsexuality. Furthermore, it helps to explain how the social marginalization of transsexuals is directly shaped by the workings of different institutions. The case study illustrates the importance and value of institutional ethnography in the work of political activism.

Yet my research also suggests some innovative directions for the future of institutional ethnography and political activist ethnography. I wish to conclude with a brief consideration of substantive issues that could be explored further. As I do so, I suggest that these kinds of issues are best understood through integrating some of the methodological questions I raised as to the coordination, or lack of coordination, among different institutions. One matter to be considered would be access to health care for urban Aboriginal people, which research in the field clearly shows is a complicated bureaucratic situation (Native Friendship Centre of Montréal 2001; Ship and Norton 2001). Often, dispute over jurisdiction results in a virtual refusal of services: in some cases, provincial governments argue that the provision of health services to urban Aboriginals is a federal matter, while some federal representatives maintain that, depending on the service, it is a provincial question. On a practical level for Aboriginal people, these disputes about jurisdiction and budgets can result in inability to access services entirely. An adequate understanding of this situation, I submit, needs to consider the ways in which both federal and provincial health ministries work, as well as the possible lack of coordination among them. To take another example, one could consider matters related to state surveillance — for instance, proposals to have electronic health cards that contain an individual's entire medical history (COPHAN 2002). Increasingly, state governments are passing laws that authorize the sharing of information between different ministries (Kinsman, Buse and Steedman 2000). What are the implications of these kinds of laws? Could such information be used to make decisions related to immigration and citizenship? Could such information be shared with prison authorities without an individual's consent? Answering these kinds of questions requires a framework that considers not one institution in isolation but the relations among different institutional sites.

The field of political activist ethnography is exciting and promising, both for academics in the university and for political activists outside of it. As the field develops and expands in the future, its innovation and relevance will be strengthened to the extent that its methodology integrates a framework for understanding the connections and disjunctures among institutions.

Critical Thinking and Discussion Questions

1. How can institutional ethnography expand its analysis to include the relations among different institutions?

2. What specific case studies would lend themselves to such an approach?

3. How could such a framework be useful for political activists?

Notes

1. For example, transsexuals function in the world as men and women, but until their legal documents are changed, they are constantly informed and treated as members of their original, biological sex within specific institutional contexts.

2. The arbitrary interpretation of the law prevalent in the late 1990s has since been regularized. Legal proceedings brought before the *Direction de l'état civil* resulted in a clarification of the Office's practice, in which the surgeries required are those equivalent to the interpretation of the law before 1996 (hysterectomy, ovariectomy, double mastectomy and hormone treatment).

EXPLORING THE GLOBALIZED REGIME OF RULING FROM THE STANDPOINT OF IMMIGRANT WORKERS[1]

Roxana Ng

Introduction

This chapter discusses two seemingly unrelated subjects. The first is substantive: the plight of garment workers in Canada in the face of globalization and work restructuring. The second is methodological: the utility of a method of inquiry developed by feminist sociologist Dorothy E. Smith called institutional ethnography. I argue that it is through institutional ethnography that I am able to develop a *political* understanding of the plight of garment workers in the present era of economic globalization.

"Globalization" and "restructuring" are buzz words of the new millennium. The proponents of globalization see it in positive economic terms. For example, governments and corporations see it as a way of enabling businesses to move around the globe in search of markets and "flexible" labour, thereby augmenting profits. Dudley Fishburn, the editor of the 2001 special issue on globalization in *The Economist* saw it thus:

> 2001 will be a year in which the world becomes a richer and sharply more decent place. Europe will expand its wealth at the fastest rate for a decade.... The 2.3 billion people of China and India will organise their societies so as to double their prosperity every ten years. Globalisation will raise the standards of human rights, law, ethics and corporate governance around the world, even in dismal Africa. The revolution in communications lies behind this imperative. No pollution, no barriers, no dogmas, no sweatshops exist in the freer exchange of information. (9)

On the other hand, organized labour and the anti-globalization movement in Canada and elsewhere argue that globalization has led to work restructuring, job loss and depression of wages, thereby impoverishing working people.

Instead of taking up this debate merely ideologically, I examine the concrete experiences of people — working people — by means of a case study. I look at the transformation of the garment and clothing industry since the 1980s, partly through institutional ethnography, and identify the processes that have led to dramatic changes in this sector. I argue that globalization is not just economic or social; rather it indicates the convergence of a number of processes that are in a state of dynamic interaction with one another, leading to the constant transformation of work and lives. Changes in one sphere will inexorably affect other spheres. So far I have identified five spheres of activities that have produced changes in garment production and thereby in the lives of garment workers in Canada and elsewhere. I call the first four spheres "a globalized regime of ruling." However, the extent to which this regime can impose its reign on the lives of working people depends on the fifth sphere of activities, which I call "global resistance." These interactive processes are in flux as I write, so it is not possible to posit the precise outcome of this interplay. However, the findings I present here and my approach point to ways in which we can investigate the workings of globalization and political action.

I first describe, in general terms, some of the changes that garment production has been and is going through. I then discuss institutional ethnography as a method of social analysis that enables me to give a more encompassing, rather than narrow, understanding of the processes at work that transform garment production. I end by identifying, albeit not definitively, the globalized regime of ruling and global resistance that shape and transform people's livelihood in garment production. My discussion and analysis are based on my involvement in this sector and with immigrant garment workers, mostly women, since 1991, when I was asked to chair a sectoral labour adjustment committee on the garment industry. This period corresponded to the culmination of drastic re-structuring and massive lay-offs in the sector, with the result that the two major unions lost many members, and many garment workers lost their jobs. Since then, I have been working with the International Ladies Garment Workers Union (ILGWU), which merged with the ACTWU (Amalgamated Clothing and Textile Workers Union) to form UNITE (the Union of Needletrade and Industrial Textile Employees) in 1995, to document the history of this re-structuring and how it affected immigrant women workers. Between 2001 and 2005, I conducted a project, with UNITE as a partner, further investigating changes in the garment industry from the vantage point of workers, entrepreneurs, owners and others involved in the sector.[2] Unless otherwise stated, my discussion here draws on over ten years of experience working with key players in this sector, and especially from statistics and interview data collected in the study with UNITE (referred to as the 2001 study).

Re-structuring Garment Production

The garment industry in Canada is predominantly Canadian-owned. It is the eighth largest provider of manufacturing jobs and has historically occupied a secure position in Canadian manufacturing. As an industry that makes use of what are assumed to be women's skills (that is, sewing), the garment trade has always been an employer of female immigrant workers, first from Europe and later from Asia. According to Statistics Canada data in 1986 for Toronto, for instance, 94 percent of sewing machine operators were born outside of Canada, as were 83 percent of pattern-makers and cutters, and 83 percent of the employees in various textile industry occupations (reported in *The Toronto Star* September 21, 1992: A1). Whereas women constituted just 29 percent of the workforce in manufacturing, 80 percent of them were in the garment industry (Borowy and Johnson 1995).

There is a gender hierarchy within garment production. Men are the cutters; they are seen as skilled and are paid higher wages. Women are the sewers, and because their skills are acquired from domestic settings, they are seen as unskilled and earn much less than men (for a detailed discussion, see Ng 1998 and Steedman 1997). While garment production has always been cyclical, in that the production cycle ebbs and flows with the seasons, this sector had produced steady long-term employment for many immigrant women and men since the post-war period in Canada.

In the 1980s, however, this sector went through dramatic and contradictory changes. According to Borowy, Gordon et al. (1993), between 1985 and 1992, the ILGWU membership dropped by 60 percent, bringing the unionization rate from a high of up to 80 percent to below 20 percent. These authors assert that these changes corresponded to the signing of the U.S.-Canadian Free Trade Agreement (FTA) and the North America Free Trade Agreement (NAFTA), a picture corroborated by government statistics. According to Industry Canada (1996), between 1989 and 1993 the sector experienced a staggering loss of 800 plants and over 33,000 jobs, leading to the notion that the garment industry had become a "sunset" industry.

Meanwhile, statistics since the mid-1990s indicate that the industry has been growing, with both shipments and employment increasing (Gunning et al. 2000). Some segments of the industry, for example, private-label manufacturing, are booming, while others have undergone drastic downsizing. For example, the size of plants has decreased. In the early 1970s, 22 percent of shops employed less than twenty workers. By the early 1990s, 75 percent of shops employed less than twenty workers; in 2000, 85 percent of plants employed less than twenty workers. The majority of this 85 percent employed less than four people in their establishment (Yanz et al. 1999). It should be noted that this sector is highly complex, comprising twenty-one sub-sectors, from men's, women's and children's wear to uniform and shoe manufacturing. Thus, the effects of work restructuring are not uniform and do not affect sub-sectors and localities in the same way. For instance, the garment industry in Winnipeg, which uses workers from Third World countries on work permits and which produces heavy clothing such as winter coats, and the men's suit sub-sector, are less affected by restructuring because their production requires more standardization and machinery. Ladies' and children's wear, on the other hand, are subject to fashion and seasonal changes. They do not require heavy machinery and can therefore be sewn more easily by home sewers. These sub-sectors are therefore more susceptible to downsizing (Ng 2002).

Furthermore, since the 1980s control within the industry has shifted from manufacturers to large retail chains, such as Hudson's Bay (which owns Zellers), and increasingly to transnational chains, such as Wal-Mart, the largest retail chain in the world. Manufacturers in Toronto responded to their slip of control and technological changes in different ways, some adopting more than one method in order to survive. Since garment production is a relatively old industry and since many manufacturers have been in the business since the post-war period, one response by factory owners was to retire and close down their business. Some decided to produce off-shore, either by setting up factories in cheaper locations, e.g., Mexico, Bangladesh or China, or by contracting production to factories established in these areas. Off-shore production is also a major strategy used by retailers to keep production costs low, thereby further undermining local manufacturers. Another adaptive strategy was to become sub-contractors to retailers by becoming jobbers. This was done by reducing the production plant, retaining one to two cutters and laying off most sewers. The latter workers were re-employed as home-based sewers, thereby rendering the production process more "flexible." In our 2001 study, one of the vice-presidents of a medium-sized uniform manufacturing plant told us that in order to remain competitive, the company began to contract out to factories in Pakistan and other South Asian countries. Its Toronto plant was downsized from over forty sewers, when his father bought the business over twenty-five years ago, to under twelve sewers, who mainly did alternations from their off-shore plants and sewed customized uniforms. The Toronto plant was also used as a warehouse and distribution centre for off-shore shipment. The garment industry is now structured as a pyramid, with large retailers at the top, layers of contractors and sub-contractors in the middle, and workers at the bottom. Home-based sewing is an example of how the sub-contracting system works to maximize profit at the top (see Dagg 1996).

What are the effects of these changes on garment workers in general and sewers in particular? The kind of restructuring, partly in response to globalization (to be explicated below), I described above, means there is an overall decrease in wages and a corresponding deterioration of working conditions. Our 2001 study indicates that overall hourly earnings in Ontario have declined, from $7.13 in 1984, to $9.66 in 1993, to $11.16 in 2000 (O'Connell 2003: 7). These figures are in real dollars, therefore constituting a drop in constant dollars. A 1999 study I conducted also indicates that wages have not increased since the 1980s, when Laura Johnson (1982) did her study on home-based workers. The following quote from a home-based sewer interviewed in my 1999 study illustrates this point:

> The lowest salary I earned was about $3 per hour, with the same employers I'm now working. [I asked why she didn't complain about the low rate.] I didn't say anything at the beginning. I dared not. But now I start to talk to them about this. The kind of pocket-cover sewing I'm now doing also requires me to cut certain fabric before I can start sewing. But the employers don't count the cutting time. I told the employers about this. But they said that almost every homeworker asks them for a raise. But they get no raise from their contractor who gives them the fabric. I don't know other homeworkers who also work for them. It would be better if I know. Their factory is very small. They only have two workers in their factory, plus some part-timers, and the two owners.
>
> The highest salary I earned was around $8 per hour. That was the beginning when I first worked for these employers, when they let me know the piece-rate before I sewed. But now they don't tell me the piece rate before I sew.
>
> Every time I ask them for the piece-rate, they always say they haven't had time to think about it yet. At the beginning they gave me the piece-rate before I sewed. But now they don't. They never tell me the piece-rate until I finish sewing the garments. (Ng 1999: 7)

Concomitant with decreasing real wages is the erosion of union protection, benefits (such as some degree of job security in the heyday of the garment industry), and other labour rights as contractors/manufacturers downsized and cut overhead costs. As plants become smaller and workers are laid off, they lose their former union status and hence job security. As home-based sewers, workers experience increased isolation, not only from other workers but from labour monitoring processes. For instance, although in Ontario, home-based workers are covered under the *Labour Standards Act*, their isolation and anonymity make it extremely hard to monitor and enforce the legislation. Home-based workers and workers in small establishments also feel much more vulnerable and unable to bargain with employers. Thus, by the 1990s, sweatshops and home-based work (popularly known as homeworking), the early scenario of the garment sector, which disappeared in the heyday of the sector due to unionization, once again became an integral part of the garment industry in Canada.[3]

Understanding Restructuring and
Globalization from the Standpoint of Garment Workers

The picture I paint of garment production illustrates both the positive and negative aspects of work restructuring in the context of globalization. Rising levels of shipment and export indicate statistically that the industry on the whole was doing well, at least up to September 11, 2001.[4] At least some retailers and manufacturers are augmenting their profits and market share. Smaller shops, depressed wages and working conditions indicate that workers and smaller sub-contractors are increasingly squeezed out of a decent livelihood. The issue here is not a matter of whether the proponents or the detractors are right about globalization. It is: how do we understand the contradictions and changes we find in garment production? Here, I move away from seeing the world as having one truth to an attempt at understanding it based on a particular standpoint. What is considered "true" depends on *where you stand* and *how you look*.

The standpoint of garment workers, the standpoint I adopt in my analysis, identifies an epistemological and methodological starting point located outside of the institutional order that nevertheless gives rise to the experiences of the workers I study and work with. The term "standpoint" is a stronger word than perspective because it indicates a *political* vantage point from which one views the world and identifies the seer as an interested and invested knower, rather than a disinterested, neutral and "objective" one. Dorothy Smith first used the term, "the standpoint of women," as an epistemological point of departure in criticizing how knowledge is constructed in sociology, from the perspective of men who take for granted how the world appears to them.

Based on this critique, Dorothy Smith calls the subsequent method of inquiry she developed institutional ethnography. Institutional ethnography is, accordingly to Smith, decidedly *not* the study of institutions. The term, "institutional," identifies a complex of relations forming part of the ruling apparatus. "It does not only refer to a determinate form of organization, but rather to the *intersection and coordination* of more than one relational mode of the ruling apparatus" (Smith 1986: 8, my emphasis). That is, it draws attention to how institutionalized processes intersect and work together, albeit not always intentionally, to produce particular local effects. Put in another way, terms such as "institution" and "ruling apparatus" do not refer to fixed entities; they are through and through *relations* enacted by sensuous living individuals in particular settings, occupying particular social locations. One of the features of modern, or perhaps postmodern, societies is that regardless of the intentions of these individuals, their action, by virtue of their locations in the institutions, affect others in determinate ways. This theorization therefore shifts social investigation from human intention to an examination and analysis of social courses of action.

According to Smith, the term "ethnography," "commits us to an exploration, description and analysis of such a complex set of relations, not conceived in the abstract but from the entry-point of some particular people or a particular person whose everyday world of working is organized thereby" (1986: 8). Taking up the standpoint of garment workers and utilizing institutional ethnography as a method of inquiry thus allows me to link garment workers' (which are at once immigrant women's) experiences to the concurrent globalizing processes happening at the municipal, regional, national and international levels that are (re)shaping garment production and hence workers' experiences. This method closes the empirical and methodological gap between different levels of analysis (macro, mezo or mid-level, micro) common in sociological investigation and analysis.

Taking this approach, I identified at least four sets of processes that gave rise to the transformation I witnessed in the Canadian garment industry. Working together, these processes constitute what I call a "global regime of ruling," which produces many of the local conditions I saw in garment production that have the contradictory effect of augmenting production and profit on the one hand and creating sweatshop conditions on the other. I use the term, "regime" after George Smith, to indicate that these are not accidental processes (see G. Smith 1995; the term has also been used by Foucault 1980b). They are planned and effected by actual people in their actual everyday activities, working toward the integration of markets, including labour markets, on a global scale. I describe these processes in the next section, giving indication of how they affect the changes I described above. While my focus is on garment production in Canada, it will be seen that my discussion inevitably touches on conditions around the globe.

Exploring the Globalized Regime of Ruling

1. Corporate mergers and takeovers
The increasing concentration of capital through corporate mergers and takeovers has had a tremendous impact on the present-day configuration of the garment industry. The shift of control away from manufacturers to large, increasingly transnational, retail chains has centralized control of the industry, ironically rendering the production process more fragmented. Production is now carried out, not through large manufacturers located close to the market, but by layers of contractors and sub-contractors through a pyramid structure (Dagg 1996) dispersed throughout the world. As mentioned, this has forced the closing and downsizing of many local plants, displacing the livelihood of many garment workers and weakening processes of unionization and collective bargaining not only locally, but nationally and even internationally.

The shift of control in the garment sector and fragmentation of the production process is enabled by the electronic revolution. Computerized stock market activities are a good example of how trading is facilitated by this revolution. Internet technology enables money and goods to be moved faster and faster around the world. Companies are being traded and profits made by speculation virtually, instantaneously and simultaneously every day in stock exchanges around the world. It is through these activities that large mergers and takeovers are effected.

Another example, one that affects garment production specifically, is the electronic data interchange system (EDI). This kind of computerized technology enables retailers to keep better records of their stock and to keep less stock. Information on sales of garments on the rack can be communicated to production plants almost instantaneously anywhere in the world. This cuts down on mass production, storage and other overhead costs (see Borowy, Gordon et al. 1993). It was partially the use of this kind of technology that enabled retailers to wrestle control of the industry away from manufacturers.

2. The forging of trade agreements

The capacity of retailers and manufacturers to move across national borders in search of the cheapest labour cost is facilitated by trade negotiations and agreements between and among nation-states and international trade organizations such as the WTO (World Trade Organization). The Canadian government has taken a progressively active role in these trade agreements for over three decades, beginning notably with the negotiation and implementation of the Canada-U.S. Free Trade Agreement (the FTA) in 1989. Here I highlight only the major agreements that concern the garment industry directly and then look at the implications of these agreements for the industry and for workers' security and working conditions.[5]

Until the 1980s, Canada's garment industry was relatively protected by tariffs and quotas. Trade liberalization in the garment sector began with the signing of the FTA in 1989. Before the FTA, Canada's major apparel suppliers were China, Hong Kong and Korea. Since then, there has been a huge jump in the value of U.S. garments imported to Canada. According to Industry Canada statistics (1996), between 1988 and 1995, apparel imports from the U.S. increased at an average annual rate of over 25 percent. Although as a bilateral agreement, the scope of the FTA was limited, it is an important legal document because it set precedents for future trade negotiations, such as those around the North American Free Trade Agreement (NAFTA).

Trade liberalization was accelerated with NAFTA, implemented in January 1993. It played a major role in the re-configuration of the garment sector because it enables the movement of production and goods more freely between/among Canada, the U.S. and Mexico. Specifically, it enables manufacturers to invest in, set up or out-source to garment plants in Mexico, where labour costs are much lower relative to those in the U.S. and Canada. Indeed major Canadian companies such as Nygard International, which manufactures women's wear, and Gildan Activewear, the largest T-shirt manufacturer in Québec, now have plants in Mexico and elsewhere in Latin

America and the Caribbean Basin (see MSN 2000). This has led directly to job loss, depression of Canadian wages and the restructuring of garment manufacturing in the Canadian context. One strategy used by U.S. manufacturers, for example, is to ship U.S.-produced textiles to Mexico, where garments can be made much more cheaply, and then import the finished products back to the U.S. market, taking advantage of the free tariff and quota agreement of NAFTA (Vosko 1993).

Since the signing of NAFTA, Canada's apparel export to the U.S. has also increased. However, the advantage of NAFTA to Canadian manufacturers is contradictory. According to one analyst, the "rules of origin" in NAFTA limit Canadian manufacturers in two ways. First, these rules stipulate that duty is only exempted for products containing textiles made in North America. The high-end clothing produced in Canada, however, is made mainly with textiles imported from Europe. Since much Canadian-made clothing would be considered non-originating, the work of Canada's apparel manufacturers and their employees is effectively devalued. Thus, NAFTA sets unfair export limits and duties on Canada's most competitive garments. Second, the same rules also force Canada and Mexico to import yarn from the U.S., thus giving U.S. textile and apparel manufacturing an unfair advantage (Vosko 1993).

In terms of international agreements, Canada first participated in the Multi-Fibre Arrangement (MFA), negotiated through the WTO in 1974. The MFA involved negotiation, country by country, of bilateral quotas on garments that exporting countries from the South could send into Canada and other northern countries. This has protected the Canadian industry from southern countries that have a competitive edge in terms of lower labour costs, lower labour standards and fewer workplace health and safety requirements. In 1995, a new agreement, the Agreement on Textiles and Clothing (ATC) replaced the MFA. Under the ATC, worldwide apparel and textile quotas will be phased out by 2005. This will enable countries such as China to dramatically increase apparel and textile exports to western markets, thus significantly affecting garment production within Canada. The ATC will completely restructure garment production in Canada and globally, leading to further deterioration of workers' job security and working conditions in Canada.

Economic globalization, through trade agreements, has led to increasing competition among workers across national borders. For example, Canadian workers, who historically received protection through unionization and strict tariffs and quotas, now face intense competition from workers in countries such as Mexico and China, who are paid much less. This has led and will lead to further depression of wages and erosion of labour protection for Canadian workers. To keep existing manufacturers and investors and attract new ones, provincial governments will likely respond by further de-regulating labour standards. This has indeed been the strategy of the Conservative Ontario Harris and the Alberta Klein governments and is being valiantly pursued by the Liberal government in British Columbia. While the Ontario Liberal government has increased the minimum wage, it has not improved industry monitoring mechanisms. Thus we can expect that problems of enforcing the labour code will continue to plague the workers in this sector.

3. Legislative and coercive regulation of worker mobility

The adoption of the concept of "globalization" has been accompanied by a shift, by all levels of the state, in how to think about the economy and economic development. Analysts suggest that whereas in the 1950s and 1960s there was widespread consensus that national governments needed to play a key role in relation to economic activities, the opposite assumptions have been operative since the 1980s. Essentially, the new discourse of globalization, dominated by neoliberalism, subscribes to the view that the markets are uncontrollable and the only way to avoid being a loser is to be as competitive as possible. According to du Gay (2000), the globalization discourse both "defines the circumstances in which states find themselves and advocates particular mechanisms through which security might conceivably be obtained under those circumstances," suggesting that "survival is only possible by devolving responsibility for the 'economy' to 'the market'" (116).

This devolution has led, at the provincial level, to legislation and policies involving cutbacks of or privatizing social provisions, deregulating industries and services, and liberalizing employment standards. For example, in spite of the increasing phenomenon of home-based work, the Ontario government has consistently resisted reforming labour legislation to enable home-based workers such as domestic and garment workers to unionize across work sites. Furthermore, in Ontario the legal work week has been increased to sixty hours, without giving workers protection against employer exploitation. In Québec, the decree system, which offered sector-wide, rather than plant-by-plant, protection to garment workers, has been lifted, thereby weakening the ability of workers to bargain on a sectoral basis. By now, it is clear that cutbacks have seriously undermined the healthcare and education systems for many Canadians. What is more significant is the destabilization and erosion of the sense of security and community that many Canadians enjoyed previously.

This development works in concert with federal policies, albeit not in deliberate coordination, that support the mobility of investors and entrepreneurs while limiting that of workers and their families. For example, the expansion of independent-class and contraction of family-class immigrants[6] serves to produce and reinforce a workforce that meets the short-term needs of industries and businesses. The lack of social and educational provisions for family-class immigrants means that the capacity of a whole sector of the immigrant population is under-utilized. Another pitfall of Canada's immigration policy is the lack of fit between recruitment, settlement and labour-market placement once immigrants arrive. Although recently, Canadian immigration has focused on recruiting highly educated and skilled immigrants, once they enter the country, they almost always end up in jobs that have little to do with their prior education and work experience. To our surprise, in our 2001 study, fourteen out of the twenty-three workers interviewed had college education and had occupied professional jobs prior to immigration. The lack of "Canadian work experience" and at times the lack of English language proficiency meant that they were unable to find work commensurate with their education and experience, and they entered positions in the garment industry as a temporary measure. This mismatch in immigration and settlement policies and strategies has received a lot of government and media attention lately, and all three levels of government are allocating funds to retrain foreign professionals. What is important to point out here is that the effects of existing policies, working in relation to other policies and measures, have produced a captive labour force, many of whom are immigrants of colour and vulnerable to exploitation.

Legislative restriction of worker mobility is further evidenced since the September 11, 2001, terrorist attacks on the U.S. Accompanying the trend of restricting immigration and increased surveillance of immigrants and refugees is the increasing use of work permits, which effectively restrict the mobility and citizenship rights of groups of workers, frequently from Third World countries (Sharma 1999). Such workers are especially vulnerable to the whims of employers. Government action, especially increased monitoring of goods by the U.S., has served to curtail its trade with Canada. This has had a negative impact on the garment industry beyond the control of labour (O'Connell 2003). It can be seen, from this brief discussion, that while not designed in a coordinated manner, policies and legislation developed at different levels interact to produce particular effects on a sector and its workers.

4. The global movement of people

Globalization is frequently seen in economic terms; the term is used to refer to either the electronic revolution, or the integration of national economies and markets into a singular market, or both. What is frequently overlooked, and which I argue is an integral part of globalization, is the movement of people resulting from economic displacement, political unrest such as warfare or environmental disasters such as the tsunami that occurred on December 26, 2004. Whereas migrants such as farmers, labourers and convicts were recruited by nations and businesses to "open up" (read colonize) the New World during earlier periods of colonization in North America, in recent years we see the movement of people from the economic South to the economic North. There is, however, increasing evidence to pinpoint the link between the movement of capital and of people. Saskia Sassen's work on international migration, for example, shows the direct link between trade (in terms of export), foreign investment and foreign aid by the U.S. to Mexico and the Caribbean, and migrants from these localities to the U.S. (Sassen 1998). A similar pattern occurs between Japan, the dominant economic power in Asia, and illegal migrants into Japan from Korea, Bangladesh, Thailand, the Philippines, Pakistan and Malaysia (Sassen 1998, 2001). This is both because people from the South are in search of better economic opportunities and employment and because there is a demand for cheaper labour in selected sectors of the economy (see Sassen 1998; Kwang 1997). The garment industry, as we have seen, is a classic example, having thrived on immigrant labour since its inception in the post-war period. Indeed, immigrant labour has allowed this sector to maintain its competitive edge during the present period of economic globalization.

The movement of people is a complicated phenomenon, and involves legal and illegal migration. In Canada, legal migration involves individuals entering the country as permanent residents (called landed immigrants) in accordance with a rather elaborate classification system, or as temporary workers, whose length of stay and working conditions are strictly controlled. As mentioned, the garment industry has always relied heavily on landed immigrants, and to a lesser extent temporary workers, for its labour supply.[7] What is seldom discussed is the use of undocumented workers (that is, illegal migrants) to provide a cheap and vulnerable labour supply for industries and as a means to depress the wages and working conditions of local workers.

Frequently, illegal migration and human trafficking are seen to be illicit phenomena occurring outside the legal institutions and apparatuses of globalization (such as governments and the WTO). However, a recent exposé by investigative journalists and the work of U.S. historian Peter Kwang demonstrate convincingly the elaborate character of human trafficking. Kwang's long-term study of undocumented migrants on both sides of the Pacific shows that human trafficking is a highly coordinated transnational activity that involves international *business* networks facilitated by governments (more appropriately government officials), business agents, transportation companies and so forth (Kwang 1997). Indeed, he argues that the trafficking of people is a more profitable venture than drug trafficking (see also Murphy 2000). He and investigative journalists found that most illegal migrants eventually end up in the thriving (though restructured) garment industry in New York, Toronto, Montréal and Vancouver.[8] While the employers and union members we interviewed vehemently denied the use of undocumented migrants in the factories they owned and organized, a key informant in our 2001 study, who operated mainly in the U.S., confirmed their extensive use in garment production in Toronto and elsewhere. He quipped that of course no one in his or her right mind would admit to this; otherwise it would be a legal, not illegal, activity.

These studies indicate that economic globalization (that is, the integration of national economies and markets into a singular entity to facilitate the augmentation of capital) involves institutionalized activities at many sites and levels. Not only does it involve so-called legal activities that are coordinated and effected through documentary processes inscribed in laws, trade agreements, policies, reports, records and so forth, it also involves institutionalized processes that are illegal and undocumented, which feed directly into the documented and legal organization of society. The power of institutional ethnography is precisely its ability to bring these seemingly contradictory processes into a relation of dependence with one another and open them up to empirical scrutiny. Although recent iterations of institutional ethnography analyses tend to focus on textual analysis as the key component of present forms of capitalist social organization, my work on garment production reminds us of the importance of undocumented activities and how these two spheres of action dovetail each other.

Resistance and Mobilization: Institutional Ethnography as a Political Tool

I have sketched some of the institutional processes that are part of the regime of ruling underpinning globalization. Institutional ethnography enabled me to take up the standpoint of immigrant garment workers as a starting point, in order to map the complex intersecting relations and processes that affect the lives of these workers. For me, the power of institutional ethnography lies in its ability to link local experiences to broader social and global processes, which are not always immediately apparent at the local level. It also enables me to see the social organization of garment production as dynamic and changing, rather than static. If we see globalization as generated out of social relations that are interconnected in and through human activities, intentional and otherwise, then we see that all of us can and do play a role in this seemingly overarching and unalterable force. Mapping ways in which forces of globalization affect workers negatively can contribute to developing strategies of resistance and mobilization. Counter-forces of globalization, in turn, alter the contours of economic globalization by curtailing the relentless advent of capital in search of profit at the expense of the well-being and security of workers.

In terms of garment production, an example of a group which is a part of the anti-sweat movement is the Maquila Solidarity Network (MSN) in Toronto, Ontario. The MSN is a non-profit research and advocacy network of 400-plus organizations concerned with the detrimental impact of the globalized production circuit on workers. It traces Canadian manufacturers' involvement in garment production worldwide, tracking their movement and employment practices in Mexico, Central America, the Caribbean Basin, and more recently in Asia. Data generated by the research are used as the basis for campaigns to bring to light the situation of these workers and what Canadians can do to help. The group also collaborates with women's and labour rights organizations in the economic South, for example, by advocating for the development and implementation of codes of conduct governing garment production.

The work of MSN is an instance of how institutional ethnography research can be used to analyze and expose the interconnection between different processes that lead to the impoverishment of workers worldwide. This understanding, in turn, serves to inform strategies for resistance and mobilization. A recent action, coordinated by the Ethical Trading Action Group (ETAG), housed by the MSN, is the Fallout from the Phase-Out forum held on March 17 and 18, 2005, in Toronto, Ontario. This forum brought together a wide range of interested people, including unionists, activists, researchers, students, retailers (including the Mountain Equipment Co-op and GAP), investment advisors and others to explore the effects of and strategize around the complete phase out of the Multi-Fibre Arrangement and the institution of the Agreement of Clothing and Textile by the WTO.[9] In addition to information sharing, the aim of the forum was to develop strategies to curtail the exploitative and predatory practices of large retail chains. My own research is both informed by and informs the work of the MSN and people working in this sector.[10]

For me, the power of institutional ethnography goes beyond its academic and analytical utility. Its stance, located outside the ruling regime, enables the researcher to identify how ruling gets done and how to develop alternative modes of action to challenge regimes of ruling. It is thus through and through a political tool. Indeed, Dorothy Smith thinks of institutional ethnography as a subversive enterprise (1987: 222–25) that continuously opens the world as we know it up for examination. Since its aim is to problematize and investigate complex interconnecting institutional processes, institutional ethnography is also by definition a collaborative enterprise. It requires that people share information on what they know on the basis of their locations within institutional modes in order to gain an overview of how the system works as a whole and how to challenge and transform it. In the final analysis, it is only through action that we can rescue research from its position in the ivory tower, so that it can be used to transform the world for the better.

Critical Thinking and Discussion Questions

1. How can two radically different experiences of globalization arise from the same set of social relations? How does Ng's investigation, which begins from the standpoint of garment workers, help to make sense of this disjuncture?

2. How would a political activist ethnographer trace changes in the garment sector? What may s/he look for? Who may s/he talk with?

3. In what ways can a more concrete understanding of the organization of the garment industry contribute to more effective anti-sweatshop activism?

Notes

1. This chapter owes its beginning to a public lecture bearing a similar title that I gave at the University of Victoria in February 2001. I thank Marie Campbell for inviting me to test out my ideas there. The present chapter is based on a paper with the same title I presented at the Political Activist Ethnography Conference at Laurentian University, November 8–10, 2002, organized by Gary Kinsman. I thank Gary and Andrew Thompson, co-editors of the collection, for feedback on earlier versions of this chapter.
2. The project, "Changing Work, Changing Lives: Mapping the Canadian Garment Industry," was funded by the Social Sciences and Humanities Research Council of Canada. The financial support of SSHRCC is gratefully acknowledged, as is the work of the entire research team.
3. This phenomenon is corroborated by a documentary entitled, "Made in Canada," produced by Zone Libre of the Canadian Broadcasting Company, aired in French in November 2003 and in English in January 2004.
4. In our 2001 study, when we interviewed garment workers and employers about changes in the industry, a few mentioned September 11, 2001, as a marker for the downturn in the sector, rather than larger global trends such as trade agreements. Apparently orders from the U.S. practically ceased after 9/11 due to the unstable conditions in the U.S. Our study also discovered changes in custom regulations, which began to have an impact on cross-border movements of goods after this time (O'Connell 2003: 8).
5. This information is corroborated by presentations at the Ethical Trading Forum on "The Fallout from the Phase-Out," sponsored by the Ethical Trading Action Group on March 17, 2005.
6. Landed immigrants to Canada are classified in terms of their application status. Independent-class immigrants are those who apply on the basis of "points" obtained on the basis of their education, language ability, skills and other considerations. Family-class immigrants do not earn enough points and are sponsored by the independent-class immigrant or a relative already residing in Canada. There have been a lot of recent changes in naming different classes of immigrants, and therefore the terms used in this chapter should not be seen as necessarily current.
7. The city where this sector makes use of large number of workers on temporary permits is Winnipeg, through a special arrangement between the garment sector and the federal department of immigration (personal communication with Dr. Ray Weist and his research team at the University of Manitoba).
8. See the CBC Zone Libre documentary "Made in Canada" mentioned in Note 3.
9. The Multi-Fibre Arrangement, to be completely phased out by 2005, designated quotas for import from cheap labour countries in the South to the North. Thus its phase-out will enable the flooding of cheaper clothing from countries such as China in North American markets, further decimating its declining garment sector. Instead of blaming countries in the South for flooding North American markets, ETAG and the MSN, working with concerned companies, labour organizations and consumer groups, attempt to develop coordinated transnational strategies to curtail the relentless advent of large retailers and their contractors in both the North and the South.
10. The Homeworkers Association (HWA), consisting of mainly Chinese immigrant garment workers who work in factory and home-based production, is the local group that I work with most closely.

AGAINST ILLEGALITY: NEW DIRECTIONS IN ORGANIZING BY AND WITH NON-STATUS PEOPLE IN CANADA[1]

Cynthia Wright

I think that nobody should be prevented to go somewhere because the world is for everybody. —non-status person living in Canada (Khandor et al. 2004: 5)

In his essay, "What We Owe to the *Sans-Papiers*," French philosopher Etienne Balibar passionately argues that political contestation by undocumented immigrants in France has made a fundamental challenge to notions of democracy, politics, civil rights and citizenship (Balibar 2000). Interventions such as Balibar's are essential in the European context, where "immigration is threatening to become the central issue of politics," as it is in many other parts of the world (Sutcliffe 2003: 278). But Balibar's own work, as he acknowledges, is highly indebted to the autonomous formations of undocumented people in France who, since 1996, have carried out spectacular protests against the state production of their illegality and have developed their own highly sophisticated analyses of migration, illegality, exploitation and the politics of free movement (Hayter 2000).

In France, as elsewhere in Europe, the United States, Australia and Asia, organizing by and with undocumented and non-citizen people has in recent years become a pressing priority; it has also begun to unsettle longstanding assumptions within political theory and practice about borders, nations, sovereignty and the regulation of immigration. But as we look back since September 11, 2001, and observe the systematic tearing up of immigrant, refugee and indeed civil rights — not to speak of detentions, deportations, racist killings, physical and verbal harassment, burnings of mosques and Hindu temples, draconian anti-terrorist and domestic security bills, and much else — Balibar's essay and the various manifestoes of the *sans papiers* calling for an end to global apartheid appear wildly utopian, even as they remain politically more necessary than ever. For, as Muneer Ahmad has argued in an article on racial violence after September 11, "it is exactly in moments of nationalist, nativist, and militarist excess that we might develop greater acuity not only in our critique of prevailing politics, but in the imagined alternatives" (Ahmad 2002: 101).

In Canada, detentions, deportations and "national security" sweeps are not going uncontested, and immigrant and refugee rights struggles — rather than disappearing — have heated up significantly in the country since 2001. Daily my e-mail box fills with wrenching stories but also with accounts of resistance: a Brazilian woman goes underground with her children rather than be deported; a Pakistani man held in a bogus "national security" sweep is deported while his allies are pepper-sprayed and arrested; a non-status Afro-Latina woman living underground recalls the underground railroad in a letter to allies; a group of Arabs and Muslims assert their right to photograph Toronto's CN Tower free of surveillance and harassment by staging a day to do just that. In this chapter, I draw on my own direct involvement with immigrant rights campaigns — as well as on the collective work of others — to consider how the contestations of non-status and non-citizen people, together with their allies, have slowly begun to challenge media and official discourses that frequently position undocumented people as terrorists, criminals and a problem for "removal" from the national space. This chapter builds on political activist ethnography in order to locate those contestations and the standpoint of non-status people as a concrete resource — as the grounding — for understanding the making of key aspects of our social world.

Indeed, the campaigns of non-status people have made a very small opening to question ruling narratives and categories of official multiculturalism, citizenship and national security and to understand them as ideological practice. Specifically, such struggles have underlined the ways in which the institution of citizenship fundamentally relies on the production and reproduction of states of illegality and on the making of non-citizen "others" with inferior access to labour and other rights within the space of the nation-state. Nandita Sharma argues, "Categories of legality and illegality are... deeply ideological. They help to conceal the fact that both those represented as foreigners and those seen as Canadian work within the same labour market and live within the same society" (Sharma 2003a: 62). Such categories of legality and illegality, and the stratified statuses that accompany them, are more and more organized through documents that define access not just to paid work but also to social services, including basic ones such as food banks, and indeed many other aspects of everyday life (Lahn 2004). Crucially, such categories also structure "the forms of surveillance, discipline, and normalization to which they [migrants] will be subjected" (Luibheid 2005: xi).

Generated from the standpoint of ruling, the social construction of "illegality" appears wholly outside the daily lived experience of non-status people living in Canada. As one non-status Algerian woman living in Québec comments, "even though you are a non-status person you do not even realize it. You are working; you have friends; you go out; you try to have a life despite all the barriers, despite everything — which is just normal, just human" (Lowry and Nyers 2003: 67). It is only in the course of trying to carry out particular everyday activities, such as enrolling in school, that many non-status people realize the extent to which their ordinary courses of action place them in full confrontation with an immigration system that denies them a "just normal, just human" existence. This line of fault — the brutal rupture between the everyday courses of action (working, studying, socializing) that non-status people initiate and the violence visited upon these same human beings through detention and deportation — forms the central location from which powerful interrogations of the immigration system (and its ruling categories, including "legal citizen" and "illegal") are generated.

It has also become very clear — from the work of important groups formed to help security detainees, such as Project Threadbare and the Campaign to Stop Secret Trials in Canada — that "the nation's security" rests, crucially, on non-citizen insecurity (Murray 2004). Canada's new anti-terrorism and security legislation, passed after 9/11 following massive public and media debate about citizen civil liberties, is scarcely being used. The fact is that the *Immigration and Refugee Protection Act*, which originated before September 11 and came into effect on June 30, 2002, gives the state all the powers that it needs to easily detain and deport non-citizen people, and that power is being used. Law professor Audrey Macklin points out, "immigration law has long done to non-citizens what the Anti-terrorism Act proposes to do to citizens–without public outcry and with judicial blessing" (Macklin 2001: 394). A good example is the very notion of "terrorism as a discrete legal category of conduct"; before Bill C-36, this legal category "only existed within the confines of the immigration legislation," thereby locating "in law the figure of the immigrant as archetypal menace to the cultural, social, and political vitality of the nation" (Macklin 2001: 391, 392). This has been dramatically illustrated by the detention on "national security" grounds of some two dozen non-citizen South Asian men in Toronto on evidence that clearly would not hold up in a criminal court (Piepzna-Samarasinha 2004).

This chapter offers only a very preliminary analysis of how, post-9/11, "race" and citizenship in Canada are being reconstructed in the context of calls for a security perimeter, "illegal immigrant" squads, and limitations on the mobility and other rights of immigrants, refugees and citizens of colour in the name of national security. As Sunera Thobani has recently pointed out, what we are looking at is the institutionalization of racial and national profiling (Thobani 2002, 2003). Indeed, the whole question of what is new and not new about the forms of racialization and criminalization we are seeing now is an extremely important one with some clear implications for strategy and alliance-building (Ahmad 2002).

Rather, this chapter attempts to map some moments of emergence — to describe and begin to account for some of the important new directions in the immigrant and refugee rights scene in Canada: groups and actions that are a clear departure, politically and in social base, from many — not all — of the earlier formations and which are also linked to some of the *international* campaigns and political arguments around the demand for open borders. While I have already gestured to the critical importance of campaigns focused on the detention of non-citizens on security grounds, my primary focus here is on the community anti-deportation campaigns articulated to the demand for the regularization of all non-status people and in defence of the right of free movement. I hope these strategic reflections contribute in some small way to bringing our interlocking movements and campaigns — including anti-racist, labour, Aboriginal, immigrant rights, anti-globalization and anti-war among others — in closer alliance. While in many cases immigrant rights activists are focused on apparently highly localized campaigns — for example, to stop a particular deportation of a particular community member — the mass migration of people in a context of capitalist globalization is frequently central to the analysis offered by many. Moreover, given the centrality of "race," migration and citizenship to the formation of "national" labour markets and to constructions of nation and nationalism, immigrant rights campaigns are no mere sectoral issue but are at the core of the very possibility of politics in the contemporary context (Balibar 2004).

It is vital, therefore, that activists and activist academics begin to piece together some historical and contemporary accounts of grassroots and non-institutionally located anti-racist practice and to begin to situate them within a transnational framework (Lentin 2004). While we now have some fine scholarly accounts of the operations of racism in a number of areas of social life, we need historically specific and dynamic accounts of the agency of non-status people and of all the campaigns and actions carried out by those committed to anti-racist and immigrant rights struggle in Canada — or indeed elsewhere. As the contributors to the collection, *Rethinking Anti-racisms*, comment on the British case: "media and political anxieties around immigration have coexisted alongside a largely unwritten history of the struggle against immigration and asylum laws" (Anthias and Lloyd 2002: 11). And, as Chandra Mohanty reminds us, it is "imperative that we rethink, remember, and utilize our lived relations as a basis of knowledge" (1991: 34–35). Starting from the lived relations of everyday life provides us with a powerful place from which to challenge both ruling categories (citizen, refugee, migrant, "illegal") and also to re-invigorate our understanding of how processes of racialization and nation-making concretely work through, among other things, the erasure of non-status people as political subjects with their own standpoints.

Across Europe people are mobilizing under the banner of No Borders and in other campaigns to contest the terms of Fortress Europe, with its regime of greater movement within Europe while simultaneously subordinating people from the South. An issue of *New Internationalist* magazine is devoted to the theme, "The Case for Open Borders," and features an excerpt from the best-known English-language manifesto for an end to immigration controls, Teresa Hayter's *Open Borders* (Hayter 2000; Stevens 2001). The choice of theme for this issue is testimony to the new confidence and growth of such international campaigns and perspectives. The European Social Forum, held in London in 2004, provided a space for the framing of "migration as a social movement" and for the rejection of borders and of theoretical frameworks that can only understand the migrant as "victim" rather than political subject (Kelly 2005: 51). In France, the activism of the *sans-papiers* and *sans-papieres* — autonomous formations of undocumented people who insist on speaking for themselves — has provided an important model for undocumented people and their allies everywhere (Gutierrez Rodriguez 2004).

Outside Europe, in Australia, we have seen dramatic instances of refugees breaking out of detention and of direct-action campaigns to free, and give sanctuary to, refugees warehoused outside the country's main cities and on Aboriginal territories. And while most discussions focus on the so-called "migrant-receiving" nations in the North, people in the global South, for example, indigenous people and people of African descent in Colombia, have continued to draw attention to the ways in which they have been displaced by war, paramilitaries, capitalist "development" and their own states.

In the North American context, massive setbacks in immigrant rights in the U.S. since the 1990s have produced a new generation of tough and creative activists, many of whom are younger first- and second-generation immigrants of colour. Clustered in groups like the National Network for Immigrant and Refugee Rights (NNIRR), Desis Rising Up and Moving (DRUM), and around the publication *Colorlines* — to name a few — many articulate a total break with the politics of the U.S. melting pot and the myth of "immigrant America" (Chang 2000; Honig 2001; Khokha 2001; Kumar 2000; Lowe 1996; Martinez 1998; Sun-Hee Park 1998). Struggles led by migrant domestic workers and other emblematic figures (whether "legal" or undocumented) of the global city have led many to question the ideological framework of U.S. citizenship, the construction of "illegality" and the assumptions of nationally bounded organizing (Poo and Tang 2004).

Meanwhile, key alliances between the mainstream U.S. labour movement and immigrant groups, and renewed labour organizing among working-class immigrants, meant that a significant victory was achieved on the eve of September 11. A central — if not *the* central — demand of the immigrant rights movement, legalization for that country's estimated six to nine million undocumented, was moved onto the national political agenda (Bacon 2001). Unlike many Republicans, Bush seemed prepared then to back a limited legalization plan, no doubt with a view to capturing the sizeable number of Latino/a voters and shifting their loyalties from the Democratic to the Republican Party (Waslin 2001).

September 11 has been a catastrophe for all such legalization and workers' rights campaigns, and indeed for anti-racist and economic justice projects generally (Lee 2001). In the celebration of the heroic white masculinity of firefighters, police and (then) New York City mayor Rudolph Giuliani, the tremendous struggles waged largely by the city's African-American community for accountability from those same police and Giuliani were buried (Marable 2003). The number of undocumented people who died in the twin towers once again revealed the extent to which glittering world cities rely on a service sector with large numbers of both documented and undocumented immigrants (Sassen 1999a). In an article on 9/11 and New York City's Latino/a community, Arturo Ignacio Sanchez notes that some activists tried to effect a "symbolic shift" by talking about the undocumented people who died in the attack as "working heroes"; one goal of this move was to further the "struggle to secure immigrant amnesty in the United States and other nations" (Sanchez 2002: 149). But such a strategic move was no match for what Neil Smith calls the "manufacturing of nationalism" in the aftermath of 9/11: while the victims of the WTC attack came from some eighty-three countries, that story was quickly re-written in the interests of a United States bent on a permanent "war on terrorism"; for this reason, the victims had to be symbolically "nationalized" in media and political discourses and represented as American citizens in the name of whom the state could conduct war (Smith 2002: 98). Meanwhile, "illegal immigrants" and non-U.S. citizens were offered a visa if they provided tips about "terrorists" — even if no criminal conviction resulted from that information (*Globe and Mail* December 3, 2001).

The U.S. amnesty movement had planned to establish its strength and visibility in a September 25, 2001, demonstration in Washington, DC; it was called off. Attendance dropped off in organizations for the undocumented, and public events became very difficult. Many undocumented and non-citizen people feared they were about to be rounded up. And, of course, many were. Indeed, much-expanded powers of detention and the requirement for male visitors over sixteen from some twenty-five countries to register themselves by March 21, 2003, dramatically underlined the insecurity and precariousness of undocumented, non-citizen and refugee lives (Featherstone 2002; Lee 2003). Meanwhile, the ongoing militarization of the Mexico-U.S. border, not to speak of the presence of vigilante white ranchers who murder suspected "illegals," means that migrants continue to risk their freedom and their lives crossing that border (Davis 1999; Chaddha 2003–4). The demand for legalization was almost forced off the *public* agenda in the United States and may yet be sacrificed altogether, although Bush has floated a proposal for what is essentially a limited guest worker program.

While some activists have sharply (and correctly) criticized the failure of the mainstream U.S. labour movement "to challenge what is fundamentally oppressive to the undocumented migrant worker: American citizenship itself" (Poo and Tang 2004: 162), projects such as the Immigrant Workers' Freedom Ride, a labour-led campaign for legalization and immigrant workers' rights, have recently mobilized tens of thousands of people across the United States (Calpotura 2004).

Here in Canada, where organizations by and for the undocumented and their allies have been weak or non-existent until relatively recently, such regularization or amnesty campaigns have few precise parallels. Of course, the shift to the right in immigration policy in Canada, particularly evident since the early 1990s, did not go uncontested: groups such as the now-defunct Toronto Coalition Against Racism, for example, did for a number of years lead important campaigns, and there was significant grassroots organizing in Vancouver when several hundred migrants from China arrived in boats on the BC coast in the summer of 1999 (Wright 2000; Sharma 2003a). These formations may in some ways be understood as among the precursors for today's campaigns for free movement and for the regularization of all non-status people.[2] But radical immigrant rights work, with some exceptions, has historically had relatively little public or media profile in Canada. At one level, this is a question of scale; there are millions of undocumented people in the U.S., while the figures for Canada range widely from 20,000 to 200,000 (Lawton and Thompson 2001). But it is also, crucially, a question of political context and contest. A series of highly charged cases surrounding "illegals," as well as the mass campaign to stop Proposition 187, have contributed to a fierce public and media debate in the U.S. about immigration and opened up space for advocating the rights of undocumented people. Most importantly, undocumented people have also begun to come forward and speak on their own behalf — crucial in the North American media context, where literally putting a "face" to a political issue is key to how it gets framed (Berlant 1996).

An overview of current groups, campaigns and activities directed at the rights of undocumented and non-citizen people living in Canada reveals that, unsurprisingly, most appear to be clustered in Vancouver, Toronto or Montréal — the cities with the largest immigrant populations and with important and ongoing histories of anti-racist/immigrant rights organizing. In Vancouver, the Open the Borders! group, some of whose members had worked with the Asian migrants of 1999, organized an international activist/academic conference with a view to building a movement calling for an end to displacement and for no borders (Wright 2002). More recently, groups such as No One is Illegal–Vancouver are among those taking the lead in coordinating militant grassroots campaigns against detention, deportation and racial profiling. NOII–Vancouver has also been very active in forming alliances with Aboriginal people in the B.C. area.

In Toronto, Status Coalition formed in May 2001 when a group of undocumented Latino men in the construction sector approached a Toronto lawyer about their situation; the lawyer in turn put out a call to agencies serving immigrants to see who might be interested in initiating a campaign for regularization. The Ontario Coalition Against Poverty (OCAP), also based in Toronto, has expanded its powerful and galvanizing direct action approach to housing and poverty issues to include immigration case work, including undocumented people and refugees (Landsberg 2002; Lowry and Nyers 2003). No One is Illegal–Toronto, which often allies with OCAP on key campaigns, has carried out an impressive amount of work in its relatively short history, including public education and the coordination of anti-deportation and anti-detention campaigns. The group advocates for regularization for non-status people and is committed to the principle of free movement and to indigenous sovereignty. Other groups based in the city are leading related campaigns, among them working with migrant agricultural workers on temporary work permits and developing among Church-affiliated people a sanctuary space for refugees, especially now that the "safe third country agreement" has been implemented. People in smaller Ontario cities have been active as well, for example, in resistance to the building of detention centres in their communities.

Montréal is home to what is probably still the most visible and well-known campaign for regularization of non-status people, one that provides important testimony to what may be accomplished even in unfavourable conditions when non-status people self-organize and build a campaign with committed allies (Nyers 2003; Lowry and Nyers 2003). Based in the Algerian community, this campaign has provided an important model for subsequent organizing among other affected non-status communities in that city and for campaigns in other Canadian centres. The Algerian campaign was also notable for the way in which it mobilized the political energies of women through autonomous actions such as occupying immigration offices and leading women's marches. It began in the spring of 2002 when the federal government removed Algeria from the short-list of countries to which Canada does not deport. For Québec's thousand-plus failed Algerian refugee claimants, this removal was deeply disturbing news. They were to be deported to a country locked in a decade-long and deadly violent conflict — an Algeria so dangerous that the Canadian government warned its citizens to avoid tourist visits there. In response, the Comité d'Action des Sans-Statut Algériens (CASSA) advanced three basic demands: 1) stop the deportations; 2) return Algeria to the moratorium list; and 3) regularize non-status Algerians. By the fall of 2002, the last demand had expanded to include a call for the regularization of all non-status people living in Canada — a move that recognized the slow but growing support for such a demand in other parts of the country, particularly Toronto.

Working with the allied group, No One is Illegal–Montréal, and with the support of numerous individuals and labour, faith and women's organizations, the Comité put together a well-organized campaign of activities, including holding press conferences and rallies; making unscheduled visits to immigration offices; seeking sanctuary in a church; and giving public talks in Montréal and Toronto, all of which have garnered a significant amount of press coverage in both French and English. Certainly, the French-language ability of many Algerians has been a major asset in enabling the community to speak directly to Québec's francophone media and immigration officials at all levels; in this regard, they have an advantage not enjoyed by those non-status people who are not fluent in English or French and who may also lack effective allies who can act as interpreters. Much of the coverage is sympathetic to the claims of the non-status Algerians — particularly striking given that the campaign began not long after the events of September 11 and Montréal's Algerian community had been targeted as home to terrorist plots. CASSA members and their allies have repeatedly drawn attention to dangerous political conditions within Algeria but also to Canada's complicity in constructing that country as "safe" for North American business interests — and for sending people back "home." Indeed, as more than one analyst has argued, the two go together in the current neoliberal order: within the E.U., for example, "repatriation agreements" are becoming "an explicit condition of new trade deals: We'll take your products, the Euros say to South America and Africa, as long as we can send your people back" (Klein 2003: 10; Nyers 2003; Lowry and Nyers 2003).

CASSA members have insisted on their claims as *refugees*, and indeed such a strategy is important in a context in which claims for the right to permanent residence of non-status *immigrants* can often, by comparison, be more difficult to argue successfully. Bob Sutcliffe put it succinctly, "Political migrants are in principle characterized as helpless victims who deserve help. Economic migrants are increasingly portrayed as selfish, grasping people, only out to get more money. The distinction has therefore been made into a moral one between good and bad migrants" (Sutcliffe 2001: 76). Yet it must also be acknowledged that the category of "political migrant" or "refugee" is itself increasingly under attack in the neoliberal context (Pittz 2002; Sassen 1999b) and the figure of the "bogus refugee," as well as the "illegal immigrant," is ubiquitous in popular and media immigration debates (Sutcliffe 2003). What is more, such distinctions are not mere weightless ideological constructions, for they currently find concrete manifestation in the greater use of detention — now made easier with the new *Immigration Act* — to hold the "illegals" and the "bad and the bogus" among refugee claimants. Moreover, the construction of both "bogus refugee" and "illegal immigrant" is occurring in a context in which rates of acceptance of refugees are declining rapidly and in which it is considerably harder now to enter the country under the points system. At the same time, the system relies more and more on temporary workers, on proliferating categories of workers each with different (or no) entitlements to services, family reunification and citizenship (Cohen 2002).

But there is still another category at work here: "immigrant criminals." In the French context, in particular, the so-called "double penalty," whereby non-citizens convicted of crimes and who serve their sentences are also deported (a form of second penalty that obviously does not affect citizens), has been the object of important mobilizations as well as appeals to the European Court of Human Rights (ECHR). Here, then, is another important line of fault: the production of two types of criminals (citizen and non-citizen) with *different* penalties for *identical* criminal acts has been revealed as ideological by those persons who are most subject to it: so-called "non-nationals" — often people with long residencies in France. As Jacqueline Bhabha comments in her review of such cases at the ECHR, "deportation of third country nationals has become an arm of post factum immigration control, a mechanism for the current French administration to produce a 'fictive ethnicity' and to concretize the sense of a racially homogeneous French national identity" (Bhabha 1998: 617). Such deportations have also long been an issue in Canada, and the new *Immigration Act* makes the deportation of "immigration criminals" still easier. Regularization programs, such as the one that Algerians in Québec eventually won, threatened to exclude some in the community based on minor criminal convictions. This experience suggests that confronting directly the process whereby immigrants are criminalized and subject to the "double penalty" will continue to be a major challenge. Moreover, the resignification of the terms we have been using in working within immigrant and refugee rights campaigns suggests that the strategic implications of working within and against state categories such as "immigrant," "refugee," and "temporary worker," among others, will need to become the focus of much greater scrutiny and reflection by activists.

What is clear is that the figure of the failed refugee claimant is the most politically visible non-status person, rather than the (undocumented) "immigrant worker" more characteristic of other national settings, such as the United States. When one is faced with a relatively immediate threat of deportation, as is the case for people who are "failed" refugee claimants, organizing with others in the same situation often makes a good deal of sense. Indeed, the activity of "failed claimants" in resisting their own detention and deportation has created new standpoints for producing knowledge about how the system operates and for opening up political space for challenging "removals" even if the ruling category of "refugee" does not always itself come under explicit challenge. It has proven much more difficult for non-status immigrants to organize themselves; those who are not refugee claimants, who have lived without status in the country often for many years and who do not face an *immediate* threat of deportation are often made invisible. Organizing can appear too much of a risk. This exchange between two people living without status captures the point: "A:

I asked a person to come to this meeting and this person said to me, 'You go and if you get anything let me know.' What do you call that? Laziness. B. No, that's called security" (Khandor et al. 2004: 6). Very often, the best strategy is to remain underground. Those underground are not, however, wholly silent even if they are often made to disappear in ruling discourses and even if they cannot be present in street-level mobilizations. Those who are undocumented and underground in fact live, love and work alongside those who are "legal." In many cases, those living underground are assisted by those with status — by people who in one way or another live the bonds of human solidarity. In some cases, undocumented people are also able to access the social services of those few community organizations that have undertaken to meet the needs of human beings regardless of citizenship status. In these often unrecognized ways, undocumented people appear as active agents within their own lives and with a clear knowledge of how the economic system rests on their unacknowledged exploitation.

These diverse formations and campaigns in Vancouver, Toronto and Montréal are exciting, and many are breaking new ground. It is clear that a "no borders/no one is illegal" politic is capturing the political imagination of many anti-globalization and anti-war activists, many of whom are younger people of colour with immigrant or refugee backgrounds who want a much stronger anti-racist analysis integrated throughout these movements. This is obviously reflective of some of the international conversations in the anti-globalization movement. Radical anti-deportation, anti-detention and no border campaigns in Europe and, more recently, Australia are an obvious major influence, but conditions in Canada are also radicalizing many. These conditions include increasing detentions, deportations, racial and national profiling, arbitrary treatment, surveillance and the general *normalization* of official violence against undocumented and non-citizen people.

Tired of the racism and not inclined to take up old defensive arguments about "the contributions of immigrants to Canada" or indeed about the basic fairness and soundness of the immigration system in the face of attacks on it from the right, younger activists are elaborating a different political language that speaks both to the causes of displacement globally and to the right of people to move across borders freely with full labour, social and political rights. It is a politics that, for some, may also be explicitly linked to an anti-national and anti-colonial perspective and one which attends to the need to bring together Aboriginal rights and im/migrant rights through a common critique of displacement, dispossession and of the power of nation-states to construct regimes of racialized and gendered citizenship (Marmon Silko 1994; Moreton-Robinson 2003; Wright 2002).

It is important not to overestimate the strength of these autonomous groups; many are relatively new, somewhat fragile and all are under-resourced. There is no social movement around migration in Canada, only small networks of very hard-working activists. Typical of grassroots organizations, the work is often highly labour intensive, unpaid and involves a willingness to confront bureaucracies and officials head-on. Such an approach differs distinctly from that of more long-standing refugee rights groups or agencies serving immigrants — many of which have long emphasized strategies based on lobbying and changes to the law, and many of which may be reluctant to publicly defend those whom the state constructs as "illegals," much less advocate an open-borders position. Service agencies facing funding cuts, restructuring and a conservative political climate may be unwilling — or too burdened by existing demands — to implicate themselves in high-profile campaigns.

At their best, allied organizations may embody what is most effective about a grassroots organizing approach: working directly with those most affected — whether they be detained, undocumented, migrant workers, refugees, deportees — in order to make concrete change in everyday lives and, in the process, democratizing knowledge and analysis about the law and much else. The emphasis is on collective decision-making, democratic involvement of affected and allied people, and building solidarity. As one immigrant rights activist in Montréal has commented, "The important point is that any campaign has to be based on the lived reality of immigrants, refugees, non-status, of illegals, of people on the front lines. Their lived reality. And that lived reality, again, is about fake passports, the indignities, all the things to do with the system. But also that lived reality is that these are acts of self-determination" (Lowry and Nyers 2003: 68).

For both non-status people and their allies, the immigration system is experienced (at best) as wholly arbitrary and bureaucratic and (at worst, and often) racist. As one non-status person commented about immigration officers, "There are rules, but they turn their back on the rules. Identical cases get treated differently" (Khandor et al. 2004: 17). As George Smith shows in his discussion of political activist ethnography, how the system actually works, how it is organized and coordinated through particular texts and ruling categories is very often invisible and only begins to become visible to those located outside it through moments of confrontation and contestation. Collective organizing makes visible to people that the immigration system has a way of doing things but also that it can be interrupted. As one non-status Algerian woman commented on the women's occupation of (former immigration minister) Denis Coderre's office in Montréal: "This would take away from their image of their administrative life, of things done normally. This would ruin that. So that's how we approached it" (Lowry and Nyers 2003: 70). What is more, non-status people and their allies have rendered visible the often-invisible and violent parts of the system of detentions and removals by staging actions at each part of the process and making of them a site of contestation. The recent deportation of the non-status community activist, Wendy Maxwell, for example, was accompanied throughout by such interventions — including at the airport the morning of her removal.

Anti-deportation campaigns, whether organized around an individual or a group, remain fundamental to our organizing for obvious reasons; one of them is that, without secure residency, a person cannot claim other rights. But case work has major limits and is ultimately unsustainable (Lowry and Nyers 2003: 71). For one thing, very few anti-deportation campaigns are successful these days. The immense amount of work involved means that little energy is left over for broader community organizing, much less sustaining long-term, transformative struggles around immigration and borders. Hard-won interim or partial successes in individual immigration cases or, more rarely, an affected community such as the Algerians are simply not translated into long-term change. In Toronto, groups and individuals have come together in a "city sanctuary" campaign, a popular strategy in the United States, where a number of cities have adopted a "Don't ask, don't tell" policy. This means local authorities may not ask about immigration status and individuals do not have to reveal it. Along with broad campaigns for the regularization of all non-status people, the "Don't ask, don't tell" demand is one way activists are trying to raise immigration issues beyond the immediate and incredibly labour-intensive space of the anti-deportation campaign (Amuchastegui 2004).

But without national coordination and, ultimately, transnational alliances of all kinds, gains will be limited. Such work in Canada is, in many ways, still in formation, although there have been important attempts in conferences in Montréal and Toronto to hammer out a nationally coordinated, long-term campaign with a core set of demands, a basis of unity, a plan of action and an organizational structure flexible enough to accommodate existing local formations/campaigns. Recently, Solidarity Across Borders organized an historic week-long march of non-status people and their allies from Montréal to Ottawa to press for regularization, an end to deportations and detentions, and the abolition of the security certificate used to hold non-citizens indefinitely.

Coordination is indeed evident in the way in which local campaigns are able, increasingly, to articulate similar broad demands and to mobilize in response to key emergencies such as the seizure of non-status Algerian activist, Mohamed Cherfi, from a Québec City church where he had sought sanctuary, or to the arrest of non-status activist, Wendy Maxwell, on International Women's Day in Toronto. However, there is no equivalent of the U.K.-based National Coalition of Anti-Deportation Campaigns. Links between activist campaigns and important allies such as the labour movement remain underdeveloped, despite the important work carried out by individual labour activists in unions such as the Canadian Auto Workers. Compared to the U.S. and the U.K., the conversations in the organized labour movement in Canada about organizing undocumented and non-citizen people are limited, and largely confined to the hotel, construction and agricultural sectors, where many temporary workers and undocumented people work.

So, what now? On both sides of the Canada/U.S. border, immigrant rights movements and organizations have been re-grouping, re-building and re-thinking strategy since September 11. In the Canadian case, as we have seen, significant new organizing has in fact emerged *since* 9/11 in spite of — and indeed because of — conditions that increasingly become more deeply unfavourable. But the crucial fact still remains that the current "war on terrorism" and its associated projects of homeland and national security are making the costs of political agency too high to be sustained by racialized non-citizens, above all those without legal status. In what follows, I want to comment on some of the broad strategic dilemmas currently facing activists; such an analysis ultimately needs to consider how to bring together political questions that were alive well *prior* to September 11 (for example, struggles around Aboriginal self-determination or the deportation of Afro-Caribbean people) with the newer challenges and racialization processes/targets we currently face (Browne 2002). My focus here is on Canada and the United States. While many activists have been most influenced by European and Australian "no border/no detention" organizing, the fact is that Canada's geographical and political/economic relationship to the U.S. empire needs to be the focus of some serious analysis, reflection and cross-border action. It is in this context that the lack of ongoing coordinated work between activists on either side of the Canada/U.S. border emerges as a very serious weakness. My analysis will necessarily remain partial and preliminary given the sheer number of changes that have occurred since September 11, as well as their far-reaching implications, not all of which are clear. Moreover, the so-called "war on terrorism" — which many have argued is in essence "a war for U.S. globalism" — has created a very volatile political context, which continues to shift quite rapidly (Ali 2003; McAlister 2001; Smith 2002).

What *is* abundantly clear is that, as one U.S.-based activist commented, "The 'homeland defense' agenda and the war are two parts of the same thing" (Quiroz-Martinez 2002: 32). In his provocative essay on the "manufacturing of nationalism," Neil Smith suggests a way to elucidate this relationship by asking, "A global event and yet utterly local: how did September 11 become a *national* tragedy?" (Smith 2002: 98). His essay details some of those national practices in the immediate aftermath of 9/11, all of which were reinforced — and yet simultaneously revealed for analysis — by anxious media silences, gaps and outright censorship. One move, as we have seen, was to "nationalize" the victims as Americans ("Why do they hate us so much?"), but others included immediately shutting down the borders and airports; defining terrorism to exclude "Americans"; and closing the stock exchange for several days, thus "revealing in stark outline the very real fusion (and confusion) of an ideological Americanism with the interests of global capitalism" (Smith 2002: 101). If national victims had to be identi- fied, so too did national enemies — both abroad (Afghanistan, then Iraq) and, crucially, at home. Racial and national profiling, and much else, has been the result. The ideological and practical work of constructing the WTC attack for U.S. nationalism was necessary in order to lay the groundwork for the violence and war that followed since "nationalism *is* the discourse of war under modern capitalism, in which the national state has cornered a monopoly on violence. In this case it is a national monopoly over violence asserted at the global scale" (Smith 2002: 104).

One clear dilemma is that, despite the emergence of an international anti-war movement, its North American wing simply does not (yet) have the strength to turn back the discourses/practices of homeland and national security. But without a highly organized and broad anti-war movement that clearly addresses both the war and domestic racism, the rights of immigrants of whatever status, as well as citizen people of colour, will continue to erode dramatically, for "national security" is an extremely powerful and mobile discourse. As Kinsman, Buse and Steedman state, "Under its regime, those who are defined as 'security threats' can be excluded from regular human and citizenship right." (2000: 281). The detentions, semi-secret trials and abuses of all sorts currently taking place on both sides of the border (and beyond, as in Guantanamo) provide ample evidence (Choudry 2005; Hagopian 2004; International Civil Liberties Monitoring Group 2003; Meeropol 2005; Ratner and Ray 2004). General calls at anti-war rallies and forums to defend civil liberties, including those of immigrants, refugees and racialized communities, are certainly important at one level; they are also wholly inadequate given the dimensions of the racist nationalism that we are dealing with here for they do not confront head-on the institution of national citizenship and the exclusions it organizes (Nadeau 2002).

A broad key strategic point, then, is that we must understand immigration and anti-racist politics as deeply bound up with anti-war politics, and vice versa. In Canada, we are seeing some renewed public debate about U.S. imperial power. Deeply important as this opening has been, the force of such critiques has often been blunted by perspectives that centre the "loss of Canadian sovereignty" as the key issue; one challenge, then, is to develop a very different kind of analysis, one that asks the questions from the standpoint of immigrants, refugees, undocumented people and racialized communities (Sharma 2003b). This means, among many things, challenging directly the discourses of nationalism and "national security." We have to continually ask: whose security? whose nation? In Canada, this poses a number of particular difficulties. For a start, the national security apparatus has, historically, been *more* secretive in fact than the American one. Second, despite important books such as the accessible academic collection, *Whose National Security?*, on the history of state surveillance and its targets (Kinsman et al. 2000) and journalist Zuhair Kashmeri's *The Gulf Within* (1991), on the harassment of Arabs and Muslims in Canada during the Gulf War, it is striking how few people seem to have a working knowledge of even the recent history of the security apparatus in Canada. One consequence of this has been that the iconic memory that was frequently invoked in debates and forums about civil liberties and "national security" in the months after September 11 was that of McCarthyism and Cold War United States. Yet, without that historical memory and analysis, we will not be able to identify some of the continuities (as well as discontinuities) with past racisms and national security practices (Iacovetta et al. 2000; Oikawa 2002).

Challenging the terms of "national security" also means resisting any move to re-frame existing immigration campaigns within that discursive framework. In the United States, for example, some have sought to present the demand for legalization of undocumented people as a security measure. As an activist with the Border Network for Human Rights commented, "I have fears that some people, including our *compañeros* in unions, believe the only way to get legalization is to define it as an issue of national security, as a process for identifying everyone" (Quiroz-Martinez 2002: 32). The undocumented movement in the U.S. gained significant ground by forming a key alliance with the labour movement; therefore, the AFL-CIO's re-affirmation in December 2001 of support for legalizing undocumented workers was very important. But the AFL-CIO's acceptance of limitations on the rights of non-citizen workers was a major, though not surprising, setback (Quiroz-Martinez 2002: 32). On this side of the border, the finding by Canada's Auditor-General, Sheila Fraser, that some 36,000 "illegals" have not been deported or accounted for is being framed as a security issue by the media (Clark 2003). The various groups calling for regularization have for the most part resisted the move to pose status for undocumented people as a national security question. At the same time, such campaigns — as in the United States — have been nowhere near strong enough to form a counterweight to border panics about "illegals" and security.

While campaigns for regularization of undocumented people in both Canada and the United States continue to be deeply necessary, we also have to confront the fact that, as Jane Bai and Eric Tang have argued for the U.S., "The 'war at home' has shifted the dividing line from documented vs. undocumented to citizen vs. non-citizen" (Bai and Tang 2002: 29). The post-9/11 context makes much starker what has always been a reality: merely being "legal" is never enough in the absence of full social, labour and political rights. Being "legal" is little use if you can be easily detained and/or deported. Recent changes in U.S. legislation mean that the rights of non-citizens have once again been dramatically reduced. Canada's new *Immigration Act* makes the detention and deportation of non-citizens easier. Then Prime Minister Jean Chrétien further underlined these realities by his stunning refusal to defend the rights of permanent residents in Canada facing racial and national profiling in the United States: "If they do not have a Canadian passport, it's no longer my problem.... Let them become Canadian citizens, and we will protect them" (Clark 2001). But the fact is, as Bai and Tang also acknowledge, *citizen* rights of people of colour are always precarious; the aftermath of September 11 has dramatically served to high-light this once again. The Canadian state appears unwilling to vigorously protect the rights of Canadian citizens apprehended, detained or kidnapped by U.S. authorities; figures such as Shakir Boloch, who was detained in the U.S. for months and released through the efforts of the Ontario Coalition Against Poverty (Oziewicz 2002; Lee 2002) or, famously, Maher Arar come to mind. Challenging the terms of racialized citizenship must, therefore, be added to the long list of political priorities for the current context; one immediate implication is that we need to challenge any attempt to further widen distinctions between citizen and non-citizen, and also distinctions *within* those categories. Ultimately, however, it means challenging the institution of citizenship itself.

A key part of the U.S. "homeland defense" agenda — with its racial and national profiling, arbitrary detentions, destruction of civil rights and much else — is bringing Canada and Mexico into it through the creation of a so-called "security perimeter." Naomi Klein has commented that the U.S. is constrained both to lock down its northern and southern borders *and* to demonstrate to business interests that delays at the border will not cost them money — currently a serious problem. The way around this apparent conflict in imperatives is to harmonize borders and make Fortress NAFTA: "How do you have air-tight borders and still maintain access to cheap labor? How do you expand for trade, and still pander to the anti-immigrant vote? How do you stay open to business, and stay closed to people? Easy: first, you expand the perimeter. Then you lock down" (Klein 2003: 10). The U.S. has exerted serious pressure on both "Canada and Mexico to harmonize their refugee, immigration and visa laws with U.S. policies" (Klein 2003: 10; see also Klein 2001; Gabriel and Macdonald 2004). The ongoing and active ideological construction since September 11 of Canada's border as porous and a conduit for "terrorists" to cross into the United States must be understood in this light.

One of many ways that the terms of the security perimeter might be challenged is from the standpoint of policing, prisons and detention. The province of Ontario is highly committed to a detention system along the lines of the now-notorious Australian one (Zwarenstein 2001). It is also clear that one key component of the practical implementation of the security perimeter is the greater integration of policing *across* borders, as well as *within* each country, as Toronto's recent Great Lakes Security Summit makes clear. U.S.-based activists Bai and Tang, in an analysis of "The War at Home," argue that what can potentially provide a unifying focus for U.S. anti-racist and immigration rights activists post-9/11 is renewed organizing directed at policing and "the prison industrial complex," which are being dramatically reorganized and expanded to target a whole new range of non-citizen and undocumented people, in addition to the African-Americans and Aboriginal people who have been — and continue to be — among those most likely to be racially profiled and incarcerated (Bai and Tang 2002: 29; see also Sudbury 2005; Welch 2002). Their analysis is aimed at linking contemporary immigrant rights agendas with the historic struggles led by African-American and Aboriginal people — struggles that are often articulated separately in the U.S. context. While policing, prison and detention struggles in Canada have differed in some important ways from their U.S. counterparts, as have the respective social movements, such a political focus could be potentially unifying of Aboriginal, anti-racist and immigrant/refugee rights groups in Canada as well. In short, as Bai and Tang bluntly put it: "The immigrant rights movement can ill-afford to view state violence as peripheral to its long-term core issue, legalization of the undocumented" (Bai and Tang 2002: 29).

In recent years, we have seen the development of striking new campaigns across Europe, the United States, Asia and Australia, as refugees, immigrants, migrant workers, undocumented people and their allies have sought to challenge controls over the right of people to move freely within and across borders. They offer important examples of undocumented people as *political agents* and have captured the imagination of numerous allies, artists and political theorists. Campaigns emerging in Canada — among them renewed calls for the regularization of undocumented people, self-organizing by non-status people themselves, anti-deportation/anti-detention work, defence and sanctuary — have clearly been influenced by local developments but also by transnational conversations within the no-border and anti-globalization movements and by the campaigns for legalization south of the border.

In the United States, where millions of undocumented people live without status and full labour rights, immigrant rights campaigns have focused on the call for amnesty and have clearly demonstrated what U.S. political theorist Bonnie Honig describes as "the potential power of the undocumented as political actors, labor organizers, and community activists" (Honig 2001: 82). Her work reminds us that, while anti-immigrant legislation, policy and practice may appear to be about keeping (some) people out, the dependence of the U.S. economy on migrants suggests that the goal has been not so much stopping cross-border migration but criminalization — and making the costs of political agency and visibility too high to be sustained by immigrant communities (Honig 2001: 82). But mass organizing by immigrant communities and their allies continued in spite of this ongoing criminalization, and, after years of setbacks, it was finally looking like it might pay off as legalization began to seem like a realistic political possibility.

However, the events of September 11 — immediately appropriated for a U.S. nationalism bent on war — have led to a "homeland security" agenda that has exacted a terrible toll on all projects for racial, economic and gender justice in the United States and will have lasting effects on the political mobilization of immigrant and racialized communities within the United States and also Canada for many years to come. The so-called "security perimeter" is the extension of many aspects of the "homeland security" agenda to Canada and to Mexico; on the northern border front, this has been accompanied by numerous border panics about "terrorists" and "illegals," as well as calls for new powers of detention and so on. It has also dramatically underlined the need to deepen and internationalize our often locally and nationally bound immigration struggles.

Yet, there are some signs of hope: namely, an unprecedented anti-war movement, building in part on prior anti-globalization activism. Yet, on both sides of the Canada/U.S. border, there has been a failure to fully connect the anti-war movement with a clear and direct challenge to surveillance, detention, racialized citizenship and national security logics. One way to do that, I suggest, is to begin to examine current border panics and nationalisms from the standpoint of immigrants, refugees and the undocumented. Regularization and other immigrant rights campaigns, for their part, now face more starkly than ever the problem of state violence and criminalization and will need to re-shape alliances and strategies accordingly. The stakes are now vastly higher than when Balibar wrote his well-known manifesto in support of the French *sans-papiers*. But that fact changes nothing about his analysis. Of the undocumented, Balibar writes that they "have shown that their illegality has not been reformed by the state but rather created by it. They have shown that such a production of illegality, destined for political manipulation, could not be accomplished without constant attacks on civil rights ... nor without constant compromises with neo-fascism and the men who promote it" (Balibar 2000: 42). It is in this context that renewed challenges to borders, nationalisms and state categories must be understood — not as unrealizable and utopian — but as democratic political projects directed at dismantling "global apartheid" (Richmond 1994).

Critical Thinking and Discussion Questions

1. What does it mean that some people are constituted as "illegal immigrants" and others as "citizens" and "legal permanent residents"? What are the practices which sustain these relations within the media, policing, the labour market, law, the immigration and detention system and in other aspects of our everyday world?

2. What practices and knowledges are non-status or undocumented people and their allies developing in order to challenge the production of some people as "illegal"? What does it mean to argue that "no one is illegal"?

3. U.S. historian Mae M. Ngai writes: "It may be that illegal immigration will persist as long as the world remains divided into sovereign nation-states and as long as there remains an unequal distribution of wealth among them." What does she mean and what are the implications of this argument?

Notes

1. This article is a longer and much more developed version of talks I presented at two conferences, Open the Borders and Sociology for Changing the World: Political Activist Ethnography, and of an article published in *Refuge* 21, 3 (May 2003). I thank the organizers of these conferences, as well as my audiences, for their support and discussion. I also want to acknowledge that Peter Nyers provided the idea for this article's epigraph; he used the same quotation to begin a document we collectively wrote with Erika Khandor and Jean McDonald and which is cited in my bibliography. This is also the place to acknowledge how much I have learned from all the immigrant rights activists (status and non-status) with whom I have had the enormous good fortune to work. Finally, I would like very much to thank the editors of this collection for their patience and for encouraging me to contribute to this anthology.

2. Veteran immigrant rights activists will know the prior work on non-status people. See, for example, the conference kit from Living Without Status: Human Rights Underground, held in Toronto, 2–3 March 1998 (in author's possession). On the history of prior legalization schemes in Canada, see Hawkins 1991. For a rare account by a non-status person from the Caribbean, see Haile Telatra Edoney (n.d.) The story of the "paper sons" within the Chinese-Canadian community can also be set within the context of a long history of challenges to the state production of illegality. For the story of one "paper son" who died without citizenship after almost fifty years in Canada, see Keung 2002.

POLITICAL DE-SKILLING/RE-SKILLING: FLYING SQUADS AND THE CRISIS OF WORKING-CLASS CONSCIOUSNESS/SELF-ORGANIZATION[1]

Clarice Kuhling and Alex Levant

On September 7, 2000, we were among more than one hundred people from the Somali community and union supporters visiting an immigration office in Toronto. We were there in defence of four families facing deportation who were waiting for decisions on their appeals to stay in Canada on humanitarian and compassionate grounds. Although they were confident that their appeals would be successful, they feared that they would be deported before a decision was made — an all too common practice of Citizenship and Immigration Canada. At the families' request, the action was called to secure a commitment from the authorities that this would not happen.

The action, organized by the Ontario Coalition Against Poverty (OCAP), a direct action anti-poverty group (also see Clarke this volume), had support from union activists from the Canadian Auto Workers (CAW) locals 40, 112, 199, 397, 504, 673, 707 and 1285, the Canadian Union of Public Employees (CUPE) locals 79 and 3903, and Hotel Employees Restaurant Employees (HERE) local 75. We met at a nearby church, where members of each family explained their situation. After the briefing, we walked to the immigration office and unfurled our union flags in the lobby. Representatives from OCAP asked to meet with management to discuss the cases in question. Citizenship and Immigration Canada responded by calling security and the police. We continued to press our demands while two small groups negotiated with immigration officials and police. What occurred next marks a lesson in how decisions are often made in this state institution. The presence of so many people in the office created a situation where business as usual could not take place, making it more attractive for the officials to meet our demands than to endure the

CUPE 3903 Flying Squad in downtown Toronto

disruption caused by our presence. A commitment was secured to delay the deportation orders until the families' appeals were heard. As a result, the deportations were prevented.

What is a Flying Squad?

Most of the union activists at this action were organized in flying squads, which is an association of union activists who confront our bosses and their representatives by disrupting the normal operations of their organizations, much like during a strike. When workers go on strike we not only withdraw our labour but we also disrupt the functioning of our workplaces. Flying squads take this tactic beyond our own workplaces, challenging the effects of capitalism and forms of oppression that capitalism mobilizes. Flying Squads can channel the strength of our collective labour (often through direct action) to force changes both to government policy between elections or to corporate policies (where there are no elections). Supporting striking workers, as well as unorganized, unemployed and unpaid workers, stopping deportations, providing abortion clinic defence, challenging abusive landlords and mobilizing for mass protests against capitalist globalization are some of the activities in which flying squads in Ontario have engaged.

In the above example, the immigration office represents one of many institutions, a "political and administrative forms of organization [which] act as relations of ruling by the way they organize and manage the activities of people" (George W. Smith 1990: 637). As part of this "politico-administrative regime" the immigration office is the local setting in and through which extra-local economic and political policies are enacted.

If ruling regimes represent forces that order our lives, then activists organized in flying squads can act as a counter to these forces by directly challenging and disrupting them, as the above example illustrates. Immigration officials came face-to-face with the actual lived experience of the individuals who were most affected by, but usually least able to alter, immigration policy. Our flying squad action made visible the connections between state policies and their local implementation through disrupting and challenging the extra-local social relations of ruling that organize such settings. This same method has been used in actions at welfare offices and in mobilizations in support of strikes at workplaces, for instance during flying squad mobilizations in Sudbury in 2000–01 in support of CAW/Mine Mill Local 598 against Falconbridge/Noranda (Beck, Bowes et. al. 2005).

These flying squad actions, based on direct action and the disruption of ruling relations, build in practice an understanding of the connections between the situations of unionized workers, immigrants and refugees, and people living in poverty. Winning victories through our own actions builds a consciousness of our own power and develops capacities to bring about social transformation.

Recent History: Re-emergence of Flying Squads in Ontario

Rank-and-file organizations that use direct action to resist the effects of capitalism beyond their workplaces have existed, in one form or another, throughout the world for many decades. In North America, their prototype, cruising picket squads, first appeared during the 1934 Teamsters strikes in Minneapolis (Dobbs 1972: 23). They also played a significant role in the 1945 United Auto Workers strike against Ford in Windsor. However, after being dormant for many decades, they re-appeared as a promising force in Ontario, Canada, in the CAW during the Days of Action[2] in the mid-1990s. According to Steve Watson, National Representative in the Education Department of the CAW, the first CAW flying squad was jointly started by locals 195, 200 and 444. "In 1995–96, with the election of the Harris government, in Windsor local activists first set up a flying squad to ensure that there would be a rapid mobilization capacity around social actions." This idea spread through the CAW Education Centre and its Paid Education Program, as part of the mobilization for the Ontario Days of Action against the Tory government. There have been flying squads in CAW locals across Ontario, with the largest ones in Ingersoll, Kitchener, Oakville, Hamilton and Sudbury.

Their success at making immediate visible gains in stopping deportations and in getting people the social assistance they need sparked an interest in other unions. In the fall of 2002, following the opening of the "Pope Squat" organized by OCAP (see Clarke this volume),[3] members of the Ontario Secondary School Teachers' Federation, the Elementary Teachers of Toronto, and the Ontario English Catholic Teachers Association formed the Toronto Teachers Flying Squad. "The motivation behind this was to give teachers a more visible presence in protests as teachers," explains Rob, a founding member of the Toronto Teachers Flying Squad.

The Toronto Teachers Flying Squad is unique because it draws its members from several unions. "We are open to all educators," Rob continues. "The idea behind this coalition was to have a space, which crosses some of the unions, so that elementary teachers, secondary teachers and Catholic teachers could all work together, which we don't often see from our unions." In just a few months of operation, they had more than twenty members on call.

The Crisis of Working-Class Consciousness/Self-Organization

The re-emergence of flying squads in Ontario was welcome news for refugees fighting deportations, for tenants battling abusive landlords, for non-unionized workers struggling against their employers, for unemployed workers seeking social assistance and for unionized striking workers seeking solidarity beyond their workplace. But the significance of flying squads goes far beyond their capacity to mitigate the effects of capitalism on specific individuals. What is particularly exciting about their emergence is not only their success, albeit limited, at "beating back the corporate attack," but their potential to help end this attack altogether. By focusing on employed union-ized workers, flying squads tap into a key source of resistance to capitalist exploitation and oppression. Such workers occupy a unique structural posi-tion in society. Since the employing class depends on us selling our labour, we have a special power (and responsibility) in the struggle for social justice for the working class as a whole and against all forms of oppression.

However, our power as employed workers remains largely untapped. Unions mobilize our collective strength to improve our wages and working conditions, but they also can limit us to this terrain, which only scratches the surface of our potential. In reality, we have much more power than our employers (and many of our unions) would have us believe. There is no reason why we could not operate our workplaces democratically, reaping the full product of our labour. Instead of following the dictates of our employers and producing whatever makes them a profit, we could democratically decide what, when and how to produce, taking into consideration our collective needs and that of our shared environment.

But there is a gap between what we are able to achieve and what appears possible in the minds of most workers. While the global justice movement made considerable headway in recent years on this front, most workers in the overdeveloped world still believe that another world is not possible. This gap is the *crisis of working-class consciousness/self-organization*. This crisis limits our potential, reducing us from subjects who are able to consciously direct our productive capacities towards objects whose productive powers are regulated by our employers. But what causes this crisis, and how can it be overcome? These key questions confront those who believe that another world is possible.

The crisis of working-class consciousness/self-organization is produced not only by deliberate disinformation and propaganda of the corporate media but also by our actual life-experiences under capitalism. The way our activity is organized in today's capitalist society restricts our social capacities to self-manage our workplaces, our society and our lives in general. For example, life under capitalism trains us to follow orders rather than follow our own creative initiative, to watch rather than do, to compete rather than cooperate, to dominate rather than coexist and to possess rather than share. More specifically, the experience of having to compete with each other for work atomizes us and stunts our capacity for collective action. Similarly, experiencing our workplaces as dictatorships of our employers, where decisions are made without our involvement and imposed externally upon us, can pacify us. This contributes to our transformation into spectators rather than actors. But more than that, it presents us with a nightmare world and offers us commodities as an escape, commodities that keep us in a dream-like state, frustrating our collective awakening (Benjamin 1969: 161; Buck-Morss 2000: 104). A whole range of our social abilities atrophy as a result of life under capitalism.

Political De-skilling and the Post-War Compromise

Workers have not passively accepted this state of affairs. Our struggles have resulted in considerable victories as well as defeats. The current state of working-class movements must be understood in the context of the history of trade union struggles and their subsequent de-clawing.

Following on the heels of the first craft unions, which sprung up in North America in the early nineteenth century, the emergence of monopoly capitalism, the factory system and consequent de-skilling and loss of control over the production process led to an increasing militancy of workers. As a result, the first half of the 20th century was characterized by an ongoing ebb and flow of struggle between labour and capital, which eventually produced what is sometimes referred to as the "post-war compromise." The capitalist classes accepted aspects of welfare-state social democracy as a less threatening alternative to "communism" and other extra-parliamentary left movements[4] (Petras 2000: 26). The development of the welfare-state based on Keynesian economic theory (Smith and Smith 1990) was also an attempt to develop new technologies of ruling that would alleviate some of the internal contradictions of capitalism following the devastation of the Great Depression.

The growing strength of the working class was evident by the spread of the union movement and the militancy of its workplace actions,[5] as well as by the rise of the Co-operative Commonwealth Federation (CCF), which was the national social democratic party in Canada and the forerunner of the current New Democratic Party. The CCF had made considerable gains since its founding in 1933. By 1944 it had won election in the province of

Saskatchewan and came close to winning Ontario and British Columbia the previous year. According to a national opinion poll, the CCF had become more popular than the Liberals and Conservatives (Heron 1996: 72).

The ruling class responded by making a series of concessions (albeit on its own terms) to the working class in an effort to stop the rise of the opposition. In 1944, in a sweeping move, the Ontario and British Columbia provincial governments made it compulsory for the bosses to recognize unions if they had the support of the majority of workers at a given workplace. Striking for union recognition was no longer required. Furthermore, in 1945, Justice Ivan Rand, the arbitrator of the famous United Auto Workers (UAW) strike against Ford in Windsor, Ontario, proposed a compromise solution where the workers did not have to join a newly recognized union but did have to pay dues to the union, strengthening the dues base and bargaining power of unions. These victories, which contributed to the growth and stability of the union movement, became recognized on a national level in 1948, when the federal government passed the *Industrial Relations and Disputes Investigations Act* to establish the above two principles as the framework of labour relations in Canada (Heron 1996: 72–76).

As some labour historians have pointed out, this post-war compromise represented significant gains for trade unions in the form of winning the "right of recognition and the right to negotiate the terms of employment" (Black and Silver 2001: 105; Heron 1996: 77). But these gains came at an enormous price. Labour peace was won at the expense of labour militancy, and in exchange for gradual incremental gains in the welfare state, struggle for more profound social transformation was sacrificed. While the power of employers and management to treat workers poorly was now limited and replaced with the rule of law, the power and ability of workers to press demands, foster class consciousness and build solidarity by engaging in sympathy and wildcat strikes for instance, was now stripped from them through legislative changes and legal restrictions. The union movement became increasingly institutionalized, contained and governed by state and legal regulations. This represented a shift whereby workers were increasingly "ruled by forms of organization vested in and mediated by texts and documents" (Dorothy Smith 1987: 3), organizational forms and texts that workers had a limited part in creating. In addition, solutions to workplace problems, once the purview of workers themselves, were taken out of their hands and placed with a professional class of arbitrators, lawyers and staffers (Heron 1996: 79; Black and Silver 2001: 105–106). Problems once debated amongst and solved by rank-and-file workers through their own collective and direct actions were now displaced onto a separate layer of labour bureaucrats and professionals, who now "represented" or "stood in" for workers.

In a recent keynote address to the Alberta Federation of Labour, Canadian labour historian Bryan Palmer described the post-war compromise as follows:

> This was a victory for workers, won by wrestling concessions long denied from capital and the state. But it was largely won on capitalist terms. And a price was paid. The union check-off[6] meant the old shop floor and workplace solidarities, garnered as shop stewards and activists collected union dues and talked to union members, faded. Union recognition introduced the increasing expansion of contracts with employers, both in terms of influence and in terms of size, with management rights clauses defining what was not in the contract as the prerogative of the boss. Complicated grievance procedures, the significance of lawyers, who played more and more of a role in defining the nature of contract relations, and the rise of an expanding layer of labour officialdom, all made unionism more and more distant from its ranks. (Palmer 2004)

As power increasingly shifted from workers to bureaucrats, the agents of workplace struggle ceased to be workers and instead became bureaucrats and professionals. The self-activity of workers was transformed into the activity of others. This transformation is part of the process of political de-skilling.

When labour historians and sociologists talk about the "de-skilling" of the working class, they normally mean the effect of Taylorism on the labour process and its fragmentation into small simple tasks, which reduces the skills a workforce requires. This form of de-skilling, as Braverman notes, was the result of the fragmentation of work processes under advanced industrial capitalism which breaks down the processes involved in the creation of a product into many (simpler) operations performed by several workers. "The capitalist mode of production systematically destroys all-around skills where they exist, and brings into being skills and occupations that correspond to its needs" (Braverman 1974: 82). As a result labour is not consciously directed by the worker and becomes reduced or distorted into robotic, mechanized and monotonous activity, directed by others. Those who produce do not manage, those who execute the tasks do not direct those tasks, and those who do the work are cut off from the planning of that work. But most significantly, the fragmentation of the work process into simple isolated tasks results in a reduction of the skill level required in the production process, which contributes to the de-skilling of the workforce. This leads to the fragmentation of the knowledge of the workers and a ripping apart of the collective knowledge workers have of the production process. At the same time workers still know a great deal about how production is organized through their own activities.

Accompanying this de-skilling process was a political de-skilling — the weakening of workers' capacity for collective self-activity. Our ability to self-manage our workplaces and our society in general was, and continues to be, undermined by the way our activity is organized under capitalism. One aspect of this political de-skilling is a consequence of selling our capacity to labour in exchange for a wage. When we sell our labour power, we not only give up the product of our labour, but we also lose control over the production process (Marx 1973: 110–15). As a result, our creative capacities become damaged.

> What workers are surrendering is their capacity to *do*, the capacity for the creative planning and execution of goals. Equally if not more important, they are also handing to someone else control over how that capacity to do is *developed* over time. The new owner of their labour power determines, through the organization of work and the division of labour, which skills are used and which are ignored or allowed to atrophy. (Gindin 1998: 78)

Moreover, having to compete with one another to sell our labour to employers atomizes us and fragments us as a class. These are some of the ways we are trained by our own daily experience of life under capitalism to follow the dictates of the bosses rather than collectively self-manage our affairs. In this way, the crisis of working-class consciousness/self-organization reflects the process of political de-skilling.

Marx analyzed the impact of this alienation of our activity when capitalism was still in its infancy. However, the process of political de-skilling, a trend that was already becoming apparent in the 1920s, has considerably intensified since then. Gramsci sought to grasp this phenomenon in a different way with his conception of the relationship between the state and civil society. He tried to understand why the methods that led the Bolsheviks to successfully overthrow the ruling regime in Russia appeared to fail in other European countries. In a letter to Togliatti in February 1924, he concluded that the greater development of capitalism in Western Europe produced "political superstructures" that made the revolutionary process more complicated compared to Russia (Adamson 1979: 56). These new institutions integrated workers into bourgeois society to a degree that required a much more prolonged "war of position"[7] to prepare the working class for a "war of manoeuvre" — an open struggle for power (Gramsci 1971: 206–76).

Similarly, Walter Benjamin sought to illuminate how the development of capitalism made it increasingly difficult to consciously experience our everyday lives. This "atrophy of experience" is a result of the increasing shock effects of life under capitalism, which numb the senses and transform our consciousness from a way to stay in touch with reality into a shield against trauma (Benjamin 1969: 161). From this perspective, consciousness not only receives stimuli but also protects against potentially harmful stimuli by producing "a narrative which represses the memory of these sensory shocks and the fears they inspired" (McNally 2001: 214). "Consciousness, in other words, spins a tale of security and stability in a dangerous and frightening world" (214). The narratives with which consciousness grasps the world organizes it in a manner that protects us from traumatic shocks. The more successfully such shocks are warded off by these narratives, the less they are experienced consciously. Susan Buck-Morss puts it as follows:

> The aesthetic system undergoes a dialectical reversal. The human sensorium changes from a mode of being "in touch" with reality into a means of blocking out reality. Aesthetics — sensory perception — becomes *an*aesthetics, a numbing of the senses' cognitive capacity that destroys the human organism's power to respond politically even when self-preservation is at stake. (Buck-Morss 2000: 104)

In light of Benjamin's concept of the "atrophy of experience" we can see how our experiences in bourgeois society politically de-skill us in a manner beyond Marx's concept of alienation and Sam Gindin's articulation of our loss of creative capacities. Moreover, theorists like Gramsci and Benjamin help us to understand how some of the more recent aspects of life under capitalism contribute to the de-skilling process. Capitalism today de-skills the working class much more effectively and intensely than during Marx's time, and this process appears to be accelerating.

In addition to these new ways that capitalism impacts our capacities for self-activity, another aspect to consider is the relationship between de-skilling and re-skilling. While the various processes of de-skilling have proliferated, the counter-posing processes of re-skilling have significantly waned. The absence of organizations engaged in mass struggle today and the overwhelming presence of de-skilling mechanisms contribute to a situation where the working class continues to resist, but in a very subdued, fragmented and semi-conscious fashion. Today, in the virtual absence of experiences that re-skill workers, it is no wonder we lack confidence in our ability to transform our world.

While unions have the potential to serve as mechanisms of re-skilling by providing workers with opportunities to work together, to see the effect of their collective self-activity and to foster and develop capacities that atrophy under capitalism, the re-organization of workers' activity in unions as part of the post-war compromise has weakened this potential and has in fact contributed to the de-skilling process due to the substitution of professional union staff representatives for workers themselves. As unions became more governed by the law and by regulatory texts, the ability of most rank-and-file workers to participate in these activities became more limited.

In addition to transformations in the agents of struggle from workers to professional bureaucrats, the site of struggle increasingly shifted away from the workplace, picket line and street and onto the highly regulated and isolated terrain of the bargaining table and arbitration hearing. Time was increasingly spent on servicing, negotiating and administering collective agreements at the expense of mobilizing, agitating, organizing and educating members through political education and direct action.

This shift in the terrain of struggle is also reflected in changes in the nature of the collective agreement, the prime document that regulates relations between classes in the workplace. Palmer writes, "Signed collective agreements told the tale. Prior to 1940 the average collective agreement in even the largest of Canadian industries was no more than a dozen pages. By the late 1940s, such agreements totalled hundreds of pages, and today they look like multi-volume tomes on a library shelf, thousands of pages in length. Experts and professionals, distanced from the rank-and-file in so many ways, were seemingly needed to 'interpret' and 'understand' a myriad of 'clauses' which could well mean much to workers" (Palmer 2004). Texts, like contracts and grievance procedures, increasingly connect unions to specialized languages and skills, to professional and legal discourse and to union staffers, full-timers and lawyers. Through these texts ruling relations re-organize relations within our unions.

Here again we see how "the language of documents operates as a conceptual coordinator of social action" (G. Smith 1990: 642). From this perspective, collective agreements increasingly structure and organize our activities, decisions and understandings (both present and future) and are the concrete embodiment of social relations at a certain period of time. The collective agreement, then, can be understood as the crystallization of a particular moment in the class struggle — both the expression and coordinator of the conjuncture of class forces, which co-ordinates and maintains the set of relations established through bargaining during the life of the contract and often into the next contract.

Furthermore, as Heron, Black and Silver acknowledge, this shift toward a service-oriented bureaucratized union movement was reinforced by the legal constraints on labour struggle that expected union officials to stifle collective and direct action during the life of the collective agreement and to channel such actions into safer mechanisms. This new policing role, which some labour bureaucrats and officials continue to display with a disturbing amount of enthusiasm, meant that union officials were in essence acting on behalf of the state and against their own members.

As John Clarke notes, the price that was paid for this post-war class compromise was a legalized, compartmentalized, regularized struggle, a struggle now "managed" from above (2002). While the domestication of trade unions has happened in an uneven way across the Canadian state, this legacy still haunts and informs trade unions and their struggles. The labour movement is still largely patterned on this post-war compromise and continues to act as if this "class truce" was intact, despite the rapid ascendancy of neoliberalism, which has replaced class compromise with direct attacks on unions and the working class. The previous compromise of the "welfare state" is seen from this vantage point as giving too much power to workers and unions and as creating too many obstacles to profitability for capital. Part of this neoliberal re-orientation is accomplished through a "downloading" of "responsibilities" for containing working-class militancy onto unions.

Over the last three decades this post-war compromise has become increasingly one-sided. In response to the economic woes of the mid-1970s (high unemployment and inflation), the capitalist class and the state embarked on a concerted effort to blame the working class for these problems and to claw back the gains it made in the post-war settlement (Heron 1996: 107–26). The bosses became much more innovative in the class struggle, in their methods of production and in their ability to use state relations against workers and to rip part major aspects of the welfare-state. The government became considerably more interventionist on the side of capital, its tactics ranging from fining unions, jailing their leaders, imposing injunctions and back-to-work legislation and of course imposing wage controls. The result has been a severe erosion of the gains won by workers in the aftermath of World War II, which can be seen in the considerable drop in living standards since the mid-1970s. The unions, for their part, have largely, with some exceptions, continued to hold up their end of the compromise, playing by the old rules and policing its members to do the same. These practices are not able to address the new situations unions and working class people are facing.

To compound problems, unions have also unquestioningly retained and replicated undemocratic structures of decision-making and leadership control inherited from the past. Failure to address these weaknesses will mean that the labour movement will continue to be woefully and wilfully ill-equipped to wage an adequate fight back and will fail in its task of living up to the unique challenges the present situation poses.

The Power and Limits of Unions Today

As part of our effort to re-skill workers to self-manage our common resources and productive capacities, we must contend with the contradictory position that unions occupy in capitalist society. On the one hand, unions act to "improve workers' position *within* capitalism," but on the other, they are a "collective organization of workers *against* capital" (McNally 2002: 208). The benefits accrued from "negotiat(ing) better terms for the sale of labour to capital" (McNally 2002: 208) represent only conditional or provisional protection from the insecurities inherent in competitive labour markets — and can thus be easily retracted.

However, as one of the only mechanisms that act as a buffer against the servility of wage employment and the vagaries of an unstable labour market, unions to some extent take labour/wages out of competition (Moody 1997: 284, 303). In these ways unions contradict the principles of competition and private property inherent to capitalism and in this sense they act in opposition to capitalism. If part of the logic and imperatives of capitalism involves taking away our control over our social and economic conditions and circumstances, then forms of resistance that seek to reassert and demand control over economic life indeed challenge both the sources of power as well as the pain that these sources of power cause us. Such struggles for radical democracy, as McNally acknowledges, are implicitly anti-capitalist (McNally 2002: 195).

In addition to mitigating the effects of capitalism and challenging its monopoly over decision-making, unions can also have a transformative effect on their members. Unions can re-skill workers by uniting us on the basis of our solidarity as labourers and our struggles against the bosses. These struggles build the very social capacities that atrophy as a result of life under capitalism, including the capacity to see beyond the current horizon of possibilities.

A key aspect of the union movement's role in developing our abilities to think and act for ourselves involves what Sam Gindin, former assistant to the president of the CAW, calls an "independent orientation."

> With no alternative or independent orientation, what exists becomes "inevitable." The corporate view of the world becomes the only view of the world. Workers, demoralized and with no sense of what to struggle for, are left vulnerable not just to concessions, but to a larger disorientation that affects the future strength of their organization. (Gindin 2004: 4)

Moreover, by re-skilling workers in the process of fighting for reforms within capitalism, unions can prepare us for a post-capitalist society, where workers gain control over their productive powers and collectively and democratically self-manage their shared resources. This "transformative reformism" overcomes the old debate (which haunts us still) between reform and revolution. As Rosa Luxemburg noted more than a century ago, "the struggle for reforms is its means; the social revolution its goal" (Luxemburg 1970: 52). In this way, unions not only win reforms from the class of employers but can also re-skill workers to take what is theirs back from their employers and to run their workplaces and their society democratically.

But despite being implicitly anti-capitalist organizations, there are limits to the transformative power of unions in Canada today. The "no strike, no lockout" clause that is part of every collective agreement in the country cuts us off from our greatest power during the lives of our collective agreements: to withdraw our labour and to disrupt the functioning of our workplaces. In exchange for concessions from the employing class, unions commit themselves to maintaining a "class truce," hence limiting their objectives to operating within existing class relations. Consequently, they limit their ability to re-skill workers to self-manage their workplaces and their society; and in fact, as we have seen, they often contribute to the process of de-skilling themselves. This class truce demonstrates both the power and the limits of unions today.

Re-skilling 1: Toward a Social Movement Unionism

However, our unions have not reached their full potential even within the framework of this class truce. Throughout the period characterized by the post-war compromise the union movement has been plagued by what some commentators call "business unionism" — treating unions as businesses that provide services to members (negotiating and administering collective agreements) in exchange for dues payments. Such unions restrict their own activity far below the limit set by the "no strike, no lockout" clause, and by replicating the same decision-making structures that de-skill workers under capitalism they contribute to the de-skilling process themselves.

In contrast, a new trend in the union movement — social movement unionism — emerged in the mid-1990s. Social movement unionism is characterized by internal democracy, militancy, independence from retreating political parties, a broader agenda than the immediate economic interests of its members and an effort to develop the consciousness of its rank-and-file members (Moody 1997: 4–5, 10, 14, 278, 290). While social movement unionism originated in "Third World" countries like Brazil, South Africa and South Korea, it has spread to the overdeveloped countries like France and Canada.

Flying squads can pose a threat to business unionism by fostering membership activism, which bolsters left opposition currents in these unions. Activists in flying squads can become a base for opposition movements. By including rank-and-file members in militant struggle, where they see the power of their activity, by creating a space for workers to become active outside of political parties and by making links with members of the working class beyond their workplaces, flying squads prepare members of business unions to transform their unions into social movement unions.

For example, the flying squad in our union local, CUPE 3903, has had considerable impact on moving beyond business unionism. Since its beginning in 2000, the CUPE 3903 flying squad has been a key organizing space for progressive members in the local, particularly activists who are suspicious of and alienated from traditional union structures, processes and discourses. The flying squad has brought members who are active in other struggles — for social housing, immigrant and refugee rights, international solidarity, to name but a few — into the life of the union. Drawing on these workers' activism and their connections with the broader community, the union has, in turn, broadened the scope of its activity beyond business unionism. Moreover, through their activism in the flying squad, these workers have become more familiar with how the union functions and have become more engaged with the union. In many cases flying squad activists have gone on to run for positions on the local's executive committee. In fact, some of the most progressive union activists have come out of the flying squad. These members have also provided much of the drive behind transforming the union's constitution, making it more democratic, inclusive and participatory, as well as limiting the power of the executive committee. For example, in 2003, the local amended its constitution, changing the role of executive officers from "overseers" to facilitators and transforming the Stewards' Council into an open body focused on mobilizing members rather than simply "representing" their interests and concerns. At the same time a more general de-escalation of struggle and activity in the local has undercut the impact of these changes.

Our flying squad has also had an impact on the union beyond our local. In response to an increase in police repression of protesters, flying squad activists successfully lobbied for the establishment of a national legal defence fund for all CUPE members across the country.[8] Starting with our own local, this initiative was taken to provincial and national conventions by activists who became familiar with union politics and processes through the flying squad.

The Canadian union movement includes a broad spectrum of approaches from business unionism to social movement unionism. But even the main social movement oriented unions, like CUPE and the CAW, only begin to approach the principles of social movement unionism outlined above. Both unions have made strides in the direction of social movement unionism. For example, in the 1996 round of collective bargaining with the three large automakers, the CAW's bargaining demands exceeded the immediate interests of its members and sought to include some of the broader interests of the class as a whole. "Unlike the United Auto Workers in the U.S. that year," writes Moody, "the CAW put forth an aggressive bargaining program that would increase employment in the industry and the country. Shorter work time, restrictions on outsourcing, and guaranteed job levels for the communities in which each plant was located was the heart of the bargaining program" (Moody 1997: 278). Nevertheless, there is still much work to be done in democratizing these unions. There is still an enormous gap between elected officials and hired staff on the one hand and the rank-and-file on the other, and there appears to be no strategy to reduce and eliminate that gap.

Re-skilling 2: Toward a Democratic Social Movement Unionism

As part of developing workers' capacities to transform their unions' practices from business to social movement unionism, flying squads can facilitate the re-skilling process by developing an active and more critical working-class consciousness, which can contribute to opposition currents aimed at democratizing unions, including those that claim to practice social movement unionism. Because undemocratic unions frustrate the re-skilling process at best and serve to de-skill workers at worst, democratizing the union movement is key to overcoming the crisis of working-class consciousness.

Class collaborationism, compromise and co-optation, shaped through state and legal regulation of unions, are not the only causes of a lethargic labour movement. Democratic union practices are inextricably linked to a union's ability to mobilize and act effectively. Authoritarian, bureaucratic and unaccountable forms of leadership that control struggle from above and stifle membership initiatives are a sure fire way to demobilize and demoralize workers and lead to concessionary struggle. Lack of leadership accountability and membership control, where union practices are non-transparent and/or top-down, result in a passive membership. Such circumstances pose particular challenges for flying squads, which must then either bypass or overcome leadership control altogether.

The issue of democracy is intimately linked to that of power. Active democratic involvement strengthens union power, and practical evidence of union power encourages member involvement; conversely, a low level of power discourages participation and commitment, which in turn saps a union's strength (Camfield 2004: 25).

Moreover, as Michael Eisenscher reflects,

> [Union] democracy is not synonymous with either union activism or militancy. Members can be mobilized for activities over which they have little or no control, for objectives determined for them rather than by them.... [Unions'] responsiveness to membership aspirations and needs is determined, in part, by the extent to which members can and do assert effective control over their political objectives, bargaining strategies, disposition of resources, accountability of staff and officers, and innumerable other aspects of organizational performance. (Eisenscher in Moody, 1997: 276)

While flying squads pose a challenge to business unionism and insist on developing social movement unionism much more fully (including its focus on internal democracy), they do not conflict with the union movement as such; rather, their democratizing effect only serves to empower the union movement. As a member from the opposition caucus in the Transport Workers' Union, Local 100, said, "Democracy is power" (Moody 1997: 277).

Re-skilling 3: Transformative
Reformism beyond the Limits of Unions

While flying squads can help transform the union movement by moving it toward a democratic social movement unionism, they can also build on and exceed the achievements of unions by facilitating collective action beyond their limits. History is peppered with examples of defensive struggles around "bread and butter" issues suddenly exploding into massive social upheaval

— and where such struggles resulted in major advances for labour and other social groups (Moody 1997: 285, 301). What distinguishes defensive struggles that grow into large political confrontations from those that never develop beyond particular grievances has much to do with *how* these defensive struggles are carried out. If they are undertaken in such a way as to develop and expand our capacities for self-activity and self-organization, to provide us with a better understanding of our world and our ability to change that world, and which expand the horizons of what we think is possible (Kuhling 2002: 77–78), then defensive struggles can be transformative.[9]

There is no easy formula for the creation of socialist ideas and practices, much less organizations and parties; indeed, socialist ideas and organizations do not automatically flow out of our experiences of day-to-day struggles. What can be said with more certainty, however, is that "routine collective bargaining by bureaucratic unions in 'normal' times is not likely to lead to more than routine politics" (Moody 1997: 303).

Flying squads, however, can be used during "normal" times to break out of routine forms of struggle by resuscitating, fostering and channelling forms of opposition that can move workers beyond class compromise to class confrontation. By mobilizing workers for direct action alongside routine collective bargaining, or else between rounds of bargaining, when disruption of workplaces is prohibited by collective agreements, flying squads continue to develop our capacities for collective action.

For example, the CUPE 3903 flying squad played a significant role in the strike of 2000–01 by providing an already mobilized layer of activists who were able to work alongside the executive committee and the bargaining team by escalating and diversifying the disruption caused by our strike. Since the mid-1990s, CUPE 3903 has had the strongest collective agreements in the post-secondary sector in Canada and was the first union to successfully negotiate "tuition indexation" for graduate student teaching staff (this meant that any increase in tuition would be compensated by an equal increase in pay). The employer tried to claw back this important gain, forcing the longest (seventy-eight days) strike in English Canadian history in this sector.[10] This strike was a success in no small part due to the impact of flying squad activists, who were already mobilized and who advocated for unorthodox tactics,[11] democratic processes[12] and solidarity across the different units of the local (contract faculty, teaching assistants and graduate assistants) and with the broader community, which was far beyond the norm of the union movement at the time.

As large numbers of us participated in, and made decisions regarding, the day-to-day functioning of our strike and as we began to gain an understanding of the unequal relations of power and domination in which we were embedded, we gradually began to develop a sense of our capacities. As we gained confidence and skills, we began to exert our power as workers. And as we exerted our power as workers, we began to see how our collective power increased exponentially and how we collectively transformed into something far more than the sum of our individual members (Kuhling 2002: 80). And through the "multiplication" of our individual selves (facilitated through mechanisms that elicited our mass participation and decision making), we began to see how we could, in Gramsci's words, "obtain a change... far more radical than at first sight ever seemed possible" (1971: 353). In this way, political confrontation served as the basis of knowledge production, which in turn informed our struggle, our political activism.

As Moody points out, during periods and in places where no mass socialist organization or movement exists, day-to-day union and social struggles serve as reference points for, and are part of, what shapes the thought and practices of the working class, including those who are most organized and active (1997: 303). Part of changing how we relate to one another in the struggle for change involves creating a piece of the future in the here and now. In terms of our practices, this means forging bonds of solidarity far beyond unionized workers and implementing forms of genuine democracy where membership control is paramount. In this sense, the politics that informs the way we undertake to change a small piece of the world can be referred to as prefigurative politics (Breines 1982; Kaufman 2003: 277–78), since it prefigures the kinds of social relations for which we are fighting. These pre-figurative forms of struggle, like the forms of organizing developed during an occupation or during the squat of a building, conflict with ruling relations and build a sense of how social relations could be organized very differently.

By enabling workers to develop their own counter-power, flying squads can function to re-skill, re-politicize and empower workers. Through this process, the agents of struggle once again become the mass of workers themselves, and the site of struggle is broadened beyond the bargaining table to the workplace and the streets. As bodies that help foster our capacities for collective action, flying squads can help offset fragmentation, isolation and alienation by providing participating workers with opportunities to experience our collective power to effect change. Such experiences are transformative: they develop our abilities and feed our imaginations, extending the horizon of possibilities. By developing abilities that tend to atrophy under capitalism, flying squads can help overcome the crisis of working-class consciousness/self-organization.

Development of Flying Squads: Dilemmas and Conflicts

The efficacy and sustainability of a flying squad in large part depend on how it is structured. Typically, flying squads use a phone tree and an e-mail list (which are available to all flying squad activists) to contact members for actions on short notice. But what is key is that flying squads must work as autonomous organizations rather than as formal committees of their union. This approach is vital if flying squads are to exceed the limits of unions in their activities and if they are to help transform the union movement toward democratic social movement unionism. The CUPE 3903 Flying Squad maintains its autonomy by structuring itself as a separate organization from the union with a common membership. It is completely separate from all decision-making structures of the local. Similarly, the Toronto Teachers Flying Squad aims to maintain autonomy with respect to the unions from which it draws its members.

Flying squads have generally been received by union executives with caution and ambivalence. "They're not against it, but they're not wonder-fully supportive either," explains Rob with respect to the OSSTF executive. "They won't allow you to identify yourself as a union member" at flying squad actions. "There is no formalized relationship" between flying squads and the local and national executives in the CAW, explains Euan Gibb, of the CAW 707 Flying Squad. Watson characterizes the relationship as one of "give and take." "As a staff member of the union, I try to respect the autonomy of the flying squads. At the same time they appreciate any support they can get from the national union."

In practice, however, this has not been the case. As the CAW flying squads began to attract more members, the union's National Executive Board (NEB) took over control. Beginning in the summer of 2001, all CAW flying squad actions had to be sanctioned by the NEB or by local executive committees. This decision was ostensibly made in response to OCAP's mock eviction of Ontario's finance minister, Jim Flaherty, following the introduction of the sixty-hour work week, in which several CAW flying squad members participated. However, given the union movement's militant history[13] and the recent militancy of CAW members, which far surpasses any mock evic-tions, it is difficult to believe that the decision to control the flying squads was related to their militancy. Instead, this clamping down had more to do with the threat of independent CAW flying squads becoming a base for a left opposition to the official union leadership.

The predictable result of the CAW flying squads integration into the union structure has been a limit on their activity and efficacy. For example, they no longer participate in immigration actions to stop deportations. Because the flying squads are not as effective any more, they are not as attractive to their members; consequently, the number of union activists participating in flying squads has dwindled. Their capacity to re-skill their members no longer exceeds that of the union, and they neither pose a threat to its leadership nor constitute a democratizing force in the union. They have become scarcely more than traditional political action committees,[14] seeking direction from the union officialdom.

But perhaps the greatest (but failed) attempt at co-opting flying squads, and the greatest mockery of the flying squad phenomenon, has been the Ontario Federation of Labour's (OFL) Solidarity Network. While the objec-tives of this network were ostensibly similar to those of flying squads, its top-down structure prevented it from being effective. All actions had to be cleared by the OFL bureaucracy, including its president, Wayne Samuelson. Rather than fostering workers' participation, the Solidarity Network simply reproduced the same decision-making structures that turn people into spectators under capitalism. As a result, the Solidarity Network was a flop. The link to subscribe to it on the OFL website aptly leads to a dead end.

Given that flying squads pose a challenge to business unionism and threaten to democratize and radicalize social movement unions, it is no surprise that union officials have sought to contain and integrate them. However, it is vital that flying squads maintain not only their autonomy from but also their connection to the unions from which they draw their members. They must maintain autonomy in order to be able to exceed the limits of unions in their activities. But in order to have a transformative effect toward democratic social movement unionism, they must maintain a connection to their unions. Autonomy is vital, but isolation from their unions cuts them off from the very people who they should be attracting and re-skilling. An isolated flying squad may be able to do much more radical actions, but its efficacy will be limited. To be effective, flying squads must work both inside and outside unions. Their autonomy is based on maintaining a separate decision-making structure; their connection is based on a common membership. For example, what connects the CUPE 3903 Flying Squad to that local is that it draws its activists from that local's membership. Consequently, it is a flying squad comprised of CUPE 3903 members. Flying squads are most effective when they resist both co-optation and isolation. In order to do this, they must maintain an autonomous connection to the unions.

Conclusion

Since their re-emergence in the mid-1990s, the popularity and efficacy of flying squads in Ontario have ebbed and flowed along with other movements against capitalism. They largely continue to be limited to unions that already practice some aspects of social movement unionism. It is unclear if the flying squads will be able to live up to their potential given their current co-optation and isolation. What is vital here, however, is not so much the name "flying squads." There are a number of co-opted flying squads today that have been reduced to political action committees that mobilize and de-mobilize their activists at the request of their union's elected officials. In contrast, flying squads that are autonomously connected to their unions are rank-and-file "from below" organizations whose effect is to re-skill workers and to transform the union movement into a vehicle for re-skilling workers. Such organizations will continue to emerge in one form or another and under a variety of names.

Their project is vital for those of us who believe that another world is in fact possible, because a post-capitalist society will not be produced by benevolent parliamentarians or by progressive union leaders *on behalf* of the workers. A truly democratic post-capitalist society can only be made *by* the workers. As the provisional rules of the First International begin: "the emancipation of the working classes must be conquered by the working classes themselves" (Marx 1974: 82). The crisis of working-class consciousness — the fact that most workers do not believe that another world is possible despite the fact that they make this world through their own activity — is not a false consciousness but an accurate reflection of the fact that workers do not currently have the capacities to emancipate themselves. Decades, even centuries, of de-skilling under capitalism must be countered by a re-skilling process that develops workers' capacities to meet this challenge. The significance of flying squads is their potential role in facilitating this process.

Critical Thinking and Discussion Questions

1. What mechanisms and forms of organization enable unionists to struggle for change in ways that develop and expand our capacities for self-organization and self-activity?

2. What are some practical ways in which we can encourage the development of militancy, solidarity and democracy in our workplaces, unions and other sites of struggle?

3. How does the current form of the Canadian labour movement (since the post-war compromise) contribute to de-skilling and re-skilling?

4. Why do flying squads have the potential to transform unions into organizations that re-skill workers, and how has the labour establishment sought to contain their effect?

Notes

1. This article is based on a shorter piece (Levant 2003) as well as a presentation by Kuhling and Levant at the Sociology for Changing the World conference in Sudbury, Ontario, November 2002. We would like to dedicate this work to CUPE 3903 — a union that has demonstrated the power that can be tapped when we challenge the norms of business unionism and engage in militant forms of democratic self-organization.
2. The Ontario Days of Action were a series of one-day general strikes and mass demonstrations organized by the Ontario Federation of Labour and social justice coalitions against the neoliberal Progressive Conservative Party from 1995–98.
3. The "Pope Squat" was a successful four month occupation of an abandoned building organized by OCAP during the Pope's visit to Toronto in 2002 to create more housing for the homeless.
4. According to Petras, the rise of the welfare state was the product of certain political conditions and conjunctural phenomena — a context dependent situation whereby revolutionary movements worldwide were growing, communism

was on the rise, and the USSR's role in the defeat of Nazi Germany accorded it heightened prestige, all at the same time as capitalism's legitimacy was tarnished due to its ties to fascism.

5. "By 1943 union membership in Canada soared, and one out of every three unionists was on strike" (Heron 1996: 70).

6. A legal provision that ensured that a union automatically received dues payments from all workers holding a job that was in the scope of their collective agreement. This was one of the cornerstones of the post-war compromise, which exists to this day.

7. War of position refers to the struggle that is waged on the terrain of civil society in preparation for a war of manoeuvre — open class warfare over the means of production, the state, etc.

8. CUPE is the largest union in Canada, with over 500,000 members.

9. See Rosa Luxemburg (1970) and also David McNally (2001).

10. See Kuhling 2002 for an analysis of how this strike was won.

11. These tactics included identifying and targeting the pressure points that impacted the employer's decision-making, for example, disrupting the business, social or even personal lives of the key decision-makers.

12. These included a strike committee that made most of the day-to-day decisions and recommendations to the executive committee, which was open to all members and met on a daily basis.

13. For example, during the 2000–01 Mine Mill/CAW 598 strike in Sudbury, the union engaged in a number of militant activities. When the employer, Falconbridge/Noranda, hired scabs and Accu-Fax, a strikebreaking firm, to intimidate the workers, union members responded by slashing and spiking the tires of their vehicles. The union's "scab-mobile" "went around town causing problems for scabs — visiting their houses and calling attention to them" (Kinsman 2005b: 57).

14. Unlike flying squads, political action committees are a part of the structure of the union and are consequently limited by the current form that unions have taken.

Part D

CONCLUSION

The following two chapters provide some conclusions and propose some directions for further inquiry and activism. William Carroll's contribution is based on his presentation at the launch of the Social Justice PhD program in Sociology at the University of Windsor in 2002. A version of these comments also appear in his book, *Critical Strategies for Social Research* (2004). In this chapter Carroll reminds us of the continuing importance of both Marx's critical analysis of capitalism and the potential for sociology to become a transformative social praxis. After Carroll's discussion comes our collective Afterword. Here, we try to illuminate some future directions for political activist research and identify some of the obstacles we are bound to confront as we embark collectively on this journey.

MARX'S METHOD
AND THE CONTRIBUTIONS OF
INSTITUTIONAL ETHNOGRAPHY

William K. Carroll

When, in 1990, Stuart Hall and his colleagues presented the notion of "New Times," capitalist societies seemed in transition to a more market-oriented way of life structured around information technologies and post-modern culture. A decade and a half later, new times have grown familiar to us. We have been living a series of interrelated transformations, as neoliberal globalization has gathered force and gained a certain sense of inevitability, as poverty and privation have touched the lives of growing numbers of people worldwide — in short, as the logic of the market has colonized more and more areas of social life, including of course the academy (Drakich, Grant and Stewart 2002). The ravages of neoliberalism have been accompanied by the unprecedented pace of changes in communications, spurred on by the microelectronics revolution, wiring us into a cultural environment that is at once both local and global, and that continuously throws up a clatter of images and voices for our consideration or fascination. But if we are by now well into an era of the "posts" — postmodern, post-colonial, post-Fordist — we are emphatically not living in times of "post-scarcity" or triumphant democracy, as suggested in musings about the end of history. Indeed, if these be now-familiar yet still new times, they are times of great danger, particularly in international relations. The "peace dividend" promised at the close of the Cold War has been converted into the currency of a new Washington-centred imperialism as indifferent to the lives of those brutalized by its wars and occupations as it is keen to gain strategic and commercial advantage, all under the cover of a war on terrorism. But dangers to human welfare are evident in many other realms — in the deterioration of public health care, education and other social services, in the increased salience of racialized and anti-immigrant discourses, in the criminalization of dissent in the wake of September 11, 2001. By implication, these are also times of accentuated political contention and social-justice struggles, whether over matters of material distribution, cultural recognition or ecological well-being. Such initiatives take various forms: local community organizing to meet specific human needs, movement activism informed by alternate social visions, state-centred lobbying for human-centred policies, experiments in more democratic forms of social organization and communication, micro-political interventions to contest hegemonic codes and arrangements. Whatever their form, these are hopeful currents that might comfortably flow together under the "Another world is possible" banner, unfurled at the 2002 World Social Forum. I want to suggest some ideas, of a primarily methodological nature, on what sociology's project can be in these new times.

Sociology, of course, has conservative, even reactionary, roots. Auguste Comte's response to the social crisis of post-revolutionary French society was a Eurocentric program for top-down social engineering in which the high priests of sociology would share power with the rising industrial bourgeoisie, directing what Comte envisaged as "a new era of unlimited human progress" (Seidman 1998: 27). In the twentieth century, as its leading protagonists engaged in an inconclusive debate with the ghost of Marx (Zeitlin 1968), sociology became aligned with the welfare state. If sociology was denied the status of technocratic monarch envisaged by Comte, many sociologists did take up what C. Wright Mills called the role of "advisor to the king" (Mills 1959). It is not that sociology is hopelessly compromised when it enters the terrain of the state. Over the years, Canadian sociologists have contributed to the furtherance of social justice via public-policy venues that include royal commissions (Armstrong and Armstrong 1992; McFarlane 1992) and sociology continues to play a role in social programming, but with a diminishing margin for manoeuvre. In the policy networks that surround and permeate the neoliberal state sociologists are heavily outnumbered by economists, efficiency experts, risk-management consultants and others whose worldviews incline them toward market-driven politics.

Toward Sociology as Praxis

As Mills observed, "advisor to the king" is only one possible role for sociology. Beginning with the scathing critiques of conservative sociology forwarded by scholars such as Mills as early as the 1950s, sociology, and particularly sociology in Canada since the 1970s, has shed many of its positivist conceits, including its faith in the rational beneficence of the modern state. Key to my argument is that there now is a plurality of critical approaches to social inquiry, which can in different ways contribute to a sociology for social justice. These need to be nurtured and developed and made more widely accessible.

Sociology in Canada is well poised to embrace a praxis-oriented approach to social inquiry, which in my view is the most effective way of placing social justice directly onto our disciplinary agenda. Elsewhere (Carroll 2004), I have discussed the convergences, complementaries and tensions among five "critical strategies" for emancipatory social inquiry. Here, I want to trace out three such strategies, beginning with Marx's own method. These approaches have developed out of a dialogue between activism and reflection — practice and theory. In combination, they give us a methodological toolkit for responding to not only the New Times of neoliberal globalization but to the coming-to-voice of subaltern groups whose presence in the cultural and political fields opens new possibilities for the ways we live our lives and define ourselves.

What these approaches share is a grounding in praxis; indeed, they together recommend that we view sociology itself *as praxis*. Such a critical perspective proceeds from the recognition that social life as we know it is marked by inequities that are deeply structured yet contingent features of human organization. As a systematic knowledge of the social, sociology is inevitably caught up in these inequities. In a world marked by enduring injustice, yet open to democratic possibilities, "uncritical" sociology — blandly indifferent to injustice — does not yield objective knowledge; it reinforces entrenched power. There are two senses in which sociology as praxis takes a critical stance. First, recognizing the intimate connection between knowledge and power and the political reality of material inequity and ideological contestation, sociology as praxis situates itself on the side of the subaltern, the community, the democratic public. In producing reflexive knowledge of the social, with emancipatory intent, it contests entrenched power and knowledge. Second, recognizing the complex, stratified and historical character of social life, sociology as praxis undertakes radical inquiry — radical not in the popular, pejorative sense of extremism but in the classic sense of getting at the root of matters. As praxis, sociology makes a commitment to understand the deeper, systemic bases of the problems we face, whether social, psychological or ecological, which often means understanding the interconnections between allegedly separate issues and problems, as in the intersections of race, class and gender that constitute specific lived realities.

Marx's Method: Dialectics of Unmasking and Transformation

Marx was not a sociologist, at least not in the Comtean sense. But then Marx was also not a "Marxist." When he noticed in his later years the kinds of deterministic and reductive analyses that were being deployed in his name, Marx became the first post-Marxist. According to Engels he declared, "I am not a Marxist" (Reiss 1997: 6). Be that as it may, perhaps the most profound and epigrammatic statement of praxis can be found in Marx's "Theses on Feuerbach," written in 1845. In the Theses we find a dialectical conception of praxis as "the coincidence of the changing of circumstances and of human activity," of human activity as at once objective — sensuous — and subjective, of social life as "essentially *practical*," of human essence as "the ensemble of social relations," ever subject to critique and reconstruction.

And it is here that we find the famous adage that "the philosophers have only *interpreted* the world, in various ways; the point, however, is to *change* it" (Marx 1968: 28–30). Two years earlier, in his letter to Arnold Ruge, Marx had enunciated guidelines for the sort of critical social analysis he was to develop in the ensuing decades. Characterizing critical theory as "the self-clarification of the struggles and the wishes of the age," he wrote of "a *ruthless criticism of everything existing*, ruthless in two senses: The criticism must not be afraid of its own conclusions, nor of conflict with the powers that be" (Marx 1978: 13). These remain indispensable criteria of intellectual honesty more than a century and a half later. They advise us to refuse both the roles of cheerleader for the underprivileged and apologist for the privileged. Certainly, if we retrace Marx's own journey we find in his masterwork, *Capital*, just such a critical analysis.

Marx's was a project of *unmasking* capitalism's dirty secret: the peculiar way in which its social relations provide a persuasive basis for liberal freedoms and formal equalities while enabling a dominant class to appropriate the surplus produced by subordinates. As a post-Enlightenment thinker, Marx believed in the power of revealed truth as a catalyst for social self-understanding and dialectical change. For Marx, however, truth was the result not of detached, academic observation but of practical action within the social formation.[1] In its radical chains, the proletariat was not only the source of transformative agency, it furnished a standpoint, internal to capitalism, from which to uncover capital's secrets. With Marx, the academy loses its epistemic privilege, even if in the development of Marxist orthodoxy that privilege eventually became reinscribed within the party/state.

What kind of critical strategies for social inquiry does Marx bequeath to us? The central thrust would seem to follow the course of a post-Enlightenment critical modernism, but in a highly dialectical way. The strategy of unmasking — of penetrating the ideological, surface-level realities of bourgeois society, to show how an unjust social organization betrays the promises of liberal humanism — has an emancipatory intent. The point is not merely to interpret or to understand the world, but to change it. Such change is itself conceptualized dialectically, as a conjoint transformation of circumstances and of selves.

Indeed, what is central to Marx's strategy is the use of dialectical analysis in attempting to grasp the many-sided character of a world that is fundamentally relational and practical. As Bertell Ollman has stated in his essay, "Why dialectics, why now?" this method is indispensable in a world more integrated than ever around a highly dynamic and globalized form of capitalism. Ollman tells us that the fundamental assumption underlying Marx's method "is that reality is an internally related whole with temporal as well as spatial dimensions" (Ollman 1998: 349). To understand one social issue, such as poverty, one must uncover the ways in which it is hooked into other social issues and relations. If dialectical analysis is holistic it is also historical. Marx's method rejects metaphysical conceptions that view the present as "walled off" from either the past or the future. Such conceptions, all too common in social-science and policy discourses, can become "a prison for thinking," as the present form of something — "the family," "the economy," "retirement" — is mistaken for "what it is in full, and what it could only be" (Ollman 1998: 345). For Marx, the point is to provide categories "capable of grasping the historicity of the phenomena they describe" (Sayer 1979: 147). Marx's historical appreciation of the internal relations that constitute our world extends not only from past to present but also into the future. Just as the present is a *résumé* of past practice, the future, as potential, already inhabits the present. Thus, a careful analysis of contemporary social contradictions, emergent practices and relations, and forms of collective agency can help identify ways forward for social justice initiatives, as in possibilities for a widening and deepening of democracy or for the appropriate use of new technologies.

Such projections, however, are no more than probable eventualities. For Marx, the future is radically contingent: it depends upon what people do, how they make history. The danger in dialectics is that of a closed, totalizing formulation — a dogma of universal "laws" (Sherman 1976). In contrast, dialectic as a critical method provides questions, not answers, about the interconnected, conflictual and dynamic character of social life. Indeed, as David Harvey has suggested, since our world is dynamic, contradictory and emergent, "the exploration of 'possible worlds' is integral to dialectical thinking.... The exploration of potentialities for change, for self-realization, for the construction of new collective identities and social orders, new totalities (e.g., social ecosystems), and the like is a fundamental motif in Marxian dialectical thinking" (1996: 56).

As a critical strategy for social inquiry, Marx's dialectic provides for a radical sociology whose relevance is unabated a century and a half after its formation. As a critical research strategy, dialectical social analysis has two main strengths: 1) it enables the researcher to "make connections," to grasp the many-sided character of a social/natural world that is fundamentally relational, practical and emergent; 2) it enables the researcher to "unmask" both the underlying relations that generate social injustices and ecological maladies *and* the ideologies that legitimate entrenched power by attending only to surface-level appearances.[2]

Marx's influence is evident in other critical strategies that were formulated in the twentieth century, but nowhere more than in the corpus of work inspired primarily by the work of Gramsci and Lukács. Their protean concepts of hegemony and reification have been tools for elaborating an historical-materialist analysis of cultural and political power that effectively widens the lens of critical inquiry. There are various methodological lessons that might be drawn from the corpus of "western Marxism," but the thread I want to trace leads from Lukács through Horkheimer and Marcuse to

Dorothy Smith. The thread is not tightly woven into a dense fabric but is perhaps more of a loose end — there is much in Lukács and the Frankfurt theorists that Smith would probably question.[3] Still, there is a sense in which Dorothy Smith's work incorporates crucial insights from these thinkers.

In Lukács's concept of reification (introduced in 1923), in the contrast Horkheimer drew between traditional and critical theory in 1937, and in Marcuse's response to commentators on his Weber lecture of 1964, we find a strand of thought that challenges the facticity of contemporary realities. Lukács understood that the full-fledged development of capitalism universalized the commodity form within a rationalization process that reached well beyond the economy. With reification, a relation between people takes on the character of a thing, whose autonomy seems so rational and so all-encompassing that it conceals the social relation itself (Lukács 1968). Social processes take on the appearance of "a nature-like quality beyond human control" (Kellner 1985: 92). To the reified mind, the commodity form — the abstract, quantitative mode of calculability — is viewed as the "authentic immediacy" of the object. For Lukács, the discipline of economics, which takes up the standpoint of a capitalist class concerned with the immediacies of accumulation, adds a further layer to reification by positing modernity's permanent economic "laws."

This settled, immediate, thing-like appearance of social reality was identified by Horkheimer a decade later as the object of traditional theory. What Horkheimer and his colleagues attacked in positivist social science was the Kantian division of fact and value, the claim that one can know what *is* without making value judgments, and specifically the way in which western empiricism reified the conventional values legitimating capitalist society (Antonio 1981: 381). Here is Marcuse's response to his critics, who charged him with a "tragic reluctance to acknowledge the inevitable features of our time":

> It is the reasonable willingness, not to see facts as inevitable, but to draw the conclusions of one's own capabilities. If we have gone so far as to call it "tragic reluctance," if one does not recognize this "inevitability," all thought has become meaningless; for thought which decides beforehand that facts are inevitable is not really thought at all. (Quoted in Kellner 1985: 105)

On this account, social reality is to be judged not as an obdurate collection of "facts" but as a living and ongoing accomplishment, holding definite potentialities.

Institutional Ethnography: Problematizing the Everyday

If Lukács and the Frankfurt School introduced these ideas for critical social science, Ray Morrow has shown how with the Diaspora of the late 1930s, the School's research program moved away from interdisciplinary materialism, into philosophical critique (cf. Benhabib 1994). Yet in the past three decades one critical sociologist has contributed brilliantly to the elaboration of effective strategies for writing the social while critiquing the facticity of ruling relations and perspectives. Thirty years ago, Dorothy Smith presented her paper, "Women's perspective as a radical critique of sociology," at the meetings of the American Academy for Political Science (Smith 1992). The ensuing corpus of sociological analysis — from Smith herself, from her students, from students of her students and so on, has transfigured sociology in a most valuable way.

By placing the practical accomplishment of social life at the centre of her analysis while offering a way of explicating how extra-local relations of ruling reach into and organize the everyday, Dorothy Smith has developed a critical sociology that provides resources for challenging the reified categories of textually mediated social organization. But Smith's sociology does much more than follow the thread of ideology-critique. She incorporates lessons from feminist consciousness-raising about the need to begin inquiry with lived experience and to preserve the presence of active subjects in our sociological accounts. From ethnomethodology she derives a democratic conception of people as knowledgeable practitioners of their lives and of practice as a complex process of concentration and coordination. Smith's critique is not only of ruling relations but of conventional sociology's participation in those relations. She shows us how texts such as Emile Durkheim's *Rules of Sociological Method* transfer human agency "from actual subjects to the virtual entities of the sociological text" (Smith 1989: 45). Conventional methods such as Durkheim's "construct an objectified standpoint situating their readers and writers in the relations of ruling and subduing particular local positions, perspectives, and experiences" (Smith 1989: 43).

To recover the active agent, to explore the actualities of her life and to create awareness of possibilities for alternative organization, Smith begins her sociology in the everyday, not as descriptive ethnography but as institutional ethnography. By this she means a research strategy whose "aim is to explicate the actual social processes and practices organizing people's everyday experience ... a sociology in which we do not transform people into objects but preserve their presence as subjects" (Smith 1986: 6). To problematize the everyday world is to explore how it is articulated to the social relations of the larger social and economic process (1986: 6). Smith presents her strategy as a form of consciousness-raising "aiming to find the objective correlates of what had seemed a private experience of oppression" (1986: 7). In taking a standpoint outside the relations of ruling, the institutional ethnographer is able to develop empirically grounded sociological insight that escapes the logic and priorities of entrenched power and that shows how those priorities are instantiated and inscribed in texts and extra-local relations, including capital relations. Taking the side of those excluded from ruling does not compromise the scientific character of the project. After all, as Howard Becker (1970) noted long ago, there is no possibility for detachment in sociology: we must begin from some position in the world. Social inquiry that begins from locations of management, administration and power tends to create knowledge that is useful for the purposes of ruling and that reinforces the hierarchies of credibility and the common-sense facts of the dominant social order. Institutional ethnography offers an escape-hatch from that closed circuit. The hatch is for both the researcher and the people whose side she takes. For Dorothy Smith the crucial moment is not that of writing sociological texts in a new way, but of developing ethical-political connections such that "we who are doing the technical work of research and explication are responsible in what we write to those for whom we write" (Smith 1987: 224). In the closing sentences of their primer on institutional ethnography, Marie Campbell and Frances Gregor have stated the matter quite clearly:

> There is a commitment to making the conditions of people's everyday lives known and knowable as the basis for action. Rather than supporting a ruling perspective and approach, the new institutional ethnographic knowledge should help to form a subject's political consciousness related to equitable decision making, undermining subordination, and so on.... Our responsibility is to make texts that express the standpoint of people and to help make them available to those who will use the work's subversive capacity in their own struggles. (2002: 128)

It is precisely the value of institutional ethnography *in struggle* that informs George Smith's (1990) highly innovative approach to political activist ethnography. George Smith recognized that institutional ethnography has great significance for emancipatory politics "not only because it begins from the standpoint of those outside ruling *regimes*, but because its analysis is directed at empirically determining how such *regimes* work — that is, how they are socially organized" (1990: 631). He aptly characterized institutional ethnography as a "reflexive-materialist method," following from Marx's historical materialism, that can give the political work of activists a scientific basis. Concerned neither with the production of abstract, "objective" accounts of the social nor with abandoning science for a celebration of the subjective experiences of the oppressed, George Smith emphasized the shift, in institutional ethnography, to a reflexive stance in which the sociologist inhabits an actual world she is investigating. Equally important is the ontological shift in institutional ethnography from idealist theorizing in which social explanation is deduced from abstract theory to investigating "the everyday world as it is put together in the practices and activities of actual individuals" (1990: 635).

These epistemological and ontological shifts enable the political activist as ethnographer to understand how things work, which is crucial to effective political activism. If, following Marx, the point is not simply to understand the world but to change it, a proper understanding is nonetheless necessary for effecting that change. To change how things work, to construct an alternative future, we need clarity as to how things work in their present, problematical form. With political activist ethnography, George Smith drew an especially clear line from the reflexive-materialist method of institutional ethnography to a reflexive form of political practice attuned to the social actualities that activists need to deal with effectively, if we are to create change.

Community-based Action Research:
Empowerment and Democratization

The project of community-based action research (CBAR), also inspired by Marx's method, is in some ways complementary to institutional ethnography. As CBAR, social inquiry becomes a form of radical pedagogy. In Paulo Freire's foundational text, *Pedagogy of the Oppressed* (1970), Marx's dialectic of understanding the world in order to participate in its transformation informed an initiative of democratic empowerment. This critical tradition has elaborated the more subjective side of the dialectic, as enunciated in Marx's third thesis on Feuerbach, which states:

> The materialist doctrine that men are products of circumstances and upbringing, and that, therefore, changed men are products of other circumstances and changed upbringing, forgets that it is men that change circumstances and that the educator himself needs educating. Hence, this doctrine necessarily arrives at dividing society into two parts, of which one is necessarily superior to society. (Marx 1968)

Radical pedagogy works against this division. It insists on a two-way dialogue between scholars and communities; it recognizes the practical need to create an awareness and capacity among subaltern groups as to how they can liberate themselves.[4] But given the existential duality of the oppressed — the fact that oppression is not only experienced as such but is internalized as both prescribed conduct and self-loathing — the oppressed are often fearful of freedom (1970: 31). What Freire called *conscientization*, and what action researchers call empowerment, is a movement from passive acceptance of circumstances "beyond one's control" to active participation in democratically controlled social change, founded on a sense of autonomy and responsibility.

With roots in both the second Euro-North American wave of feminism and in the politics of decolonization that writers like Franz Fanon (1961) and Kwame Nkrumah (1964) represented in the 1960s, this notion of consciousness-raising and empowerment as a shedding of internalized elements of oppression and a creation of personal and cultural autonomy, has multiple lineages in social-justice struggles. It has notably been carried forward recently by scholars and activists focused around Aboriginal politics, such as Linda Tuhiwai Smith (1999), whose *Decolonizing Methodologies* is a landmark text.

Action research also has a mixed lineage and because of that an ambiguous relationship to critical sociology. Its historical precedents include not only the likes of Freire and Fanon but "quality of work life" programs, through which large corporations have attempted to increase productivity and loyalty on the shop floor. Many action research projects, particularly those initiated and funded by corporate or state management, are obviously co-optative, or geared instrumentally toward realizing more effective service delivery (Stringer 1996: 37). Without a firm and practical commitment to democratic empowerment and to critique in Marx's (1978) double sense (afraid neither of the powers that be nor of its own conclusions), action research becomes little more than a sophisticated form of social regulation. Even so, as Joe Feagin and Hernán Vera (2001: 177) point out, once effectively launched by extensive community participation, action research is difficult to contain, and local people, once organized, may move their organization in the direction of more radical goals than were initially intended.

This dynamic character is one of CBAR's great virtues. It is a method that puts people in motion in what Budd Hall (1979) describes as a three-pronged initiative: as a method of research involving full participation of the community, as a dialogical educational process and as a means of taking action for change. This allows "people to rediscover the realities of their lives and their potential capabilities," to build self-reliance and re-humanize their worlds (Susan E. Smith 1997). Community-based action research is a way to democratize knowledge and to erode the boundaries between knowledge and action, researchers and actors. Successful action research involves what Davydd Greenwood and Morten Levin (1998) call a double democratization. The research process is democratized through full participation and co-learning between outside facilitators and insiders, with power shifting to insiders over the course of the project. Moreover, the project yields as its output knowledge that increases participants' ability to control their own situation.

The language of "insiders and outsiders" acknowledges a breach that may itself be narrowed as subaltern groups and communities empower themselves. If, for instance, we consider the twenty-five indigenous projects presented by Tuhiwai Smith — all of them attempts to decolonize methodologies — few actually presume the facilitative involvement of "outsiders," and many are about building self-reliant capacities and breaking with colonial hegemonies. Projects such as "celebrating survival," "renaming" objects and subjects to connect with indigenous history, "re-reading" and reworking Euro-centric narratives, "remembering" a painful past and people's responses to that pain foreground the priority of contesting colonialism's cultural and psychological legacy as an integral element in an "ambitious research programme, one that is very strategic in its purpose and activities and relentless in its pursuit of social justice" (142). Ultimately, decolonized methodologies blend knowledge production with cultural, personal and political transformation, blurring the borderline between understanding the world and changing it.

Conclusion

The strategies I have sketched offer ways for sociologists and activist researchers to address the profound injustices that mark the human condition today. Each strategy has potentialities and limits. Marx's dialectical approach to unmasking modernity's contradictions and injustices yields insights particularly on issues of material inequality. As political activist ethnography, institutional ethnography is a powerful tool for explicating the reach of extra-local ruling relations into the everyday and for informing activist strategies and actions. CBAR effects a tight link between theory and practice: it empowers and mobilizes while producing knowledge of practical value to participants.

The congruencies and divergences between the strategies are also worth considering. The methods of Marx and Smith share an ontology that is explicitly historical-materialist and a commitment to ideology critique. In developing institutional ethnography, Dorothy Smith turned to Marx's critical analysis of capitalism as an extra-local complex of social relations, but her approach extends that critique to take in the characteristically textual mode through which ruling occurs in late modernity. Institutional ethnography can also be read as a critique of those interpreters of Marx who convert his analysis into an abstract theory disconnected from the lived realities of the everyday. Institutional ethnography, then, gives us a flexible yet richly detailed research strategy, grounded in dialectical social analysis. By inflecting institutional ethnography in an explicitly activist direction, George Smith accentuated institutional ethnography's value as a critical mode of inquiry.

CBAR also has a Marxist lineage, at least in its activist-oriented, Freirean version. Cantered upon the dialectical relation of theory and practice — understanding the world in order to participate in its transformation — action research is both dialectical and dialogical: it requires democratic communicative relations among the practitioners and professionals engaged in a co-generative learning process (Greenwood and Levin 1998). Indeed, without a process of democratic empowerment, through which the local practitioners gain the capacity to control their own knowledge production and action, action research degenerates into little more than a sophisticated exercise in regulation: it becomes an instrument for the ruling relations, not a catalyst of democratization.

However, if institutional ethnography and CBAR both resonate strongly with Marx's method, they do so in distinctive ways. Institutional ethnography is a sociology *for* people; CBAR is a sociology *with* them. Marie Campbell and Frances Gregor point out that "institutional ethnography attempts something different from most participatory research" (2002: 67). The "radical potential" of institutional ethnography is to rethink social settings taking power relations fully into account and on that basis "to produce an analysis in the interest of those about whom knowledge is being constructed" (2002: 68). This objective is quite distinct from the thrust of participatory research, which in Campbell and Gregor's view is to democratize the interpersonal relations among researchers and researched. In this respect, institutional ethnography is somewhat more inclined toward Marx's method, which emphasizes the conflicting interests and standpoints in knowledge/power relations; while action research highlights the importance of democratizing the knowledge generating process as a means of empowerment. In certain contexts it may be feasible to combine the two approaches, as Campbell and her colleagues did in Project Inter-Seed, a collaborative research project on disability issues and health care in which the research team (which included people with disabilities) accepted institutional ethnography as coherent with the values of the project. This meant that, as an aspect of the participatory research process, the entire research team had to learn how to take up the standpoint of people with disabilities (Campbell and Gregor 2002: 117–19), a desirable result in itself.

In other contexts and particularly where power is entrenched within ruling relations, institutional ethnography will be a more effective strategy. Consider, for instance, what we learn from Colleen Reid's (2000) attempt to implement a feminist action research (FAR) strategy at a YWCA employment training program for low-income single mothers. Despite an official organizational discourse of empowerment, the hierarchical positions of service providers and clients were deeply inscribed within the formal organization of the YWCA. The service providers occupied positions of power and were wedded to a professionalized perspective on their relation to clients; the clients lacked the time and resources to really collaborate in the project and were not entirely trusting of a researcher aligned with the formal organization, who came from an affluent background. In this situation none of the conditions for successful participatory research were in place:

> As I became more immersed in my research I began to question FAR's assumption that collaboration and negotiation were possible in a structured organizational setting. My location as a relatively privileged and educated researcher coupled with the limitations imposed by the research site became increasingly problematic. The growing awareness of my power challenged me to consistently document my assumptions and to confront the issue of voice appropriation. (2000: 179)

Reid's insightful account suggests that action research is a strategy that is most appropriate in settings where democratic, communicative action is already in play and can be drawn upon as a primary resource in building new communicative spaces and useful knowledge. In settings that are organized around ruling relations, institutional ethnography is a more effective strategy since it specifically addresses those relations. Of course, within activist movements and communities — to the extent that their everyday worlds are built around relatively democratic social relations — the very practice of institutional ethnography will typically involve a participatory dimension. In this sense, the project of political activist ethnography nudges institutional ethnography in the direction of CBAR. George Smith made clear his own commitment to participatory democracy with his insistence that the value of activist ethnography does not lie immediately in the production of a "political line":

> Doing this kind of research is not the practice of "vanguard politics." On the contrary, research studies of this sort are designed to be written up, published, and made available to all members of a grass-roots organization for their political consideration. They are not in some sense special or unique. Rather, they are intended to provide, on a day-to-day basis, the scientific ground for political action. (1990: 646)

Perhaps, within the praxis of democratic social movements, institutional ethnography and community-based action research can be creatively synthesized, so that the virtues of a reflexive-materialist ontology and epistemology combine with those of dialogue and cogenerative learning. Such a combination could bring forth a mode of critical inquiry that is both scientifically grounded and empowering, contributing to veridical political analysis and effective collective action. A synthesis of this sort between institutional ethnography and action research may prove to be one of the most important legacies of George Smith's vision of political activist ethnography.

Institutional ethnography, community-based action research, dialectical social analysis — these research strategies give critical sociology a methodological toolkit. They enable a sociology grounded in the actualities of the past and present and alert to future possibilities. They prefigure a sociology allied with oppressed groups and movements for social justice but also involved with other fields of critical knowledge — development studies, gender studies, labour studies, critical legal studies, political economy, cultural studies, environmental studies, social history. They provide resources for a critical social *science*, in the most defensible sense of the term: a systematic, disciplined inquiry into how the social world is put together and how it can be remade to enhance well-rounded human development and ecological health.

Critical Thinking and Discussion Questions

1. Discuss the ways in which "sociology as praxis" takes a critical stance toward the social world. How can such a stance be "scientific" in a deeper sense than that found within a good deal of conventional sociology?

2. Compare and contrast how institutional ethnography and community-based action research draw upon the Marx's method in offering praxis-oriented research strategies.

3. How might political activist ethnography contribute to a creative synthesis of community-based action research and institutional ethnography, within the praxis of democratic social movements?

Notes

1. "In practice, man must prove the truth, that is, the reality and power, the this-sidedness of his thinking," from the third thesis on Feuerbach (Marx 1968: 28–30).
2. The latter sort of unmasking is termed ideology critique. For a clear account of Marx's critique of liberal ideology as a world view that celebrates the freedoms and equal opportunities offered by the market — capitalism's most evident surface reality — while denying the deeper relations of class exploitation and alienation that are integral to capitalism, see Larrain (1983, Chapter 2).
3. As in Lukács's somewhat abstracted dialectic of history and class consciousness, Marcuse's heavy reliance on Freudian psychoanalytic theory and the Frankfurt School's general neglect of the everyday world as a location for knowledge and action.
4. In Freire's words, "to surmount the situation of oppression, men must first critically recognize its causes, so that through transforming action they can create a new situation" (Freire 1970: 31–32).

Afterword

NEW DIRECTIONS
FOR ACTIVIST RESEARCH

C. Frampton, G. Kinsman, A.K. Thompson and K. Tilleczek

This book has offered suggestions to activists, researchers and those of us wanting to change the world. We have written this Afterword by re-reading the book's contributions and noting suggested directions for research as well as the obstacles encountered while doing political activist ethnography. What we are left with is a series of questions and suggestions for further exploration. This conclusion is not intended to be the last word on these topics. And it perhaps raises more questions than it resolves. Rather than providing definitive assurance, our goal is to inspire and provoke further discussion and research, in a dialogical fashion.

It is in this light that we begin with objections raised by some activists themselves. These objections arise both from those who reject the need for such activist research, which is often seen as being too much inside the "system," and from those who accept more mainstream forms of research, arguing only for strategies of reform from inside this "system." We then focus on how we can use the insights of political activist ethnography to maintain the standpoints of social movements and activism while resisting both the ideological perspectives that often predominate in movements and the pressures of academic and professional institutionalization and containment. We also begin to explore how we can engage with research funding and ethics review procedures as sites of regulation in the context of neoliberalism and the capitalist university[1]; the need to engage more activists both outside and within university contexts in doing activist research; and some of the ways through which we can challenge the narrowly "textual" in developing more transformative and transgressive pedagogies and textual practices. How can we write, perform, visualize and incite an activist sociology for changing the world? How can we participate in writing new kinds of texts that help to organize and push forward social movement struggles? We hope you will join with us in strategizing about ways to resist, challenge and transform the regulatory regimes that currently constrain activist research. We hope that you will contribute to devising a means by which an activist sociology can become an integral part of social movements.

Exploding the Inside/Outside Binary

Some basic activist concerns are levelled against the activist sociological project outlined in this book. Concerns about "us versus them" and "outside versus inside" were raised at the conference where this book originates and are often raised in movements and in doing activist research. These concerns have major implications for research. Different chapters have raised further concerns about doing research that is too directly tied into the needs and interests of social movements, suggesting that this research is in danger of becoming "ideological" in character. Others have highlighted the dangers of being too tied into the worlds of institutions and professions, which can bend even the best-intentioned research in the direction of ruling relations. One standard and often well-founded objection encountered in movements is a rejection of "sociology" that uses people as research fodder and brings nothing of value back into the movements.

There are also objections that are aimed more precisely at the usefulness of doing political activist ethnography. Questions are raised about whether this type of research is necessary and why, if it is needed, it cannot simply be research of a more "traditional" kind, which does not raise profound critiques of mainstream forms of knowledge production. These concerns come from two sides. One side argues that we simply need to "smash the system" from a position of exteriority. The other argues that we need only to reform the system from the inside. The first position questions the importance of any critical social research and knowledge generation regarding ruling relations. The second does not usually challenge dominant forms of knowledge production and ruling ideologies, and uses more traditional research methods. Moving beyond this dichotomy is crucial to moving beyond ideology and speculation and toward exploring actual social relations, organization and struggle in developing knowledge *for* social movements. Here, knowledge production and the practice of changing the world are intertwined, and knowledge has a clear social character. Knowledge production and research take place within social relations produced by people and within terrains of social struggle.

Beyond the Outsider

The "smash the system" position goes something like this: What is the point of understanding ruling relations if our goal is to smash them? From the position of perceived exteriority, the call for a further elaboration and deepening of activist research capacities seems absurd. How will our assault be facilitated by a knowledge of "the system's" inner workings if our starting point for resistance is of necessity outside it. Put more poetically, these activists might steal a line from Bertolt Brecht and say, "You don't need to understand something in order to destroy it." While our account of this perspective might seem to be an uncharitable caricature of a current of anarchist thought, it is nevertheless an objection that is frequently raised within the sphere of current anti-capitalist and anti-globalization struggles. It can be detected in the opposition of some parts of the anti-capitalist wing of the global justice movement to social research within movement organizing. As Thompson points out in his chapter, direct tactics of confrontation are emphasized, often outside of any analysis of the social relations of struggle that a movement confronts.

One illustration of this is the position that starts from a very valid critique of the corporate and capitalist character of the mainstream media and leads to a rejection of all forms of activism that engage with these media outlets as sites of social struggle. This perspective argues for only building alternative media and for refusing to engage with the mass media, who are seen as part of the "enemy." While building alternative media is vital, as an exclusive focus, it works against our gaining a "framing" in the mainstream media that can allow (even if in a very distorted fashion) larger numbers of people to learn more about activist movements.

The ontological distinction rendered in ideas is that between the activist and the world. Globalization or capitalism is something apart. It can be confronted from a position of exteriority. This position assumes that our capacity to resist is contingent upon our social exteriority. A position "inside" the "system" is seen as compromised and suspect. Someone who works within the mass media or the legal profession, as a social worker or a university professor is classified as politically compromised despite their perhaps subversive and radical social practices. The injunction to be outside is thus clear.

In these outsider activist spheres, activist research is aimed principally towards developing valuable accounts of the abuses and dangers of the present state of affairs, for instance, in relation to the ravages of capitalist globalization.[2] In other instances, and on rare occasions, activists within these struggles turn their efforts towards a concrete reckoning with the ruling practices that become operative in the lead up to a confrontation with political or corporate leaders, as was the case at some of the protests against the WTO, the FTAA and the G-8. More rarely do activists involved in these struggles focus on the everyday world as their problematic or attempt to map the broader social relations of the struggles in which they are engaged.

At times these activists also produce a rather moralistic rejection of people's everyday lives. For instance, the slogan emerging from the global justice movement (and the World Social Forums, which have brought together tens of thousands of people), "Another world is possible," can have an abstract ring when not linked with struggles and the means through which social relations can be transformed (McNally 2002, Notes from Nowhere 2003).

From this position of exteriority, the solution can seem simple: build the camp of resistance along the perimeter of "the system" and embrace "the margin" as an ethical and strategic standpoint, and become — in one's own being — the antithesis of this world. Of course this impulse to embrace the outside has often amounted to a healthy hatred of the present. The Russian anarchist terrorist[3] Sergei Nechayev, for instance, insisted in his 1869 pamphlet, "Catechism of the Revolutionist," that the revolutionary must not be a part of this world:

> In the very depths of his being, not only in words but also in deeds, he has broken every tie with the civil order and the entire cultivated world, with all its laws, proprieties, social conventions and its ethical rules. He is an implacable enemy of this world, and if he continues to live in it, that is only to destroy it more effectively. (1869)

More than a century later, Nechayev's convictions can still be heard from the balaclava-covered mouths of the Black Bloc rioters. However, exteriority has also been expressed in more spiritual or transcendental forms within the anti-globalization movement. One need only think back to the scene at the protests against the FTAA in Québec City in 2001 (Chang, Or, Tharmendran et al. 2001) where several dozen activists threw down yoga mats and confronted an advancing line of riot police with the sun salutation. At that same protest, other demonstrators could be seen wearing T-shirts on which were written the word "satyagraha," in reference to the spiritual path of resistance elaborated by Gandhi. In Gandhi's formulation, the *satyagrahi* had to abandon all worldly possessions and adopt a strategy of resistance based on non-compliance. By rooting this non-compliance in asceticism, or the denials of the pleasures and desires of this world, *satyagraha* often amounted to a battle of wills, a war fought on the abstract plane of virtue. And while Ghandian derived perspectives have provided energy and inspiration to social struggles like the Black civil rights movement in the U.S. and among civil disobedience activists in environmental and pacifist movements, others — notably Ward Churchill — have pointed out the strategy's serious limitations.[4]

Below the heights of virtue and on the less lofty realm of the everyday, some anti-globalization/global justice activists have adopted small and large strategies to stay "outside the system." These include living as cheaply as possible by squatting or sharing accommodations; refusing to engage in purchasing commodities (whether by celebrating asceticism or by shoplifting), so as to alleviate the need to engage in waged work; and supporting and participating in DIY (do it yourself) cultural scenes like punk. While these strategies can often yield insights and present important survival methods, they are not in and of themselves transformative of social organization and relations. They still require the material basis and wealth produced by people through capitalist social relations to sustain them and are therefore never fully outside the system. These strategies of living "outside the system" require this very system in order to exist. In order to dumpster dive, there must first be dumpsters. In order to squat a building, someone must first have built it.

Perhaps the most explicit consolidation of these strategies of stepping into the "unregulated" sphere of exteriority for North American anti-globalization activists can be found in the insightful work of the CrimethInc Ex-workers Collective. This group, which operates anonymously or by pseudonym and which derives many of its ideas from the situationist tradition,[5] has been responsible for the publication of at least two books bent on attaining exteriority. In the first, *Days of War, Nights of Love* (2000) — a kind of anti-manifesto — the group makes every effort to break with the constraints of the present. In one provocative entry, they advocate replacing history with myth, so as not to become ensnared by "the chain of events." The book begins, appropriately, with an illustration depicting a sorcerer crawling through a rip in a kind of energetic fabric enveloping the globe. The accompanying text reads, "your ticket out of this world."

The second book, aptly titled *Evasion*, provides a first-person account by a young man living life outside the system. The book's online promotional material describes it as,

> the author's travelogue of thievery and trespassing across the country, evading not only arrest, but also the 40-hour workweek and the hopeless boredom of modern life. The journey documents a literal and metaphorical reclamation of an individual's life and the spaces surrounding them — scamming, squatting, dumpstering, train hopping and shoplifting a life worth living and a world worth fighting for.

Despite the mythic insights of CrimethInc and the potential powers of the politics of spectacle, this strategy does not facilitate analysis of the social relations of struggle in which people are engaged.[6]

While most activists would admit that it is a practical impossibility to ever be truly outside of the system, this has not prevented many of us from on occasion adopting an ethic of struggle that forges a direct link between our exteriority and our capacity to resist. At play in this process is a profound moment of philosophical idealist thought. First, "the enemy" (or "the system" or "capitalism") is constituted as a discrete entity or thing that we are somehow outside of. The enemy is rendered, as Dorothy Smith has described it, as a "blob ontology" or a "supra-individual blob" (D. Smith 1999: 7; D. Smith 2005: 58), which does not address the social organization or social relations through which this enemy is created. While this enables us to reckon with the enemy conceptually as that thing in need of being opposed and negated, it also reifies the enemy, preventing us from grasping how it is organized through social practices and relations.

Being outside of the enemy also has the effect of transposing the everyday practices and processes of the social world into the realm of conceptual abstraction. From here, activists often end up working on the *concept* of the "system," or of "capitalism," rather than on the actual social world that produces both our enemies and capitalist relations. As should by now be clear, this is precisely the ideological and speculative approach that George Smith criticizes. Further, by casting the "inside" as inconsequential (since it is to be smashed), the celebration of exteriority is of necessity at odds with political activist ethnography and institutional ethnography. A lot is at stake here.[7]

Very often, these same activists have perceived the development of social knowledge for struggle to be a symptom of an emerging complicity. Since it does not take the form of an ontological refusal of the "system"; since it acknowledges that we are also inside the "system," which has been expelled from activist purity through an idealistic sleight of hand, these activists have thought that those people who "know the game" are at risk of suffering the corruptions of reformism. Reformism gets used as a moralistic term of abuse rather than as a description of a specific social and political practice — just as "radical," "extremist" and "anarchist" become moralistic terms of abuse for many of these "reformists." The dialogue, which we are caricaturing here for the purposes of argument, is so familiar as to be painful (see cartoon on the following page).[8]

It is far easier to be radical in the field of ideas than in actual social practice. Through the process of abstract negation (overthrowing ideas in consciousness but not in social practice), it is possible to tear down entire worlds of oppression in thought. This is exactly the type of position that Marx's (1973) critique of ideology in the *German Ideology* is directed against.

However, it is equally true that those who pay close attention to the intricacies of how power actually operates within ruling relations are often in danger of becoming mesmerized by its splendour. This tendency is seen perhaps most infamously in some of Foucault's writings (1979, 1980a) and in some of the readings made of Foucault's work, including those of Nikolas Rose (1999). Despite all of Foucault's and his interpreters' insights, one might question the wisdom of marvelling over the genius of power in a fashion that renders it a purely technical accomplishment.[9] As suggested later, this can even be a danger for currents in institutional ethnography, which can become so fixated on ruling regimes that they often run the risk of becoming "trapped" within ruling textual strategies. Foucault — along with the best of the "reformists" — seems to be suggesting that what already exists shall constitute our terrain of negotiation, barring any unannounced epochal breaks[10] or the appearance of any other unspecified sources for the introduction of novelty.

It is not surprising that such a perspective finds opponents amongst members of a movement who profess that another world is possible and who have begun to live this possibility in ways of organizing (including affinity groups and spokescouncils) that rupture the alienation of oppressive capitalist and social relations (Notes from Nowhere 2003; McNally

credit: Sam Bradd

2002). In moments of resistance to the forces and institutions of capitalist globalization, like in Seattle or Québec City, people have caught a glimpse what a new world no longer defined by exploitation and oppression might look like.

Beyond Insider-Only Positions

Opposed to those who argue for a position of absolute exteriority *vis-à-vis* ruling regimes are those who argue that it is only "realistic" to always and everywhere be inside these institutional relations. This position is espoused by much of the moderate and social democratic left, many NGOs and union leaderships, and the wings of social movements influenced by these groups. Here, many activists forget that it is precisely these institutional relations that are the source of the problems that oppressed and working-class people experience, and that these relations often marginalize and exclude oppressed peoples. As we first sat down to write this Afterword, the Live8 concerts and the Make Poverty History campaign, which took place in the lead up to the 2005 G8 Summit in Gleneagles, Scotland, were very present in the news. Much of this organizing was informed by what we here are calling the insider-only approach. This organizing, involving large numbers of people in concerts and marches, generated a certain level of social aware- ness about issues of poverty but was based on the flawed assumption that the G-8, which has done so much to extend world poverty, could simply be asked to end poverty in Africa.[11] Needless to say, very little has changed, and aspects of global anti-poverty organizing have been demobilized. By focusing their efforts on influencing the existing institutional relations of the G-8 rather than on building a counter-power moving against these institutional relations, insider-only activists have not addressed the social roots of poverty in the least.

Insider-only social forces forget that activist social movements are transformative rather than incremental in character, and that they therefore entail radical reconfigurations of existing social relations. Insider positions tend to have limited and partial critiques of ruling relations and tend to accept major aspects of hegemonic social ideologies. In Marx's time, within labour and socialist organizing, this type of position led to arguing for a fair wage rather than for the social transformations needed to abolish the com- modification of labour power (Marx 1847/1891). In a capitalist society, even what can be claimed as a fair wage is based on the exploitation of workers. In a similar fashion, those who call for "fair trade" as opposed to "free trade" are not fully addressing the exploitative character of trade and exchange in the context of capitalist and imperialist social relations (McNally 2002: 60–62). Rather than ignoring the wage demands of workers, however, what Marx and others argued for was involvement in the daily struggles of workers to fight for wage advances and for more control over the conditions of production. These everyday struggles were seen as a basis for building a counter-power that could, in the end, uproot wage slavery. Insider-only positions tend to be stronger when the composition of social struggles is weaker and when there is a downturn in the cycles and circulations of struggle.

These positions also lead to a rather conservative approach to research that accepts the authority (power/knowledge)[12] of university-trained researchers, who often use the positivist methods of the natural sciences and who rely on more quantitative forms of research based on counting and quan- tification.[13] These approaches posture as being "neutral" and "objective," as somehow being outside of social power and class struggles. Ironically, insider-only positions often suggest that the social world can only be known by looking at it from "above" or "outside" so as to not get contaminated by subjective experiences and particular social standpoints. They are therefore unable to acknowledge the social character of all knowledge production.

The standard use of research in many insider-only social movement organizations is to simply marshal statistics, "facts" and data to buttress the argument the social movement is making at the time. This leads to an ideological approach to research and "facts"; it simply takes this knowledge for granted without challenging how it has been produced or questioning the power of the "experts" who produced it. It can also lead to movements relying on certain "experts" and arguments, almost as if social struggle was a clash between the "experts" opposing the social movement and those that adopt positions the movement feels it can use to buttress itself within the corridors of power. For instance, in some environmental struggles we see a battle between the "experts" who argue that corporate pollution is leading to ecological devastation and negative health impacts, and other "experts" who argue that the specific corporation is not responsible and that the problems being encountered have other causes.

Once again, the insider-only position also does not lead towards political activist ethnography. On the contrary, its process involves marshalling certain aspects of traditional research when they seem useful to its lobbying efforts, media conferences and briefs to governments and other agencies. This process often involves cobbling together various "facts" and forms of knowledge without critical thinking or a holistic methodology. Activists working from the insider-only position certainly do not see the usefulness of (and often are quite horrified by) activist breaching experiments, which can become an important way of mapping social relations of struggle.

We can see how this works in relation to research on homelessness. There are many studies of homelessness that use various techniques to count the homeless. These studies take the homeless as their object. They can be useful in showing us that homelessness is a pervasive social problem (if we did not know this already) and can even begin to help us identify some of the roots of the problem and some of the reasons why individuals report they are homeless. At the same time, these studies cannot explicate the social organization of campaigns of social cleansing. These studies can and also have been used to construct the homeless themselves as the problem. For instance, on the basis of some of these studies, social policy analysts and government officials can argue that the homeless are largely people who are mentally ill or are associated with deviance and criminality. Many of these studies deny agency to the homeless and portray them as in need of other people's help.[14]

Mainstream studies are often used to separate homelessness from more general questions of poverty and from the broader social relations through which homelessness is socially organized, and especially to separate questions of homelessness from class relations and struggles. These studies do not produce knowledge *for* the homeless or for groups like OCAP that are organizing people living in poverty as a social movement. They do not begin to map out the social relations of struggle so that activists can sort out where to exert pressure to get results in addressing the needs of the homeless.

Mainstream research and regulation have often gone hand in hand. This becomes clear in Deborah Brock's work (1998), where she shows how research done on prostitution has largely been used to stigmatize and criminalize sex workers, despite the individual intentions of the researchers. Research that was intended to "help" prostitutes has instead been used to create more problems for them. "Facts" produced regarding sex work have come to be used against prostitutes.

There is always a struggle over facts and knowledge. Sometimes the reports of state appointees can be read subversively and used for other ends. In *Capital*, Marx used the published reports of the small number of state-appointed factory inspectors, who were to ensure that the provisions of the *Factory Act* were being followed, to excavate aspects of the social organization of capital and the condition of workers. Marx read these reports from the social standpoint of the working class, so as not to cast workers themselves as the problem, which was sometimes the implication of the reports. He also did not to read them as part of a middle-class argument for moral and social reform, which is the discourse in which they were often embedded (Marx 1977: 349–53).

Political activist ethnography provides us with a means to move beyond the limitations of both abstract "moral" exteriority and abstract "realistic" interiority. Political activist ethnography re-affirms that another world is possible, not from a position of exteriority, but from the inside out. It is rooted in struggles currently going on within and against "the system." The debate between the "lunatic radical" and the "reformist pig," the debate where both are right and both are wrong, therefore finds its resolution in a mode of investigation that enables us to envision forms of counter-power as practical social accomplishments — whether it is thousands of people marching on Yonge Street in Toronto to protest the bath raids, people converting an abandoned building into housing for the homeless or the successful blockading of the WTO meeting in Seattle. Counter-power, in this instance, does not take exteriority as its precondition but rather locates its sources in social relations, organization and struggles. The wealth and resources of this "system" are based in large part in our own activities and on the exploitation and oppression we endure. Workers (used here in the broad autonomist Marxist sense, including those who do domestic and unpaid labour) produce the resources and wealth that capital appropriates for itself (Cleaver 2000). It is therefore through our own practices, relations and struggles that capitalist social relations are produced, and we have the social capacities to transform them. We are both within and against this "system."

This experience of being both within and against the "system" also provides us with a basis to expose the limitations of strategies based on the simple celebration of the marginality of the oppressed. Although celebrating cultures of resistance is crucial, there needs to be a critique of any identity politics that separates these experiences of oppression and marginality off from class relations and history (Bannerji 1995b). Celebrated marginal identities are also in part formed within ruling relations and definitions. There is no place of oppression or marginality outside the system that can serve as the privileged epistemological place from which to examine social relations.

There are major barriers to exploring the social relations of struggle when we abide by structuralist concepts and ontologies of a "system" that we are either outside of or inside of. Structuralist ontologies that assume that it is social structures that cause us to act in particular ways (producing metaphors of people as puppets on strings) and that cause oppression need to be counterposed to the ontological assumptions of political activist ethnography, where people produce the social world through our own practices. Forms of oppression are socially organized through the practices of people and can be undone. We therefore need to abandon the language of "systems" and "structures." They get in the way of the work of recovering social practices, relations and organization, and impede our social struggles. We therefore prefer a language that does not participate in the reification of our social worlds and instead focuses on the social practices and relations we actively produce.

It is in this context that we are struck by the popularity in many activist circles of John Holloway's (2002) powerful critique of the fetishization of state and power relations. Holloway points out that orthodox and political economy versions of Marxism have participated in this fetishization of power and state relations, rendering them as things and objects that are not produced through people's actions.[15] The solution offered by these approaches is to dethrone and usurp, either by getting your party elected to government or by seizing state power. Holloway points out that both these approaches end up reproducing the same relations of power that already exist in capitalist state relations. Drawing on the experiences of the Zapatistas in Mexico he raises the possibility that the relations of "power over others" that run through state relations can be subverted without a seizure of this form of power through the development of a "power to do" amongst workers and the oppressed. While many questions remain, this suggests a useful approach for building forms of counter-power. Nevertheless, this work has often been misinterpreted by those on the moderate and social democratic left as simply advancing an argument for exteriority and "extremism." In contrast, for some on the Leninist "revolutionary left," it is read as almost a form of reformism, given its refusal to adopt the strategy of seizing state power. We see Holloway's book and the discussions around it in activist circles as one important attempt to work through these questions in a way that refuses the constraints of both insider and outsider perspectives, and of the limitations of ruling relations.

Effective Activist Research

In our view, successful activist research is research that allows activists to more effectively target the forms of social organization they are facing, to pinpoint weak links and contradictions, and to figure out ways of advancing people's struggles. We are thinking of the research conducted by the Right to Privacy Committee, AIDS ACTION NOW! and OCAP. This research bypasses questions of externality/internality to focus instead on disclosing how forms of oppression are socially organized so that they can be more effectively challenged and transformed. Often these practices of research are based on "activist breaching experiments," which disrupt ruling social relations in order to uncover more about their social organization.

In undertaking direct action "case work," e.g., when organizations like OCAP and the Sudbury Coalition Against Poverty (in 2002–04) work daily to fight for the survival needs of people trying to access social service support, activists are forced to learn about how provincial social assistance and municipal social policy are organized. Learning of this kind is a practical matter. It is about how and where to apply political pressure to get the best results. Its premises are not debatable or open to interpretation. When someone's social assistance cheque is denied, what can be done that day to get the cheque released? This activist organizing leads to mapping out institutional relations and learning how to most effectively disrupt them to win victories for people. In Sudbury, those of us involved in doing direct action support work with S-CAP learned quickly that the most productive area to apply pressure was the municipal figure in charge of Ontario Works (basic social assistance). This allowed us to map out the relation between the Ontario Works worker, their supervisor, the local management of Ontario Works and (given the partial devolution of control to municipalities that occurred during the years of Tory rule), the ways the city official who had jurisdiction over Ontario Works could be the most susceptible target for action.

Similarly, groups of anti-war/anti-occupation activists in Montréal, Ottawa and Toronto opposing Canadian state and corporate complicity in the occupation of Iraq have been able to research and put relatively effective forms of disruptive pressure on companies, like SNC-Lavalin, that produce ammunition for the U.S. military (Behrens 2005, Erwin 2005). In May 2005, Toronto anti-war and anti-imperialist activists mounted an effective protest against the corporation's annual meeting in Toronto that managed to seize the day in terms of business media coverage of the meeting.

Effective activism in these situations is based on researching and producing knowledge by challenging ruling forms of social organization.

This is what effective or successful activist research is all about. Often, this activist research does not go far enough in mapping out the social relations of struggle in which activists are engaged. This means that the knowledge gained from direct action and disrupting institutional relations does not become fully social knowledge that can be communicated to others and that can thereby inform the strategy and actions of the movement as a whole.

In summary, we have begun to develop a position that contests the outsider/insider polarity that continues to trap both research and activism. When the research begins, we are already located within social relations. The problem is in whether or not and how we see this. In mapping out the social relations of struggle in which we are engaged, we need to recognize both our implications within ruling relations and our opposition to them.

Developing capacities and resources for activist ethnographic research raises questions about the relation between movement activists and those in the university world who strive to do this kind of research for or as activists. How do we go about opening up dialogue and channels of communication aimed at bridging the divides between activists and social movement researchers? One side of this is to get more activists involved in doing political activist research. Another is to challenge and move beyond the binary opposition that separates "activist" and "researcher" as identity categories. This must be done in the very process of doing activist research and knowledge production. Here, we must inevitably raise questions about the particular social locations and trajectories of many of the people doing institutional ethnography work in the university and professional worlds.

Institutional Ethnography for Whom?

As we have seen throughout this book, social movements could benefit greatly from political activist ethnography and institutional ethnography. These approaches help to challenge the power/knowledge relation of "experts"; they allow us to focus on social organization and to produce knowledge differently. At the same time, there has been an uneven and troubling gulf developing between currents in institutional ethnography and forms of activism. At institutional ethnography gatherings in the late 1990s, while there were clearly strong political roots to the work being presented, there was often less focus on political activist ethnography. This is unfortunate, although it has also been acknowledged and contested by some practitioners of institutional ethnography. Quite often, the institutional location — in the universities and in various professions — of many (but not all) of us who do institutional ethnography is having an influence on the social and political character of our work. The starting point for much of our ethnographic inquiry is often now located in and initiated from these academic and professional social locations. This has led to a limited but important shift in the character of some of the institutional ethnography work that gets done. Sometimes because of these locations and the attendant lack of connection to grassroots struggles, analysis can get trapped within shifting ruling strategies of management and regulation. We can become much more adept at detailing shifting textual strategies of management and regulation than at identifying sites for resistance and struggle. As social and historical materialists, it is clear that our social locations and starting points influence the social character of the work we produce. This is not an individual or moral problem but is a question of social standpoint and social organization.

We need to ask ourselves more clearly: whose standpoint do we take up? Whose questions are privileged? This became clear at the 1998 institutional ethnography conference at York University, which was focused on the restructuring taking place across capitalist societies.[16] Major insights were put forward at this conference. The work on restructuring in professional areas of work, however, had a different social character from research produced in relation to racism and immigration, or to refugee and migrant worker policies. The work on restructuring within social work and educational institutional relations was undertaken from professional standpoints and tended to focus on shifts in the managerial regulation of professional work, while work done in relation to immigrant, refugee and migrant workers' experiences addressed more directly relations of poverty, class and racialization (see Sharma 1998).

The restructuring of professional work is crucial to grasp as central to capitalist globalization, but we cannot simply look at this from the vantage points of those involved in professional labour. The transformation of professional work processes does not encapsulate the entire context regarding restructuring. These relations also affect people accessing services, those living in poverty, students and others who exist within and produce the institutional relations we are exploring. This focus on the restructuring of the management of professional work has echoes in the Foucauldian work on governmentality, including in the work of Nikolas Rose (1999), where we lose sight of the struggles of people from below. A similar social process of domestication and containment can be seen in the process by which feminist work, subversive by nature, became trapped by institutional stipulations with the rise of accredited women's studies programs. D. Smith has also analyzed how funding regulations can transform the character of the research that we do (D. Smith 1987, 1999: 15–28).

Social locations within both the academic world and the professions can lead to social pressures tied to the social relations and practices of class (D. Smith 1999: 15–28). For those of us in the academic world, this constructs a loyalty to departments, or disciplines, or to professional institutions. Although we might wish it to be otherwise, our loyalties are rarely to oppressed peoples or social movements for change. Those of us in these locations need to actively resist practices that attempt to contain the subversive character of institutional ethnography. More recently, institutional ethnography events — especially the "Putting Institutional Ethnography into Practice" conference in Victoria in 2002 and the "Sociology for Changing the World" conference itself— have attempted to break with this domestication and to re-connect institutional ethnography to its activist roots.

Resisting Institutionalization, Discipline and Regulatory Regimes

One important path towards clarification and resistance to institutional capture is returning to George Smith's *Political Activist as Ethnographer* and seeing its continuing and contemporary relevance. Political activist ethnography has distinct features from more traditional, or standard-funded, forms of institutional ethnography.[17] It is important that political activist ethnography not simply be subsumed under more traditional means of doing institutional ethnography since it connects institutional ethnography to activism in a very different way. Those of us doing institutional ethnography and political activist ethnography in the university need to develop alternatives to academic and professional institutionalization. At very least, we need to develop other ways of linking ourselves to social movements that can cut across some of this institutional influence. Part of this is resisting pressures to be "responsible" to the institution or discipline. Another part is resisting practices of professionalization and enforced loyalty to the disciplines. Finally, we must be negligent in our responsibility to discipline others. We need to seize spaces and resources within the academy that we can use in our fight against ruling relations. This can include developing activist research programs in universities, such as the one proposed in this volume by Clarke to address issues of housing and the class restructuring of cities, and developing other concrete links with activist organizations in doing research *for* social movements.

A Sketch Towards a Political Activist Ethnography Research Agenda and Practice

To help us in thinking this through, we have developed the following sketch of one possible way of doing political activist ethnography that brings together activists and university-based researchers. Since research of this kind must always evolve in relation to the relevancies determined by the course of struggle itself, this account is of necessity quite preliminary and general. Some readers may find it maddingly so. We can also envision more solely activist based research projects that would have different characteristics. Starting from the research agenda set out in Clarke's chapter we can envisage the possibility of setting up a joint program of political activist ethnography research on the historical and social organization of social cleansing and homelessness. This research will be directed at actively strengthening the struggles against these practices and will bring together OCAP activists, university professors and graduate students (and some of these university workers will also be activists in OCAP). While this research will require access to university resources (and we deal with some of the difficulties regarding research funding and ethics approval in a moment), it must be conceived as research being done to meet the research and analytical needs of OCAP in its campaigns against homelessness and social cleansing. It is intended to produce knowledge for activists in OCAP and to strengthen their positions in the social relations of struggle. The research must therefore not be seen as the property of the university-based research-ers and must be defined by and made accountable to activists in OCAP. But the research cannot simply be the property of activists in OCAP either. The goal of activist research is to change the world, not to simply confirm who the activist already is or how they already envision their struggle. Breaking down researcher/activist distinctions is therefore at the heart of the research and knowledge creation process itself. As G. Smith points out, it is politi-cal confrontation and the needs of the struggle that must guide research. A crucial part of this research will be involving and training a significant number of researchers in political activist ethnography who are also OCAP members and non-university workers. It will be necessary to break down the divisions of labour between researchers and activists in the process of producing knowledge for the struggle. Clearly, there will be a number of complexities and contradictions here that will have to be worked through in actually doing this research.

This research will have to include a detailed documenting of and breaking away from the forms of ideological thought that currently organ-ize research on homelessness — including among activists themselves (for instance, the attempts to separate "the poor" from working-class struggles or to view people living in poverty as being without agency and in need of help). We will have to ensure that the social standpoints of people living in poverty, homeless people and anti-poverty activists are consistently taken up in this research. The research will concentrate on mapping out the social relations of the struggles against homelessness and social cleansing, and on identifying areas for organizing that will bring about results for people liv-ing in poverty. The research will rely upon activist breaching experiments to help map these relations of struggle. The research process will include the production of varying forms of research publications that are useful to members of OCAP, which may not take the form of standard academic research (more on this later) and that can be connected to the pedagogy and organizational efforts of the group.

One can see how such a research agenda and practice will both help to strengthening the composition of struggle that OCAP can mobilize, sharp-ening the effectiveness of its activism, and also strengthen the position of people in the university world who wish to engage in this form of research. It will concretely link theory and practice, research and activism. One can also envisage extending this approach to other areas of social and class struggle. At the same time, we can see how such a research agenda and practice will be attacked by university administrations and political authorities and may become the target of security and surveillance operations. This brings us right back to our starting point in the Preface — the security surveillance of a session on activist research.

This is why, at the same time that we envision the possibilities of activist research using university resources, we also have to see the many obstacles we will confront. We now take up a number of these obstacles and challenges before returning to more general questions of activism, research and social transformation.

The placement of some of us in the university world and in the professions gives us access to resources and spaces that are denied to most people. While social organization always gives people different starting points and differential access to resources and skills, there are specific skills, capacities and resources available to academic university workers that can beneficially be appropriated by those engaged in social struggles. We need to try to systematically strategize about how to defend these resources from attempts by university officials to regulate them and deprive social movements of their use. This requires a concrete relation to student and union organizing on campuses. A relation to activism within these contexts and outside them gives us another social grounding, a different place to stand and move from. We also see that one of our central projects must be to consciously extend the capacities and skills of social movement and community activists in doing political activist ethnography.

There are major problems in doing activist research in the era of neoliberalism. This is especially true in the current university, which has succumbed to a process of ongoing corporatization (Reimer 2004; Sears 2003) and adopted an evermore resolute focus on commercial, directly "applied" (often understood narrowly as needs assessments and program evaluations for ruling relations) and managerial work. While the capitalist university has shifted in some powerful ways that make doing progressive activist research difficult, there are still spaces that can be seized to do this work and ways in which student and union movements in university contexts can help to open up and defend these spaces. These spaces must also be used to bring in and familiarize social and community activists with activist research and to provide support for them in pursuing these goals. Amongst the neoliberal strategies of containment, we invariably confront specific regulatory regimes relating to funding and ethics reviews. These regimes restrict the possibilities of gaining support for activist research in the academy. Consequently, we need to research, navigate, challenge and transform them.

Research Funding as Regulation

To do significant research in a capitalist society requires money to purchase the necessary resources, supplies, equipment and researchers' time. Funding is therefore crucial to engaging in most forms of sustained research. While George Smith had no distinct funding for his research in *Political Activist as Ethnographer*, if we are to conduct this kind of research in a more extended and systematic fashion, we will need significant research funding. If funding is denied or is only offered in ways that subvert the commitments of political activist ethnography, then major problems are presented for doing this research. Mykhalovskiy has raised concerns about the implications of the emergence of a new university research regime that will make activist and critical research more difficult. He describes how, through funding agencies, various social forces are attempting to transform universities into centres for the production of commercial, applied and/or managerial knowledge. These forms of knowledge are counterpoised to those developed for activism and for changing the world. He describes how part of this process involves the reorganization of the Social Sciences and Humanities Research Council (SSHRC), which is the main funding body for social science research in the Canadian state. This is one of the regulatory regimes that those of us located in universities are up against, and we need institutional ethnographic research done on SSHRC to help us develop strategies for shifting its guidelines, navigating its regulations and getting funding for oppositional work. Below we sketch some preliminary lines of investigation into what is happening on the research funding front.

In 2002, the federal government launched a ten-year research and funding strategy aimed at putting Canada in the front ranks of "the world's most innovative countries." What does it mean exactly to be "innovative"? The Association of Universities and Colleges of Canada (AUCC) released *"A Strong Foundation for Innovation: An AUCC Action Plan"* (2002), which evaluates the current state of university funding and makes recommendations; it stresses the idea of competition between nation states and the need for funding from the private capitalist sector. Investment in the boundaries and borders of the nation-state and its competitive advantage over others is thus at the core of this approach. In this context, "innovation" is part of the same rhetoric as that of "lean production" and "flexibility," which are key terms for the neoliberal re-organization of capitalist relations (Sears 2003). Consequently, political activist research can be seen as nothing other than a form of resistance to this strategy of "innovation." The AUCC document states throughout that Canada must be on a par with other countries in terms of its production of research. It argues that "Canadians" should be part of this empire of knowledge and at the forefront of the "knowledge based economy."[18] This discourse is based on the maintenance of elite and nation-state based forms of knowledge.

The Canadian government has decided to match any of the private monies universities secure. The public/private matching system creates university reliance upon money from corporations. This gravely affects the push towards the commercialization of research. It is therefore not surprising that, in the *Strong Foundation for Innovation* document, there is a constant appeal to the private sector. This document also states that it should be the federal government's priority to provide research grants to new and established 'innovators' for basic research.

The attempt to shift the reliance of under-funded universities from public to private funding sets up a dynamic whereby a previously publicly funded institution is being much more directly regulated by and subordinated to capital. One immediately visible effect of this shift has been the censorship experienced by Canadian university teachers when they refuse to remain silent about research findings that conflict with corporate sponsors. The most famous case is Dr. Nancy Oliveri, who was dismissed from the University of Toronto for blowing the whistle on the drug company that was funding her research (Canadian Association of University Teachers 2002; Woo 2003: 198–99). Other cases, such as the Simon Fraser University administration's attempt to block the entrance of David Noble (a York University history professor and a noted critic of the corporatization of the university world) as Canadian Research Chair, demonstrate the hierarchical investment made into what constitutes "legitimate" research when state and corporate regulation is involved (Woo 2003; O'Brien MacDonald and Jensen 2004).

In the U.S. and Canada, there is rising alarm over the disproportionate allocation of research funding among disciplines, and especially the trend in recent years toward considerably lower levels of support for the social sciences and humanities. SSHRC has been criticized as being enthusiastic to fund projects that are policy driven, commodifiable and in line with the needs of government research while at the same time not funding socially critical research. There is also a dramatically low success rate for the application process, especially when SSHRC is compared to NSERC (the main state funding body for the natural sciences) (Canadian Association for Graduate Studies 2001: 20). SSHRC is under funded and the type of research it tends to reward falls in line with the government's need to be at the forefront of the "knowledge-based economy."

Despite the fact that the government continues to put money into research, it is not usually going to be research for changing the world, at least not in the ways we are writing about it. As much as possible, we must act to establish the context, and to create spaces, for activists to be heard and to play a part in defining the research that goes on in universities and other contexts.

Alternative Funding

While we need to research, use and resist university funding regimes, we also need to investigate sources of research funding that will not have the same constraints. Most social movements will not have much access to monies for research, but there is some funding available from organizations and the union movement. Many of the larger unions have their own research departments. Sometimes these bodies produce useful research, but most often the needs of research are subordinated to bargaining and reflect the overall character of the union movement. Often times, this research is simply a left version of mainstream economics. The knowledge it produces is not really on the side of workers and the oppressed. We need to help get more people in the union movement to see the importance of doing political activist ethnography, thereby opening up more possibilities of union funding for this kind of activist research.

The research conducted by Kinsman and others regarding the important 2000–01 strike by Mine Mill/Canadian Auto Workers (CAW) Local 598 against Falconbridge (Beck, Bowes et al. 2005) secured only limited university funding. This was due in part to the fact that granting bodies perceived the research to be "biased" because it took the standpoint of the workers and community supporters. Nevertheless, the research project managed to obtain significant funding from the CAW itself. While such an approach raises a set of complexities relating to union leaderships and the constraints they may impose on research, these are of a different social character than those faced from official funding bodies.

Ethics Reviews as Regulation

Mykhalovskiy also raises important concerns about how ethics reviews with the new Tri-Council[19] policy have become part of a regulatory regime coordinated conceptually by the *Tri-Council Policy Statement on Ethical Research Conduct* (MRC, NRC and SSHRC 2003). This policy organizes university-based ethics review boards in standardized ways that privilege a formal, proceduralist interpretation of ethics and that potentially discourage ethnographic fieldwork (Van Den Hoonaard 2002). For instance, if the research is perceived as having an element of "risk," it allows methodological questions to be raised — which means that more radical or innovative forms of research get more severely challenged. The idea of "risk" is itself reified in ethics reviews as an individual, psychological problem that will be raised for the participant through talking about their social experiences and locations. Notions of risk applied in these contexts often have more to do with the possible legal liability of the university than genuine concerns for research participants.

Moreover, if one is unable to produce pre-made and reductionist research tools and procedures, ethical concerns can be raised. This is quite commonly brought up as an objection to research with reflexive epistemologies that develop their research methodology and theorizing in relation to what is discovered through the research itself. Given that political activist ethnography and institutional ethnography proceed from the locations of the oppressed, its methods, questions and procedures are also reflexively worked out in those fields — often after the research has formally begun. At present, this methodological process is often seen as inherently unethical. Critical work is thus easily open to challenges based on the type of "sample" or "research instruments" it uses. It can sometimes be hard to argue in the context of research ethics boards that the purpose of the research is not to study a population or a social movement from an administrative perspective. It can be even harder to argue that the purpose of research is to critically investigate the social and institutional relations that produce problems in people's lives and the relations a social movement confronts. The position that political activist ethnography adopts — that research participants are not a sample that we wish to generalize from but are instead people we need to learn from — is generally not accepted by research ethics boards.

This is a significant obstacle for critical research, since official ethics reviews are required of all research that involves human subjects, and all universities have ethics review boards that use the Tri-Council policy. If the ethics review board does not approve the research, it cannot go forward with institutional approval. Even more community-based research, which may not be directly tied into a university, is supposed to go through this ethical review process. While concerns about ethics in relation to "human subjects" are extremely valid and political activist ethnography is based on highly ethical relations with research participants, this new regulatory regime of official ethics can be used to curtail critical forms of research.

At the Sociology for Changing the World conference there was a workshop on this topic which identified a series of problems — including research being modified and even being shut down due to the intervention of ethics committees. Official text-mediated ethics is therefore an important area with which we need to be concerned. We need to do institutional ethnographies of the ways Research Ethics Boards and other bodies work and to empower ourselves to do activist research within these various institutions.

Transformative/Transgressive Pedagogies, Texts and Activism

This book raises, but by no means answers, important questions about how to democratize research and the production of knowledge. How can we move from monological to dialogical knowledge creation to build more effective forms of activism? How can doing research move from being an individual enterprise to a more collective practice that can inform movement activism? How can movement activism inform research and knowledge production? How do we break down distinctions between activists and researchers in doing political activist research? How do we develop new divisions of labour in doing research in order to ground that research in activism?

In pursuing these questions, we may find, as Carroll suggests, that we can learn much from some of the best forms of participatory action research. Part of this is also to focus more attention on the pedagogy of activism and the teaching, learning and knowledge creation that takes place through activism. A number of contributors to this volume have suggested ways in which Freirian notions of critical pedagogy and the transformation of people from the objects into the subjects of teaching, learning and knowledge production can be enacted through political activist ethnography. We need to take these insights further in the development of activist research. Thompson's suggestion that direct action is simultaneously a research strategy and a form of pedagogy for the oppressed has great potential in this regard.

Central to the question of pedagogy is the way in which we read and use texts, and the primacy which those of us more connected with ruling relations often give to a narrow notion of the "textual." Historically, this primacy has privileged words and written texts over images, the visual,[20] art and cultural production. If we are talking about extending political activist ethnography among activists, including people who are less hooked into written texts, we need to broaden our pedagogies and to expand our range of subversive "texts" beyond the strictly textual. We need to expand our notion of the textual, doing research, teaching and creating knowledge, so as to include performance, art, videos, films, plays, music, dance, zines, poetry, comic books and other media. These forms can capture people's imagination and can create new contexts for research and knowledge creation. They can also create forms of dialogical pedagogy that are often occluded by more traditional textual forms. Such a commitment necessarily involves breaking down some of the distinctions between art, research and knowledge production in the life of social movements. In order to get a sense of what is possible in this respect, it is useful to consider the accomplishments of the early twentieth-century Russian Constructionist Movement, which John Berger felt encouraged dialogical forms of thought by undermining the narrative conventions of bourgeois art (Berger 1998).

The placement of this dialogue on activist research within a move towards more visually based sociologies is fruitful given that issues of material culture, representation, forms of reflexivity, social relations and the treatment of people as active subjects are embedded in this movement (Tilleczek 2005). Creating and reading the visual in research reminds us that these accounts are *about* something but that they also *do* something. One example is a documentary film produced by Tilleczek in which the social organization of the children's mental health system in rural Northern Ontario is examined. This film was based on research that produced text-based reports, fact sheets and research articles that helped to communicate the struggles and lives of these marginalized children. But these means could only go so far. The researchers and filmmakers worked collaboratively to find a way in which to re-enter the communities and provide visual narratives to parents and frontline workers so as to further open up the dialogue of what was "found" and to explore questions that would be helpful to examine further. In such cases, the visual can become either an aspect of the research process itself or a way in which to tell the research story. In each case, its affective and communicative power is useful in illustrating the social (Tilleczek 2005). The process also prodded the research team through the epistemological door and towards a deeper examination of the new visual knowledge they produced. This raised questions about the relation of visual work to the "research" knowledge and about ways of mapping the social lives of marginalized children. But questions remain: for instance, what is the relationship between this visual text and the research text? What is gained and lost in new forms of telling and knowing?

Another approach to the visual as both research strategy and knowledge producer can be seen in the narrative strategy of montage used by Michael Moore rather effectively in *Roger and Me*. At one point in the film, Moore is able to illuminate the trans-local coordination of social relations by switching between an eviction in Flint, Michigan, and a speech at a General Motors Christmas party (Michael Moore 1989). We need also to remember the significant impact that activist videos like *This is What Democracy Looks Like* (Independent Media Centre/Big Noise 2000), *Fourth World War* (Big Noise 2003) or *Tear Gas Holiday* (Toronto Video Activist Collective 2003) have had. The Sociology for Changing the World conference included an activist video festival; we have to move beyond seeing this as simply entertainment, to seeing it also as research and knowledge production. This can allow us to connect with people we would never reach through more academic forms of language and research.

Part of doing sociology for changing the world involves challenging the forms of conventional academic research and developing ways of writing, modes of performance, ways of visualizing and ways of knowing that allow us to transform the social. Political activist ethnography needs to involve very serious and committed analysis. But this analysis need not be counterposed to festivals of the oppressed. By helping to develop "texts" that move beyond the narrow confines of the textual, we can participate in coordinating and pushing forward struggles for social transformation.

By moving beyond the binary of outside versus inside and locating ourselves within social organization, we produce the basis for forms of activist research that can more effectively produce knowledge for our struggles. If effective, this research allows us to map the social relations of struggle and to more effectively challenge and transform ruling relations. From here it is possible to build forms of counter-power that grow out of our struggles against ruling relations. Throughout this process, there are more specifically activist based forms of research that, along with political activist ethnography, can be drawn upon. Invariably, these research projects will come up against administrative regimes that regulating research funding and that oversee ethics reviews. We must research and struggle against these regimes. We must also seek out alternative sources of funding that will place fewer restrictions on the research we can do. Finally, we are left with questions about how to build more dialogical and pedagogical forms of research within social movements. We are faced with the challenge of communicating with people through use of subversive texts that more effectively coordinate and facilitate our struggles. This is how we can begin to make a sociology for changing the world.

Notes

1. For a useful preliminary analysis of the capitalist university as a site of labour and the struggle against this see Harry Cleaver, "On Schoolwork and the Struggle Against it" (2003) available at <http://www.eco.utexas.edu/Homepages/Faculty/Cleaver/OnSchoolwork1.pdf>. (Accessed November 2005.)
2. One very useful example of this kind of analysis is *An Anarchist Attack on Global Governance,* produced in the lead-up to the G-8 meetings in Canada in 2002 by members of Anti-Capitalist Convergence (CLAC).
3. At the same time as using this word in this historical context we also wish to trouble or problematize "terrorist" in the current context of the "war on terror," which is in so many ways a war against Muslim identified people and people of colour and which conveniently shifts our focus away from the forces of state and institutional terrorism.
4. On some of the limitations of these approaches see Ward Churchill (1998).
5. Situationism is an artistic/anti-artistic radical political movement in Europe and elsewhere that gained some influence in France in the May/June 1968 student/worker revolt and has continued to inform forms of social and political organizing since then. One central figure was Guy Debord. Situationism focuses on the development of the society of the spectacle and "détournement" or the shifting and subversion of the works and images of others as a political and artistic practice. See Debord (1967), translated by Ken Knabb, and Guy Debord, *Comments on the Society of the Spectacle* at <http://www.notbored.org/commentaires.html>.
6. While some may draw parallels between the CrimethInc perspective and what is described as individualist "lifestyle" anarchism (critiqued in Bookchin 1997), they are quite distinct. There is a great deal of practical research involved in the work CrimethInc undertakes, some of which can be seen as having similarities to ethnomethodological breaching experiments as social "norms" and "order" are challenged and violated. See <http://www.crimethinc.com/>.
7. What is at stake here? It is useful to envision this problem in the terms provided by Rene DesCartes in his *Discourse on Method and Meditations* (2003). Perhaps history's most scintillating philosophical idealist, DesCartes formalized the long-standing habit of thinking of concepts as things when he turned thought itself into an ontological proof: "I think, therefore I am." This first proposition of being necessarily begs the question "what do I think?" and also "who is this 'I' that is thinking?" The *a priori* assertion of the "I" in DesCartes' postulate suggests that, invariably, one of the first things that our intrepid individualist philosopher thinks is "I am not that." Here, ontological distinctions are rendered in accordance with categories of the imagination rather than in terms of social doing, being and

becoming. The "I" is also argued for in an individualist and not a social fashion. Thought is, however, never simply individual but always social in character and therefore to engage in thought is already to be engaged in social relations. There is no place we can think outside the social (D. Smith 1999). DesCartes' thinking "I" requires the social but at the same time his philosophical idealism erases social relations.

8. It is precisely on the grounds of the term's pejorative connection to mental ill-ness that we make use of "lunatic radical" in our comic depiction of the conflict between insiders and outsiders. We do so first because it has often been a strategy of those on the moderate left to dismiss their opponents and, second, because it reveals the epistemological dimensions of the conflict.

9. Nikolas Rose's text *Powers of Freedom: Reframing Political Thought* (1999) is so focused on the idea that shifts within ruling forms of governance are *internal* to these forms of governance that he is unable to grasp how many of these shifts and transformations have been brought about in response to class and social struggles from below. These transformations are themselves part of the social relations of struggle.

10. On Foucault's notion of epochal breaks, which are never fully accounted for, see Michel Foucault (1973).

11. On this see Pilger (2005), Shabi (2005), Monboit (2005) and Mirrilees (2005).

12. There are also problems with Foucault's insightful formulation of power/knowledge relations since the ontological basis for power is never specified and it implies that all knowledge is always tied up with relations of social power putting in question liberatory knowledge projects. See D. Smith 1990a: 70, 79–80. Here we are using power/knowledge relations to get at the relations of social power that produce and operate through ruling forms of knowledge.

13. We are not trying to construct the methodological division as between quanti-tative ("bad") and qualitative ("good"). There are ways that critical quantitative methods, when used in combination with critical qualitative approaches, can be useful for making knowledge for social movements.

14. Vancouver's Downtown Eastside is one example of an over-studied neighbour-hood. There has been a large amount of research done in the area and on the people living there, but most of it does not benefit those living in this impover-ished neighbourhood. In contrast, the most effective work is done in consulta-tion and connection with the people living in the area such as through the Safe Injection Site. When the government-approved site was slow in progressing, members of the Vancouver Area Network of Drug Users (VANDU) opened their own unauthorized clinic. On this see <http://vancouver.cbc.ca/regional/serv-let/View?r=112338571 0&filename=bc_vandu20031001>. (Accessed Nov. 2005.)

   More generally on the Downtown East Side there are many studies including Currie (1995). For a more critical perspective see Bentley (2004). We wish to thank Erin Bentley for sharing some of her research with us.

15. This overlaps with and pushes further the critique of the use of "the state" that Corrigan and Sayer develop in *The Great Arch* (1985).

16. The conference was titled "Exploring the Restructuring and Transformation of Institutional Processes: Applications of Institutional Ethnography" and was held October 30–Nov. 1, 1998.

17. In her "Foreword," Dorothy E. Smith (1999: 3) describes this more traditional institutional ethnography work: "A definite project, questions, and methods of investigation were developed; bibliographies were prepared; applications were made for funding; individual or focus-group interviews, addressing predefined

topics, created a body of data that became the basis of reports, papers, and so on."

18. For a very different autonomist Marxist approach to these questions, with which we are sympathetic, see Dyer-Witheford (1999).
19. The Tri-Council brings together SSHRC, NSERC and the Medical Research Council.
20. For some crucial insights on extending textual analysis to photographs, see McCoy (1995).

REFERENCES

Adam, Barry D. 1997. "Post-Marxism and the New Social Movements." In William K. Carroll (ed.), *Organizing Dissent, Contemporary Social Movements in Theory and Practice, Second Edition*. Aurora, ON: Garamond.

Adamson, Walter. 1979. "Towards the Prison Notebooks: The Evolution of Gramsci's Thinking on Political Organization, 1918–1926." *Polity* (Fall): 38–64.

Agletta, Michel. 1979. *A Theory of Capitalist Regulation: The U.S. Experience*. London: New Left.

Ahmad, Muneer. 2002. "Homeland Insecurities: Racial Violence the Day after September 11." *Social Text* 72.

Ali, Tariq. 2003. *The Clash of Fundamentalisms: Crusades, Jihads and Modernity*. London: Verso.

Allen, Max, and Coleman Jones, producers. 1987–89. "The AIDS campaigns." CBC Radio, Ideas series.

Althusser, Louis. 1971. *Lenin and Philosophy and Other Essays*. New York: Monthly Review.

_____. 1977. *For Marx*. London: New Left.

Amin, Samir. 1988. *Eurocentrism*. New York: Monthly Review.

Amuchastegui, Maria. 2004. "Shadowy Survival." *Now Magazine*, July 29.

Anthias, Floya, and Cathie Lloyd. 2002. "Introduction: Fighting Racism, Defining the Territory." In Floya Anthias and Cathie Lloyd (eds.), *Rethinking Anti-racisms: From Theory to Practice*. London: Routledge.

Anti-Capitalist Convergence (CLAC) and Montreal@tao.ca. 2002. *An Anarchist Attack on Global Governance*. Montreal.

Antonio, Robert J. 1981. "Immanent Critique as the Core of Critical Theory: Its Origins and Developments in Hegel, Marx and Contemporary Thought." *British Journal of Sociology* 32, 3.

Armstrong, Pat, and Hugh Armstrong. 1992. "Better Irreverent than Irrelevant." In William K. Carroll et al. (eds.), *Fragile Truths*. Ottawa: Carleton University Press.

Association of Universities and Colleges of Canada. 2002. *A Strong Foundation for Innovation: An AUCC Action Plan*. At <www.aucc.ca/_pdf/english/reports/2002/innovation/innoactionpl_e.pdf>. (Accessed Dec. 2, 2005).

Bacon, David. 2001. "Which Side Are You On?" *Colorlines* 4, 2 (Summer)

Bai, Jane, and Eric Tang. 2002. "The War at Home." *Colorlines* 5, 1 (Spring)

Bakhtin, Mikhail. 1981. *The Dialogical Imagination: Four Essays*. Edited by Michael Holquist, translated by Carly Emerson and Michael Holquist. Austin: University of Texas Press.

Balibar, Etienne. 2000. "What We Owe to the *Sans-Papiers*." In Len Guenther and Cornelius Heesters (eds.), *Social Insecurity*. Toronto: Anansi.

_____. 2004. *We, the People of Europe? Reflections on Transnational Citizenship*. Translated by James Swenson. Princeton: Princeton University Press.

Bannerji, Himani. 1994. "Writing 'India', Doing Ideology." *Left History* 2, 2.

_____. 1995a. "Beyond the Ruling Category to What Actually Happens: Notes on James Mill's Historiography in the History of British India." In Marie Campbell and Ann Manicom (eds.), *Knowledge Experience and Ruling Relations*. Toronto: University of Toronto Press.

_____. 1995b. *Thinking Through: Essays on Feminism, Marxism and Anti-Racism*. Toronto: Women's Press.

Beck, Kaili, Chris Bowes, Gary Kinsman, Mercedes Steedman, and Peter Suschnigg (eds.). 2005. *Mine Mill Fights Back, Mine Mill/CAW Local Strike 2000–2001 Sudbury*. Sudbury: Mine Mill/CAW Local 598.

Becker, Howard. 1970. "Whose Side Are We on?" In Larry T. Reynolds and Janice M. Reynolds (eds.), *The Sociology of Sociology*. New York: David Mackay Company Inc.

Behrens, Matthew. 2005. "Canadian Firms Soaked in Iraqi and Afghan Blood." *Counterpunch*. At <www.counterpunch.org/behrens10062004.html>. (Accessed Dec. 2, 2005.)

Benhabib, Seyla. 1994. "The Critique of Instrumental Reason." In Slavoj Zizek (ed.), *Mapping Ideologies*. London: Verso.

Benjamin, Walter. 1969. "On Some Motifs in Baudelaire." *Illuminations*. New York: Schocken.

Bentley, Erin. 2004, "(No)Where to Go: Street-Involved Queer, Lesbian, and Bisexual Young Women and 'Relations of Ruling,'" MA Thesis in Sociology, UBC, Vancouver.

Berger, John. 1998. *Art and Revolution, Ernst Neizvestny, Endurance, and the Role of the Artist*. New York: Vintage.

Berlant, Lauren. 1996. "The Face of America and the State of Emergency." In Cary Nelson and Dilip Parameshwar Gaonkar (eds.), *Disciplinarity and Dissent in Cultural Studies*. New York: Routledge.

Best, Steven. 1995. *The Politics of Historical Vision*. New York: Guilford.

Beyer-Arnesen, Harold. 2000. "Direct Action: Toward an Understanding of a Concept." Anarcho *Syndicalist Review* 29 (Summer).

Bhabha, Jacqueline. 1998. "'Get Back to Where You Once Belonged': Identity, Citizenship, and Exclusion in Europe." *Human Rights Quarterly* 20, 3.

Big Noise. 2003. *The Fourth World War*. Film.

Black, Errol, and Jim Silver. 2001. *Building a Better World: An Introduction to Trade Unionism in Canada*. Halifax: Fernwood.

Bloor M. 1995. "A User's Guide to Contrasting Theories of HIV-related Risk Behaviour." In J. Gabe (ed.), *Health and Risk: Sociological Approaches*. Oxford: Blackwell.

Bloor, M.J., N.P. McKeganey, A. Finlay and M.A. Barnard. 1992. "The Inappropriateness of Psycho-social Models of Risk Behaviour for Understanding HIV-related Risk Practices among Glasgow Male Prostitutes." *AIDS Care* 4, 2.

Bologh, Roslyn Wallach. 1979. *Dialectical Phenomenology: Marx's Method*. Boston: Northeastern University Press.

Bookchin, Murray. 1997. *Social Anarchism or Lifestyle Anarchism: An Unbridgeable Chasm*. San Francisco: AK Press.

Borowy, J., S. Gordon et al. 1993. "Are These Clothes Clean? The Campaign for Fair Wages and Working Conditions for Homeworkers." In L. Carty (ed.), *And Still We Rise: Feminist Political Mobilizing in Contemporary Canada*. Toronto:

Women's Press.

Bowes, Chris. 2003. "Direct Action: Fighting to Win Locally." *New Socialist* 42 (July-August).

_____. 2004, "Culture-Jamming: Confronting the Capitalist Colonization of Social Space," MA Thesis in Applied Social Research, Laurentian University, Sudbury.

Braverman, Harry. 1974. *Labor and Monopoly Capital*. New York: Monthly Review.

Breines, Wini. 1982. *Community and Organization in the New Left, 1962–1968: The Great Refusal*. South Hadley, MA: J.F. Bergin.

Brock, Deborah. 1998. *Making Work, Making Trouble: Prostitution as a Social Problem*. Toronto: University of Toronto Press.

_____. 2003. *Making Normal: Social Regulation in Canada*. Toronto: Thomson/Nelson.

Browne, Simone. 2002."'Of Passport Babies' and 'Border Control': The Case of *Mavis Baker v. Minister of Citizenship and Immigration*." *Atlantis* 26.

Bruner, Arnold. 1981. "Out of the Closet: A Study of Relations between the Homosexual Community and the Police." Report to Mayor Arthur Eggleton and the Council of the City of Toronto. Toronto: City Clerk's Office.

Buck-Morss, Susan. 2000. *Dreamworld and Catastrophe*. Cambridge: MIT Press.

Burawoy, Michael et al. 2000. *Global Ethnography: Forces, Connections and Imaginations in a Postmodern World*. Berkeley: University of California Press.

Butler, Judith. 1990. *Gender Trouble: Feminism and the Subversion of Identity*, London: Routledge.

_____. 1999. "A 'bad writer' bites back." *New York Times*, March 20.

Calpotura, Francis. 2004. "Riding with the Wind." *Colorlines* 7, 1 (Spring).

Camfield, David. 2004. "Union Renewal in the Canadian Public Sector: Challenges, Prospects and Choices." Paper presented at the International Colloquium on Union Renewal: Assessing Innovations for Union Power in a Globalized Economy, organized by the Inter-university Research Centre on Globalization and Work, University of Montréal.

Campbell, Marie. 2002. "Disability Research and Institutional Ethnography: Exploring 'Social Organization' from Inside It." Paper presented at the Nordic Network on Disability Research, Reykjavik, Iceland, August 22–24.

_____. 2003. "Dorothy Smith and Knowing the World We Live In." *Journal of Sociology and Social Welfare* 30, 1 (3–22) March.

Campbell, Marie, and Frances Gregor. 2002. *Mapping Social Relations: A Primer in Doing Institutional Ethnography*. Toronto: Garamond.

Campbell, Marie, and Ann Manicom (eds.). 1995. *Knowledge Experience and Ruling Relations: Essays in the Social Organization of Knowledge*. Toronto: University of Toronto Press.

Campbell, M., B. Copeland and B. Tate (with assistance from the research team). 1999. "Project Inter-Seed: Learning from the health care experiences of people with disabilities." Final Report submitted to B.C. Health Research Foundation December.

Canadian Association for Graduate Studies. 2001. "Educating the Best Minds for the Knowledge Economy: Setting the Stage for Success," A position paper for the Executive Committee of the Canadian Association for Graduate Studies. At <www.cags.ca/pdf/knowledge-economy.pdf>. (Accessed Dec. 2, 2005.)

Canadian Association of University Teachers. 2002. "Supplement to the Report to the Committee of Inquiry." At <www.caut.ca/en/issues/academicfreedom/ol-ivierireport.asp>. (Accessed Dec. 2, 2005.)

Canel, Eduardo. 1992. "New Social Movement Theory and Resource Mobilization: The Need for Integration." In William K. Carroll (ed.), *Organizing Dissent, Contemporary Social Movements in Theory and Practice.* Toronto: Garamond.

Carroll, William K. 2004. *Critical Strategies for Social Research.* Toronto: Canadian Scholars' Press.

Chaddha, Anmol. 2003–4. "Borderland Security." *Colorlines* 6, 4 (Winter).

Chang, Grace. 2000. *Disposable Domestics: Immigrant Women Workers in the Global Economy.* Cambridge: South End.

Chang, Or, Tharmendran et al. (eds.). 2001. *Resist, a Grassroots Collection of Stories, Poetry, Photos and Analyses from the Québec City FTAA Protests and Beyond.* Halifax: Fernwood.

Cheng, L., and G. Gereffi. 1994. "U.S. Retailers and Asian Garment Production." In E. Bonacich, L. Cheng, N. Chincilla, N. Hamilton and P. Ong (eds.), *Global Production: The Apparel Industry in the Pacific Rim.* Philadelphia: Temple University Press.

Choudry, Abdul Aziz. 2004. "Institutional Ethnography, Political Activist Ethnography, and 'Anti-Globalization' Movements." Unpublished paper.

_____. 2005. "Crackdown." *New Internationalist* 376 (March).

Church, Kathryn. 1993. "Breaking Down/Breaking Through: Multi-voiced Narratives on Psychiatric Survivor Participation in Ontario's Community Mental Health System." Doctoral Dissertation, University of Toronto.

_____. 1995. *Forbidden Narratives: Critical Autobiography as Social Science.* Amsterdam: International Publishers Distributors. Reprinted by Routledge in 2003.

_____. 1997. "Because of Where We've Been: The Business Behind the Business of Psychiatric Survivor Economic Development." Toronto: Ontario Council of Alternative Businesses. Available from the author and to be posted on the website for the School of Disability Studies at Ryerson University. At <www.ryerson.ca/ds>.

Church, K., E. Shragge, R. Ng and J.M. Fontan. Forthcoming. "While no one is watching: Learning in social action among people who are excluded from the labour market."

Churchill, Ward. 1998. *Pacifism as Pathology, Reflections on the Role of Armed Struggle in North America.* Winnipeg: Arbeiter Ring.

Clark, Campbell. 2001. "PM shrugs off immigrants' travel trouble." *Globe and Mail,* November 6.

_____. 2003. "Alarm sounded over border control." *Globe and Mail,* April 9.

Clarke, John. 2002. "Allies in Conflict? The Labour Movement and Other Social Movements." Paper presented at Sociology For Changing the World: Political Activist Ethnography Conference, Laurentian University, Sudbury, ON, November 9.

Cleaver, Harry. 1998. "The Zapatistas and the International Circulation of Struggle: Lessons Suggested and Problems Raised." At <http://www.eco.utexas.edu/facstaff/Cleaver/hmchtmlpapers.html>. (Accessed Dec. 2, 2005.)

_____. 2000. *Reading Capital Politically.* London and San Francisco: AK Press.

_____. 2003. *On Schoolwork and the Struggle Against it.* At <http://www.eco.utexas.edu/Homepages/Faculty/Cleaver/OnSchoolwork1.pdf>. (Accessed Dec. 2, 2005.)

Code civil du Québec. 1991. Québec: Éditeur officiel du Québec.

Cohen, Nicole. 2004. "York U Stumbles." At <eye.net/eye/issue/issue_05.13.04/city/york.html>. (Accessed Dec. 2, 2005.)

Cohen, Steve. 2002. *No One Is Illegal: Asylum and Immigration Controls Past and Present*. London: Trentham Books.

Collins, Patricia Hill. 1990. *Black Feminist Thought: Knowledge, Consciousness, and the Politics of Enlightenment*. Boston: Unwin Hyman.

Conway, Janet. 2004. *Identity, Place, Knowledge: Social Movements Contesting Globalization*. Halifax: Fernwood.

Cophan. 2002. "Avant-projet de loi sur la carte de santé du Québec." Mémoire résenté à la Commission des affaires sociales, 8 février.

Correctional Services of Canada. 1991. Directive 800 (Health Services). Ottawa.

Corrigan, Phillip, and Derek Sayer. 1985. *The Great Arch: English State Formation as Cultural Revolution*. Oxford/New York: Basil Blackwell.

CrimethInc. 2000. "Days of War, Nights of Love: Crimethink for Beginners." At <http://www.crimethink.com/library/english/libdays.html>. (Accessed Dec. 2, 2005.)

_____. 2001. "Evasion." At <http://www.crimethinc.com>. (Accessed Dec. 2, 2005.)

Currie, Dawn, and Anoja Wickramasinghe. 1998. "Engendering Development Theory from the Standpoint of Women." In D. Currie, G. Noga and P. Gurstein (eds.), *Learning to Write: Women's Studies in Development*. Vancouver: Collective Press,

Currie, Sue. 1995. *Assessing the Violence Against Street-Involved Women in the Downtown Eastside / Strathcona Community*. Vancouver, BC: Downtown Eastside Youth Activities Society and Watari Research Society for the Ministry of Women's Equality.

Dagg, A. 1996. "Organizing Homeworkers into Unions: The Homeworkers' Association of Toronto, Canada." In E. Boris and E. Prugl (eds.), *Homeworkers in Global Perspective: Invisible No More*. New York: Routledge.

Dalla Costa, Mariarosa, and Selma James. 1972. *The Power of Women and the Subversion of the Community*. Bristol: Falling Wall.

Darder, Antonia, Marta Baltodano and Rololfo D. Torres (eds.). 2003. *The Critical Pedagogy Reader*. New York: Routledge.

Davis, Mike. 1999. "Magical Urbanism: Latinos Reinvent the Big City." *New Left Review* 234 (old series).

Debord, Guy. 1967. *The Society of the Spectacle*. Translated by Ken Knabb. Detroit: Black and Red.

_____. *Comments on the Society of the Spectacle*. At <http://www.notbored.org/commentaires.html>. (Accessed Dec. 2, 2005.)

Derrida, Jacques. 1978. *Writing and Difference*. Chicago: University of Chicago Press.

DesCartes, René. 2003. *Discourse on Method and Meditations*. Couriere: Dover Publications.

Dobbs, Farrell. 1972. *Teamster Rebellion*. New York: Monad.

Drakich, Janice, Karen R. Grant and Penni Stewart. 2002. "The Academy in the 21st Century: Editors' Introduction." *Canadian Review of Sociology and Anthropology* 39, 3.

Draper, Hal. 1978. *Karl Marx's Theory of Revolution, Vol. II: The Politics of Social Classes*. New York: Monthly Review.

du Gay, P. 2000. "Representing 'Globalization': Notes on the Discursive Orderings of Economic Life." In P. Gilroy, L. Grossberg and A. McRobbie (eds.), *Without Guarantees in Honour of Stuart Hall*. London: Verso.

DuBois, W.E.B. 1903. *The Souls of Black Folks*. Chicago: A.C. McClurg.

Dyer-Witheford, Nick. 1999. *Cyber-Marx: Cycles and Circuits of Struggle in High-Technology Capitalism*. Chicago: University of Illinois Press.

Edoney, Haile Telatra. n.d. but c1970s. *Cry of the Illegal Immigrant*. Photocopy in author's possession.

Erwin, Steve. 2005, "Protests Overshadow SNC-Lavalin Shareholders Meeting." *Canadian Press*, May 5.

Feagin, Joe, and Hernan Vera. 2001. *Liberation Sociology*. Boulder, CO: Westview.

Fanon, Franz. 1961. *The Wretched of the Earth*. New York: Grove.

Featherstone, Liza. 2002. "Fighting the War at Home." *The Nation*, April 1.

Federici, Silvia. 1975. *Wages Against Housework*. London: Power of Women Collective and Falling Wall.

Fishburn, Dudley. 1999. "Editor's Introduction" (Special issue on globalization). *The Economist*, The World in 2000.

_____. 2000. "Editor's Introduction." *The Economist*, The World in 2001.

Fishman, Mark. 1988. *Manufacturing the News*. Austin: University of Texas Press.

Foucault, Michel. 1973. *The Order of Things: An Archaeology of the Human Sciences*. New York: Random House.

_____. 1974. *The Archaeology of Knowledge*. London: Tavistock.

_____. 1979. *Discipline and Punish: The Birth of the Prison*. New York: Vintage.

_____. 1980a. *The History of Sexuality, Vol. 1. An Introduction*. Translated by Robert Hurley. New York: Vintage.

_____. 1980b. *Power/Knowledge: Selected Interviews and Other Writings, 1972–1977*. Colin Gordon (ed.). New York: Pantheon.

Freire, Paulo. 1970. *Pedagogy of the Oppressed*. New York: Seabury.

_____. 1996. *Pedagogy of the Oppressed*. New York: Continuum.

Gabriel, Christina, and Laura Macdonald. 2004. "Of Borders and Business: Canadian Corporate Proposals for North American 'Deep Integration.'" *Studies in Political Economy* 74 (Autumn).

Garfinkel, Harold. 1967. *Studies in Ethnomethodology*. Englewood Cliffs, NJ: Prentice-Hall.

Gindin, Sam. 1998. "Socialism 'With Sober Senses': Developing Workers' Capacities." *Socialist Register* 34 (February).

_____. 2004. *The Auto Industry: Concretizing Working Class Solidarity, Internationalism Beyond Slogans*. Toronto: Socialist Project.

Globe and Mail. 2001. "Trading citizenship for a terrorism tip." Editorial, December 3.

Gould, C. Carol. 1978. *Marx's Social Ontology*. Cambridge, MA: MIT Press.

Gramsci, Antonio.1971. *Selections from the Prison Notebooks*. New York: International.

Green Mountain Anarchist Collective. 2000. *A Communiqué on Tactics and Organization*. December. Montpellier, VT.

Greenspan, Edward L. 1984. "Martin's Annual Criminal Code, 1984." Aurora: Canada Law Book.

Greenwood, Davydd J., and Morten Levin. 1998. *Introduction to Action Research*. London: Sage.

Greffier, Ethel. 1975. "De certains aspects juridiques du transsexualisme dans le droit québécois." *Revue de droit Université de Sherbrooke* 6.

Gunning, J., J. Eaton, S. Ferrier, M. Kerr, A. King and J. Maltby. 2000. "Dealing with work-related musculoskeletal disorders in the Ontario clothing industry." Report submitted to the Research Advisory Council of the Workplace Safety and Insurance Board, UNITE, November 3.

Gutierrez Rodriguez, Encarnacion. 2004. "'We Need Your Support, but the Struggle is Primarily Ours': On Representation, Migration and the Sans Papiers Movement, ESF Paris, 12–15 November 2003." *Feminist Review* 77.

Hagopian, Elaine (ed.). 2004. *Civil Rights in Peril: The Targeting of Arabs and Muslims*. London: Pluto.

Hall, Budd L. 1979. "Knowledge as a Commodity and Participatory Research." *Prospects* 9, 4.

Hall, Stuart, Charles Critcher, Tony Jefferson, John Clarke and Brian Roberts. 1978. *Policing the Crisis: Mugging the State and Law and Order*. London: Macmillan.

Hall, Stuart, and Martin Jacques (eds.). 1989. *New Times*. London: Lawrence and Wishart.

Harding, Sandra. 1986. *The Science Question in Feminism*. Ithaca: Cornell University Press.

Hardt, Michael, and Antonio Negri. 2000. *Empire*. Cambridge: Harvard University Press.

_____. 2004. *Multitude: War and Democracy in the Age of Empire*. New York: Penguin.

Hartsock, Nancy. 1985. *Money, Sex, and Power: Toward a Feminist Historical Materialism*. Boston: Northeastern University Press.

Harvey, David. 1996. "The Principles of Dialectics." In David Harvey (ed.), *Justice, Nature and the Geography of Difference*. Oxford: Blackwell.

Hawkins, Freda. 1991. *Critical Years in Immigration: Canada and Australia Compared*. Second edition. Montréal: McGill-Queens.

Hayter, Teresa. 2000. *Open Borders: The Case Against Immigration Controls*. London: Pluto.

Herman, Edward S., and Noam Chomsky. 2002. *Manufacturing Consent: The Political Economy of Mass Media*. New York: Pantheon.

Heron, Craig. 1996. *The Canadian Labour Movement: A Short History*. Second Edition. Toronto: Lorimer.

Hickling-Johnson, Inc. 1981–82. *Metropolitan Police Management Study*. Toronto.

Hofstadter, Douglas R. 1979. *Goedel, Escher, Bach: An Eternal Golden Braid*. New York: Random House.

Holloway, John. 2002. *Change the World Without Taking Power*. London: Pluto.

Holquist, Michael (ed.). 1981. *The Dialogic Imagination, Four Essays by M.M. Bakhtin*. Austin: University of Texas.

Honig, Bonnie. 2001. *Democracy and the Foreigner*. Princeton: Princeton University Press.

hooks, bell. 1994. *Teaching to Transgress: Education as the Practice of Freedom*. New York: Routledge.

_____. 2003. *Teaching Community: A Pedagogy of Hope*. New York: Routledge.

Horowitz, Irving Louis. 1961. *Radicalism and the Revolt Against Reason: The Social Theories of Georges Sorel*. London: Routledge.

Hurl, Chris. 2005. "Anti-Globalization and Diversity of Tactics." *Upping the Anti... A*

Journal of Theory and Action 1, 1. Autonomy and Solidarity Network, Toronto.

Iacovetta, Franca, Roberto Perrin and Angelo Principe (eds.). 2000. *Enemies Within: Italian and Other Internees in Canada and Abroad.* Toronto: University of Toronto Press.

Independent Media Centre. 2003. *KM.0 (Kilometer Zero).* Video.

Independent Media Centre/Big Noise. 2000. *This Is What Democracy Looks Like.* Video.

Industry Canada. 1996. *Clothing Industry Statistical Data.*

International Civil Liberties Monitoring Group. 2003. "In the Shadow of the Law: A Report by the International Civil Liberties Monitoring Group (ICLMG) in response to Justice Canada's 1st annual report on the application of the *Anti-Terrorism Act* (Bill C-36)."

Jackson, D. 1990. *Unmasking Masculinity: A Critical Autobiography.* London: Unwin Hyman.

Johnson, L., and R. Johnson. 1982. *The Seam Allowance: Industrial Home Sewing in Canada.* Toronto: Women's Educational Press.

Jordan, Grant. 1994. *The British Administrative System: Principles versus Practice.* London: Routledge.

Kashmeri, Zuhair. 1991. *The Gulf Within: Canadian Arabs, Racism, and the Gulf War.* Toronto: Lorimer.

Kaufman, Cynthia. 2003. *Ideas for Action: Relevant Theory for Radical Change.* Cambridge, MA: South End Press.

Kellner, Douglas. 1985. "Critical Theory, Max Weber, and the Dialectics of Domination." In Robert J. Antonio and Ronald M. Glassman (eds.), *A Weber-Marx Dialogue.* Lawrence: University of Kansas Press.

Kelly, Susan. 2005. "Is Another World Possible? Report on the European Social Forum, London 2004." *Fuse* 28, 1 (February).

Kessler, Suzanne J., and Wendy McKenna. 1978. *Gender: An Ethnomethodological Approach.* Chicago and London: University of Chicago Press.

Keung, Nicholas. 2002. "Final dignity for a homeless man." *Toronto Star*, 11 March.

Khandor, Erika, Jean McDonald, Peter Nyers and Cynthia Wright. 2004. "The Regularization of Non-Status Immigrants in Canada, 1960–2004: Past Policies, Current Perspectives, Active Campaigns." At <http://www.ocasi.org/STATUS/index.asp>. (Accessed Dec. 2, 2005.)

Khokha, Sasha. 2001. "Paper Chase." *ColorLines* 4, 2.

Kidd, Dorothy. 2004. "From Carnival to Commons: The Global IMC Network." In Eddie Yuen, George Katsiaficas and Daniel Burton-Rose (eds.), *Confronting Capitalism: Dispatches from a Global Movement.* New York: Soft Skull.

Kinsman, Gary. 1995. "The Textual Practices of Sexual Rule: Sexual Policing and Gay Men." In Marie Campbell and Ann Manicom (eds.), *Knowledge, Experience, and Ruling Relations: Studies in the Social Organization of Knowledge.* Toronto: University of Toronto Press.

_____. 1996. *The Regulation of Desire.* Montréal: Black Rose.

_____. 1997. "Managing AIDS Organizing: 'Consultation,' 'Partnership,' and 'Responsibility' as Strategies of Regulation." In William Carrol (ed.), *Organizing Dissent: Contemporary Social Movements in Theory and Practice.* Second Edition. Toronto: Garamond.

_____. 2000. "Constructing Gay Men and Lesbians as National Security Risks." In

Gary Kinsman, Dieter K. Buse and Mercedes Steedman (eds.), *Whose National Security? Canadian State Surveillance and the Creation of Enemies*. Toronto: Between the Lines.

_____. 2003a. "National Security as Moral Regulation: Making the Normal and the Deviant in the Security Campaigns Against Gay Men and Lesbians." In Deborah Brock (ed.).

_____. 2003b. "Queerness Is Not in Our Genes: Biological Determinism Versus Social Liberation." In Deborah Brock (ed.).

_____. 2004. "The Canadian Cold War on Queers: Sexual Regulation and Resistance." In Richard Cavell (ed.), *Love, Hate, and Fear in Canada's Cold War*. Toronto: University of Toronto Press/Green College Thematic Series.

_____. 2005a. "The Politics of Revolution: Learning from Autonomist Marxism." *Upping the Anti... A Journal of Theory and Action* 1, 1. Autonomy and Solidarity Network, Toronto.

_____. 2005b. "'Waking Up a Sleeping Dog': The Significance of the Strike." In Kaili Beck et al. (eds.).

Kinsman, Gary, Dieter K. Buse and Mercedes Steedman (eds.). 2000. *Whose National Security? Canadian State Surveillance and the Creation of Enemies*. Toronto: Between the Lines.

Klein, Naomi. 2001. "The legacy of austerity? A really 'great' border." *Globe and Mail*, December 12.

_____. 2003. "The Rise of the Fortress Continent." *The Nation*, February 3.

Kouri, Robert. 1973. "Comments on Transsexualism in the Province of Québec." *Revue de droit Université de Sherbrooke* 4.

_____. 1975. "Certain Legal Aspects of Modern Medicine (Sex Reassignment and Sterilization)." PhD dissertation, Institute of Comparative Law, McGill University.

Kuhling, Clarice. 2002. "How CUPE 3903 Struck and Won." *Just Labour: A Canadian Journal of Work and Society* 1(Winter). At <http://www.yorku.ca/julabour/volume1/index2.htm>. (Accessed Dec. 2, 2005.)

Kuhn, Thomas S. 1970. *The Structure of Scientific Revolutions*. Chicago: University of Chicago Press.

Kumar, Amitava. 2000. *Passport Photos*. Berkeley: University of California Press.

Kurasawa, F. 2002. "Which Barbarians at the Gates? From the Culture Wars to Market Orthodoxy in the North American Academy." *Canadian Review of Sociology and Anthropology* 39, 3.

Kwang, P. 1997. *Forbidden Workers: Illegal Chinese Immigrants and American Labor*. New York: New Press.

Lachance, E., K.Church, E. Shragge and J.M. Fontan. 1999. "Appropriating Evaluation: A Guide to Critically Examining Our Practice." Ottawa: Human Resources Development Canada. Available from K. Church and available on the website for the School of Disability Studies at Ryerson University. At <www.ryerson.ca/ds>. (Accessed Dec. 2, 2005.)

Laclau, Ernesto, and Chantal Mouffe. 1985. *Hegemony and Socialist Strategy: Toward a Radical Democratic Politics*. London: Verso.

Lahn, Peg. 2004. "Identifying the Excluded: ID Documents and Targeted Communities." *New Socialist* 47.

Landsberg, Michele. 2002. "Officials hound woman fighting deportation." *Toronto Star*, April 13.

Larrain, Jorge. 1983. *Marxism and Ideology*. London: Macmillan.

Lawton, Valerie, and Allan Thompson. 2001. "Still in Canada? No one knows." *Toronto Star*, October 7.

Lee, Chisun. 2001. "The Other Disaster: Tough Times Ahead Bode Worst for City's Poorest." *Village Voice*, October 16.

_____. 2002. "INS Detainee Hits, US Strikes Back: Canadian Attempts Freedom on Habeas Suit but Gets Charged." *Village Voice*, February 5.

_____. 2003. "Defending America's Least Wanted." *Village Voice*, January 15–21.

Lemert, Charles. 1992. "Subjectivity's Limit: The Unsolved Riddle of the Standpoint." *Sociological Theory* 10, 1.

Lentin, Alana. 2004. *Racism and Anti-racism in Europe*. London: Pluto.

Levant, Alex. 2003. "Flying Squads and the Crisis of Self-Organization." *New Socialst* 39 (March\April).

Levine, Robert J. 1986. *Ethics and Regulation of Clinical Research*. Baltimore: Urban.

Lilley, P.J., and Jeff Shantz. 2004. "The World's Largest Workplace, Social Reproduction and Wages for Housework." *The Northeastern Anarchist, Publication of the Northeastern Federation of Anarcho-Communists* (NEFAC) 9 (Summer/Fall).

Lowe, Lisa. 1996. *Immigrant Acts: On Asian American Cultural Politics*. Durham: Duke University Press.

Lowry, Michelle, and Peter Nyers. 2003. "'No One Is Illegal': The Fight for Refugee and Migrant Rights in Canada." *Refuge: Canada's Periodical on Refugees* 21, 3 (May).

Luibheid, Eithne. 2005. "Introduction: Queering Migration and Citizenship." In Eithne Luibheid and Lionel Cantu Jr. (eds.), *Queer Migrations: Sexuality, U.S. Citizenship, and Border Crossings*. Minneapolis: University of Minnesota Press.

Lukcás, Georg. 1968. *History and Class Consciousness*. London: Merlin.

_____. 1978. *Marx's Basic Ontological Principles*. Translated by David Fernbach. London: Merlin.

Luxemburg, Rosa. 1970. *Reform or Revolution*. New York: Pathfinder.

Macklin, Audrey. 2001. "Borderline Security." In Ronald J. Daniels, Patrick Macklem and Kent Roach (eds.), *The Security of Freedom: Essays on Canada's Anti-Terrorism Bill*. Toronto: University of Toronto Press.

Maquila Solidarity Network (MSN). 2000. "A Needle in a Haystack: Tracing Canadian Garment Connections to Mexico and Central America." At <http://www.maquilasolidarity.org/resources/garment/haystack/Introduction.PDF>. (Accessed Dec. 2, 2005.)

Marable, Manning. 2003. "9/11: Racism in a Time of Terror." In Stanley Aronowitz and Heather Gautney (eds.), *Implicating Empire: Globalization and Resistance in the 21st Century World Order*. New York: Basic.

Martinez, Elizabeth. 1998. *De Colores Means All of Us: Latina Views for a Multi-Colored Century*. Cambridge: South End.

Marx, Karl. 1849/1891. *Wage Labour and Capital*. Edited/translated by Frederick Engels; First Published (in German): Neue Rheinische Zeitung, April 5–8 and 11, 1849.

_____. 1962. *Capital: A Critique of Political Economy*. Translated by Eden and Cedar Paul. London: J.M. Dent and Sons.

_____. 1968. "Theses on Feuerbach." In *Karl Marx and Frederick Engels: Selected Works*. New York: International.

_____. 1973. *Economic and Philosophic Manuscripts of 1844*. New York: International.

_____. 1974. "The Provisional Rules of the International." In *The First International and After*. London: New Left Review.

_____. 1975. *Early Writings*. Translated by R. Livingstone and G. Benton, introduction by L. Colletti. Harmondsworth: Penguin.

_____. 1977. *Capital: A Critique of Political Economy, Volume One*. Translated by Ben Fowkes. New York: Vintage/Random House.

_____. 1978. "For a Ruthless Criticism of Everything Existing." In Robert C. Tucker (ed.), *The Marx-Engels Reader*. New York: Norton.

Marx, Karl, and Frederick Engels. 1976. *The German Ideology*. Moscow: Progress.

McAlister, Melanie. 2001. *Epic Encounters: Culture, Media, and U.S. Interests in the Middle East, 1945–2000*. Berkeley: University of California Press.

McCaskell, Tim. 1988. "The Bath Raids and Gay Politics." In Frank Cunningham and Sue Findlay, et al. (eds.), *Social Movements/Social Change: The Politics and Practice of Organizing*. Toronto: Between the Lines.

McCoy, Liza. 1995. "Activating the Photographic Text." In M. Campbell and Anne Manicom (eds.), *Knowledge, Experience and Ruling Relations*. Toronto: University of Toronto Press.

_____. 1999. "Accounting discourse and textual practices of ruling: A study of institutional transformation and restructuring in higher education." PhD Dissertation. University of Toronto.

McFarlane, Bruce A. 1992. "Anthropologists and Sociologists, and their Contributions to Policy in Canada." In William K. Carroll et al. (ed.), *Fragile Truths*. Ottawa: Carleton University Press.

McKinlay, John B. 1984. *Issues in the Political Economy of Health Care*. New York: Tavistock.

McNally, David. 1997. "Language, History and Class Struggle." In Ellen Meiksins Wood and John Bellamy Foster (eds.), *Defense of History, Marxism and the Postmodern Agenda*. New York: Monthly Review Press.

_____. 2001. *Bodies of Meaning*. Albany: State University of New York Press.

_____. 2002. *Another World is Possible*. Winnipeg: Arbeiter Ring.

Medical Research Council of Canada (MRC), Natural Sciences and Engineering Research Council (NSERC), and Social Sciences and Humanities Research Council (SSHRC). 2003. "Tri-Council Policy Statement: Ethical Conduct for Research Involving Humans." At http://www.pre.ethics.gc.ca/english/pdf/TCPS%20June2003_E.pdf>. (Accessed Dec. 2, 2005.)

Meeropol, Rachel, ed. 2005. *America's Disappeared: Secret Imprisonment, Detainees, and the "War on Terror."* New York: Seven Stories.

Midnight Notes (eds.). 2001. *Auroras of the Zapatistas, Local and Global Struggles of the Fourth World War*. Brooklyn, NY: Autonomedia.

Mills, C. Wright. 1959. *The Sociological Imagination*. New York: Oxford University Press.

Mirrilees, Tanner. 2005. "Live 8 for G8: Musical Hegemony and "Hidden" Neoliberal Messages." *Relay: A Socialist Project Review* 7 (Sept./October).

Mohanty, Chandra Talpade. 1991. "Cartographies of Struggle: Third World Women and the Politics of Feminism." In Chandra Talpade Mohanty, Ann Russo and Lourdes Torres (eds.), *Third World Women and the Politics of Feminism*. Bloomington: Indiana.

Monboit, George. 2005. "The Man Who Betrayed the Poor, Even as the G8 Promises Fall Apart, Geldof Stays Silent." *ZNet*, Sept. 6.

Moody, Kim. 1997. *Workers in a Lean World*. London: Verso.

Mooers, Colin, and Alan Sears. 1992. "The 'New Social Movements' and the Withering Away of State Theory." In William K. Carroll (ed.). *Organizing Dissent, Contemporary Social Movements in Theory and Practice*. Garamond.

Moore, Michael. 1989. *Roger and Me*. Film.

Moreton-Robinson, Aileen. 2003. "I Still Call Australia Home: Indigenous Belonging and Place in a White Postcolonizing Society." In Sara Ahmed, Claudia Castaneda, Anne-Marie Fortier and Mimi Sheller (eds.), *Uprootings/Regroundings: Questions of Home and Migration*. Oxford: Berg.

Morrow, Raymond. 1994. *Critical Theory and Methodology*. London: Sage.

Moynihan, Daniel P. 1965. *The Negro Family: The Case for National Action*. Washington, DC: US Department of Labour, Office of Policy Planning and Research.

Murphy, B. 2000. "International NGOs and the Challenge of Modernity." *Development in Practice* 10, 3/4.

Murray, Nancy. 2004. "Profiled: Arabs, Muslims, and the Post-9/11 Hunt for the 'Enemy Within.'" In Elaine Hagopian (ed.), *Civil Rights in Peril: The Targeting of Arabs and Muslims*. London: Pluto.

Mykhalovskiy E., and L. McCoy. 2002. "Troubling Ruling Discourses of Health: Using Institutional Ethnography in Community-Based Research." *Critical Public Health* 12, 1.

Mykhalovskiy, E., L. McCoy and M. Bresalier. 2004. "Compliance/Adherence HIV/AIDS and the Critique of Medical Power." *Social Theory and Health* 2, 4.

Mykhalovskiy, E., and G.W. Smith. 1994. *Getting "Hooked Up": A Report on the Barriers People Living with HIV/AIDS Face Accessing Social Services*. Research report prepared for National Welfare Grants, Health Canada. Toronto: Ontario Institute for Studies in Education.

Nadeau, Mary-Jo. 2002. "Who is Canadian Now? Feminism and the Politics of Nation After September 11." *Atlantis* 27

Namaste, Viviane. 1995. *Access Denied: A Report on the Experiences of Transsexuals and Transgenderists with Health Care and Social Services in Toronto, Ontario*. Report submitted to Project Affirmation/Coalition for Lesbian and Gay Rights in Ontario, Toronto.

_____. 1998. *Évaluation des besoins: Les travesti(e)s et les transsexuel(le)s au Québec à l'égard du vih/sida*. Rapport soumis au Centre québécois de coordination sur le sida, mai.

_____. 2000. *Invisible Lives: The Erasure of Transsexual and Transgendered People*. Chicago: University of Chicago Press.

Native Friendship Centre of Montréal. 2001. *Community Consultation on Aboriginal Homelessness Montréal Region: Workshop Proceedings and Final Report*. Montréal.

Nechayev, Sergei. 1869, "Catechism of the Revolutionist." At <http://www.nbp-info. org/library/SergeiNechaevKat.htm>. (Accessed Dec. 2, 2005.)

New Internationalist. 2002. "The Case for Open Borders." Special issue, 350. At <http://www.newint.org/issue350/keynote.htm>. (Accessed Dec. 2, 2005.)

Ng, Roxana. 1996. *The Politics of Community Services, Immigrant Women, Class and State*. Toronto: Fernwood.

_____. 1998. "Work Restructuring and Recolonizing Third World Women: An

Example from the Garment Industry in Toronto." *Canadian Woman Studies* 18, 1 (Spring).

_____. 1999. *Homeworking: Home Office or Home Sweatshop? Report on Current Conditions of Homeworkers in Toronto's Garment Industry.* Ontario Institute for Studies in Education, University of Toronto.

_____. 2002. "Globalization and Garment Workers in Canada: Implications for Social Policy." In *Changing Work, Changing Lives: Mapping the Canadian Garment Industry.* Working Paper No. 3, August.

Ng, Roxana, and Anne O'Connell. 2003. *Changing Work, changing lives: Mapping the Canadian Garment Industry.* Working Paper No. 3, August.

Nicol, Nancy. 2002. "Stand Together, A History of the Lesbian and Gay Liberation Movement in Ontario from 1967 to 1987." Intervention video.

Nkrumah, Kwame. 1964. *Consciencism: Philosophy and Ideology for De-Colonization.* New York: Monthly Review.

Notes from Nowhere (ed.). 2003. *We are Everywhere: The Irresistible Rise of Global Anticapitalism.* London: Verso.

Nyers, Peter. 2003. "Abject Cosmopolitanism: The Politics of Protection in the Anti-Deportation Movement." *Third World Quarterly* 24, 5.

O'Brien, M. 1978. *The Politics of Reproduction.* London: Routledge.

O'Brien MacDonald, Karen and Stefan Jensen. 2004. *CFS National Graduate Caucus Report.* Canadian Federation of Students, Feb. 25–29.

O'Connell, A. 2003. "Industry Trends." Community Roundtable Proceedings, Ontario Institute for Studies in Education, University of Toronto, Toronto, June 20.

Oikawa, Mona. 2002. "Cartographies of Violence: Women, Memory and the Subject(s) of 'Internment.'" In Sherene H. Razack (ed.), *Race, Space, and the Law: Unmapping a White Settler Society.* Toronto: Between the Lines.

Ollman, Bertell. 1998. "Why Dialectics? Why Now?" *Science & Society* 62, 3.

Otero, Gerardo, and Heidi A. Jugenitz. 2003. "Challenging National Borders from Within: The Political-Class Formation of Indigenous Peasants in Latin America." In *Canadian Review of Sociology and Anthropology* 40, 5 (December).

Oziewicz, Estanislao. 2002. "Man held 7 months, sent home with no ID." *Globe and Mail*, April 17.

Padgham, Oona. 2005. "Drawing Detention: A Conversation with No One Is Illegal." *Fuse* 28, 2 (May).

Palmer, Bryan. 2004. "System Failure: The Break-Down of the Post-War Settlement and the Politics of Labour in our Time." At <www.candiandimension. mb.ca/frame.htm>. (Accessed Dec. 2, 2005.)

Panem, Sandra. 1988. *The AIDS Bureaucracy.* Cambridge, MA: Harvard University Press.

Park, Lisa Sun-Hee. 1998. "Navigating the Anti-Immigrant Wave: The Korean Women's Hotline and the Politics of Community." In Nancy Naples (ed.), *Community Activism and Feminist Politics: Organizing Across Race, Class, and Gender.* New York: Routledge.

Pearlston, Karen. 2000. "APEC Days at UBC: Student Protesters and National Security in the Era of Trade Liberalization." In Gary Kinsman, Dieter K. Buse, and Mercedes Steedman (eds.).

Petras, James. 2000. "The Third Way: Myth and Reality." *Monthly Review* 51, 10.

Piepzna-Samarasinha, Leah Lakshmi. 2004. "Even in Canada." *ColorLines* 7, 3.

Pilger, John. 2005. "The G8 Summit: A Fraud and a Circus." *New Statesman* At

<www.newstatemen.co.uk>. (Accessed Dec. 2, 2005.)

Pittz, William. 2002. "No Safe Haven." *ColorLines* 5, 1.

Polster, C. 2002. "A Break from the Past: Impacts and Implications of the Canada Foundation for Innovation and the Canada Research Chairs Initiative." *Canadian Review of Sociology and Anthropology* 39, 3.

Poo, Al-Jen, and Eric Tang. 2004. "Domestic Workers Organize in the Global City." In Vivien Labaton and Dawn Lundy Martin (eds.), *The Fire This Time: Young Activists and the New Feminism.* New York: Anchor.

Pue, Wesley W. (ed.). 2000. *Pepper In Our Eyes: The APEC Affair.* Vancouver: University of British Columbia Press.

Quiroz-Martinez, Julie. 2002. "For War and Workers?" *ColorLines* 5, 1.

Ratner, Michael, and Ellen Ray. 2004. *Guantanamo: What the World Should Know.* White River Junction, VT: Chelsea Green.

Ray, Larry. 1993. *Rethinking Critical Theory.* London: Sage.

Rebick, Judy. 2000. *Imagine Democracy.* Toronto: Stoddart.

Reid, Colleen. 2000. "Seduction and Enlightenment in Feminist Action Research." *Resources for Feminist Research* 28, 1–2.

Reimer, Marilee (ed.). 2004. *Inside Corporate U, Women in the Academy Speak Out.* Toronto: Sumach.

Reiss, Edward. 1997. *Marx: A Clear Guide.* London: Pluto.

Richmond, Anthony. 1994. *Global Apartheid: Refugees, Racism, and the New World Order.* Toronto: Oxford.

Rose, Nikolas. 1999. *Powers of Freedom: Reframing Political Thought.* Cambridge University Press.

Said, Edward. 1979. *Orientalism.* New York: Vintage.

Salas, Daniel. 1994. *Sujet de chair, sujet de droit. La justice face au transsexualisme.* Paris: Presses universitaires de France.

Sanchez, Arturo Ignacio. 2002. "From Jackson Heights to *Nuestra America*: 9/11 and Latino New York." In Michael Sorkin and Sharon Zukin (eds.), *After the World Trade Center: Rethinking New York City.* New York: Routledge.

Sassen, Saskia. 1998. *Globalization and Its Discontents.* New York: New Press.

_____. 1999a. "Analytic Borderlands: Race, Gender and Representation in the New City." In Rodolfo Torres, Louis F. Miron, and Jonathan Xavier Inda (eds.), *Race, Identity, and Citizenship.* Oxford: Blackwell.

_____. 1999b. *Guests and Aliens.* New York: New Press.

_____. 2001. *The Global City.* Second Edition. Princeton: Princeton University Press.

Sayer, Derek. 1979. *Marx's Method.* Sussex, UK: Harvester.

Schutz, Alfred. 1962. *Collected Papers, Vol. 1. The Problem of Social Reality.* The Hague: Martinus Nijhoff.

Scraton, Philip. 1985. *The State of the Police.* London: Pluto.

Sears, Alan. 2003. *Re-Tooling the Mind Factory: Education in a Lean State.* Aurora, ON: Garamond.

Seidman, Steven. 1998. *Contested Knowledge.* Second Edition. Oxford: Blackwell.

Shabi, Rachel. 2005. "The War on Dissent." *The Guardian*, July 2.

Sharma, Nandita. 1998. "Capitalist Restructuring and the Social Organization of 'Non-Immigrants' in Canada: The (Re)-Formalization of Non-Membership." Unpublished paper.

_____. 1999. "The Social Organization of 'Difference' and Capitalist Restructuring in Canada: The Making of 'Non-immigrants' and 'Migrant Workers' Through the Formation of the 1973 Non-employment Authorization Program." PhD Dissertation, Department of Sociology and Equity Studies in Education, OISE/University of Toronto.

_____. 2000. "'Race,' Class and Gender and the Making of 'Difference': The Social Organization of 'Migrant Workers' in Canada." *Atlantis: A Women's Studies Journal* (Special Issue: "Whose Canada Is It? Immigrant Women, Women of Colour, Citizenship and Multiculturalism") 24, 2 (Winter).

_____. 2001. "On Being Not Canadian: The Social Organization of 'Migrant Workers' in Canada." *The Canadian Review of Sociology and Anthropology* 38, 4): 41 (November).

_____. 2003a. "Travel Agency: A Critique of Anti-Trafficking Campaigns." *Refuge: Canada's Periodical on Refugees* 21, 3 (May).

_____. 2003b. "No Borders Movements and the Rejection of Left Nationalism." *Canadian Dimension* 37, 3 (May/June).

Sherman, Howard. 1976. "Dialectics as a Method." *Insurgent Sociologist* 6, 4.

Ship, Susan, and Laura Norton. 2001. "Breaking the Walls of Silence: Aboriginal People and HIV/AIDS in Montréal." HIV/AIDS needs assessment final report. Montréal: Native friendship Centre of Montréal.

Silko, Leslie Marmon. 1994. "The Border Patrol State." *The Nation*, October 17.

Smith, Dorothy E. 1974. "The Ideological Practice of Sociology." *Catalyst* 8 (Winter).

_____. 1982. "The Active Text: A Textual Analysis of the Social Relations of Public Discourse." Paper presented, World Congress of Sociology, Mexico City.

_____. 1983. "No one commits Suicide: Textual Analysis of Ideological Practices." *Human Studies* 6.

_____. 1984. "Textually-mediated Social Organization." *International Social Science Journal* 36.

_____. 1986. "Institutional Ethnography: A Feminist Method." *Resources for Feminist Research* 15, 10.

_____. 1987. *Everyday World as Problematic: A Feminist Sociology*. Toronto: University of Toronto Press.

_____. 1989. "Sociological Theory: Methods of Writing Patriarchy." In Ruth A. Wallace (ed.), *Feminism and Sociological Theory*. London: Sage.

_____. 1990a. *The Conceptual Practices of Power: A Feminist Sociology of Knowledge*. Toronto: University of Toronto.

_____. 1990b. *Texts, Facts, and Femininity: Exploring the Relations of Ruling*. London and New York: Routledge.

_____. 1992. "Remaking a Life, Remaking Sociology: Reflections of a Feminist." In William K. Carroll, et al. (eds.), *Fragile Truths*. Ottawa: Carleton University Press.

_____. 1999. *Writing the Social: Critique Theory and Investigations*. Toronto: University of Toronto Press.

_____. 2002. "Institutional Ethnography." In Tim May (ed.), *Qualitative Research in Action*. Thousand Oaks, CA: Sage.

_____. 2005. *Institutional Ethnography: A Sociology for People*. Lantham, NY, Toronto, Oxford: AltaMira.

Smith, Dorothy E., and S. Dobson. 2002. "Storing and Transmitting Skills: The Expropriation of Working Class Control." *New Approaches to Lifelong Learn-*

ing (NALL). At <www.oise.utoronto.ca/depts/sese/csew/nall>. (Accessed Dec. 2003.)

Smith, Dorothy E., and George Smith, 1990. "Re-organizing the Job-Skills Training Relation: From 'Human Capital' to 'Human Resources.'" In Jacob Muller (ed.), *Education For Work, Education As Work: Canada's Changing Community Colleges*. Toronto: Garamond.

Smith. G.W. 1982. "In Defence of Privacy: Or Bluntly Put, No More Shit." *Action! Publication of the Right to Privacy Committee* 3, 1.

_____. 1988a. *Occupation and Skill: Government Discourse as Problematic*. Occasional Paper No. 2, The Nexus Project: Studies in the Job Education Nexus. Toronto: Ontario Institute for Studies in Education.

_____. 1988b. "Policing the Gay Community: An Inquiry into Textually-Mediated Social Relations." *International Journal of the Sociology of Law* 16; Reprinted 1990 as "Policing the Gay Community." In Roxana Ng, Gillain Walker, and Jacob Mueller (eds.), *Community Organization and the Canadian State*. Toronto: Garamond.

_____. 1989. "AIDS Treatment Deficits: An Ethnographic Study of the Management of the AIDS Epidemic, the Ontario Case." Paper presented at Fifth International AIDS Conference, Montreal.

_____. 1990. "Political Activist as Ethnographer." *Social Problems* 37, 4. 6; Shortened revised version 1995 "Accessing Treatments: Managing the AIDS Epidemic in Ontario." In Marie Campbell and Ann Manicom (eds.), *Knowledge Experience and Ruling Relations: Studies in the Social Organization of Knowledge*. Toronto: University of Toronto Press.

_____. 1995. "Accessing Treatments: Managing the AIDS Epidemic in Toronto." In Marie Campbell and Ann Manicom (eds.), *Knowledge Experience and Ruling Relations: Studies in the Social Organization of Knowledge*. Toronto: University of Toronto Press.

_____. 1998. "The ideology of 'Fag': Barriers to Education for Gay Students." *Sociological Quarterly* 39, 2.

Smith, G.W., E. Myhalovksiy and D. Weatherbee. 2006 (forthcoming). Research proposal "Getting 'hooked up:' An organizational study of the problems people with HIV/AIDS have accessing social services." In D.E. Smith (ed.), *Institutional Ethnography as Practice*. New York: Rowman and Littlefield.

Smith, Neil. 1996. *The New Urban Frontier: Gentrification and the Revanchist City*. New York: Routledge.

_____. 2002. "Scales of Terror: The Manufacturing of Nationalism and the War for U.S. Globalism." In Michael Sorkin and Sharon Zukin (eds.), *After the World Trade Center: Rethinking New York City*. New York: Routledge.

Smith, Susan E. 1997. "Introduction." In Susan E. Smith, Dennis G. Williams and Nancy A. Johnnson (eds.), *Nurtured by Knowledge: Learning to Do Participatory Action-Research*. Ottawa: International Development Research Centre.

Sorel, Georges Eugene. 1908. *Reflections on Violence*. New York: Collier.

Steedman, Mercedes. 1997. *Angels of the Workplace: Women and the Construction of Gender Relations in the Canadian Clothing Industry, 1890–1940*. Toronto: Oxford University Press.

Stevens, Jacob. 2001. "Barring the Doors." *New Left Review* 12 (new series).

Stringer, Ernest T. 1996. *Action Research: A Handbook for Practitioners*. London: Sage.

Sudbury, Julia. 2005. *Global Lockdown: Race, Gender and the Prison-Industrial Complex.* New York: Routledge.

Sutcliffe, Bob. 2001. "Migration and Citizenship: Why Can Birds, Whales, Butterflies and Ants Cross International Frontiers More Easily than Cows, Dogs and Human Beings?" In Subrata Ghatak and Anne Showstack Sassoon (eds.), *Migration and Mobility: The European Context.* New York: Palgrave.

_____. 2003. "Crossing Borders in the New Imperialism." In Leo Panitch and Colin Leys (eds.), *The New Imperial Challenge, Socialist Register.* London: Merlin.

Tanner, Mirrilees. 2005. "Live 8 for G8: Musical Hegemony and 'Hidden' Neoliberal Messages." *Relay: A Socialist Project Review* 7 (Sept./October).

Thobani, Sunera. 2002. Oral presentation at the conference on Racism and National Consciousness held at New College, University of Toronto, October 26.

_____. 2003. "Saving the West: Reflections on Gender, Race and the War on Terrorism." *Fireweed* 80.

Thompson, A.K. Forthcoming. *Black Bloc, White Riot: Anti-Globalization and the Genealogy of Dissent.*

Thorne, B. 1983. "Political Activist as Participant Observer: Conflicts of Commitment in a Study of the Draft Resistance Movement of the 1960s." In R. Emerson (ed.), *Contemporary Field Research: A Collection of Readings.* Boston: Little Brown.

Tilleczek, Kate. 2005. "Research Goes to the Cinema: Visuality, Textuality and Reflexivity in Visual Sociology." Manuscript in preparation following a paper presented at the Fifth Conference on the Canadian Rural Health Research Society, Sudbury, ON., October 21–23.

Tuhiwai Smith, Linda. 1999. *Decolonizing Methodologies.* New York: Zed.

Turk, J. (ed.). 2000. *The Corporate Campus: Commercialization and the Dangers to Canada's Colleges and Universities.* Toronto: Lorimer.

Van den Hoonaard, W.C. (ed.). 2002. *Walking the Tightrope: Ethical Issues for Qualitative Researchers.* Toronto: University of Toronto Press.

Vosko, L.F. 1993. *The Last Thread: Analysis of the Apparel Goods Provisions in the North American Free Trade Agreement and the Impact on Women.* Ottawa: Canadian Centre for Policy Alternatives. February.

Walker, Gillian. 1990. *Family Violence and the Women's Movement: The Conceptual Politics of Struggle.* Toronto: University of Toronto Press.

Warner, Tom, interviewed by Gary Kinsman. 2004. "Fighting the Anti-Queer Right-Wing." *New Socialist* Jan./Feb.

Waslin, Michele. 2001. *Immigration Policy in Flux.* NACLA Reports XXXV.

Weir, Lorna. 1993. "Limitations of New Social Movement Analysis." *Studies in Political Economy* 48.

Weitz, Rose. 1991. *Life with AIDS.* New Brunswick, NJ: Rutgers University Press.

Welch, Michael. 2002. *Detained: Immigration Laws and the Expanding I.N.S. Jail Complex.* Philadelphia: Temple University Press.

White, David, and Patrick Sheppard. 1981. *Report on Police Raids on Gay Steambaths.* Report to Toronto City Council, Feb. 26.

Woo, Deborah. 2003. "University, Industry, and Government Alliances: Escalating Conflicts with the Public Interest." *Public Adminstration and Management, An Interactive Journal* 8, 3.

Wright, Cynthia. 2002. "Open the Borders! Interview with Nandita Sharma." *New Socialist* 37.

_____. 2000. "Nowhere at Home: Gender, Race and the Making of Anti-Immigrant

Discourse in Canada." *Atlantis* 24.

Yanz, Lynda, Bob Jeffcott, Deena Ladd and Joan Atlin. 1999. *Policy Options to Improve Standards for Women Garment Workers in Canada and Internationally*. Ottawa: Status of Women Canada.

York University. 2004. "University Policies, Procedures and Regulations Database." At <www.yorku.ca/secretariat/legislation/u_pol/spaceuse.htm>. (Accessed Dec. 2, 2005.)

Yuen, Eddy, George Katsiaficas and Daniel Burton-Rose. 2004. *Confronting Capitalism: Dispatches from a Global Movement*. New York: Soft Skull.

Zeitlin, Irving. 1968. *Ideology and the Development of Sociological Theory*. Englewood Cliffs, NJ: Prentice-Hall.

Zimmerman, Don. 1974. "Fact as Practical Accomplishment." In Roy Turner (ed.), *Ethnomethodology: Selected Readings*. Markham, ON: Penguin.

Zwarenstein, Carolyn. 2001. "Our Human Chicken Coop." *Eye*, December 13.

INDEX